D1617467

Controlled Open Economies

Controlled Open Economies

A Neoclassical Approach to Structuralism

David Bevan, Paul Collier, and Jan Willem Gunning
with Arne Bigsten and Paul Horsnell

CLARENDON PRESS · OXFORD
1990

Oxford University Press, Walton Street, Oxford OX2 6DP

Oxford New York Toronto
Delhi Bombay Calcutta Madras Karachi
Petaling Joya Singapore Hong Kong Tokyo
Nairobi Dar es Salaam Cape Town
Melbourne Auckland
and associated companies in
Berlin Ibadan

Oxford is a trade mark of Oxford University Press

Published in the United States
by Oxford University Press, New York

British Library Cataloguing in Publication Data
Bevan, David 1944–
Controlled open economies: a neoclassical approach to
structuralism.
1. Open economies. Macroeconomic aspects
I. Title II. Collier, Paul III. Gunning, Jan Willem
330.12'2
ISBN 0–19–828620–1

Library of Congress Cataloging in Publication Data
Controlled open economies: a neoclassical approach to structuralism/
David Bevan, Paul Collier; Jan Willem Gunning with Arne Bigsten and Paul
Horsnell.
Includes bibliographical references.
1. Developing countries—Economic policy. 2. States, Small-
Economic policy. 3. Macroeconomics. 4. Neoclassical school of
economics. 5. Agricultural prices—Government policy—Kenya.
6. Agricultural prices—Government policy—Tanzania.
I. Bevan, David. II. Collier, Paul. III. Gunning, Jan Willem.
HC59.7.C632   1990   338.9'009172'4--dc20   89-25480
ISBN 0–19–828620–1

Typeset by Macmillan India Ltd., Bangalore 25

Printed and bound in Great Britain by
Biddles Ltd, Guildford and King's Lynn

Acknowledgements

This book has benefited from the comments of seminar participants at the Delhi School of Economics, the London School of Economics, the School of Oriental and African Studies, and the Universities of Amsterdam, Clermont 1, Columbia, Gothenberg, Harvard, Oxford, Sussex, and Princeton. Dr Amani and Dr Ndulu of the Department of Economics, University of Dar es Salaam provided an informed commentary on the Tanzanian component of the work. Major funding was provided by the World Bank, where Shankar Acharya participated in the original design of the research, and our work was monitored helpfully by Robert Liebenthal and David Greene. The manuscript has been typed by Sarah Smith who has retained her equanimity in the face of severe provocation.

Contents

List of Figures

List of Tables

1

Introduction

Most modern macroeconomics originates in America. Applied work uses American data, and theoretical work assumes an economic structure consistent with the salient features of the United States. Even for the analysis of other developed market economies this has proved unsatisfactory: these economies behave differently and face different problems, as the following examples illustrate. The relationship between unemployment and wages, which has long been indeterminate on US data, has recently been found to be robust in virtually all other developed market economies (Bean *et al.*, 1986). The relationship between inflation and the exchange rate in small open economies, irrelevant for the United States, was pioneered in Sweden and Australia. The analysis of permanent terms of trade shocks, 'Dutch Disease', again irrelevant for the United States, was pioneered by Australian, Dutch, and Irish economists. For developing countries the problems posed in applying modern macroeconomics are far more severe because economic structures are so different. Financial markets are often virtually absent, many economies are small, open, and periodically hit by temporary trade shocks, and most of them are heavily regulated by government controls wholly unfamiliar in America.

Because of this evident gap between modern macroeconomics and the characteristics of many developing countries two mutually hostile approaches have coexisted. Modern neoclassical macroeconomists, to the extent that they have worked on developing countries, have tended to make little concession to different economic structures; meanwhile, 'structuralists' have paid great attention to the particular features of the economies they have studied, but have not attempted to demonstrate rigorously how these features affect the applicability of 'orthodox' policy advice. Instead they have tended to use *ad hoc* theories. The lack of attention to institutional characteristics in the neoclassical approach and the absence of viable micro-foundations in the structuralists' theories have tended to make the exchanges between the two polemical. Meanwhile, many developing economies have experienced dramatic macroeconomic events, and have embarked upon large policy experiments, in an alarming vacuum of comprehension. This vacuum has arisen because both the structuralist and neoclassical critiques are right: theory must be tailored to structure to be applicable, but an atheoretic approach is inadequate. We are convinced that the misgiving of most structuralists that 'orthodox' policies are inappropriate in developing economies is at least partly right and that this concern can be accommodated within a neoclassical methodology.

The neoclassical approach is, in our view, characterized by its choice-theoretic microeconomic foundations. The present study attempts to provide a body of neoclassical theory (thus defined) which is purpose-built for a class of developing countries, namely small, open economies with weak domestic financial markets, subject to a variety of government controls and liable to periodic temporary shocks in their terms of trade. We refer to this class of country by the shorthand term 'controlled open economies'. We make no claims to generality beyond this class of country; for example, we would not expect our work to have much bearing upon the behaviour of the American economy (this being a corollary of our hypothesis that much macroeconomics designed around the American economy has little bearing on the class of economy we consider). The theory we develop is firmly rooted in the characteristics of controlled open economies because it was motivated by a particular event in particular countries (the coffee boom of 1976–8 in Kenya and Tanzania). As a result, part of the study is general to the class of economies described above, and part is a detailed quantitative application of the generic analysis to a particular historical episode in two countries. The application is, however, integral to the study, rather than being intended primarily for country specialists. It demonstrates that the theory is pertinent, capable of being used given the data available in developing countries, and that the postulated effects are quantitatively important. For example, we show that the Kenyan control regime entailed very poor use of the largest opportunity the country had ever experienced, with powerful repercussions for both growth and income distribution, while the Tanzanian control regime was driving the economy into an alarmingly rapid income collapse.

The particular event which motivated the attempt to construct a macroeconomics for controlled open economies was the Brazilian frost of 1975, which caused a large but temporary increase in the price of coffee. This was the major export of Kenya and Tanzania so that they experienced a windfall which was known to be temporary. Such a temporary windfall poses two types of macroeconomic policy question.

The more obvious policy question is, how should the government 'manage' the windfall? Should it tax it? Should it increase public expenditure, and if so, on what? The governments of Kenya and Tanzania arrived at radically different answers to this question: in Kenya virtually the entire price increase was passed on to coffee farmers (most of whom were peasants), whereas in Tanzania almost the entire windfall was taxed. This might appear to provide a convenient control experiment as to the efficacy of these different policy responses. However, the two responses turn out not to be directly comparable, owing to key differences in policies in place before the windfall. These differences constitute the second, less obvious but probably more important, type of policy issue, namely the way in which private behaviour is constrained by government regulations which pre-date the windfall. For even if the private sector is permitted to receive the windfall, its responses will be shaped by the control regime.

Like most other developing economies, the governments of Kenya and Tanzania had introduced a wide array of controls on the behaviour of private agents. The central thrust of this study is to analyse the macroeconomic consequences of these 'control regimes'. Superficially, the Kenyan and Tanzanian control regimes appear similar: both imposed foreign exchange controls, made imports subject to quotas, and had agencies responsible for fixing the prices of many commodities. However, we show that there was a critically important difference between them. The Kenyan policies we refer to as an example of a 'compatible' control regime. By this we mean that the policy configuration gave rise to a sustainable equilibrium. Policies were, however, as we shall demonstrate, grossly sub-optimal. Not only were resources misallocated, but the regime was peculiarly ill-suited to the efficient utilization of temporary windfalls, which are a recurring feature of the economy. In Chapter 2 we develop a theory of the macroeconomic properties of such control regimes, focusing upon the compatibility of trade, exchange rate, monetary, and budgetary policies. We show how these policies jointly determine the relative prices of exportable, importable, and non-tradable goods, and how only some configurations of relative prices are sustainable.

The Tanzanian policies are an example of an incompatible control regime. The central aspect of such policy configurations is that they are not sustainable and so must eventually be changed. In Chapter 3 we show why the particular policy combination adopted by the Tanzanian government gives rise to a disastrous cumulative contraction in the economy, which we refer to as an 'implosion'. This theory is an extension of the fix-price temporary equilibrium theory of Malinvaud and others, which incorporates neoclassical microfoundations of maximizing agents into a model in which markets are not cleared by price changes. However, whereas that theory provides no account as to why prices should be sticky downwards, in our analysis the upwards stickiness of prices is a direct consequence of universal price controls. Instead of excess supply of goods giving rise to unemployment (the reasonable focus of European-centred analysis), excess demand for goods induces reduced peasant labour supply. In turn this reduced labour supply has dynamic repercussions for goods availability in subsequent periods.

For each type of control regime we analyse the problems which must be confronted in dismantling it. For compatible control regimes policy reform may be highly desirable, while for incompatible regimes it is at some stage imperative. However, reform is by no means technically straightforward. A policy configuration can be disastrously wrong, we may know an alternative set of policies which, had they been in place, would have been far more suitable, and yet the transition from the existing to the desired set of policies can be deeply problematic. A reasonable supposition would be that the further policies diverged from some desired configurations, the easier it would be to improve matters by altering them. Regrettably, this seems not to be the case.

Because in Tanzania the control regime was incompatible, giving rise to an imploding economy, the temporary windfall was in some sense peripheral (except to the extent that it contributed indirectly to the maintenance of these policies). In Kenya, however, where the control regime was compatible, the way in which the controls shaped private responses to the windfall which private agents received is central to policy analysis. The theory of how agents respond to temporary windfalls under different behavioural constraints is developed in Chapter 4. The starting-point for this development is the existing theory of Dutch Disease. However, that analysis focuses only upon a permanent windfall in an economy without controls. Yet if the windfall is transient, the savings rate will rise so that in addition to the familiar disaggregation into tradables and non-tradables it is necessary to distinguish capital from consumer goods. Controls restrict how private agents make use of the windfall: foreign exchange controls inhibit the acquisition of foreign financial assets; import quotas may restrict the volume of imports, or alter their composition; interest rate ceilings may alter the volume and composition of investment.

It is one thing to develop theories for controlled open economies and another to show that they are capable of application. Part II applies the theory of temporary windfalls to the Kenyan coffee boom of 1976–9 and the theory of incompatible control regimes to the Tanzanian economic collapse of 1978–84. Chapter 5 develops two complementary approaches to the analysis of the Kenyan coffee boom and its aftermath. The first approach is to use the National Accounts, and related data, to quantify the effects of the windfall using simple counterfactuals. The advantage of this approach is that it is easy to follow what assumptions are being made and how variations in the assumptions would alter the results. The second, more sophisticated, approach is the construction of a computable general equilibrium model. This enables us to investigate several issues, notably distributional and long-term growth consequences, which would otherwise be unresearchable. Chapter 6 is a more limited analysis of the Tanzanian economy. The thrust of the chapter is to demonstrate the applicability of the theory of incompatible control regimes (Chapter 3), the central aspect of which was the cumulative repercussions of behavioural responses to disequilibria. Chapter 7 provides a brief comparison, using the theory of compatible and incompatible control regimes developed in Part I, and Chapter 8 concludes.

I

The Theory of Controlled Open Economies

2

Compatible Control Regimes

1. Introduction

Governments in developing countries commonly use an array of policies
which have macroeconomic effects: they set the exchange rate, trade and
other taxes, import quotas, price controls, foreign exchange controls, interest
rate ceilings, liquidity ratios for banks; they determine the magnitude and
composition of public expenditure; and they incur domestic and foreign
liabilities. Because many of these policies regulate private behaviour to a far
greater extent than is usual in developed economies, we describe them
collectively by the shorthand term 'control regime'. Many controls generate
undesirable micro-level inefficiencies which are well understood. Here we are
concerned less with the optimality of policy than with its feasibility. From this
perspective, an appropriate minimal property of a system of controls is that
they should be consistent with each other at the macro level. We refer to such
a control regime as 'compatible': all compatible control regimes give rise to
sustainable equilibria, even though some of them might be highly inefficient.
Although governments may at times wish to adopt incompatible control
regimes, these can at best be temporary stages in the transition between
compatible regimes. In this chapter we analyse the interdependence of some
major components of the control regime. We begin in section 2 with a
minimalist control regime: the only policy interventions are that the exchange
rate is set by the government, import quotas are imposed, and the government determines the money supply. A simple model is developed which
shows the set of those policy choices which are compatible and the consequences of choices which are incompatible. The analysis is then extended in
section 3 to include a more detailed treatment of taxation and public
expenditure, and to permit analysis of fiscal deficits. This requires us to move
beyond the comparative static framework adopted in section 2, since a
continuing fiscal deficit necessarily induces continuing changes in the stocks
of money and/or government debt. We investigate circumstances in which
the use of import controls does or does not permit the government to sustain
a larger deficit than otherwise. It also emerges that accurate diagnosis of fiscal
problems may require the budget to be disaggregated between tradable and
non-tradable sectors.

The control regimes studied in the chapter are far less complex than those
commonly found in developing countries. Even so, we demonstrate that the
transition between compatible regimes, for example the achievement of a

sustainable trade liberalization, is by no means straightforward. In Chapter 3 a further policy is introduced, namely generalized price controls, and it is shown that the inclusion of such a policy makes the control regime incompatible. In Chapter 4 foreign exchange, liquidity, and interest rate controls are introduced in the context of a temporary trade shock.

2. Compatible Trade, Monetary and Exchange Rate Policies

2.1. *The Macroeconomic Trade Policy Model: An Introduction*

In developed countries trade policy is generally peripheral to macroeconomic performance: trade taxes are usually low and do not change markedly. By contrast, in many developing countries governments impose high barriers to trade (often in the form of quotas), and actively vary them as a key instrument of macroeconomic policy. Indeed, behind the rhetoric of import-substituting industrialization, it has often been the Central Bank which has determined the height of trade barriers, with an eye on the foreign exchange reserves. The standard macroeconomic model for small open economies (the Salter model) was designed for the analysis of developed countries and abstracts from trade policy. Exportable and importable goods are treated as a single aggregate, 'tradables'. The focus of the analysis is then the relative price of these tradables to non-tradables, a price commonly referred to as the real exchange rate. The concept of the real exchange rate has come to be applied to the analysis of structural adjustment policies for developing countries (Ahamed, 1986). But here the application encounters a difficulty. Structural adjustment, as most other changes in macroeconomic policy in developing countries, involves major changes in trade policy. As a result, for given world prices, the domestic relative price of exportable to importable goods is substantially altered. In these circumstances tradable goods can no longer be treated as a Hicksian composite commodity. The three aggregates, exportables, importables, and non-tradables, thus give rise to two independent relative prices, both of which change. With the loss of the fundamental simplifying assumption of constant relative prices among tradable goods the concept of the real exchange rate becomes problematic. For example, in his major development of the Salter model, Prachowny (1984) omits trade taxes from his discussion of taxation because 'a reduction in an import tariff would change the relative price of importables to exportables and would make it impossible to use the composite good, tradables' (p. 83, n. 7).

We incorporate trade policy into the analysis of policy compatibility, identifying the relationship between equilibrium vectors of relative prices and the trade, monetary, and exchange rate policies which sustain those prices. We draw on Dornbusch (1974), Mussa (1976), and Neary and van Wijnbergen (1986). Dornbusch adopts the commodity aggregation used here and investigates the effect of a tariff upon two key relative prices. However, his analysis is confined to real variables; there is no money supply and hence continuous balance-of-payments equilibrium is imposed. Mussa analyses the monetary consequences of a tariff but adopts a more restrictive commodity aggregation in which there are no non-tradable goods, the only relative price being the terms of trade. Finally, Neary and van Wijnbergen incorporate non-tradable goods into a monetary model, but treat tradables as a composite commodity so that trade policy cannot be considered. A macroeconomic model suitable for developing countries must therefore extend the Salter model by disaggregating tradables, enabling the interaction between trade, monetary, and exchange rate policies to be investigated. In this section we present a simplified diagrammatic exposition of such a model. The microeconomic foundations of the model, and the assumptions which must be made, are presented more rigorously in section 2.2.

Let the three commodity aggregates, exportables, importables, and non-tradables, all be produced domestically, but assume that exportables are not consumed domestically. Production is characterized by the Sector-Specific Capital model (Neary, 1978): two factors are used in the production process, both being fully employed. Labour is mobile between sectors, while capital is sector-specific.

Preferences are assumed to be homothetic. World prices (denoted by superscript *) are treated as exogenous. The domestic consumer price of importable goods is determined by a fixed exchange rate, e, and an import quota, at the tariff-equivalent rate, t_q. For simplicity no trade restrictions on exports are introduced. Nominal income is the sum of production and the value of quota entitlements. The only asset is money. The transactions demand, C, is treated as proportional to planned expenditures. In equilibrium, households are assumed not to accumulate assets, income equalling expenditure at domestic prices. The money supply, c, is endogenously determined by the fiscal deficit, the payments deficit, and the government's decreed cash-to-deposit ratio, $1/\beta$.

The fiscal deficit may have trade restrictions as a direct argument depending upon whether they take the form of tariffs or quotas, and how government expenditure reacts to extra revenue. Mussa (1976) analyses the balance-of-payments effects of tariffs, but under the assumption that the revenue from tariffs does not affect the budget since it is redistributed to consumers. In this section we consider only the pure quota case. Government revenue is a function of an income tax, t, and expenditure, g takes the form of redistributions to consumers. At this stage we assume budget balance.

Now consider how relative prices and the trade balance are affected by an alteration in the trade regime. We begin by identifying loci of notional equilibria in the non-tradables and money markets. The space in which the model is developed is defined on the two independent domestic relative prices, p_X/p_M being the vertical axis and p_N/p_M being the horizontal axis.

Along any ray from the origin p_X/p_N is thus constant, vertical movements have no effects upon the pattern of demand, and horizontal movements, since they preserve relative prices among tradable goods, collapse the model back into standard open economy analysis.

In Fig. 2.1 the schedule N–N is the locus of notional equilibria in the non-tradables market. Dornbusch derives such a locus only for constant real income. That is, changes in the trade regime are not permitted to have any effects on real income and hence are only investigated in the neighbourhood of free trade. With such a restriction the N–N locus is unambiguously steeper than a ray through the origin. Point A denotes the relative prices which clear the market under free trade (so that w is both the terms of trade and the domestic relative price). At B import restrictions have lowered p_X/p_M but there is no change in p_N/p_M. This induces a shift of resources out of exportables into the production of both importables and non-tradables, causing an excess supply of the latter. To maintain equilibrium in the non-tradables sector a lower relative price of non-tradable goods is needed. At H p_N is reduced so that p_N/p_X has reverted to its value at A. Thus the incentive for resources to shift from exportables into non-tradables has been entirely eliminated while an incentive for consumption to switch into non-tradables has been created. Hence, H must be a point of excess demand for non-tradables, so that the locus of equilibria through A must be steeper than a ray

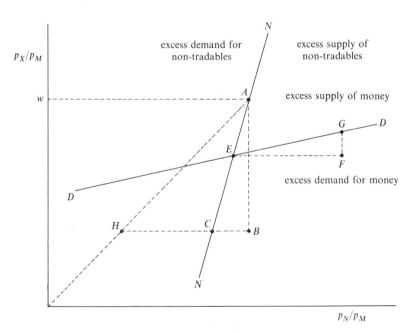

FIG. 2.1. *Loci of notional equilibria*

through the origin. Now consider a finite increase in trade restrictions, so that real income falls. With this additional income effect the move from A to H could involve an absolute reduction in the consumption of non-tradables. The $N-N$ schedule could therefore be flatter than a ray through the origin once income effects are incorporated, a possibility considered in section 2.2.

The $D-D$ locus represents equilibrium in the money market for given income and money supply valued in foreign currency (which we shall refer to as the dollar-equivalent money supply). For given relative prices, a change in e causes an equal, proportionate change in the demand for money, so that the maintenance of monetary equilibrium requires a corresponding change in the money supply. This is why monetary equilibrium is defined upon the dollar-equivalent money supply c/e. Letting E be a point of monetary equilibrium, at F there is an increase in p_N/p_M. With constant e and t_q the nominal price of importables is unchanged so p_N has risen. Hence, nominal expenditure must rise to maintain real income and so there is excess demand for money. The move from F to G restores monetary equilibrium: the implicit tariff rate is reduced, lowering the nominal price of importables. But since p_N/p_M is unchanged the nominal price of non-tradables also falls. Hence, the move from F to G represents a reduction in the price level.

Combining the two loci, we now introduce the concept of a compatible policy set $\{e, t_q, \beta\}$ which generates a sustainable equilibrium. Point E denotes such a position in which e and t_q fix p_M, and p_N is then determined by the money supply. At these prices the non-tradables market clears. By assumption there is no net asset accumulation and so the budget is in balance. The money market clears, and hence by Walras's law the balance of payments is in equilibrium. This in turn implies that there is no change in the money supply.

2.2. *The Formal Model*

We now formalize the presentation of the previous section. First, we consider a very simple model in which there is a single private agent who produces three goods: exportables (X), importables (M), and non-tradables (N). There is, in addition to sector-specific factors, at least one factor which is mobile between all three sectors. Factor supplies are given. An increase of one of the prices, say p_X, induces a reallocation of the mobile factors in favour of the X sector at the expense of the other two sectors. Hence own-supply effects are positive and cross effects are negative. The agent has a transaction demand for domestic currency (C), proportional to his expenditure on M and N goods. There is no domestic consumption of the X good. The money supply, c, is given. Write r for the revenue function, s for the expenditure function, u for the utility function and x, m, and n for net compensated domestic demand (consumption minus production) of the three goods. The model may then be written as:

$$r(p_X, p_M, p_N) + c = (1 + \alpha)s(p_M, p_N, u) \tag{1}$$

$$s_{p_N} - r_{p_N} = n(p_X, p_M, p_N, u) \tag{2}$$

$$\alpha s(p_M, p_N, u) = c. \tag{3}$$

Equation (1) is the budget constraint: the opening money stock, c, plus revenue, r, equals expenditure, s, plus transaction demand for money αs. Since the partial derivative of the expenditure function with respect to a price equals the Hicksian compensated demand for the corresponding good, s_{p_N} equals compensated demand for the non-tradable. Similarly, the partial derivative of the revenue function with respect to that price equals the production of that good. These results are used in (2) to write net compensated demand for the non-tradable, n, as $s_{p_N} - r_{p_N}$. By definition, there can be no exports or imports of the N good. Hence $n = 0$ in equilibrium. The third equation is an equilibrium condition for the money market: demand αs must be equal to supply, i.e. to the opening money stock, c.

We assume that the M and N goods are normal in demand:

$$m_u, n_u > 0 \tag{4}$$

and that the income effect is not too strong in the following sense:

$$(m + \alpha s_{p_M})n_u < (1 + \alpha)n_{p_M}. \tag{5}$$

Finally, by choice of units:

$$s_u = 1. \tag{6}$$

For the time being, we consider the price of the exportable as given. The model (1), (2), and (3) then determines the endogenous variables p_M, p_N, and u. This model is illustrated in Fig. 2.2, where the N–N locus represents equations (1) and (2) and the C–C locus equations (1) and (3). First consider the N–N locus. Total differentiation of (1) and (2) gives:

$$(m + \alpha s_{p_M})dp_M + (n + \alpha s_{p_N})dp_N + (1 + \alpha)du = 0 \tag{7}$$

and

$$n_{p_M}dp_M + n_{p_N}dp_N + n_u\,du = 0. \tag{8}$$

Hence, taking into account that $n = 0$, the slope of the N–N locus is given by:

$$\frac{dp_N}{dp_M} = -\{n_{p_M} - n_u(m + \alpha s_{p_M})/(1 + \alpha)\}/\{n_{p_N} - n_u\alpha s_{p_N}/(1 + \alpha)\} \tag{9}$$

which, because of assumption (5), implies that the locus has a positive slope.[1]

---

[1] For in the denominator α, n_u, and s_{p_N} are positive while n_{p_N} is negative (substitution effect). In the numerator n_{p_M} is positive but this is not sufficient to ensure that the N–N locus has positive slope: assumption (5) is necessary. This follows from the budget constraint. Neary and van Wijnbergen (1986: 35) present a similar model but fail to take the budget constraint correctly into account, assuming that real income (i.e. the utility level u) can remain constant along the locus.

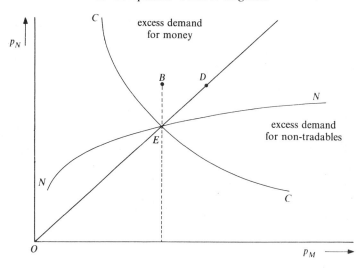

FIG. 2.2. *Equilibrium in the model without a public sector*

Consider a move along a ray through the origin, from E to D. Prices p_M and p_N increase, but in proportion, so that there is no substitution effect in demand while the increase in the relative price p_N/p_X increases production of the N good. Hence substitution effects alone cause excess supply of non-tradables at D. From (7) an outward move along a ray (starting at E, where $n=0$) implies a fall in utility. Hence the income effect is negative (demand for N falls because u falls and n_u is positive) so that it reinforces the substitution effect. There is therefore at point D unambiguously excess supply of N goods. Now consider a move from E to B. As before there is a substitution effect in production, leading to excess supply of N. This is now reinforced by a substitution effect in demand, since p_N rises while p_M remains constant. Again from (7) the income effect is negative, reinforcing the substitution effects. Hence at B there is excess supply of N. Since there is excess supply both at B and at D, the N–N locus must be less steep than the ray, as shown in the figure. There is excess supply above the curve, and excess demand for non-tradables below it. Now consider the C–C locus, defined by (1) and (3). Total differentiation of (1) after substituting $c=\alpha s$ from (3) gives:

$$m\,dp_M + n\,dp_N + du = 0 \tag{10}$$

and total differentiation of (3), taking into account that c is constant:

$$\alpha(s_{p_M}\,dp_M + s_{p_N}\,dp_N + du) = 0. \tag{11}$$

Dividing (11) by α and using $m = s_{p_M} - r_{p_M}$ and $n = s_{p_N} - r_{p_N}$ we obtain:

$$\frac{dp_M}{dp_N} = -r_{p_N}/s_{p_N}. \tag{12}$$

The C–C locus therefore has a negative slope.

The intersection of the two loci at E gives the solution of the model. Note that the price of the importable is determined endogenously. This reflects the exogeneity of the money supply. For suppose that world prices (p_X, p_M) were given, the model (1), (2), (3) would then determine the equilibrium money supply c endogenously. Making c rather than p_M exogenous amounts to asking what the world price of M goods would have to be for the exogenously given money supply to be consistent with equilibrium.

We now modify the model by introducing a public sector. The government taxes the private agent's income from production at a fixed rate t. Budget balance is imposed: government expenditure, g, equals tax revenue, tr. In addition we assume that government spending is distributionally neutral in the sense that its distribution between tradables and non-tradables is the same as the private sector's allocation. Under these assumptions (which will be relaxed in section 3) the government's fiscal operations have no effect on the private sector: it is as if the government returns its tax revenue as a lump-sum transfer to the private agent (equation (18) below).

The government issues money. As before, the supply of currency, c, is exogenous. But now the private sector's transactions demand is a demand for bank deposits, d, rather than currency. The government sets a cash ratio, β, and thereby controls the money supply (in the sense of bank deposits). In the previous model, government policy could not directly affect the position of the C–C locus. Here there is a D–D locus (on which demand for bank deposits equals supply) and, while c is still constant (within a period), the government can shift the D–D locus by changing the cash ratio. The public sector has a monopoly over external trade, importing and exporting at world prices and selling imports and buying exports at domestic prices from the private sector. Imports are subject to quantitative restrictions which, we assume, are always effective so that the volume of imports is given. The rent generated by import controls accrues to the private sector. The government has a transactions demand for foreign currency, proportional to its spending on imports. It sets a fixed exchange rate, e, using foreign exchange reserves to maintain this rate. Table 2.1 summarizes the disaggregation and notation for this model. The government has four instruments: the tax rate (t), the cash ratio (β), the exchange rate (e), and the quantitative restrictions (QRs) determining the level of imports ($\bar{m}$). These policies cannot be chosen independently: as we shall see, the model is overdetermined, so that only certain combinations of the policy variables are compatible.

TABLE 2.1. *Disaggregation in the model with a public sector*

	Domestic price	World price
X (exportable)	p_X	p_X^*
M (importable)	p_M	1
N (non-tradable)	p_N	(n.a.)
C (domestic currency)	1	$1/e$
D (bank deposits)	1	(n.a.)
F (foreign exchange)	e	1

The model consists of eight equations:[2]

$$(1-t)r(p_{\dot{X}}, p_M, p_N) + (p_M - e)(s_{p_M} - r_{p_M}) + g + d = (1+\alpha)s(p_M, p_N, u) \qquad (13)$$

$$(s_{p_N} - r_{p_N}) = n(p_X, p_M, p_N, u) = 0 \qquad (14)$$

$$\alpha s(p_M, p_N, u) = d \qquad (15)$$

$$(s_{p_M} - r_{p_M}) = m(p_X, p_M, p_N, u) = \bar{m} \qquad (16)$$

$$p_X = e p_X^* \qquad (17)$$

$$g = tr \qquad (18)$$

$$d = c/\beta \qquad (19)$$

$$f \geqslant \gamma(s_{p_M} - r_{p_M}). \qquad (20)$$

Equation (13) is the private agent's budget constraint. Compared with (1) there are three changes. First, revenue r is taxed.[3] Secondly, the private agent receives an (untaxed) rent equal to the volume of imports $(s_{p_M} - r_{p_M})$ valued at the difference between the domestic price and the equivalent in domestic currency of the world price, $(p_M - e)$. Thirdly, since the allocation between tradables and non-tradables is the same for the private and the public sector, government expenditure, g, is equivalent to a transfer. It therefore appears as a source of income for the private agent. Equations (14) and (15) are the equilibrium conditions for non-tradables and for bank deposits (these equations correspond to (2) and (3) in the previous model). Equation (16) says that imports m are equal to the controlled level $\bar{m}$. Note that m represents notional demand for imports: the quantitative restriction is not reflected in rationing. The domestic price p_M adjusts to clear the market. There is no intervention in

---

[2] The equations describe a static equilibrium. Out of equilibrium there would be a dynamic adjustment process involving changes in the two stocks, c and f. Here the stocks are treated as constants.

[3] We simplify by assuming that rent income is untaxed and that all other income is taxed at the same rate, irrespective of its source. These assumptions are relaxed in the model of section 3.

the market for exportables so that the world price and the exchange rate determine the domestic price of X goods: equation (17). Equation (18) imposes budget balance and (19) links the supply of bank deposits to the stock of currency through the cash ratio. Note that for given p_X (determined by (17)), given d (determined by (19)) and with g satisfying (18), equations (13), (14), and (15) determine p_M, p_N, and u, as in the previous model. Hence one possibility for incompatible policies is immediately evident. There is no guarantee that the level of imports determined by these equations will satisfy equation (16). For arbitrary values of the policy instruments the model's equations will be satisfied only by accident. In order to ensure compatibility they cannot all be set independently. The last equation has no counterpart in the earlier model. The government's transaction demand for foreign currency is proportional to the value of imports and (20) states that foreign reserves cannot be less than this. Since the functions r and s are linear homogenous in prices, Euler's law gives:

$$r = p_X r_{p_X} + p_M r_{p_M} + p_N r_{p_N} \tag{21}$$

$$s = p_M s_{p_M} + p_N s_{p_N} \tag{22}$$

and since $m = s_{p_M} - r_{p_M}$, $n = s_{p_N} - r_{p_N}$, we have:

$$r - s = p_X r_{p_X} - p_M m - p_N n. \tag{23}$$

From (14) $n = 0$, hence the last term drops out:

$$r - s = p_X r_{p_X} - p_M m. \tag{24}$$

Substitution of (15), (17), (18), and (24) gives:

$$e(p_X^* r_{p_X} - m) = 0. \tag{25}$$

Hence the model implies external equilibrium: the value of exports (at world prices), $p_X^* r_{p_X}$, equals the value of imports (which is m since the world price of M goods is unity).

We now introduce some new notation:

$$\zeta_1 = n_{p_N} - \xi \{\alpha s_{p_N} - (p_M - e)m_{p_N}\} \tag{26}$$

$$\zeta_2 = n_{p_M} - \xi \{\alpha s_{p_M} - (p_M - e)m_{p_M}\} \tag{27}$$

$$\zeta_3 = \alpha s_{p_N} - (p_M - e)m_{p_N} \tag{28}$$

$$\zeta_4 = r_{p_M} + (p_M - e)(m_{p_M} - m_u s_{p_M}) \tag{29}$$

$$\zeta_5 = r_{p_N} + (p_M - e)(m_{p_N} - m_u s_{p_N}) \tag{30}$$

$$\xi = n_u / \{(1 + \alpha) - (p_M - e)m_u\} \tag{31}$$

Note that

$$(1 + \alpha) > 1 = s_u = p_M m_u + p_N n_u > p_M \ m_u \geqslant (p_M - e)m_u. \tag{32}$$

Hence, since n_u is positive:

$$\xi > 0. \tag{33}$$

We assume, for reasons which will become clear later, that:

$$\zeta_i > 0 \qquad (i = 2, 3, 4, 5). \tag{34}$$

Since $\zeta_1 = n_{p_N} - \xi\zeta_3$, this implies:

$$\zeta_1 < 0. \tag{35}$$

Note that most of these expressions involve rent income $(p_M - e)m$. In the absence of import controls $p_M = e$ and ζ_3, ζ_4, and ζ_5 are necessarily positive. Hence, except for ζ_2, assumption (34) amounts to saying that the effect of rent income is not so strong as to upset the 'normal' effect.

As before, we begin by deriving the slope of the N–N locus. Total differentiation of (13) and (14), using (18) and $n = 0$ in (13), gives:

$$\alpha s_{p_M} dp_M + \alpha s_{p_N} dp_N + (1 + \alpha)du = (p_M - e)(m_{p_M} dp_M + m_{p_N} dp_N + m_u du) \tag{36}$$

$$n_{p_M} dp_M + n_{p_N} dp_N + n_u du = 0. \tag{37}$$

Substituting (36) in (37) and using the definition (31) we obtain:

$$n_{p_M} dp_M - \xi\{\alpha s_{p_M} - (p_M - e)m_{p_M}\}dp_M +$$
$$n_{p_N} dp_N - \xi\{\alpha s_{p_N} - (p_M - e)m_{p_N}\}dp_N = 0 \tag{38}$$

or, using (26) and (27):

$$\zeta_1 dp_N + \zeta_2 dp_M = 0. \tag{39}$$

Hence, given our assumptions, the slope of the N–N locus is positive, as before:

$$\frac{dp_N}{dp_M} > 0. \tag{40}$$

The locus is shown in Fig. 2.3. As before, we consider moves from E to B and from E to D to establish that the locus is less steep than the ray through the origin.[4] Moving from E to D, substitution effects lead to excess supply of N goods: their production increases while demand is unaffected, since p_M and p_N change in proportion. To derive the income effect we write (36) in the following form:

$$\{\alpha s_{p_M} - (p_M - e)m_{p_M}\} dp_M + \zeta_3 dp_N + (n_u/\xi)du = 0. \tag{41}$$

The term in curly brackets is positive.[5] Also ζ_3 is positive by assumption and the coefficient of du is also positive. Hence when (moving from E to D) p_M and p_N increase, utility falls. The income effect is therefore negative, reinforcing the conclusion that there is excess supply of N at point D.

---

[4] This is a diagrammatic device only. The changes considered in the algebra are infinitesimally small and since we start from E, which lies on the locus, we substitute $n = 0$, which would not be legitimate for discrete changes such as shown in the diagram.

[5] Note that m_{p_M} is necessarily negative because m is not the Marshallian (uncompensated) but the Hicksian (compensated) import demand function.

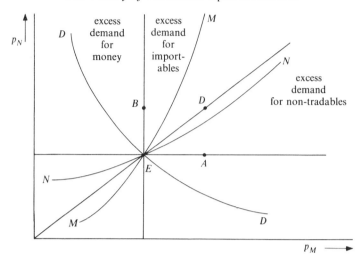

FIG. 2.3. *Equilibrium in the model with a public sector (compatibility: all loci go through E)*

Now consider a vertical move in the diagram, from E to B. Since p_N rises, substitution effects lead to excess supply: demand for N falls while production increases. The income effect is again negative. Since p_M remains constant, (41) reduces to:

$$\zeta_3 dp_N + (n_u/\xi)du = 0. \tag{42}$$

Hence the move from E to B reduces u so that the income effect reinforces the substitution effects: there must be excess supply of N at point B. Hence the locus cannot pass between points B and D; it must be flatter than the ray, as shown.

The D–D locus is defined by (13) and (15). Since g and c (and therefore d and s) are constant, total differentiation of (13) and (15) now gives:

$$(r_{p_M}dp_M + r_{p_N}dp_N) + (p_M - e)(m_{p_M}dp_M + m_{p_N}dp_N + m_u du) = 0 \tag{43}$$
$$s_{p_M}dp_M + s_{p_N}dp_N + du = 0. \tag{44}$$

Substituting (44) in (43) and using (29) and (30) we obtain:

$$\zeta_4 dp_M + \zeta_5 dp_N = 0 \tag{45}$$

and since ζ_4 and ζ_5 are both assumed to be positive it follows that the D–D locus has negative slope.

Since QRs determine the volume of imports, the M good behaves as a non-tradable: the domestic price adjusts to eliminate excess demand. This introduces a third curve, the M–M locus, defined by (13) and (16). Total differentiation of these two equations gives:

$$\alpha s_{p_M} dp_M + \alpha s_{p_N} dp_N + (1+\alpha)du = 0 \tag{46}$$

$$m_{p_M} dp_M + m_{p_N} dp_N + m_u du = 0. \tag{47}$$

Hence:

$$\{m_{p_M} - m_u(\alpha s_{p_M})/(1+\alpha)\}dp_M + \{m_{p_N} - m_u(\alpha s_{p_N})/(1+\alpha)\}dp_N = 0. \tag{48}$$

The first term in curly brackets is negative but the second one can have either sign. We assume that the income effect is weak, so that:

$$m_{p_N} > m_u \alpha s_{p_N}. \tag{49}$$

Hence the M–M locus has positive slope. If we move to the right, from E to A, substitution effects increase the production of, and reduce the demand for, M goods. This gives excess supply at A. Equation (46) shows that u falls if p_M rises, so that the income effect reinforces the substitution effects. Moving from E to D there are no substitution effects in demand while production of M increases, leading to excess supply at D. The income effect is, from (46), again negative, reinforcing the conclusion. Hence points D and A must lie on the same side of the locus: the M–M locus is steeper than the ray.

In Fig. 2.3 the three curves all pass through E. In this case policies are compatible. This need not be the case. As we noted above for the case of import controls, any one of the policies cannot be set independently of the others. Note that we have not represented the last equation of the model, (20), in the figure. The inequality defines a half space in which policies are feasible in the sense that foreign exchange reserves are sufficient. Note that compatible policies can become infeasible. Point E in Fig. 2.3 represents a set of compatible policies. If, however, these policies lead to a fall in reserves then eventually (20) will no longer be satisfied. In order not to clutter up the diagram we do not show the half space, but it should be kept in mind that the corresponding inequality, (20), further restricts the government's options.

Still keeping p_X constant, we now move the loci from the (p_M, p_N) space used so far to the $(p_X/p_M, p_N/p_M)$ double relative price space. (Note that this is possible only because p_X is kept constant. Otherwise the diagram would suggest that only relative price changes matter, but this is not true, since the real variables in the model are not homogeneous of degree zero with respect to prices.) This mapping yields Fig. 2.1, which has already been introduced in the previous section.

2.3. *Disequilibrium Behaviour*

In order to investigate the disequilibrium zones of the model we must derive effective as opposed to notional equilibrium loci, these being depicted in Fig. 2.4. Consider first the N–N locus. When there is an excess supply of

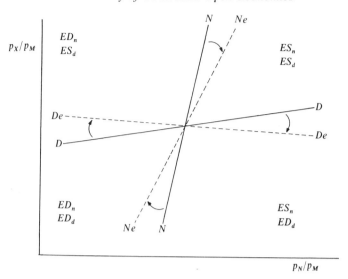

Key: ED = excess demand; ES = excess supply; n = non-tradable; d = money

FIG. 2.4. *Loci of effective equilibrium and payments balance*

money, plans will be revised so as to increase expenditure on non-tradables. Conversely, an excess demand for money reduces the demand for non-tradables. These effects flatten the *N–N* locus to *Ne–Ne*. Now consider the *D–D* locus. Excess supply in the non-tradables market reduces current income below planned income. To maintain planned expenditures the demand for money is reduced. Excess demand for non-tradables can raise or lower the demand for money, depending upon expectations and preferences. Agents may choose temporarily to build up money balances in the expectation of market-clearing in the next period. Offsetting this, since available expenditures generate lower utility, they may reduce planned income (by lowering labour supply), thereby lowering the demand for money. Finally, as we elaborate in Chapter 3, the random access which may be associated with excess goods demand can even increase the transactions demand. In Fig. 2.4, the first and third effects are shown as predominating, altering the *D–D* locus to *De–De*. This locus of monetary equilibrium is also the locus of balance-of-payments equilibrium.

The disequilibrium dynamics of the model are generated partly by endogenous changes in prices, the money supply, and investment, and partly by changes in the policy variables, e, t_q, β, t, and g. Endogenous changes in prices can occur only in the non-tradables sector and are determined by excess supply or demand as classified by *Ne–Ne*. Endogenous changes in the money supply are determined by the payments and fiscal deficits, an increase in the money supply shifting the *D–D* locus downwards. The payments deficit is signed by the *De–De* locus. The extent of any payments deficit is constrained by the requirement that reserves may not fall below the minimum needed to finance imports of $\bar{m}$. The fiscal deficit is for the present treated as exogenous and set to zero, changes in g offsetting endogenous changes in tax revenue. Endogenous changes in investment occur as the capital stock is gradually reallocated towards the sector in excess demand. For example, at F (in Fig. 2.1) the excess supply of non-tradables is gradually removed by depreciation of the non-tradable-specific capital stock and net investment in the tradables sector, leading to an eastward shift in $N–N$.

2.4. *Policy Changes*

We now use the model to illustrate the effects of policy changes designed to achieve either stabilization or liberalization. We define the former as indicating a move from an unsustainable to a sustainable position, and the latter as a movement between sustainable positions to a lower level of trade protection. Liberalization thus involves choices between compatible policy sets.

We begin by considering the consequences of departures from a compatible policy set. Although the model contains five policy variables, e, β, t_q, t, and g, it is convenient to treat the money supply as a policy instrument achieved by combinations of the ultimate policy variables, thereby reducing the policy set to t_q, d, and e. We distinguish between the impact effect and the eventual effect of policy changes. Fig. 2.5 illustrates the impact effect of changing each of the three policy instruments and of a policy package. The three policy changes illustrated are quantitatively common, each satisfying the equation

$$(1+t'_q)/(1+t_q)=e/e'=d'/d. \tag{50}$$

The impact effect of a trade liberalization from t_q to t'_q is to lower the price of importables, shifting the economy from E to a point such as L. The $D–D$ and $N–N$ loci are unaffected. A reduction in the money supply from d to d' lowers the dollar-equivalent money supply and thereby shifts the $D–D$ locus to $D'–D'$. However, it has no impact effect upon prices. A devaluation from e to e' has an impact effect upon both prices and the $D–D$ locus. The effect on prices is to raise the domestic price of tradables, shifting the economy from E to K. By reducing d/e the $E{\rightarrow}K$ devaluation also shifts the $D–D$ locus to $D'–D'$, as will be explained below. Finally, consider the policy package comprising the trade liberalization $E{\rightarrow}L$ and the devaluation $E{\rightarrow}K$. This particular policy change has the property that it has no impact effect upon the price of importables, which is kept constant by virtue of satisfying (50). The impact effect of the package on prices is confined to an increase in the nominal price of exports, shifting the economy from E to J. Since there can be no impact effect upon the price of non-tradables the above policy package has no

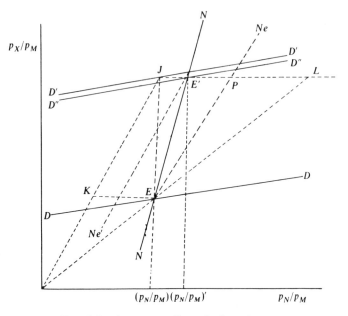

FIG. 2.5. *The impact effect of policy changes*

impact upon the price level and so the demand for money is unaltered (except for income effects). Hence, if E was a monetary equilibrium so must be J, the D–D locus therefore having shifted upwards to pass through $J(D'$–$D')$. As discussed above, proportional devaluations and money supply reductions have equivalent effects upon D–D.

The objective of an effective stabilization programme can be regarded as being to choose a policy set whose impact effect returns the economy directly to a sustainable position. Thus, were the economy to be characterized by an initial disequilibrium such as K, L, or J, the appropriate choice of the above policy changes would achieve this objective. In the absence of a policy initiative, a disequilibrium will generate endogenous adjustments, and we consider these by reanalysing these four above policy departures from equilibrium.

Following trade liberalization, at L there are excess supplies of money and non-tradables and a payments deficit. The non-tradables market will gradually equilibrate through a fall in the price of non-tradable goods, though this process will cease at P. However, the trade liberalization only becomes sustainable in conjunction with a fall in the dollar-equivalent money supply which shifts the D–D schedule to D''–D''. This will eventually occur automatically once the payments deficit depletes c, unless the implied reserve loss is infeasible.

Following the reduction in the money supply, at E there is an excess supply of non-tradables and hence a gradual reduction in p_N. This is despite the fact that E is on the N–N locus, for it lies to the right of the Ne'–Ne' locus which passes through E': the excess demand for money reduces the demand for goods. This adjustment accentuates the payments disequilibrium. The economy is accumulating financial assets, which eventually restores the money supply. Following devaluation, at K there is again a payments disequilibrium which will increase the money supply. However, the short-run dynamics of the price of non-tradables is *a priori* ambiguous. The increased demand for non-tradables generated by the fall in their relative price may be offset by the rise in the price level which raises the demand for money at the expense of the demand for goods. In Fig. 2.5 this ambiguity is reflected in that the Ne' locus could pass either to the right or to the left of K. Following the devaluation–liberalization package, at J there is an excess demand for non-tradables, and so p_N is rising towards E'. At J there is a payments surplus, and so the D'–D' locus gradually shifts so as to pass through E', at which point a sustainable equilibrium is reached.

If the government starts from a compatible set of policies it may still wish to change them. In particular, trade liberalization is likely to generate improved resource allocation. However, for the liberalization to be sustainable other policies must be changed in such a way that a new set of compatible policies is eventually established. Unless the economy moves directly to this set, the transition path of policy may be infeasible. A constraint upon the transition path is that the economy must throughout remain on the feasible side of the F–F locus: that is, reserves must not fall below the minimum needed to finance imports. Hence, a trade liberalization may abort either because the new set of policies are incompatible, or because the adjustment of policies to their new compatible levels is too slow. The extent of policy choice depends upon the initial level of reserves. If the economy is already on the F–F locus before liberalization (i.e. if it does not have spare reserves) then it has no choice of transition paths but must move directly to a new compatible policy set.[6]

There is a unique set of policies which for a particular trade liberalization will switch the economy directly to a new compatible set. Two conditions must simultaneously be satisfied: the impact effect upon relative prices must shift the economy directly to E', and monetary equilibrium must be maintained throughout. Consider first the former condition. The move $E \rightarrow E'$ raises the relative price of non-tradables to importables from (p_N/p_M) to $(p_N/p_M)'$. No policies have an impact effect upon the price of non-tradables,

---

[6] Of course, even if the economy starts on the F–F locus, it has the choice of all transition paths which have payments surpluses. However, the policy problem only arises because trade liberalization alone normally tends to worsen the balance of payments. Those policy choices which induce a payments surplus are therefore unlikely to be interesting.

but the exchange rate has an impact effect upon the price of importables.[7]

Hence, the increase in the relative price of non-tradables requires a reduction in the nominal price of importables. This in turn implies that the trade liberalization $(t_q \to t'_q)$ must exceed the required devaluation $(e \to e^*)$:

$$1 < \frac{(p_N/p_M)}{(p_N/p_M)'} = \frac{(1+t'_q)e^*}{(1+t_q)e}$$

so

$$1 > e/e^* > (1+t'_q)/(1+t_q). \tag{51}$$

The locus of exchange rates which achieve the required reduction in the price of importables for different magnitudes of trade liberalization is shown as T–T in the lower right-hand panel of Fig. 2.6.

However, such a devaluation–liberalization package, while it has the correct impact effect upon relative prices, shifts the economy to a monetary disequilibrium. This is because $\{t'_q, e^*\}$ unambiguously lowers the price level so that at the initial money supply there is an excess supply of money (unless this is fully offset by income effects). In terms of Fig. 2.5, the monetary equilibrium locus associated with the devaluation $e \to e^*$ thus lies below D''–D''. Thus, although the policy package $\{t'_q, e^*, d\}$ has an impact effect which shifts the economy from E to E', the new position, though the desired equilibrium, cannot be sustained in the short run. The excess supply of money will make E' a position of excess demand for goods, raising the nominal price of non-tradables and generating a payments deficit.

Now consider the satisfaction of the condition of monetary equilibrium. Recall that for given relative prices, proportionate changes in the exchange rate and the money supply are equivalent: an x per cent devaluation raises the price level by x per cent and thereby increases the demand for money by that amount, requiring an offsetting change in the money supply. The maintenance of monetary equilibrium consequent upon a trade liberalization can therefore be specified only in terms of the required change in the dollar-equivalent money supply, (d/e). We have already seen that for a given money supply, d, the trade liberalization to t'_q leads to an excess demand for money when combined with an exchange rate devaluation to e', whereas the smaller devaluation to e^* gives rise to an excess supply. Hence, there is an optimal reduction in the dollar-equivalent money supply to $(d/e)^*$, such that:

$$d/e > d/e^* > (d/e)^* > d/e' = d'/e. \tag{52}$$

The locus of values of the dollar-equivalent money supply which preserve

---

[7] Non-tradables prices will be changed only in relation to excess demand or supply, since the informational requirements for firms to infer the change in the market-clearing price consequent upon a policy change would be prodigious. In contrast, the informational requirements for firms to alter the price of importables in direct response to exchange rate and import quota changes are modest.

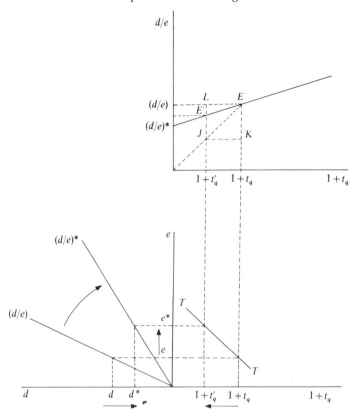

FIG. 2.6. *Compatible policies*

monetary equilibrium in response to a trade liberalization is shown in the upper panel of Fig. 2.6.

We now bring together the two conditions for a direct shift between sustainable equilibria. A given trade liberalization, $t_q \rightarrow t'_q$, requires a particular devaluation, $e \rightarrow e^*$, in order to have the correct impact upon relative prices, but this generates monetary disequilibrium. Monetary equilibrium, however, requires only a particular value of the dollar-equivalent money supply, so that monetary equilibrium can be reconciled with the correct impact effect upon relative prices by means of an appropriate reduction in the money supply to d^* ($d > d^* > d'$). The required reduction in the money supply is depicted in the lower left panel of Fig. 2.6. The policy instrument which would achieve this instant reduction in the nominal money stock is not government expenditure or taxation, which can only affect flows, but rather the cash ratio, $1/\beta$, which the government imposes on banks.

Thus, if the economy starts with a binding reserve constraint, trade liberalization requires the immediate transition to a new compatible policy set. For any particular magnitude of liberalization there is a unique combination of monetary contraction by means of the cash ratio and devaluation which achieves this. If the reserve constraint is not initially binding then choices open up. It is obvious that reserves enable choice between transition paths (such as the required speed of price adjustments). They also enable choice between compatible policy sets by relaxing the constraint imposed by the absence of a policy instrument which has an impact effect upon the price of non-tradables. Instead of thereby being constrained to the initial price, Walrasian processes can be allowed to operate, although these processes will at the same time generally give rise to a payments disequilibrium. The new compatible policy set must still be characterized by the same dollar-equivalent money supply, $(d/e)^*$, but there is some freedom to choose the exchange rate. For example, if the exchange rate is not devalued, but the dollar-equivalent money supply is reduced to $(d/e)^*$ by a larger change in the cash ratio, the initial nominal price of non-tradables will be above the market-clearing level. If the demand for non-tradables is elastic this will give rise to a payments deficit.

Governments may wish to reconcile trade liberalization with either nominal price or sector-specific real output objectives. The only nominal objective which is reconcilable with a direct switch between sustainable equilibria is the maintenance of the price of non-tradable goods. If instead the government attempts to maintain constant the price of importables, this objective can only be achieved by the policy set $\{t_q', e'\}$, as discussed above. However, it is evident that this fails to have an impact effect upon relative prices, which switches the economy to E', so that even with a correct monetary policy, excess demand will be required to raise the price of non-tradables. In the process, there will be a payments deficit, reducing the money supply, so that as relative prices approach E' the money stock will be too low. This will give rise to a subsequent phase of payments surplus while the money stock is restored.

Similarly, governments sometimes have sector-specific output objectives, particularly for importables. The concept of 'exchange rate protection' (Corden, 1985) has been developed to explain that governments have a choice in achieving such an objective by means of either trade restrictions or the exchange rate. Fig. 2.7 depicts the locus of constant output of the importable, m–m. It is at once apparent that any degree of choice in the attainment of target importable output can only be temporary unless the N–N locus is shifted. A sustainable equilibrium must lie upon the N–N locus, uniquely determining t_q, and upon D–D, uniquely determining the dollar-equivalent money supply. Only by shifting the N–N locus, for example through the public direction of investment on non-market criteria, can choices be sustained.

Finally, governments might have some assignment of policy instruments to policy targets. We consider one such assignment common to many develop-

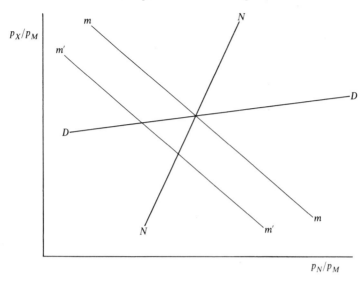

FIG. 2.7. *Exchange rate protection* ($m' > m$)

ing countries. Import controls are used to achieve balance-of-payments equilibrium. The exchange rate is maintained constant so as to defend the domestic price level, and the money supply is used to accommodate the desired budget deficit. Suppose that again starting at E (Fig. 2.8) the government incurs a budget deficit. This increases the money supply, temporarily

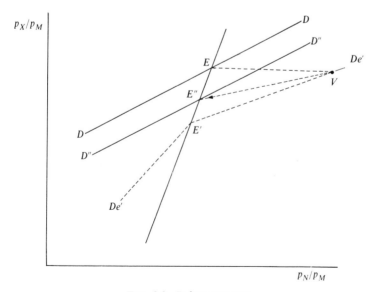

FIG. 2.8. *Policy sequence*

shifting the locus of monetary effective equilibrium to $De'-De'$. For given import controls this excess supply of money generates a payments deficit and a tendency for p_N to rise towards V. Faced with inflation, policy makers are resistant to devaluation, so the payments deficit is corrected by a tightening of import restrictions. The impact effect of this is further to stimulate inflation, reinforcing policy makers' commitment to the exchange rate. The economy thus settles at a new sustainable equilibrium such as E''. The money supply has been endogenously reduced, generating the locus $D''-D''$, and trade restrictions have been endogenously increased. This simple policy sequence illustrates how economies can accumulate import restrictions as a result of defective macroeconomic policies, though changes may be disguised in the rhetoric of import-substituting industrialization.

3. Compatible Trade and Fiscal Policies

3.1. *Introduction*

One shortcoming of the models discussed so far is their very restrictive treatment of fiscal policy. This is restrictive in two senses. First, fiscal policy has been subsumed under monetary policy. For some developing countries, including the cases of Kenya and Tanzania analysed in Part II, it is quite satisfactory to focus on only one of these, since the existence of foreign exchange controls and the absence of a bond market means that there is a very close correspondence between them. However, fiscal policy is logically prior to monetary policy in this setting, so it is appropriate to bring this into the centre of the stage. More generally, the analysis of policy compatibility should cover the case where monetary and fiscal policy can be chosen independently, and this requires a fuller specification than that adopted in the previous section.

The second sense in which the earlier treatment is restrictive is the requirement that the money stock be stationary in equilibrium (the specification of the D–D locus in Fig. 2.1). Taken together, these two restrictions confine the set of compatible policies to those characterized by a balanced budget. In practice, most developing countries run substantial budgetary deficits, financed by some combination of foreign capital inflow, domestic bond issue, and money creation. The central questions in the context of compatibility are, how large a deficit is sustainable, and how does the sustainable deficit depend on the nature of the control regime? In particular, can controls enable a government to sustain a larger fiscal deficit than would otherwise be possible and, as a corollary, is some sort of fiscal rectification a necessary component in any programme of dismantling controls?

This section addresses these questions. However, the simplest model capable of doing so is already extremely complex, and it is not possible to carry out a general qualitative analysis with minimal restrictions on functional forms. Instead, we adopt very specific functional forms and analyse their behaviour by a combination of algebraic and numerical methods. In consequence, the model and results of this section are illustrative only: they are designed to demonstrate the logical possibility of various phenomena.

An application of this apparatus would require deployment of an appropriately specified and calibrated computable general equilibrium (CGE) model. One purpose of the illustrative model is to gain an insight into the relevant fiscal structure for such a CGE model. There is an important distinction between tradable and non-tradable goods (or, more generally, a spectrum of substitutability between home and foreign goods), and another important distinction between the public and private sectors of the economy. These two dimensions for disaggregating the economy are invariably analysed separately. The model of this section utilizes the double disaggregation to analyse the ways in which trade policy and fiscal policy interact, uncovering relationships which are not apparent in a more highly aggregated model. It turns out that the interpretation of a fiscal deficit may depend sensitively on whether it is incurred within the tradable or non-tradable sectors.

In section 2 we treated stock changes as disequilibrium phenomena, and hence were able to use comparative statics. However, this device rules out the analysis of fiscal policy. Persistent deficits (or surpluses) require continual change in one or more of the stocks of the model, and preclude use of the simplest organizing framework, comparative static exercises involving alternative stationary equilibria. A fully fledged dynamic analysis would be difficult and, for the present illustrative model, not particularly illuminating. The simpler device adopted here is that of comparative dynamic analysis, involving alternative balanced growth equilibria. Transitions between those equilibria are discussed only in the briefest and most informal terms.

The section is organized as follows. First, the model is described; it bears repeating that the model is a special one, and the detailed results are of course contingent on this. However, it appears clear that the same broad type of result would arise in more general models. Then, the equilibrium conditions (derived in the Appendix) are used to analyse two questions. First, what combinations of fiscal and trade regime are sustainable? Second, what fiscal changes should accompany a programme of liberalization?

3.2. *The Model*

Formal details of the model and the equilibrium conditions are given in the Appendix. In the text, we restrict ourselves to an informal sketch. As before, the country produces three goods: an importable, a non-tradable, and an exportable. These are indexed by m, n, and x respectively. There is one mobile factor of production, labour. Production in each sector is a function of labour only, and we now assume that the elasticity of output with respect to labour input is constant within each sector and common between sectors. In the notation introduced in the Appendix, the inverse of this elasticity is a, with $a > 1$. As before, domestic private expenditure is confined to the first two goods; we now assume that it is determined by maximization of a constant elasticity of substitution (CES) utility function, with elasticity of substitution ε.

Government expenditure may be either or both of two types: it may purchase final output, or it may directly employ labour for its own production. For simplicity, it is assumed that purchases are confined to the importable and the non-tradable goods, and these are purchased in a ratio which is proportional to the corresponding ratio for private purchases. In other words, the composition of public expenditure may exhibit a bias relative to private expenditure, but this bias is uniform and does not vary with changes in relative prices. Public production affects private activities only via the reduction in the supply of labour to the private sector. This would follow if public sector output entered private utility additively, as is often assumed. It would also follow if the ouput were not valued by private agents, or in the case where public sector labour is unproductive.

The trade regime is as follows. There is an import tariff at the rate t_t; even so there may be an effective import quota with a further implicit equivalent tariff rate of t_q. There is no tax or subsidy on the export good. Associated with the import quota are rents, r, and these accrue to the private sector.

The private sector has a transactions demand for money, which is proportional to expenditure and inversely related to the anticipated inflation rate. It also has a propensity to acquire interest-bearing financial assets, at the rates s_w, s_π, and s_r, out of net disposable wages, profits, and rents respectively. These s_i can be thought of as the excess of a propensity to save over the propensity to invest out of each category of factor income.

Government expenditure is potentially financed from four sources, not all of which may be available. The first is tax revenue. This is obtained from proportional taxes on factor incomes at the rates t_w and t_π, and on the rents at the rate t_r; the tariff t_t; and domestic indirect taxes on the two locally consumed goods at the rates t_m and t_n respectively. The second source is net capital inflow, assumed to be set at an exogenously determined fraction, z, of the country's import requirements, evaluated at world prices.[8] We shall call z the capital inflow ratio. The third is the issue of domestic interest-bearing debt, the counterpart to the private sector's willingness to acquire financial assets. These government bonds are assumed to carry a constant real interest rate, that is they are invariant to the inflation rate. Finally, the government obtains seigniorage from the issue of money. This is composed partly of the growth in real balances associated with real growth in the economy, and partly of the inflation tax.

The equations formalizing this model are listed in the Appendix. The equilibrium conditions can be represented in a large variety of ways. In the Appendix an equation for non-tradable equilibrium is obtained (Appendix equation (20)) and shown to have the qualitative properties discussed earlier in the text. In place of the monetary equilibrium locus of section 2, an equation for private financial equilibrium is obtained (Appendix equation (27)). These two equations are combined to give the solution to the entire system (Appendix equation (30)). It would of course have been equally appropriate to obtain this by substituting an expression for public sector financial equilibrium in place of that for private.

The equilibrium condition (Appendix equation (30)) is a non-linear function of the tax and expenditure factors $(1+t_t)$, $(1+t_q)$, $(1+t_n)$, $(1+t_m)$, $(1+g_m)$, $(1+g_n)$; the monetary factor $(1+\mu)$, where μ is the ratio of money growth to expenditure; the domestic share of the import bill $(1-z)$; various production and preference parameters, notably the elasticity of substitution, ε, and the elasticity of output with respect to labour, $1/a$; and finally of two composite terms y, and $\hat{y}$. These are defined in the Appendix in equations (37) and (38), reproduced here as equations (53) and (54)

$$y=(1+s_w)(1-t_w)(1+g_L)/[a(1+\mu)]+(1-s_\pi)(1-t_\pi)(1-1/a)/(1+\mu) \quad (53)$$
$$\hat{y}=(1-s_r)(1-t_r)/(1+\mu) \quad (54)$$

where g_L is the ratio of public to private employment. Suppose for a moment that $g_L=0$. Then y can be interpreted straightforwardly as the private propensity to spend out of gross factor income and $\hat{y}$ as the private propensity to spend out of the rents arising from import quotas. When $g_L>0$ it can be seen that this is directly analogous to a rise in the propensity to spend out of wage income. A rise in public employment reduces the private supply of goods, given demand; a rise in the propensity to spend maintains supply but increases demand. In each case the government's access to private output is squeezed. For convenience, we continue to describe y as a propensity to spend out of factor income.

The equation is too complex to provide easy intuitive interpretation of the general case, but several key features may be elucidated by considering a number of special cases.

3.3. *Special Cases of Compatible Regime*

The purpose of the special cases is to illuminate the role of capital inflows, import controls, and tariffs in altering the restrictions which tax and expenditure instruments must satisfy if equilibrium is to be attained. To establish a bench-mark, the first case considered is that of free trade equilibrium in the absence of capital flows. Next, a capital inflow is introduced, while maintaining the free trade assumption. Third, the symmetric case is considered, where equilibrium is maintained by import controls in the absence of capital flows. These preliminary investigations clarify the relationships and permit consideration, fourthly, of a more general and interesting case, that of a tariff-ridden equilibrium with capital flows, with and without quotas. Lastly, the analysis is put in perspective by examining the simpler case of logarithmic preferences: as so often happens, this defines a special pivotal class of equilibria. In the present analysis, this is the class of fiscal equilibrium where quotas are irrelevant; that is, they do not permit the government to sustain a fiscal stance which would be infeasible in their absence.

(a) Free trade equilibrium; no capital flows

Consider a free trade equilibrium $(t_t = t_q = 0)$ with no capital flows[9] $(z = 0)$ and with the propensity to spend out of rental and factor income the same $(\hat{y} = y)$. Then the fiscal structure must satisfy one of the conditions:

$$\frac{1+t_n}{(1+g_n)y} = \frac{1+t_m}{(1+g_m)y} = 1 \tag{55a}$$

$$\frac{1+t_n}{(1+g_n)y} > 1 > \frac{1+t_m}{(1+g_m)y} \tag{55b}$$

$$\frac{1+t_n}{(1+g_n)y} < 1 < \frac{1+t_m}{(1+g_m)y}. \tag{55c}$$

To interpret these conditions, let the fraction of private sector expenditure going to non-tradables be f_n (at market prices), with $(1-f_n)$ going to importables. Then, with present assumptions, a unit of factor income must generate a unit of spending at factor prices and this entails[10]

$$f_n \frac{(1+g_n)y}{(1+t_n)} + (1-f_n)\frac{(1+g_m)y}{(1+t_m)} = 1. \tag{56}$$

Now

$$(1+g_n)y \gtrless (1+t_n)$$

as

$$g_n y \gtrless t_n + (1-y). \tag{57}$$

Consider an incremental unit of factor income; a fraction y of it is spent. If all of this were spent on the non-tradable, net government expenditure would rise by $g_n y/(1+t_n)$; and government financing by $t_n y/(1+t_n) + (1-y)$, where

---

[9] In fact, results for $t_t = 0$, $z = 0$ invariably generalize for $t_t + z = 0$.
[10] This is another way of writing the financial equilibrium condition, Appendix equation (13), when $t_t = t_q = z = 0$.

$t_n y/(1+t_n)$ is net incremental indirect tax revenue, and $1-y$ is the sum of incremental direct tax revenue, incremental seigniorage, and incremental domestic borrowing.

The relation (57) therefore determines whether private non-tradable spending tends to induce self-financing government spending or not. Equation (56) states that non-tradable and tradable activities together must be exactly self-financing. Hence the conditions (55) simply state that either both activities are exactly self-financing, or, if not, that one subsidizes the other. If (56) also holds, this may be characterized as 'fiscal rectitude under free trade'.

(b) Free trade equilibrium; capital inflow
Now consider a free trade equilibrium with capital inflow $(z>0)$. It is no longer possible for (55a) to hold. Either (55b) or (55c) could still hold, but it is now necessary that the surplus-inducing activity is insufficient to balance the deficit-inducing activity. (The left-hand side of (56) is greater than one.) It is also possible for both activities to be deficit-inducing, i.e.

$$\frac{1+t_n}{(1+g_n)y}<1 \qquad \frac{1+t_m}{(1+g_m)y}<1. \tag{58}$$

Relation (58) describes a fiscal structure that is unambiguously in deficit, in the sense that the government financing requirement spills over into the balance of payments. If the associated rate of capital inflow, z, is unsustainable, there will eventually be a foreign exchange crisis. One solution would be to raise taxation, adopting a sustainable fiscal stance (such as (55) if the equilibrium $z=0$); another might appear to be the adoption of import quotas.

(c) Import controls; no capital flows
Now consider the case of import controls but no import tariffs $(t_t=0, t_q>0)$ and no capital flows $(z=0)$.

Provided $\hat{y}=y$, the equilibrium conditions remain those given in (55). Hence import quotas cannot solve the disequilibrium caused by an unambiguously lax fiscal stance. The quota-ridden equilibrium requires the fiscal structure to be reformed in exactly the same way, though not necessarily to the same extent, as would be required for free trade equilibrium.

The reason for this result is that the underlying problem is the failure of the fiscal system to reduce private spending sufficiently to accommodate public spending. Under the quota, purchasing power is diverted from imports but remains in the hands of the private sector.[11] Productive resources are transferred from exportables to importables and non-tradables, and the balance of payments remains in deficit. A tighter quota raises the price of the importable and hence deflects demand towards the non-tradable, reinforcing these effects.

---

[11] A similar phenomenon arises in black markets. It is analysed in detail in Chapter 3.

A cumulative contraction of trade, accompanied by progressively more severe import quotas and progressively larger rents, would only be terminated by the appropriate fiscal reform. At that point, the quota-ridden equilibrium becomes established. The level of the quota and associated value of t_q depends on the nature of the fiscal reform. If it establishes the structure (55a), the value of t_q is arbitrary. In principle, it will be frozen at whatever value it has reached at the time of the reform.[12]

If the reformed structure conforms to either (55b) or (55c) t_q ceases to be arbitrary (provided $\varepsilon \neq 1$). It becomes, instead, a function of the 'cross-subsidy' ratio, θ,[13] where

$$\theta = \left\{ \frac{\dfrac{1+t_n}{(1+g_n)y} - 1}{1 - \dfrac{1+t_m}{(1+g_m)y}} \right\}.$$

The feasible variation in θ is very circumscribed in the absence of quotas, and may also be fairly circumscribed even if the quota can vary freely. In particular, there is a unique value of θ for given t_n, t_m, g_m, g_n at which t_q is exactly zero. It is straightforward to show that this is the value of θ associated with fiscal rectitude, that is when either (55b) or (55c) satisfies (56).

To summarize, three types of fiscal equilibrium are possible in the present case. First, there is an exactly self-financing equilibrium of the type (55a) (which necessarily satisfies (56)); associated with this is an arbitrary quota t_q. Second, the equilibrium may be characterized by fiscal rectitude with 'cross-subsidization ((55b) or (55c) plus (56)). There is no room for an effective quota and $t_q = 0$, unless $\varepsilon = 1$, in which case t_q again becomes arbitrary. Third, for limited divergence from fiscal rectitude, an equilibrium of the type (55b) or (55c) may be sustainable even when (56) fails, provided the quota is set at the appropriate level; t_q is > 0 and determinate.

If $\hat{y} < y$, these conclusions are somewhat qualified. For appropriate (restricted) parameter combinations, a quota may now suffice to stabilize the economy even when conditions (55) and, *a fortiori*, the fiscal rectitude condition (56) fail, as under (58). The reason is that the quota now acts a little like a tax, either because a higher than average rate of direct tax is levied on quota rentals, or because a higher than average rate of net saving is associated with these.

(d) Tariffs and capital flows with and without import quotas
First consider the impact of tariffs and the equilibrium capital inflow ratio (z^*) in the absence of quotas $(t_q = 0)$. If $t_t + z^* > 0$, so that the algebraic sum of

---

[12] This follows from the fact that all terms involving t_q drop out of Appendix equation (30) when the structure (55a) holds.
[13] The specific equation is given in endnote A, p. 42 below.

the tariff rate and the equilibrium capital inflow ratio is positive, then the economy can again achieve equilibrium with a 'deficit' fiscal structure such as (58), either because the external deficit can be financed, or because there is an additional source of revenue. If $t_t + z^* = 0$, so that the tariff is just sufficient to finance the capital outflow, equilibrium again requires (55); if $t_t + z^* < 0$, a more conservative (surplus) fiscal structure than this is required.

If quotas are also in force ($t_q > 0$) the discussion of section (c) again goes through for $t_t + z^* = 0$. If $t_t + z^* > 0$, so that a deficit fiscal structure is sustainable, the existence of a quota may raise, lower, or leave unaffected the scale of deficit. Under the special case of fiscal rectitude (55a), equilibrium requires either $\hat{y} = y$, $t_t + z^* = 0$, and t_q arbitrary, as already noted; or

$$\left(1 - \frac{\hat{y}}{y}\right)t_q = -\frac{(z^* + t_t)}{1 + t_t}. \tag{59}$$

Then an effective quota ($t_q > 0$) is associated with a rate of capital outflow in excess of the tariff rate. In particular, if $\hat{y} = 0$ (no private spending out of import rentals) and $t_t = 0$, then $t_q + z^* = 0$. In this case the explicit tariff t_t and the implicit equivalent tariff t_q are indistinguishable.[14]

(e) *The special case of logarithmic preferences*
If $\varepsilon = 1$, the pattern of private spending is fixed, and $f_n = 1 - b$. Then if $t_t + z = 0$, $\hat{y} = y$, the equilibrium condition reduces to:

$$\frac{(1+t_n)}{(1+g_n)y} - 1 = \frac{(1+g_m)b(1+t_n)}{(1+g_n)(1-b)(1+t_m)}\left[1 - \frac{1+t_m}{(1+g_m)y}\right].$$

On rearrangement, this yields

$$(1-b)\frac{(1+g_n)y}{(1+t_n)} + \frac{b(1+g_m)y}{(1+t_m)} = 1. \tag{60}$$

This is identical to the fiscal rectitude condition (56), as the previous argument demonstrated. The particular feature of the logarithmic case is that terms in t_q cancel entirely out of the equilibrium condition. Hence not only is fiscal rectitude necessary for equilibrium: if it obtains, the quota rental t_q is arbitrary for all the conditions (55), rather than being arbitrary only for the special case (55a). That is, equilibrium requires (60); if this fails to hold, no value of t_q can ensure it; if it does hold, any value of t_q is consistent with it.

3.4. *Choices between Compatible Policy Sets*

Having established the properties of different compatible regimes, we now consider what is involved in switching from one regime to another. Specifi-

---

[14] Inspection of Appendix equation (30) shows that with $\hat{y} = 0$, t_t and t_q everywhere appear in the form $(1 + t_t)(1 + t_q)$, so this equivalence carries over to all fiscal regimes.

cally, we investigate how quotas might be eliminated, either via fiscal reform, or via substitution by tariffs.

3.4.1. *Fiscal retrenchment with quotas*

Suppose that the economy is in a quota-ridden equilibrium, and that the government wishes to liberalize trade, undertaking fiscal reform as necessary. Assuming exact self-financing does not apply, and if $t_t + z = 0$, $\hat{y} = y$, then either (55b) or (55c) must hold; the instrument of fiscal reform will be assumed to be an equiproportional change in the rates of indirect tax, but equivalent results would follow for equiproportional changes in the rates of direct tax or (in the opposite direction) in the level of public spending.

From the equation in θ_q (endnote A, p. 42 below), the following conclusions are obtained. First, under logarithmic preferences ($\varepsilon = 1$), equation (56) must hold. Hence fiscal reform is neither necessary nor desirable, and the quota is arbitrary. Provided production responds quickly, and there are adequate foreign exchange reserves, imports can be liberalized immediately and there will be a realignment of prices, production, and consumption to the free trade equilibrium. If these conditions do not hold, it may be necessary to undertake a temporary deflationary reform to generate the foreign exchange and 'shake out' labour from the contracting industries.

When $\varepsilon \neq 1$, there are four cases to consider, depending on whether $\varepsilon > 1$ (importables and non-tradables are net substitutes) or $\varepsilon < 1$ (complements); and on whether the surplus-generating good is the non-tradable (55b) or the importable (55c). Under the optimal regime of a uniform indirect tax, (55b) will hold when the government spends relatively heavily on the importable, and (55c) when it spends relatively heavily on the non-tradable. Alternatively, (55b) will hold if the government is better able to tax the non-tradable than the importable, and vice versa. Table 2.2 displays the implications for the level of t_q of raising taxes for each of the four cases.

TABLE 2.2. *Tax increase and quota rentals*

Surplus generating good	Net substitutes $\varepsilon > 1$	Net complements $\varepsilon < 1$
Non-tradable $\dfrac{1 + t_n}{(1 + g_n)y} > 1 > \dfrac{1 + t_m}{(1 + g_m)y}$	$t\uparrow \Rightarrow \theta\uparrow \Rightarrow t_q\downarrow$	$t\uparrow \Rightarrow \theta\uparrow \Rightarrow t_q\uparrow$
Tradable $\dfrac{1 + t_n}{(1 + g_n)y} < 1 < \dfrac{1 + t_m}{(1 + g_m)y}$	$t\uparrow \Rightarrow \theta\downarrow \Rightarrow t_q\uparrow$	$t\uparrow \Rightarrow \theta\downarrow \Rightarrow t_q\downarrow$

If $\varepsilon > 1$, then an effective quota implies that θ_q is too low (below the fiscal rectitude value) and it should be raised if t_q is to be lowered. Raising taxes equiproportionately will achieve this only if non-tradables are the surplus-generating good. Otherwise, such a tax change will lower θ, exacerbating the problem. The converse argument applies if $\varepsilon < 1$.

What the table shows is that the conventional fiscal reform of raising taxes or lowering government spending will permit liberalization only when *either* non-tradables are the surplus generator and the goods are net substitutes *or* importables are the surplus generator and the goods are net complements. In the alternative pairings, the appropriate liberalizing reform, paradoxically, is to lower taxes. It is to be stressed that this bizarre result does not depend on special assumptions. It arises directly from the presence of quantity restrictions and taxes in a two-sector model.

The conclusion is that a quota-ridden equilibrium is (analytically) as likely to be associated with a fiscal stance that is too tight as with one that is too lax. Of course, it is most unlikely that a country would enter the quota-ridden state by adopting too tight a fiscal policy. The initial impetus is almost certain to be a lax fiscal policy and/or an adverse external shock. However, as already noted, quotas will be unable to stabilize the economy if the fiscal regime is sufficiently irresponsible (such as (58)). The quota-ridden economy is therefore likely to lurch along from crisis to crisis, with periodic reforms, until it achieves some sustainable equilibrium structure. This path will necessarily include a measure of fiscal tightening, and it is perfectly possible for fiscal policy to overshoot, even though in the normal case equilibrium would be achieved before this happened. These dynamic questions are considered further below.

3.4.2. *Replacing quotas with tariffs*

It is frequently argued that any attempt to liberalize a quota-ridden economy should proceed in two stages, thus reducing the transitional difficulties. First, the quotas should be replaced by tariffs of equivalent protective value; and second, the tariffs should be tapered off over time.

First, consider what fiscal changes should accompany the introduction of the tariff. Suppose the tariff rate is set at the old implicit equivalent tariff rate $(t_t = t_q)$ and quota restrictions are lifted.[15] Inspection of the equilibrium condition shows that equilibrium will only continue to hold if $\hat{y} = 0$, in which case tariffs and quotas are equivalent from the perspective of government finance. If $\hat{y} > 0$, the tariff substitution must be accompanied by fiscal relaxation; if these are again represented by equiproportional changes in indirect tax rates, given expenditure rates, then all production and expenditure quantities remain at their pre-tariff levels.

---

[15] The argument is unaffected if the reform is partial, provided the new values (starred) satisfy $(1 + t_t^*)(1 + t_q^*) = 1 + t_q$.

Now consider the second stage, where tariffs are reduced or eliminated. Returning to the equilibrium condition, a tariff analogue (θ_t) to the quota condition (θ_q) can be derived.[16]

Again, attention is restricted to equiproportional changes, with indirect taxes used for illustration. As in the quota case, the relationship between tariff and tax changes depends on the elasticity of substitution and on the surplus-generating good. Qualitative results are gathered in Table 2.3.

Whichever good is the surplus good, when $\varepsilon = 1$ tariff reductions must be compensated by other tax increases or expenditure reductions. These conclusions are reinforced for the combination of non-tradables as surplus good and the goods being net substitutes (top left corner) and for the combination of tradables as surplus good and the goods being net complements (bottom right corner). These were the combinations producing the standard fiscal relation in the quota case, with quota reductions requiring tax increases. In the alternative combinations (top right and bottom left in the table) the tariff/tax relation is ambiguous, whereas the quota/tax relation was perverse.

Let a fiscal regime where the non-tradable is the surplus-generating good be described as an 'outgoing' regime, and that where the importable is the surplus-generating good as an 'ingoing' regime. An outgoing fiscal regime spends relatively heavily on the importable, or taxes the non-tradable relatively heavily, and vice versa for an ingoing fiscal regime. An optimal regime where $t_n = t_m$ would be ingoing if the government spent disproportionately on non-tradables, for example.

It is now convenient to distiguish between 'well-behaved' and 'badly behaved' parameter combinations. One well-behaved case comprises low substitutability in consumption combined with an ingoing fiscal regime; the other comprises high substitutability and an outgoing regime. The badly

TABLE 2.3.   *Tariff reductions and tax changes*

Surplus-generating good	Net substitutes $\varepsilon > 1$	Independent $\varepsilon = 1$	Net complements $\varepsilon < 1$
Non-tradable $\dfrac{(1+t_n)}{(1+g_n)y} > 1 > \dfrac{(1+t_m)}{(1+g_m)y}$	$t_t \downarrow \Rightarrow \theta \uparrow \Rightarrow t \uparrow$	$t_t \downarrow \Rightarrow \theta \uparrow \Rightarrow t \uparrow$	ambiguous
Tradable $\dfrac{(1+t_n)}{(1+g_n)y} < 1 < \dfrac{(1+t_m)}{(1+g_m)y}$	ambiguous	$t_t \downarrow \Rightarrow \theta \downarrow \Rightarrow t \uparrow$	$t_t \downarrow \Rightarrow \theta \downarrow \Rightarrow t \uparrow$

[16] The specific equation is given in endnote B, p. 43 below.

behaved cases are the remaining pairings of high (low) substitutability with an ingoing (outgoing) regime.

The implications of the analysis for staged liberalization may now be summarized as follows. In all cases, replacement of quotas with equivalent tariffs implies a relaxation of the remaining fiscal instruments.[17] In well-behaved cases, tariff reduction then requires these instruments to be tightened. If tariffs are eliminated, this second effect is dominant, and the net change is to a tighter fiscal stance. This follows from the earlier analysis of fiscal retrenchment with quotas for the well-behaved case.

In the badly behaved cases, it is ambiguous whether tariff reduction requires a further relaxation or a tightening of the other fiscal instruments. However, it is clear that any tightening will not be sufficient to offset the initial relaxation, and that the net change is to a slacker fiscal stance. This again follows from the previous analysis of fiscal retrenchment for the badly behaved case.

In practice, it might be neither sensible nor plausible for a government that was fully committed to liberalization to attempt to partition the fiscal complement to liberalization between these two phases, particularly if this involved policy reversals. While this simplifies the problem of identifying the appropriate fiscal reform, it remains very difficult. It is quite likely that a government will not have the information to determine whether the economy is in a well- or badly-behaved configuration, so that the appropriate direction of reform, let alone its magnitude, is unknown.

It might appear that this ambiguity is largely a consequence of the assumption of initial (quota-ridden) equilibrium. Suppose instead that the initial condition is one of disequilibrium, with a cumulative deterioration in import availability; does this make it more likely that fiscal retrenchment is the appropriate policy? There are two answers to this, since there are really two different questions here, an analytic one and historical one. The analytic question is whether deterioration in import availability is a diagnostic of fiscal laxity any more than is a quota-ridden equilibrium. The answer is that it is not. If the fiscal regime is too tight in the quota-ridden equilibrium, fiscal retrenchment will tighten the quota.

The historical question is how the economy entered into the disequilibrium in the first place. It is very likely that this was triggered by a period of fiscal laxity, or by a failure to respond to a deterioration in the terms of trade. In either case, the balance of payments deteriorates, and the appropriate initial moves involve fiscal retrenchment. However, if the disequilibrium is not quickly resolved, and the economy stumbles through a period of quotas and cumulative import contraction, it is perfectly possible for the authorities to over-correct.

---

[17] The discussion assumes that the economy was in a quota-ridden equilibrium before liberalization.

3.4.3. *Numerical illustrations*

Tables 2.4 and 2.5 provide three illustrations of the preceding points. In each case, $A_M = A_N = 1$, $A_X = 0.25$, $a = 2$, $b = 0.5$, $t_n = t_m = t$, $y = \hat{y} = 1$, and world prices are set at unity.[18] Column (1) gives values of the variables in free trade equilibrium; the remaining three columns suppose that the uniform tax rate has been raised by 10 per cent. Column (2) portrays the outcome when free trade is maintained and the system is equilibrated by capital flows. Column (3) portrays the quota-ridden equilibrium, and column (4) the equivalent tariff equilibrium, which requires offsetting reductions in the expenditure tax.

Since particular interest attaches to the badly behaved cases, Table 2.4 concentrates on these. Table 2.4A combines high substitutability ($\varepsilon = 3$) with an ingoing fiscal regime ($g_n = 0.5$, $g_m = 0.2$); Table 2.4B combines low substitutability ($\varepsilon = 0$) with an outgoing regime ($g_n = 0.2$, $g_m = 0.5$). Table 2.5 combines the intermediate logarithmic case ($\varepsilon = 1$) with the outgoing regime, for purposes of comparison.

TABLE 2.4.   *Trade equilibria in the badly behaved case* (%)

A ($\varepsilon = 3$, $g_n = 0.5$, $g_m = 0.2$)

	Free trade equilibrium (1)	Capital flows (2)	Quota-ridden equilibrium (3)	Tariff equilibrium (4)
t	28.6	30.0	30.0	−19.8
z	0	−2.0	0	0
t_q	0	0	81.8	0
t_t	0	0	0	81.8
Import volumes as % of free trade volume	100.0	98.2	73.4	73.4

B ($\varepsilon = 0$, $g_n = 0.2$, $g_m = 0.5$)

	Free trade equilibrium (1)	Capital flows (2)	Quota-ridden equilibrium (3)	Tariff equilibrium (4)
t	25.0	27.5	27.5	15.0
z	0	−10.4	0	0
t_q	0	0	100.0	0
t_t	0	0	0	100.0
Import volumes as % of free trade volume	100.0	96.1	82.3	82.3

[18] The A_i are scale parameters in the production functions: see Appendix, equation 1.

TABLE 2.5. *Trade equilibria in the intermediate case* (%)

$(\varepsilon = 1, g_n = 0.5, g_m = 0.2)$

	Free trade equilibrium (1)	Capital flows (2)	Quota-ridden equilibrium (3)	Tariff equilibrium (4)
t	35.0	38.5	35.0	−1.8
z	0	−7.4	0	0
t_q	0	0	100.0	0
t_t	0	0	0	100.0
Import volumes as % of free trade volume	100.0	94.6	69.9	69.9

In each table, column (2) shows that in the absence of restrictions, the tax increase is associated with a capital outflow ($z < 0$) or surplus on current account. In these circumstances, there would be no problem in recognizing the fiscal stance as too restrictive (assuming for simplicity that the desired capital flow is nil), and relaxing to the column (1) value.

In column (3) of Table 2.4 values are given for the quota-ridden equilibrium with this restrictive stance. If liberalization were attempted, the natural course of action would appear to be further fiscal tightening, but this simply induces a further contraction in the quota. In a determinate, stationary world, this perverse relation would be easily inferred; in a stochastic, dynamic one, it would not. For Table 2.5, the restrictive stance cannot be underpinned by a quota, so column (3) gives an (arbitrary) illustration of a quota-ridden equilibrium under the original fiscal regime.

Column (4) gives values of the reduced expenditure tax rate which would sustain the same equilibrium as the quota-ridden equilibrium under a tariff.

The preceding analysis is of course contingent on the particular specification adopted, and it is clear from work not reported here that detailed results are sensitive to the detailed specification. However, that goes only to reinforce the main conclusion, which is that it is likely to be extraordinarily difficult within a controlled economy to get fiscal policy right, to respond to changed circumstances, or to pursue liberalization effectively. Once the economy has stumbled into a quota-ridden state, it may prove difficult to exit at all unless the quotas are first translated into tariffs. Such a two-stage procedure is much less problematic, though it is cumbersome and far from straightforward, especially during a temporary windfall, as we show in the counterfactual policy simulations of Chapter 5.

4. Conclusion

In this chapter, we have attempted to do four things. First, we have argued that it is impossible adequately to analyse the macroeconomic problems of developing countries within the confines of the standard small open economy model. Trade policies, either explicitly or implicitly, are central to this analysis, but are suppressed if exportable and importable goods are aggregated into a single tradable category. Most of the important macroeconomic problems facing these countries, such as stabilization, liberalization, and structural adjustment, have substantial trade policy components. It is necessary to maintain, at a minimum, a three-way disaggregation, between nontradables, exportables, and importables, if these problems are to be addressed.

Second, we have constructed a simple apparatus for using this disaggregation, involving a diagram in the double relative price space, $(p_X/p_M, p_N/p_M)$. Third, we have illustrated how this apparatus may be used to look at a variety of policy issues, including attempts at stabilization and liberalization of the economy. In particular, we have used it to investigate the properties of compatible control regimes, that is to say, combinations of controls which yield sustainable, though typically not optimal, outcomes.

Finally, we have shown that the problems posed to policy makers may be extraordinarily difficult to resolve when proper account is taken, within this aggregation structure, of even a relatively restricted set of economic controls. Familiar and apparently straightforward questions, such as whether the budget is overly lax, may become complex and opaque in this context. In effect, it may be necessary to carry this disaggregation within both public and private sectors.

Endnotes

A. Let the cross-subsidy ratio in the presence of import controls and in the absence of tariffs be θ_q. Then the equation for θ_q is

$$\theta_q^{\varepsilon - \frac{\varepsilon-1}{a}} = \frac{(1+g_m)}{(1+g_n)}\left[\frac{b(1+t_n)}{(1+b)(1+t_m)}\right]^{\varepsilon}\left\{\frac{\left[\frac{A_N}{A_X}\right]^{\frac{1}{a-1}}}{(1+t_q)^{\frac{1}{a-1}}}+\left[\frac{A_N}{A_M}\right]^{\frac{1}{a-1}}\right\}^{(\varepsilon-1)(1-1/a)}$$

In the more general case of $t_t + z = 0$, the term $(1+t_q)^{\frac{1}{a-1}}$ is replaced by $(1+t_q)^{\frac{1}{a-1}}(1+t_t)^{\frac{1}{a-1}}$.

B. Let the cross-subsidy ratio in the presence of tariffs and in the absence of import controls be θ_t. Then the equation for θ_t is

$$\theta_t = \left\{ \frac{\left[\dfrac{A_M}{A_X(1+t_t)}\right]^{\frac{1}{a-1}} \left[1 - \dfrac{t_t}{(1+t_t)\left(1-\dfrac{1+t_m}{(1+g_m)y}\right)}\right] + 1}{\left[\dfrac{A_M}{A_X(1+t_t)}\right]^{\frac{1}{a-1}} + 1} \right\} \times$$

$$\left\{ \frac{\left[\left[\dfrac{A_M}{A_X(1+t_t)}\right]^{\frac{1}{a-1}} + 1\right]^{(\varepsilon-1)(1-1/a)}}{\left(\dfrac{A_M}{A_N}\right)^{\frac{\varepsilon-1}{a}} \dfrac{(1+g_n)}{(1+g_m)}\left[\dfrac{(1-b)(1+t_m)}{b(1+t_n)}\right]^{\varepsilon}} \right\}^{\frac{1}{\varepsilon - \frac{\varepsilon-1}{a}}}$$

Appendix
Compatible Trade and Fiscal Policies: The Model

The Model

The private sector produces three goods, an importable, a non-tradable, and an exportable. These are indexed by M, N, and X respectively for prices, quantities, and expenditures, and by m, n, x for tax and expenditure rates. Domestic expenditure is confined to the first two, and is divided into private expenditure, E_i, and government expenditure, G_i, $i = M, N$.

There is one mobile factor of production, labour. Production in each sector takes the form

$$Q_i = (L_i/A_i)^{1/a} \qquad (a > 1, i = M, N, X) \tag{1}$$

where Q_i is output of i produced by a labour force L_i, and A_i, a are constants.

Hence the transformation frontier is defined by

$$\Sigma A_i Q_i^a \leqslant L \tag{2}$$

where L is the total private labour force.

Production in each sector is competitive,[1] with rents accruing to the

---

[1] To make this consistent with (1), suppose that there is a large number of firms in the sector, each producing according to a constant-returns-to-scale Cobb–Douglas function of immobile capital, k, and mobile labour, l. Firm j's output is given by $q_j = z_j k_j^{1-1/a} l_j^{1/a}$. Profit maximization faced with wage w yields the linear relation $p_i q_j = wa l_j$. Hence, aggregating over all firms in the sector, $p_i Q_i = wa L_i$, so the aggregate relation (1) holds. It then follows from substitution that $Q_i = [p_i/(wa A_i)]^{1/(a-1)}$.

owners of firms at the rate $(1 - 1/a)$ per unit of value added after they have paid labour at the wage w.

Private sector expenditure is determined by the maximization of a function

$$U = \begin{cases} [bE_M^{1-1/\varepsilon} + (1-b)E_N^{1-1/\varepsilon}]^{\frac{1}{1-1/\varepsilon}} & \text{if } \varepsilon \neq 1 \\ E_M^b E_N^{1-b} & \text{otherwise} \end{cases} \tag{3}$$

where b, ε are constants, $\varepsilon > 0$, $1 > b > 0$.

Public sector expenditure may be of two types: the purchase of final output, or the direct employment of labour for public production. We defer consideration of the latter for the present. For simplicity, public purchases of final output are assumed to be related to private expenditure as:

$$G_M = g_m E_M \tag{4a}$$

$$G_N = g_n E_N \tag{4b}$$

where g_i are constants. Equations (4) could have a number of different interpretations. For example, public expenditure could be determined by a function similar to (3), having the same elasticity of substitution ε, but a different distribution parameter b. Alternatively, public expenditure could be contingent on, or activated by, private expenditure on each good. For the present, public expenditure is assumed not to enter private utility directly, but this assumption is relaxed later.

Let the domestic producer price be p_i, and consumer prices be $(1 + t_i)p_i$, where t_i is the indirect tax rate on good i. World prices, denoted by superscript *, are again treated as exogenous. It is assumed that there is no tax or subsidy on the export good, so that the domestic producer price is related to the world price by

$$p_X = p_X^* e \tag{5}$$

where e is the nominal exchange rate, whose determination is discussed later.

In the case of imports, there is a tariff at the rate t_t; even so there may be an effective import quota with a further implicit equivalent tariff rate of t_q.[2] Hence the relation between the domestic producer price and the world price of the importable is

$$p_M = p_M^* (1 + t_t)(1 + t_q)e. \tag{6}$$

---

[2] It is convenient to carry out the analysis in terms of relative prices, using t_q to measure the severity of the quota. This is not problematic in the present model. It is straightforward to show that a binding quota always implies a positive t_q and vice versa, and that a tightened quota (given other parameters) is always associated with a higher t_q. Solving in terms of relative prices involves using t_q as a solution variable and treating the quota as endogenous. However, this has no bearing on which of the policy instruments would actually be adjusted to achieve an equilibrium.

In the absence of a quota, $t_q = 0$; in the absence of a tariff, $t_t = 0$. The tariff t_t accrues to the government as revenue; t_q accrues to private sector importers as rent.

Maximization of (3) at the prevailing consumer prices yields the expenditure condition

$$E_M = \left[\frac{b(1+t_n)p_N}{(1-b)(1+t_m)p_M} \right]^\varepsilon E_N. \tag{7}$$

The private sector budget constraint is

$$S + p_M(1+t_m)E_M + p_N(1+t_n)E_N = w(1-t_w)L + (1-t_\pi)\left(1 - \frac{1}{a}\right)\Sigma p_i Q_i +$$

$$\frac{p_M t_q}{1+t_q}[E_M + G_M - Q_M](1-t_r) \tag{8}$$

where t_w, t_π, and t_r are the direct tax rates on wage income, firm profits, and importer rentals respectively, and S is the sector financial surplus. If the wage rate moves to equilibrate the labour market, $\Sigma p_i Q_i = awL$. Hence, using (4), (8) can be rewritten

$$\left[(1+t_m) - \frac{t_q(1-t_r)(1+g_m)}{(1+t_q)}\right]p_M E_M + (1+t_n)p_N E_N$$

$$= awL\left[\frac{(1-t_w)}{a} + (1-t_\pi)(1-1/a)\right] - p_M Q_M\left[\frac{t_q(1-t_r)}{(1+t_q)}\right] - S. \tag{9}$$

2. Government Budget Constraint

The government spends $p_M G_M$ and $p_N G_N$ at tax inclusive prices. It obtains revenue from taxes on imports of $(E_M + G_M - Q_M)$ at the rate t_t on the world price p_M^*; from taxes on expenditure at rates t_m, t_n; from taxes on income at the rates t_w, t_π, and t_r. It also obtains net financing from the domestic private sector in the amount S, and from the foreign sector in the amount F, valued in units of domestic currency. Hence the budget constraint is

$$p_M G_M + p_N G_N = p_M t_m E_M + p_N t_n E_N + t_w wL + t_\pi(1-1/a)\Sigma p_i Q_i +$$

$$t_t[E_M + G_M - Q_M]p_M^* + \frac{t_r p_M t_q}{1+t_q}[E_M + G_M - Q_M] + S + F. \tag{10}$$

It is assumed here that the net capital inflow is set at an exogenously determined fraction (z) of the country's import requirements, evaluated at world prices, i.e.

$$F = \frac{z[E_M(1+g_m) - Q_M]p_M}{(1+t_t)(1+t_q)}. \tag{11}$$

Hence the domestic financing requirement is given by

$$S = p_M E_M(g_m - t_m) + p_N E_N(g_n - t_n) - \left[\frac{t_w}{a} + t_\pi(1 - 1/a) \right] awL -$$

$$\frac{p_M}{(1+t_t)(1+t_q)} [E_M(1 + g_m) - Q_M][t_t + z + t_r t_q(1 + t_t)]. \quad (12)$$

For equilibrium, this requirement must equal the private sector financial surplus. Eliminating S from (12) using (9), the condition is

$$p_N E_N(1 + g_n) + p_M E_M \frac{(1 + g_m)(1 - z)}{(1 + t_q)(1 + t_t)} + \frac{p_M Q_M}{(1 + t_q)} \left[t_q + \frac{t_t + z}{1 + t_t} \right] = awL = \Sigma p_i Q_i. \quad (13)$$

Notice that the direct tax parameters do not appear in (13). There are two reasons for this. First, it has been assumed that private expenditure patterns depend only on relative prices and total disposable income, not on the factor composition of this. (In effect, the composition of an individual's income is assumed uncorrelated with his spending pattern.) Second, there are no incentive effects on labour supply in the model (L is invariant to the tax structure). However, there could be incentive effects on savings; in this case the movement of the transformation frontier over time would depend on the tax structure, and government expenditure would in general crowd out more than 100% of private expenditure.

3. Non-Tradable Equilibrium

Substitution of (7) into (13) yields an equation relating private sector demand for the non-tradable to the set of relative prices and tax rates:

$$E_N = \frac{awL - \frac{p_M Q_M}{(1 + t_q)} \left[t_q + \left(\frac{t_t + z}{1 + t_t} \right) \right]}{p_N \left\{ 1 + g_n + \frac{(1 + g_m)(1 - z)}{(1 + t_q)(1 + t_t)} \left[\frac{b(1 + t_n)}{(1 - b)(1 + t_m)} \right]^\varepsilon \left(\frac{p_N}{p_M} \right)^{\varepsilon - 1} \right\}}. \quad (14)$$

Recall from n.1 above the profit maximization condition:

$$Q_i = \left[\frac{p_i}{wa A_i} \right]^{\frac{1}{a-1}}. \quad (15)$$

Substitution into the transformation frontier (2) produces:

$$\Sigma_i \left\{ \left[\frac{p_i^a}{(wa)^a A_i} \right]^{\frac{1}{a-1}} \right\} \leq L. \quad (16)$$

For labour market clearing, the wage must settle at the level required for the equality to hold, i.e.

$$(wa)^{\frac{a}{a-1}} = \frac{1}{L} \Sigma_i \left[\left(\frac{p_i^a}{A_i} \right)^{\frac{1}{a-1}} \right]. \quad (17)$$

Hence production of the non-tradable can be written:

$$Q_N = \frac{(p_N/A_N)^{\frac{1}{a-1}} L^{1/a}}{\left\{\sum_i [(p_i^a/A_i)^{\frac{1}{a-1}}]\right\}^{1/a}}. \tag{18}$$

Now demand for the non-tradable can only be met from domestic production. Hence equilibrium in the non-tradable sector requires:

$$Q_N = (1 + g_n) E_N. \tag{19}$$

Substitution of (14), (15), (17), and (18) yields, after some manipulation, the equilibrium condition for non-tradables as a function of relative prices:

$$\left(\frac{p_N}{p_M}\right)^{\varepsilon + \frac{1}{a-1}} \left(\frac{A_M}{A_N}\right)^{\frac{1}{a-1}} \left(\frac{1+g_m}{1+g_n}\right) \left[\frac{b(1+t_n)}{(1-b)(1+t_m)}\right]^{\varepsilon} \frac{(1-z)}{(1+t_t)(1+t_q)}$$

$$= \left(\frac{p_X}{p_M}\right)^{\frac{a}{a-1}} \left(\frac{A_M}{A_X}\right)^{\frac{1}{a-1}} + \frac{(1-z)}{(1+t_t)(1+t_q)}. \tag{20}$$

First assume that p_X/p_M varies, with no alteration in t_t, t_q; in other words, that there is a shift in world prices, with no alteration in trade policy. Then three implications of (20) may be noted. First, the equilibrium locus does exist (i.e. there are positive values of p_N/p_M and p_X/p_M which solve (20)). Second, p_N/p_M is continuously increasing in p_X/p_M. (Recall $a > 1$, $\varepsilon \geqslant 0$, $1 > b > 0$, and similarly for all the t's and g's and z.) Third, p_N/p_M tends to a finite positive value as p_X/p_M tends to zero.

Now consider the impact of a shift in trade policy, with given world prices. Setting $p_X^* = p_M^*$ by choice of units,

$$\frac{p_X}{p_M} = \frac{1}{(1+t_t)(1+t_q)}. \tag{21}$$

Hence (20) becomes

$$\left(\frac{p_N}{p_M}\right)^{\varepsilon + \frac{1}{a-1}} \left(\frac{A_M}{A_N}\right)^{\frac{1}{a-1}} \left(\frac{1+g_m}{1+g_n}\right) \left[\frac{b(1+t_n)}{(1-b)(1+t_m)}\right]^{\varepsilon} (1-z)$$

$$= \left(\frac{p_X}{p_M}\right)^{\frac{1}{a-1}} \left(\frac{A_M}{A_X}\right)^{\frac{1}{a-1}} + 1 - z. \tag{22}$$

Also by choice of units, set the free trade real exchange rate at unity; i.e. let $p_N/p_M = 1$ when $p_X/p_M = 1$. Then, for these units,

$$\left(\frac{A_M}{A_N}\right)^{\frac{1}{a-1}} \left(\frac{1+g_m}{(1+g_n)}\right) \left[\frac{b(1+t_n)}{(1-b)(1+t_m)}\right]^{\varepsilon} (1-z) = \left(\frac{A_M}{A_X}\right)^{\frac{1}{a-1}} + 1 - z.$$

Hence, provided $(1+g_m)/(1+g_n)$ and $(1+t_n)/(1+t_m)$ are invariant to changes in trade policy, equation (22) can be written:

$$\left(\frac{p_N}{p_M}\right)^{\varepsilon+\frac{1}{a-1}}\left[\left(\frac{A_M}{A_X}\right)^{\frac{1}{a-1}}+1-z\right]=\left(\frac{p_X}{p_M}\right)^{\frac{1}{a-1}}\left(\frac{A_M}{A_X}\right)^{\frac{1}{a-1}}+1-z. \qquad (23)$$

This is the equation of the non-tradable equilibrium locus N–N introduced in Fig. 2.1 of the text.

Inspection of (23) shows that p_N/p_M tends to a positive value as p_X/p_M tends to zero. The slope of the locus, evaluated at the free trade equilibrium, is

$$\left.\frac{d(p_X/p_M)}{d(p_N/p_M)}\right|_{t_t,\,t_q=0}=[\varepsilon(a-1)+1]\left[1+(1-z)\left(\frac{A_X}{A_M}\right)^{\frac{1}{a-1}}\right]>1.$$

Hence the locus does indeed have the shape of the N–N curve in Fig. 2.1.

The other notable feature of (22) or (23) is that it makes no difference how total protection of the importable is divided between tariffs (t_t) and quotas (t_q).

4. Tradable Equilibrium

Balance-of-payments equilibrium requires that the value of exports is just sufficient to finance the fraction $(1-z)$ of imports, valued at world prices.

$$p_X^*Q_X=(1-z)p_M^*[E_M+G_M-Q_M]$$

therefore

$$p_XQ_X=\frac{(1-z)p_M[E_M[1+g_m]-Q_M]}{(1+t_t)(1+t_q)}. \qquad (24)$$

Substitution of (7), (14), (15), and (17) would yield the condition for tradable equilibrium. There is no need to derive this separately, however, since equilibrium in the labour and non-tradable markets ensures it. Hence equation (20) is the locus for equilibrium in the tradable sector also.

5. Financing the Budget Deficit

Foreign financing has been assumed to be a function of the country's import requirement. So far, no restriction has been placed on the government's capacity to mobilize domestic savings. In general, this might be a complex function of the various fiscal instruments employed. For the present, it is convenient to assume that S is obtained by issuing government bonds paying a constant real interest rate. Money, and the possibility of monetizing part of the deficit, is introduced later. It will be assumed for simplicity that the private sector has fixed propensities both to save and invest out of different categories of disposable income, with the former exceeding the latter by s_j for category j. Hence the private sector runs a financial surplus (i.e. the excess of saving over investment) of

$$S = s_w w(1 - t_w)L + s_\pi(1 - t_\pi)(1 - 1/a)\Sigma p_i Q_i +$$

$$s_r \frac{p_M t_q}{(1 + t_q)}(1 - t_r)[E_M + G_M - Q_M]$$

$$= awL\left[\frac{s_w(1 - t_w)}{a} + s_\pi(1 - t_\pi)(1 - 1/a)\right] +$$

$$s_r \frac{p_M t_q(1 - t_r)}{(1 - t_q)}[(1 + g_m)E_M - Q_M]. \quad (25)$$

Substitution into the private sector budget constraint (9) yields

$$\left[1 + t_m - \frac{t_q(1 - t_r)(1 - s_r)(1 + g_m)}{(1 + t_q)}\right]p_M E_M + (1 + t_n)p_N E_N$$

$$= awL\left[\frac{(1 - s_w)(1 - t_w)}{a} + (1 - s_\pi)(1 - t_\pi)(1 - 1/a)\right] -$$

$$p_M Q_M \frac{t_q(1 - s_r)(1 - t_r)}{1 + t_q}. \quad (26)$$

Using (7), (15), (17), and (19), an expression for private financial equilibrium is obtained:

$$\left(\frac{p_N}{p_M}\right)^{\frac{a}{a-1}}\left(\frac{A_M}{A_N}\right)^{\frac{1}{a-1}}\left[\frac{(1 + g_m)}{(1 + g_n)}\left[\frac{(1 + t_m)}{(1 + g_m)y} - \frac{t_q \hat{y}}{(1 + t_q)y}\right]\right. \times$$

$$\left.\left[\frac{b(1 + t_n)}{(1 - b)(1 + t_m)}\right]^\varepsilon\left(\frac{p_N}{p_M}\right)^{\varepsilon - 1} + \frac{(1 + t_n)}{(1 + g_n)y} - 1\right]$$

$$= \left(\frac{p_X}{p_M}\right)^{\frac{a}{a-1}}\left(\frac{A_M}{A_X}\right)^{\frac{1}{a-1}} + 1 - \frac{t_q \hat{y}}{(1 + t_q)y} \quad (27)$$

where

$$y = \frac{(1 - s_w)(1 - t_w)}{a} + (1 - s_\pi)(1 - t_\pi)(1 - 1/a) \quad (28)$$

is the private propensity to spend out of gross factor income, and

$$\hat{y} = (1 - s_r)(1 - t_r) \quad (29)$$

is the private propensity to spend out of the rents arising from import quotas.

Substituting (20) into (27) to eliminate p_N/p_M, and setting $p_X/p_M = 1/(1 + t_t)(1 + t_q)$ as before,

$$\left\{ \frac{(A_M/A_X)^{\frac{1}{a-1}}}{[(1+t_t)(1+t_q)]^{\frac{1}{a-1}}(1-z)} + 1 \right\} \left(\frac{A_M}{A_N} \right)^{\frac{\varepsilon-1}{a}} \left[\frac{(1+t_n)}{(1+g_n)y} - 1 \right]^{\varepsilon - \frac{(\varepsilon-1)}{a}}$$

$$= \left(\frac{1+g_m}{1+g_n} \right) \left[\frac{b(1+t_n)}{(1-b)(1+t_m)} \right]^{\varepsilon} \times$$

$$\left\{ \frac{(A_M/A_X)^{\frac{1}{a-1}} \left[1 + \dfrac{t_q \hat{y}(1+t_t)}{(1-z)} - \dfrac{(1+t_q)(1+t_t)(1+t_m)}{(1-z)(1+g_m)y} \right]}{[(1+t_t)(1+t_q)]^{\frac{a}{a-1}} + 1 - \dfrac{(1+t_m)}{(1+g_m)y}} \right\}^{\varepsilon - \frac{(\varepsilon-1)}{a}}.$$

$$\tag{30}$$

Equation (30) gives the condition for equilibrium in all markets. It is a complicated expression, but several key features may be elucidated by considering a number of special cases, and this is the procedure followed in the text.

6. *Public Sector Employment*

The analysis has so far assumed that the public sector simply purchases final output: now suppose that it also pre-empts part of the labour force. This labour may be wasted in unproductive activities, or it may be used to produce an output which enters private utility in additive form, so that it does not affect private production and spending decisions. Let L continue to symbolize productive (private) labour, and let government labour be a fraction g_L of this, so the total labour force is $(1 + g_L)L$.

The effect of this extension is to augment the right-hand side of the private sector budget constraint (equation (8)) by $w(1 - t_w)g_L L$, and similarly for the left-hand side of the government budget constraint (equation (10)). The financing equilibrium (equation (13)) is unchanged, and so is the non-tradable equilibrium condition (equation (20)). The private sector financial surplus expression (equation (25)) has the right-hand side augmented by $s_w w(1 - t_w)g_L L$.

Making these substitutions, and solving the system, it turns out that the whole previous analysis goes through, provided expression (28) is redefined as:

$$\bar{y} = (1 - s_w)(1 - t_w)(1 + g_L)/a + (1 - s_\pi)(1 - t_\pi)(1 - 1/a). \tag{31}$$

The government's propensity to divert labour from productive activity is directly analogous to an increased private propensity to spend out of wage income. With this reinterpretation, equation (27) remains valid as the condition for private financial equilibrium, and equation (30) as that for equilibrium in all markets.

7. The Role of Money

So far, the analysis of fiscal policy has been conducted entirely in real terms. This has been made possible by the way in which the two mechanisms for financing the budget deficit have been modelled. It seems perfectly plausible to specify the capital inflow from the rest of the world as a real flow, but this is less satisfactory for the domestically financed component. Invariance of this to the rate of inflation implies one of two things: either all incremental government liabilities are fully indexed, or the elasticity of substitution between goods and money (factor inputs and money) in the utility function (production function) is unity. In either case, this rules out any inflation tax and makes the rate of inflation irrelevant to fiscal policy (though not to welfaçe). In this section, we adopt an alternative formulation which emphasizes the role of money.

It is assumed that domestic money demand for high-powered money takes the form:

$$C = \delta E (h + \pi)^{-\beta} \tag{32}$$

where δ, $h > 0$, and $\beta > 1$ are constants,[3] and π is the rate of domestic inflation, i.e. the joint rate of increase of p_N and p_M, and $E = P_M E_M (1 + t_m) + p_N E_N (1 + t_n)$. In an economy growing at real rate g, $h > \beta g$ is necessary to ensure that the optimum inflation tax is positive, and $\beta > 1$ is necessary to ensure that it is finite.

The demand for money is modelled as a function of private expenditures only, since this is the only component of the money stock on which a net inflation tax can be levied. The coefficient δ embodies any binding monetary controls, such as reserve ratios.

For a stationary inflation rate π, the equilibrium rate of money creation is

$$\Delta C = (g + \pi) C = (g + \pi) \delta E (h + \pi)^{-\beta}. \tag{33}$$

Assuming $h > \beta g$, this reaches its maximum at

$$(h + \bar{\pi}) = \beta (g + \bar{\pi})$$

or

$$\bar{\pi} = \frac{h - \beta g}{\beta - 1}. \tag{34}$$

ΔC is a composite of the seigniorage associated with real growth in the economy and the inflation tax. The maximum value of this composite in this economy is

$$\Delta C_{max} = \frac{\delta E}{\beta^{\beta} \left[\dfrac{h - g}{\beta - 1} \right]^{\beta - 1}}. \tag{35}$$

---

[3] In a more general application, h could be thought of as some function of the real rate of interest.

Any attempt to obtain a larger tax by greater money creation will be unsustainable: it will induce an acceleration of the inflation rate into hyper-inflation, with the real resources obtainable by government falling continuously. Of course, higher stable rates of π than $\bar{\pi}$ are possible: they are simply associated with lower $\Delta C/p$.

We assume that the rate of money creation is set (and known to be set) at some arbitrary sustainable level.[4] Hence the rate of resource mobilization from the private sector is now the sum of ΔC and S as given by equation (25).

Substituting into the private sector budget constraint, as before, we can derive the equation of private financial equilibrium:

$$\left(\frac{p_N}{p_M}\right)^{\frac{a}{a-1}}\left(\frac{A_M}{A_N}\right)^{\frac{1}{a-1}}\left[\frac{(1+g_m)}{(1+g_n)}\left[\frac{(1+t_m)}{(1+g_m)y}\left[1+\frac{(g+\pi)\delta}{(h+\pi)^\beta}\right]-\frac{t_q\hat{y}}{(1+t_q)y}\right]\times\right.$$

$$\left[\frac{b(1+t_n)}{(1-b)(1+t_m)}\right]^\varepsilon\left(\frac{p_N}{p_M}\right)^{\varepsilon-1}+\frac{(1+t_n)}{(1+g_n)y}\left[1+\frac{(g+\pi)\delta}{(h+\pi)^\beta}\right]-1\right]$$

$$=\left(\frac{p_X}{p_M}\right)^{\frac{1}{a-1}}\left(\frac{A_M}{A_X}\right)^{\frac{1}{a-1}}+1-\frac{t_q\hat{y}}{(1+t_q)y}. \quad (36)$$

Comparison with equation (27) shows that this is the same as the earlier expression if the indirect tax factors $(1+t_i)$, $i=m$, n are everywhere multiplied by the monetary factor

$$1+\mu=1+\frac{(g+\pi)\delta}{(h+\pi)^\beta}=1+\frac{\Delta C}{E}.$$

To examine the slope of this equation in p_X/p_M and p_N/p_M space, given all tax and expenditure parameters, differentiation yields an expression of the form:

$$\frac{d(p_X/p_M)}{d(p_N/p_M)}=Xp_N^{\frac{1}{a-1}}+Yp_N^{\frac{1}{a-1}}+\varepsilon-1$$

where X has the sign of

$$\left(\frac{1+t_n}{(1+g_n)y}\right)[1+\mu]-1$$

and Y has the sign of

$$\left[\left[\frac{(1+t_m)}{(1+g_m)y}\right][1+\mu]-\frac{t_q\hat{y}}{(1+t_q)y}\right](\varepsilon-1/a).$$

---

[4] Hence we abstract from the expectational and reputational issues which have been the principal concern of the recent literature on the inflation tax.

Provided nominal growth is non-negative a set of sufficient conditions for the locus to be upward-sloping is that $(1 + t_n > (1 + g_n) y)$, or, in the language of the text, that the non-tradable be the surplus-generating good, that the elasticity of substitution in consumption exceed the elasticity of output with respect to input, and that quota restrictions be 'sufficiently' small. If, instead, the tradable is the surplus-generating good and the substitution elasticity is low, the converse will apply. In general, however, there is no reason to expect a monotonic relationship. Indeed, the possible configurations are so various that a diagrammatic analysis does not appear to illuminate the issues and is not provided here.

Now consider a change in the equilibrium rate of inflation. Provided $\pi < \bar{\pi}$, this raises the monetary factor $1 + \mu$ and hence the left-hand side of (36) for given p_i. Hence, for given p_N/p_M, p_X/p_M must rise and the financial equilibrium locus shifts upward in the diagram. As π approaches $\bar{\pi}$, this upward movement ceases, and further increases lead to a downward shift in the locus.

If the equilibrium is characterized by an excessive rate of inflation (in the sense $\pi > \bar{\pi}$) then we have another fiscal paradox. The fiscal stance is overly restrictive. The non-tradable equilibrium locus (20) is unaffected by the inclusion of money demand, and the financial equilibrium locus is invariant to changes that leave $(1 + t_i)(1 + \mu)$ constant, $i = m, n$. Hence a fall in the excessive inflation rate π, which raises μ, could be accompanied by an across-the-board reduction in indirect taxes, leaving the economy at the same real equilibrium. Of course, engineering a reduction in π would typically require a pump-priming *increase* in taxation, to set the process under way.

The upshot of this analysis is that equation (30) continues to represent the balanced growth equilibrium of the monetized system, provided the indirect tax factors $(1 + t_i)$ are everywhere replaced by the product of these and the monetary factor, $(1 + t_i)(1 + \mu)$, $i = m, n$. The interpretation of this is straightforward. The (private) demand for money is here represented as a transactions demand: hence seigniorage is exactly analogous to an indirect tax on expenditure, at the uniform rate μ.

It is most convenient to represent this, by a further redefinition of y and $\hat{y}$, as

$$y = (1 - s_w)(1 - t_w)(1 + g_L)/[a(1 + \mu)] +$$
$$(1 - s_\pi)(1 - t_\pi)(1 - 1/a)/(1 + \mu) \quad (37)$$
$$\hat{y} = (1 - s_r)(1 - t_r)/(1 + \mu). \quad (38)$$

The interpretation is as before: the propensity to spend is simply reduced by the factor $(1 + \mu)$ representing the need to set income aside to keep real money balances in line with expenditure.

In this comparative dynamic setting, the price level at a point in time is fixed by the arbitrary, historically determined nominal money stock. The rate of monetary expansion, together with the real growth rate, determines the equilibrium inflation rate (π) in the domestic currency. In turn, the relation between this and the world inflation rate (π^*) fixes the equilibrium rate of change in the nominal exchange rate, that is the movement in e that is compatible with balanced growth.

This raises the question of how the exchange rate is actually set. The present model abstracts from foreign exchange holdings, so foreign exchange acquired from exports is continually used to purchase imports. If this is achieved by a free auction market in the absence of controls, then e follows the path along which $t_q \equiv 0$. Otherwise, the government can proceed in one of two ways. It can set import quotas and hence, indirectly, t_q, and allow e to equilibrate the system. (Of course, if $\pi \neq \pi^*$, this implies continuous change in e.) Alternatively it can set the path of e directly, and leave t_q to equilibrate the system. Governments often try to do both, but in general these policies are incompatible, and lead to periodic unintended adjustments in the nominal exchange rate, or to effective import quotas being tighter than official ones (because the foreign exchange is not available to honour the import licences issued).

3

Incompatible Control Regimes

1. Introduction

The previous chapter was concerned with compatible control regimes. These produce equilibria which, while possibly grossly inefficient, are sustainable. The present chapter analyses policy configurations which are unsustainable. As is implicit in the concept of unsustainability, we are here concerned with dynamics, both of the process by which a control regime becomes unsustainable and of the process by which an economy can be returned to sustainability, i.e. the sequencing of liberalization policies.

While obviously many control regimes can become unsustainable, our focus is on those which involve price control. Price control is sometimes imposed for ideological reasons, but it often originates in an unsustainable budget deficit. A common initial response is to resort to external borrowing. This is at best a temporary remedy, since eventually the country will be constrained by a borrowing limit. An alternative response is to rely on the inflation tax for the financing of the deficit. This policy too can be used only temporarily. These responses are sometimes used in sequence. Price controls are commonly a response to inflation: the government attempts to inhibit with one policy instrument a process which it generated with another.[1]

Partial price control is usually sustainable and even aggregate price control, applying to all goods, can often be evaded. We shall consider evasion of price control in section 3. Initially we assume the controls to be fully effective.

The case on which we focus is an economy in which the government controls the prices peasants receive for their crops and of the non-agricultural goods they purchase.[2] This leads to a model similar to that of Malinvaud (1977). We shall be concerned with the case in which there is excess demand for export crops (because of the government's revenue requirements) and also excess demand for urban goods, so that peasant demand for consumer goods

---

[1] The controls we are thinking of apply to non-agricultural goods. Producer prices are often controlled for quite different reasons. Hence when a budget deficit triggers control of goods prices, this often happens in a regime in which crop prices already are controlled.

[2] We use the term peasant rather than farmer. Both terms have many connotations. Our choice is based on only two considerations. First, farmer is too narrow a term: peasants typically are involved in both agricultural and non-agricultural activities. Secondly, a peasant controls his labour supply, whereas a farmer may rely much more on hired labour and to that extent have less flexibility.

is rationed, while in the market for crops they can sell as much as they want. The focus is therefore, in Malinvaud's terminology, on the repressed inflation regime.

The plan of the chapter is as follows. In the next section we consider the microeconomic repercussions of the rationing of peasants, taking into account that the ration is often not known with certainty. In section 3 we discuss the macroeconomic consequences of rationing in the case when peasants produce tradables. In the following section we consider evasion of controls (including black markets and overinvoicing), and in section 5 the dismantling of controls.

2. The Microeconomics of Enforced Price Controls

2.1. *Rationing in a Barter Economy*

Consider a peasant who produces one crop for sale (e.g. an export crop[3] such as coffee) and another one (e.g. a food crop) for own consumption. His utility function has three arguments: consumption of non-agricultural, urban goods; consumption of the own-produced food crop; and leisure. Prices of the cash crop and of urban goods are controlled at a level such that the peasant is rationed in the market for consumer goods. If this constraint is effective the peasant maximizes utility (one of the arguments of which is now predetermined) subject to a budget constraint. Since labour use on the cash crop is total time minus leisure minus the time devoted to the food crop, leisure and consumption of the food crop enter symmetrically in the budget constraint. Provided both goods are normal we can aggregate over them since the changes we want to consider (in prices and in availability) work entirely through changes in (full) income, and if both goods are normal the two income effects work in the same direction. This means that we can ignore the choice between leisure and the time spent working on food crops, focusing on the allocation of time between leisure (now understood as including time spent on food crops) and work on the cash crop.

In a barter economy, in which the cash crop is exchanged directly for consumer goods, peasants will optimize by working on their cash crop up to the point at which the marginal benefit of working harder (the utility of the consumer goods which can be obtained in exchange for the extra output) equals the marginal cost (the utility of forgone leisure). As long as the supply of consumer goods to rural areas is sufficient to meet peasants' demand at the optimum, their behaviour is not qualitatively affected by price control. But when the controls lead to shortages, the peasant will choose to reduce his

---

[3] Food crops are of course tradable. We here assume that rural food markets are unreliable and that the farmer therefore chooses to be self-sufficient in food.

work on the cash crop in response to a producer price increase, producing only sufficient to pay for the consumer goods which he expects to be available: extra effort would be wasted since it could not lead to additional consumption. Denoting cash crop production by q, its relative price (in terms of consumer goods) by p, and expected availability of consumer goods by $\bar{c}$, the farmer will choose a level of effort (and hence, if we assume for simplicity that production is proportional to labour input, of cash crop production) such that $pq = \bar{c}$. In this situation cash crop output would fall if the producer price were increased, provided the peasant's expectation of availability is constant. Hence supply response is perverse: output of the cash crop is inversely proportional to its price. Conversely, an increase in the availability of consumer goods (which would have no effect at the unrationed optimum) induces a proportional increase in output of the cash crop.

Hence, in this simple model an increase in the price of the cash crop will reduce cash crop output unless it coincides with an increased availability of consumer goods. With constant availability (and hence expenditure), the peasant will wish to maintain constant his crop income, so an increase in the price of the cash crop will induce a proportionate reduction in supply. Thus, the supply elasticity is minus unity regardless of its value in the absence of shortages. While supply response to price is perverse, an increase in the availability of consumer goods at a given cash crop price will induce a corresponding increase in cash crop production, since peasants wish to buy more goods in exchange for crops than is possible at prevailing prices.

2.2. *Stochastic Rationing and Money Stocks*

This simple analysis of perverse response to price and positive response to increased availability is complicated once we move from a barter economy to one in which goods can only be purchased for money.

To simplify, suppose that peasants receive cash from their crop sales at the close of the harvest, consume goods evenly throughout the year, and hold money balances only to finance this consumption. Hence, when goods are fully available, the maximum money stock held by the peasant (which he has upon being paid for his crop) is equal to his planned annual expenditure. When the availability of goods is limited, the money stock which the peasant chooses to hold depends critically upon the form of the rationing regime. When there is a known ration, future expenditure is also known so the desired maximum money stock is equal to this (reduced) annual expenditure.

However, rationing is sometimes a matter of chance: then, although shortage is the norm, a household may sometimes strike lucky, in which event its ability to purchase goods is determined by the money stock held. This has important consequences for the relation between goods availability and the money stock held. If the household knew the amount available for certain, this relation would be proportional. Since the household could not buy as much as it wanted, it would want to nold just enough money to buy the amount available, hence money stocks would decline if rationing became more severe. If, however, availability is uncertain (and the household has no access to credit), there is a second effect working in the opposite direction. If the household were to hold a money stock sufficient to buy the mean quantity available, for lack of money it would not be able to profit from above-average availability. Hence it may want to hold a larger money stock to reduce the probability of being constrained. The strength of this effect depends on the utility of leisure (since money can be accumulated only by working more), on the riskiness of availability, and on the household's aversion to risk.

We now present a simple model of the peasant household which formalizes the previous discussion. To keep the model as simple as possible, the peasant household is assumed to produce the cash crop as a function of labour input subject to constant returns. One unit of the crop is produced by one unit of labour and is paid for one period in arrears. The price of a unit of the crop is the same as the price of a unit of the purchased commodity. The peasant is assumed to maximize expected utility, taking into account that money left over from the current period may, depending on uncertain future availability, enable him to buy more in future.

As an illustration, consider the following two-period model:

$$\max_{c_t,\, h_{t+1}} W = u(c_t) + v(t - h_t) + \delta E[u(c^*_{t+1})] + \delta v(t - h_{t+1})$$

subject to

$$c_t \leqslant m_t \tag{1}$$

$$c_t \leqslant x_t \tag{2}$$

$$m_{t+1} = m_t - c_t + h_{t+1} \tag{3}$$

$$c_t \geqslant 0 \tag{4}$$

$$0 \leqslant h_{t+1} \leqslant t \tag{5}$$

and m_t, x_t, and h_t given and non-negative.

We assume: $f(x) > 0$ for all $x > 0$; $u' > 0 > u''$ and $v' > 0 > v''$; and $\delta < 1$; u' and v' finite and:

$$\lim_{h \to t} v'(t - h) = \infty. \tag{6}$$

The peasant's utility function is assumed to be additively separable in its two arguments: consumption of urban goods (c) and leisure ($t - h$, i.e. the difference between the total time available, t, and the number of hours, h, devoted to work on the cash crop). The price of the urban good and the producer price of the cash crop are fixed (and equal to unity by choice of units). The peasant chooses the value of the decision variables c_t and h_{t+1} when the amount of the urban good available for purchase in period t, x_t, has become known. Consumption of the urban good is subject to a cash constraint (1), an availability constraint (2), and a non-negativity constraint (4). Effort, h_{t+1}, can obviously not be negative or exceed total available time: this gives constraint (5). Equation (3) links the two periods: the money balance available in the next period (m_{t+1}) equals the present balance (m_t) minus the amount spent in the current period (c_t) plus the value of the cash crop in the next period (h_{t+1}).

Hence the effort in period ($t + 1$) generates income which can be spent in that same period: there is no lag between work on the cash crop and the consumption which it makes possible. This dynamic specification may seem artificial. But consider the implications of the alternative. If there is a lag we have:

$$m_{t+1} = m_t - c_t + h_t. \tag{3'}$$

In that case the result of current effort becomes available for financing purchases of consumption in the next period. But this specification is unacceptable in a two-period model. There would be no reason to work in period two, since this would only affect consumption in period three. Specification (3), however, does not suffer from this problem since there is no lag. Note that a different dynamic structure is possible, even if equation (3) is accepted. For while we have chosen a formulation in which the peasant decides in period t on the level of effort in the next period (h_{t+1}), it would be possible for current (h_t) rather than future effort to be decided in period t. This case is unattractive for a quite different reason: in this formulation risk would be relatively unimportant. For suppose that availability in the second period (x_{t+1}) turns out unexpectedly low. It would then still be possible to react to this outcome by working less hard in that period, for the decision on h_{t+1} would not need to be taken until all uncertainty was resolved.[4] In this case an essential element would be missing: the fact that the peasant has to take production decisions (and use his labour) before he knows how much will be available. Hence there are two reasons for the dynamic specification which we have adopted: a technical one (preventing zero effort in the second period) and an economic one (incorporating the risk of wasted effort).

In period two all uncertainty is resolved, and since there is no concern with future periods optimal consumption is clearly the minimum of availability and the money balance:

$$c_{t+1}^* = \min(x_{t+1}, m_{t+1}). \tag{7}$$

This implies that the expected utility of c_{t+1}^* in period t, when availability in

---

[4] No effort would be wasted. Since h_{t+1} would be decided when x_{t+1} was known, the peasant would choose to work just enough to finance the purchase of the amount on offer. Taking into account that an amount ($m_t - c_t$) is left over from the first period, this implies $h_{t+1} = x_{t+1} - m_t + c_t$. There still is risk in this version, but the possibility of working on the cash crop and not being able to use the proceeds is eliminated.

period $t + 1$ is still uncertain, is given by:

$$E[u(c_{t+1}^*)] = \int_0^{m_{t+1}} u(x)f(x)\,dx + u(m_{t+1}) \int_{m_{t+1}}^\infty f(x)\,dx. \qquad (8)$$

For consumption is equal to availability if that is less than the value of the money balance, while if availability is larger than the money balance then consumption is cash-constrained.

The Kuhn–Tucker conditions for this problem are analysed in the Appendix. Usually, but not necessarily, it is optimal to buy as much as possible in this current period:

$$c_t^* = \bar{c}_t = \min(x_t, m_t) \qquad (9)$$

and to decide upon a positive amount of effort ($h_{t+1} > 0$) in the next period. In that case (case III in the Appendix) the optimal amount of effort is given by the first-order conditions

$$\varphi(m_{t+1}) = u'(m_{t+1}) \int_{m_{t+1}}^\infty f(x)\,dx = v'(t - h_{t+1}) \qquad (10)$$

where $m_{t+1} = m_t - \bar{c}_t + h_{t+1}$, because of (9). Condition (10) is illustrated in Fig. 3.1. The marginal cost of effort (the increasing function v') is the forgone utility of leisure.

This is equated to the marginal benefit, which, as (10) indicates, equals the marginal utility of consumption if the peasant is liquidity constrained (i.e. if $c_{t+1} = m_{t+1}$), multiplied by the probability that this is the case, i.e. the probability that availability exceeds the money stock:

$$Pr(x_{t+1} \geqslant m_{t+1}) = \int_{m_{t+1}}^\infty f(x)\,dx. \qquad (11)$$

For given values of the predetermined variable and for a known distribution of availability, the two-period problem may be solved for c_t and h_{t+1}. The

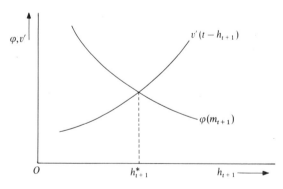

FIG. 3.1. *Marginal cost and benefit of effort*

problem can then be rolled forward one period and solved again. Money balances at any point in time will then depend on initial conditions plus the history of rationing experiences, i.e. the drawings $x_1, x_2, x_3, \ldots$, from the availability distribution. The distribution of money stocks is of interest if it is ergodic, i.e. independent of initial conditions (so that a fixed point has been reached in the stochastic sense that solving the two-period problem one more time does not affect the probability distribution of money stocks). In the Appendix we show for a numerical example that the distribution of money stocks is, after a sufficient number of periods, indeed ergodic. The question of interest at this stage is how this ergodic distribution of money stocks is affected by changes in availability. This is illustrated in Fig. 3.2, which is based on the results of the Monte Carlo simulation experiments discussed in the Appendix.[5] In unrationed equilibrium consumption would be equal to c^* and money balances to m^*. If rationing were certain then the relation between money stocks and availability would be given by the 45° line. In that case a fall in availability would lead to an equiproportional reduction of money balances. However, in the stochastic case the relation between the two variables may, as the figure shows, be negative. When availability falls, money

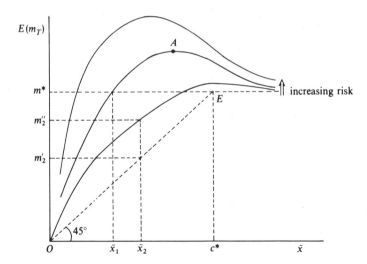

FIG. 3.2. *Money stocks as a function of mean availability of consumption goods*

[5] The distribution of availability is assumed to be log-normal in the numerical example. For a given choice of the parameters of this distribution (i.e. for a given value of mean availability, $\bar{x}$, and log standard deviation, σ), the model is solved for fifteen periods. This is repeated (with the same values of the parameters but, of course, different values for the stochastic variables $x_1, \ldots, x_{15}$) until thirty points on the distribution of m_{15} (the money stock after fifteen periods) have been obtained. The mean of these thirty points is shown in Fig. 3.2 as $E(m_T)$. Hence a point in the figure is obtained by solving the two-period problem 450 times.

stocks rise initially. Only for sufficiently severe rationing does the relation between money stocks and availability become a positive one. As one would expect, the difference from the 45° line, i.e. from the deterministic case, becomes larger as the riskiness of availability increases. In the three cases shown the functions lie everywhere above the 45° line. Hence, controlling for mean availability $\bar{x}$, the uncertainty of rationing leads to an increase in optimal long-run money stocks. For example, for mean availability equal to $\bar{x}_2$, $E(m_T)$ would, for the lowest of the three functions shown, be equal to m_2'', versus m_2' in the deterministic case. Secondly, and more importantly, money stocks can be higher even than m^*, i.e. what they would be in the absence of rationing, except if rationing is extremely severe.[6] This we call the honeymoon result. It implies that after the onset of rationing the situation looks temporarily rosier for the government than in the long run.[7] For as peasants try to increase their money balances to the new optimal level, the government obtains the cash crop at improved terms of trade. Conversely, a point to which we shall return, a liberalization attempt will have to take into account that, if full availability is restored, peasants will want to reduce their money stock (e.g. moving from point A to point E in Fig. 3.2). Hence rationing unambiguously reduces money stocks only in the deterministic case. In the stochastic case this negative effect is at least partly (and in the honeymoon case more than fully) offset by the effect of risk.

This implies that peasants are holding a claim against the government which may frustrate a subsequent liberalization attempt. For even if the government succeeds in restoring full availability, they will, starting from a point such as A, not instantaneously choose point E: they will wish first to run down their excess money balances $(m - m^*)$ and this they will do partly by (temporarily) producing less of the cash crop and partly by increasing expenditure. The liberalization attempt may then fail because an increase in imports leads (in the short run) to a fall in export volumes.

In addition to this comparative static point, a dynamic point arises from the figure. In the absence of availability risk, peasants will respond to rationing by reducing their cash crop production (supply response to availability changes is normal). In the presence of such risk, however, peasants will, in order to reach a point such as A, temporarily work harder to build up money balances. A reduction in availability still leads to a fall in cash crop production, but this effect is now mitigated by the effect of risk on money demand. The severity of the macroeconomic problem will thereby be masked. It is to the macroeconomic implications of the reactions of peasants to rationing that we now turn.

---

[6] For the second curve the exception applies for $\bar{x} < \bar{x}_1$. For all $\bar{x} > \bar{x}_1$ we have $E(m_T) > m^*$: the expected value of the money stock is higher than in unrationed equilibrium.

[7] Here we are concerned with the honeymoon result only as a theoretical possibility, but in *Peasants and Governments* we present empirical evidence of it.

3. The Macroeconomics of Enforced Price Controls

So far we have focused upon the cash crop production of the peasant as determined by some unexplained level of goods availability. We now allow for the fact that, in aggregate, since cash crop production is typically a major component of exports, it determines foreign exchange earnings. Hence, it determines the ability to import both consumer goods and the inputs needed to produce such goods locally. Thus, depending upon the system which allocates consumer goods between peasants and other groups in the economy (typically the urban sector), the availability of consumer goods to peasants is indirectly determined by the level of cash crop production as well as directly determining it, as discussed previously. If a reduction in crop sales worsens availability, this will in turn further reduce crop sales.

As with the microeconomic analysis, we begin with a barter economy and then develop a monetary analysis.

The macroeconomics of the barter model are depicted in Fig. 3.3. Cash crops are treated as being synonymous with exports, their volume measured along the vertical axis, and that of imports along the horizontal axis. The world price of the export crop is given and equal to the slope AH/OA, so that the foreign offer curve is represented by the line through O and H. The relation between the amount of the cash crop peasants produce and their consumption of imports in the absence of rationing is the concave function through O, B, and I, the peasants' offer curve. Along this curve the domestic price of the cash crop varies. If, for example, the producer price were equal to AB/OA, then the peasants would choose point B on the offer curve. They would then produce a quantity OA of the cash crop, which would be exported

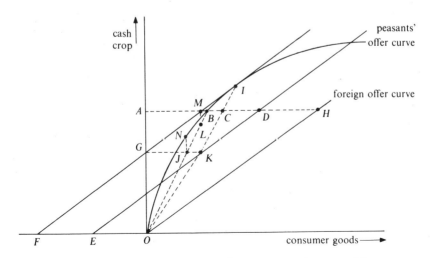

FIG. 3.3. *The macroeconomics of rationing in a barter model*

in exchange for a volume AH of imports, of which peasants would consume AB so that the quantity BH would be available for the urban sector. Note that the domestic price is lower than the world price, the difference BH/OA representing the rate at which the cash crop is implicitly taxed.

The macroeconomic effects of price controls depend upon the government's export crop taxation policy. We shall assume the government to be predatory on the peasant sector, using its revenue from crop taxation to reward client groups such as urban wage earners, who receive priority claims on consumer goods at official prices. In Fig. 3.3 this exogenous claim is set equal to DH. Its effect on rural availability may be represented in the diagram by a shift OE to the left of the foreign offer curve. The allocation of imports to urban areas can exceed this minimum level, but a lower allocation is not politically feasible.

Now suppose that this claim increases from DH to MH, for example because the government embarks upon an import-intensive investment programme. If the producer price remains unchanged then peasants will initially continue to produce a quantity OA of coffee, but now, after deduction of the urban claim, only AM of imports is available for rural consumption. Hence peasants are rationed: they cannot realize their intended consumption AB.

When peasants realize that availability is reduced, they will react by producing a smaller volume of cash crops such that their income is only sufficient to sustain available purchases. This implies a cumulative contraction. The economy gets caught in a downward spiral: cash crop production decreases, exports fall, less can be imported, peasants are more severely rationed, they revise their expectation of availability downwards and produce even less. This process does not converge; it stops once peasants move beyond point J. Cash crop output will then be less than OG and the urban claim can no longer be honoured. The government then has to give up its policy, either by changing the producer price or by reducing the urban claim on imports.

Note that the initial situation is a sustainable one: the external terms of trade, the producer price set by the government, and the allocation of importables between peasants and the urban sector are compatible. The government does not aim at rationing of peasants' consumption demand, but this may be the unintended effect of its policies if a change makes the combination of the three variables incompatible. The economy then stumbles into a rationing regime and hence into the process of cumulative contraction which we have just described.

There are three changes which may trigger this process. First, there may be, as in Fig. 3.3, an increase in the amount of the urban claim. Secondly, rationing may be caused by a reduction in the domestic relative price of the cash crop, i.e. by an increase in the rate at which coffee production is implicitly taxed. This is illustrated in Fig. 3.4 where, initially, peasants are again at point B. If the producer price is lowered from AB/OA to CG/OC then

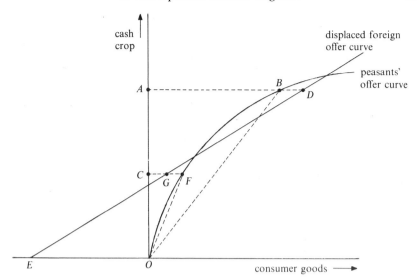

FIG. 3.4. *Rationing as a result of an increase in the taxation of export crops*

peasants become rationed, rural availability falling *GF* short of their intended consumption. The attempt to increase urban availability through heavier taxation of export agriculture in that case ultimately becomes self-defeating.

Finally, rationing may result from a deterioration of the terms of trade. In Fig. 3.5 this is shown as a rotation of the foreign offer curve: the world price of the cash crop (in terms of importables) falls from *FD/EF* to *FG/EF*. A small terms-of-trade loss would not lead to rationing, since urban consumption in the initial situation exceeds the urban claim, so that a reduction is politically feasible. But if the terms-of-trade loss is sufficiently large (as in Fig. 3.5) then the government loses this room for manœuvre: it then has to reduce rural availability of consumer goods and this leads to rationing.

Two points deserve to be emphasized at this stage. First, the contraction of the economy does not depend on policies being 'wrong' in the initial, pre-rationing situation. It is perfectly possible that initially policies are optimal in some sense. What matters is rather the rigidity introduced by the political commitment to the urban claim and to price control. It is this rigidity which explains why a change in the terms of trade or in domestic policies may make policies incompatible and may plunge the economy into a rationing regime.

Once peasants are rationed, normative statements about crop prices to producers cannot be made unambiguously. The price may be too high in the sense that for given rural availability of imported consumer goods, peasants would produce more if the price were lowered. At the same time the producer price may be too low in the sense that it would have to be increased (along with rural availability) if the 'optimum' were to be reached. The ambiguity of

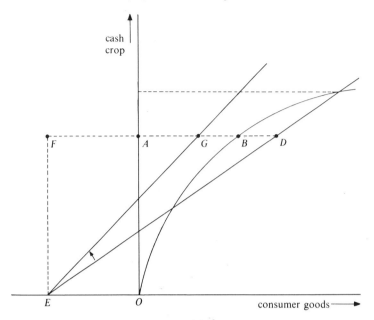

FIG. 3.5. *Rationing as a result of a deterioration of the terms of trade*

statements on the appropriateness of the level of the producer price in the case of rationing is illustrated by point J (Fig. 3.3). As long as rural availability does not change, the producer price at J is too high: if the price were lower, cash crop production would increase until the peasants' offer curve was reached at the unrationed equilibrium point N. On the other hand, reaching the 'optimum' I requires a producer price which is higher than at N and, indeed, higher than at J. Whether the price can be called too high or too low depends on the extent, if any, to which price changes are accompanied by changes in availability.

The barter analysis is now extended to an explicitly monetary analysis. The government is, in a non-trivial way, constrained by its own price controls: it loses a degree of freedom in the financing of its budget deficit, since price control makes the level of the money stock endogenous. The government can set tax rates, but total tax revenue, and hence the size of the budget deficit, will depend on the behaviour of private agents. The deficit can be financed by money creation, by domestic borrowing, and by foreign borrowing. Domestic borrowing (the bulk of which arises from portfolio requirements laid on provident funds and the like) is often very limited, and the scope for discretionary variation in it more or less negligible. Similarly, foreign commercial borrowing is often virtually impossible because of the effect of previously accumulated arrears on creditworthiness. There is some more scope for varying the amount of concessionary loans, but these are not only generally tied to projects (in which case fungibility might still qualify them as a means of general deficit financing) but increasingly also to macroeconomic performance. Hence deficit financing must come entirely (or at least largely) from money creation.

Were prices flexible, the government would be able to alter the nominal stock of money. At the initial price level, this would create a divergence from the demand for real balances, and so prices would adjust accordingly. However, to the extent that the government succeeds in controlling prices, changes in the nominal money stock necessarily involve equivalent changes in the real money stock. Except temporarily during an adjustment to a shock, the government is unable to induce the private sector to hold excess real money balances. Peasants will simply cut their marketed production and thereby reduce their money holdings. Hence the level of the money stock becomes endogenous. Price control therefore forces the government to exercise greater fiscal discipline. Given the restrictions on borrowing, the path of government expenditure and that of tax revenue must be consistent with an evolution of the money stock that the country's citizens are prepared to hold at the controlled prices. If the government does not accept the need for greater fiscal discipline implied by its own set of controls, then the infeasibility of its policies will show up directly.

For the analysis in Fig. 3.3, which portrayed the barter model, only relative prices were required. The introduction of money requires explicit consideration of nominal prices. In Fig. 3.6 the space is defined upon the two nominal prices; c, the price of the cash crop, and g, the price of goods. The schedules $C–C$ and $G–G$ denote the loci of notional equilibrium in these two markets respectively during a single period. Notional equilibria are defined on the

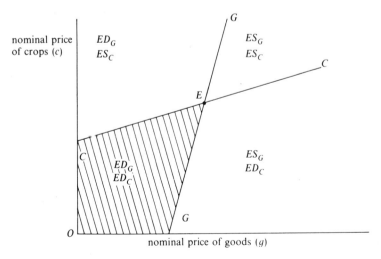

FIG. 3.6. *Notional equilibrium loci in the goods and crops markets*

assumption of equilibrium in all markets other than that of the locus being derived. Notion equilibrium in the goods market is achieved by variations in demand, supply being treated as exogenous within the period. Hence, an increase in the goods price leads to excess supply of goods unless offset by the higher incomes generated by an increase in the price of cash crops. However, proportionate increases in both prices are not neutral because of a real cash balance effect, causing the *G–G* locus to be steeper than a ray through the origin. Notional equilibrium in the cash crops market is achieved by both supply and demand responses to prices. An increase in the price of crops leads to excess supply unless offset by an increase in the price of goods. Again, proportionate increases in prices are not neutral, because as prices rise the real cash balance effect induces an increase in crop supply. Hence, the *C–C* locus is flatter than a ray through the origin. The two loci divide the space into four zones of disequilibrium. In these disequilibria not all plans can be fulfilled, so that agents change their behaviour. These changes in behaviour alter the loci of market equilibria from notional to effective. The change implied by our previous theory is that in response to an excess demand for goods peasants revise downwards their marketing of crops. This expands the zone of excess demand for crops, shifting the crops equilibrium locus to *C'–C'*, shown as effect (1) in Fig. 3.7. For completeness, we note a second effect: were there to be an excess supply of cash crops, then, because peasants would receive a lower income than planned, they would revise downwards their demand for goods. This Keynesian effect would shift the goods market locus to *G'–G'*.

We can now use the analysis to distinguish different ways is which crop and goods prices may be set wrongly. Suppose the economy is indeed charac-

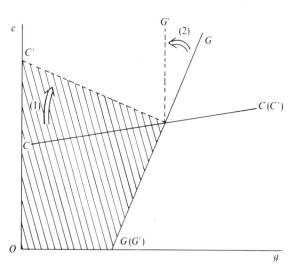

Fig. 3.7. *Effective equilibrium loci*

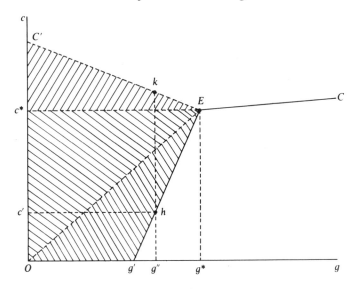

FIG. 3.8. *Regions of crop mispricing*

terized by repressed inflation, that is the combination of excess demands for both goods and crops shown in the shaded zone of Fig. 3.8. Does the excess demand for crops imply that their price is set too low, as is generally inferred in policy advice? Prices c^*, g^* secure full market clearing. Since the government's demand for crops reflects its revenue desires, c^* can be thought of as the revenue-maximizing crop price denoted by the slope OI in Fig. 3.3. First, consider whether repressed inflation implies that crop prices are below c^*. From Fig. 3.8 it is evident that no such inference can be made. Three regions of the repressed inflation zone can be distinguished. In the region bordered by C', E, c^* the nominal price of crops is too high, even though there is an excess demand for them. In the region c^*, E, O the nominal price of crops is too low, but the relative price of crops to goods is too high. Only in the third region, O, E, g', are both the nominal and the relative prices of crops too low. Hence, it is not possible to infer how crop prices differ from their equilibrium levels merely from the symptom of excess demand for crops once the goods market is also in disequilibrium. The comparison between the actual price of crops and their optimum price, c^*, is relevant only if the goods price is simultaneously raised to g^*. If instead the goods price is to be left unaltered at a level below g^* then quite different considerations determine the appropriate change in the price of crops.

As shown in the previous section, given excess demand for goods, crop supply response to price changes is perverse. Lowering the crop price will not only raise the supply of crops, it will reduce the notional demand for goods. At a sufficiently low price the notional demand will fall to coincide with the effective demand and the goods market will clear. We distinguish between three ranges of the goods price, $O-g'$, $g'-g''$, and $g''-g^*$. The point g' denotes the intersection of the G–E locus with the horizontal axis. At goods prices below g' it is not possible to achieve equilibrium in the goods market in the period depicted by lowering the crop price. Real money holdings are so large that even if crop prices, and hence cash incomes, are zero, there is still excess demand for goods. Next consider g'', which is determined by the crop price c'. Recall that c^* is the revenue-maximizing crop price. Hence, reductions in the crop price below c^* reduce revenue as the tax is increased on the wrong side of the Laffer curve. The price c' is defined as that below which the revenue accruing to the government is less than its minimum needs (i.e. below the 'urban claim' OE in Fig. 3.3). The goods price g'' is that which clears the goods market if crop prices are set at c'. Hence, if goods prices are in the range $g'-g''$, although the government can achieve goods market clearing by lowering the crop price, the resulting supply of crops is not compatible with its minimum expenditure requirements. Only in the range $g''-g^*$ will a sufficient reduction in crop prices take the economy out of the repressed inflation zone to a position which, though not optimal, is sustainable: peasants are not rationed, and the minimum urban claim is satisfied.

To summarize, if the economy is characterized by repressed inflation there is invariably a need to raise the price of goods. However, even if this is done, the nominal price of crops should be lowered if the economy starts in region C', E, c^*, and the relative price lowered if it is in region c^*, E, O. If the goods price is not raised then a sustainable position compatible with the urban claim can only be reached if the economy is in region h, k, E. The sustainable position is reached by reducing the nominal price of crops. However, such a strategy is dangerous because it runs the risk of the crop price inadvertently being lowered below c'.

We now turn from the analysis of the intra-period disequilibrium to a portrayal of the implosive dynamics of shortages. If the economy enters the repressed inflation zone and prices are not altered so as to restore equilibrium, then, as we have argued, marketed supply contracts as peasants reduce planned income to expected expenditure. In aggregate this reduces foreign exchange earnings and hence the supply of goods in the next period. This process is depicted in Fig. 3.9. The reduction in the supply of goods shifts the goods market locus to the north-east, enlarging the repressed inflation zone from C', E, G', O to C'', E'', G'', O.

The reduction in planned income, and hence demand for goods, thus reduces their supply to the peasant economy. We now consider what happens to the magnitude of excess demand as the economy implodes. Consider first the case in which the net effect of price controls on consumer goods and crops is to leave the real crop price, c/g, at that which prevails on world markets. The controls reduce the whole price level but do not alter relative prices. In this case, a reduction in crop sales reduces both the demand for goods and the

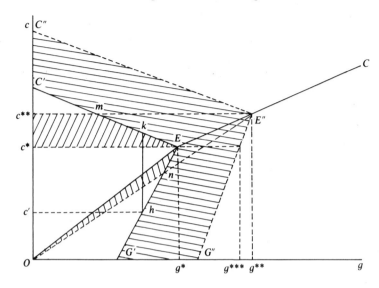

FIG. 3.9. *The dynamics of shortages*

supply of goods to the peasant economy by the same amount. For example, setting the relative price on the world market equal to unity, a one-unit reduction in crop sales will reduce both demand and supply by one unit of consumer goods. Hence, the excess demand for goods stays constant as planned incomes are successively reduced. Excess demand induces a reduction in crop sales, but this does not reduce excess demand and so the peasant economy continues to implode to an equilibrium at subsistence. Now consider the more likely case in which the net effect of price controls is to reduce the real price of crops below the world price (so that peasants are being taxed as we have previously assumed). In this case a reduction in crop sales reduces the supply of goods to the peasant economy by more than it reduces demand. A one-unit reduction in crop sales again lowers the supply of goods to the economy by one unit, but because peasants receive less than the world price for their crops their demand for goods is reduced by less than one unit. As before, excess demand induces a reduction in crop sales, but now this reduction in crop sales increases the extent of excess demand. Again the economy implodes to a subsistence equilibrium, but since there is likely to be some relationship between the extent of excess demand and the magnitude of the reduction in crop sales, the implosion will tend to accelerate. Finally, consider the case in which the net effect of price controls is that the real price of crops is above their world level, so that the government is subsidizing peasants. Only in this case may the implosion cease at an equilibrium above the subsistence floor. As crop sales are reduced, peasant demand for goods falls more rapidly than their supply to the economy, and so it is possible, though not necessary, that the excess demand is eliminated by a partial contraction in crop sales.

Now reconsider what can be said about the desirable changes in the prices of crops and goods. The period-two equilibrium prices are now higher, at c^{**} and g^{**}, than those which would have cleared the markets in period one, namely c^* and g^*. Our previous characterization of the various regions of the repressed inflation zone applies in period two to these new equilibrium prices. Suppose the economy lies in the area bounded by c^*, c^{**}, m, E. In period one this was characterized by the nominal price of crops being too high relative to market-clearing prices. In period two, however, the same crop price is below the equilibrium price. Analogously, if the economy lies in the area bounded by O, E, n, the relative price of crops was too high in period one, but the same relative price is too low in period two. Finally, if the economy lies in area k, E, h, in period one it is feasible to achieve a sustainable position compatible with the urban claim by reducing crop prices, whereas in period two this policy option is no longer available.

The analysis of Fig. 3.9 shows that if pricing policies are the only instruments available, the longer reform is delayed the more must prices temporarily overshoot their equilibrium levels, c^*, g^*. Once supply has contracted in response to shortages of goods, merely restoring prices to c^*, g^* does not constitute a compatible policy set, even though, were there no prehistory of prices below these levels, c^*, g^* would be compatible with the urban claim. These policies are compatible only if peasants expect goods market clearing, so that if peasants' expectations are adaptive, a prehistory of shortages makes the policy set incompatible.

So far we have discussed the possibility of a cumulative contraction in crop output implicity in terms of certainty. When rationing is a matter of chance, our earlier discussion on optimum money holdings suggests that this process of implosion can be divided into two phases. In the first phase, as availability deteriorates, desired money holdings rise, so peasants temporarily sell more crops than when their money stocks are at their chosen levels. Hence, although the rationing point presents an unstable equilibrium the decline in output will initially be damped. However, once availability deteriorates to the point at which peasants choose to reduce their money stocks, the long-run tendency to implosive output reductions is accelerated by short-run monetary dishoarding. Hence, once a price-controlled economy stumbles into a regime of shortages which peasants expect to be sustained, output is subject to initially creeping but eventually rapid cumulative decline.

4. The Evasion of Controls

Price control creates rents and therefore induces rent-seeking. One form of rent-seeking we have already encountered in section 2: the building up of money stocks in the case when price control leads to a stochastic form of rationing. A peasant who, confronted with an unusually large ration, is able to buy it only because he has increased his money stock, obtains more goods at the expense of others. For, within a period, total availability is pre-determined. At the village level, therefore, the response is costly: total leisure time has been reduced (since the peasant had to increase his work on the cash crop to build up his money balance), while aggregate availability of consumption goods is unaffected.[8] However, at the national level this rent-seeking is socially productive. By hypothesis, too few cash crops are pro-duced, so that extra supply in return for socially costless domestic currency is beneficial. Another form of rent-seeking involves search for places or times with better availability, in the sense of a more favourable function $f(x)$. In this case the private benefit is the only one. As before, improved availability must be at the expense of other peasants, but there is now no offsetting benefit for the rest of the economy: the resources (including time) devoted to search are socially unproductive.

Black markets may be seen as the marketing of the value added from search activity. The black marketeer sells privileged access, i.e. that which in the absence of a black market could only be obtained by search. Rents accruing to final consumers are of course reduced by a black market. But they are not eliminated. This is the result of the illegality of black market activity. The marketeer cannot advertise and each time he makes an offer to sell he runs the risk of getting caught. To him the cost of fully exploiting the willingness of his clients to pay is that he would have to make many offers. In order to reduce risk it is optimal for him to set his price below the market-clearing level. Hence, black markets cannot be seen as a way of achieving market clearing indirectly. Rents will not be completely eliminated (see Bevan *et al.*, 1989 *b*).

4.1. *Black Markets*

The textbook treatment of black markets uses partial equilibrium analysis. It thereby ignores what happens to the income earned by black marketeers. This income is either spent on consumption or saved. If it is used for consumption, the supply of goods available to other agents is reduced (since black marketeers have privileged access). For a given total supply of con-sumer goods, as the black market price rises so the incomes of black marketeers are increased, and so goods supply to other agents is reduced. With excess demand at official prices, the black market price can only equilibrate supply and demand if either desired expenditure falls as the price rises, or black marketeers hoard money. The black market supply curve has

---

[8] This intra-period loss might be compensated by a later gain if cash crop production positively affects future allocations of consumer goods to the village. In practice such a link seems rare; we assume that the allocation to the village is independent of its production.

an elasticity of minus unity. If the marketeer acquires a quantity q at the official price (unity) and sells what he does not consume himself $(q - c)$ at the black market price p, then it follows from his budget constraint

$$(p - 1)q = pc \qquad (12)$$

that the supply curve is

$$(q - c) = q/p \qquad (13)$$

There is an important difference in the demand elasticity between rural and urban black markets. There is no reason why the demand of peasants in the black market would be unit-elastic. In the stable case (shown in Fig. 3.10) it is more elastic. The equilibrium black market price is then determined by the intersection of the supply curve S–S' and the demand curve D–D', at point E. However, in the urban economy, where both the labour supply and the wage can be treated as fixed, aggregate desired expenditure is not reduced as black market prices rise. In particular, the 'urban claim' introduced in the previous section, which can be thought of as the public sector wage bill, is invariant. The demand elasticity is therefore minus unity, as the supply elasticity, and there is no equilibrium. We now present a simple general equilibrium model in which this urban claim is the only demand for goods, though it exceeds their supply. The point we demonstrate is that with such a fixed demand for goods, the black market price only equilibrates the market if black marketeers hoard money out of their income. This in turn has macroeconomic repercussions analogous to the honeymoon effect.

Suppose a black marketeer acquires (at the official price of 1) a fraction α of total supply q. Workers, who receive an income w, can therefore buy $(1 - \alpha)q$

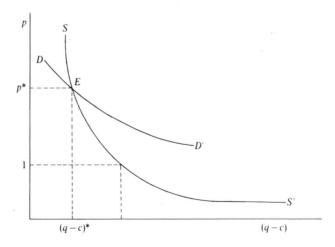

FIG. 3.10. *Rural black market equilibrium*

officially, spendng the rest of their income in the black market, where the price is p. Hence the black market demand of workers is given by:

$$q^D = [w - (1 - \alpha)q]/p. \tag{14}$$

In equilibrium this is equal to the quantity supplied by the marketeer, so that of the goods he has acquired $(\alpha q - q^D)$ remains for his own consumption. The marketeer's income is equal to his profits $(p - 1)q^D$. Hence, if he were to spend his income entirely on the good in question, his budget constraint would be:

$$(p - 1)q^D = (\alpha q - q^D). \tag{15}$$

But this implies $pq^D = \alpha q$, substitution of which in (14) gives:

$$\frac{w - (1 - \alpha)q}{p} = \frac{\alpha q}{p}. \tag{16}$$

If wage income is equal to total supply valued at the official price $(w = q$, hence $w - (1 - \alpha)q = \alpha q)$ then the left-hand side and the right-hand side of (16) are equal, irrespective of the value of p: the black market price is then indeterminate. Conversely, if wage income exceeds the value of total supply $(w > q)$ then there is excess demand in the black market at all prices: the black market price will then tend to infinity.

To avoid this pitfall marketeers must be modelled as being willing to accumulate cash balances (or other financial claims), so that (15) no longer holds: they will then use only part of their profits for their own consumption of the rationed goods. This implies an asset demand for money.

The existence of a black market may also affect the transactions demand for money. In its crudest form (a version used by the IMF to explain increases in money demand in Tanzania) the argument is that the transactions demand for money must increase, because, while the total quantity of goods is unchanged, part of it is now sold at a higher price. However, the value of peasants' purchases is unaffected, the higher price being offset by a lower quantity. There is of course the transactions demand of black marketeers themselves. But this does not imply an increase in national money demand, for any good acquired by the marketeer at the official price (to be resold at the higher black market price) would otherwise have been bought by a shop at the same price. Hence there need be no change in transactions demand: black market supply is at the expense of official supply. As discussed above, there is a hoarding demand of black marketeers. This may be reinforced by the possibility that buying in the black market will increase the incentive to build up excess money balances. Whether this will be the case depends on the extent to which the black market succeeds in achieving exchange efficiency.

Consider a polar case: risk is unaffected. This would be the case if, for example, marketeers as a group managed to acquire a share s of rural supplies and the rationing system was such that this resulted in all individual availabilities being reduced by this fraction. The incentive to have high money balances (in order to profit from unusually high availability at the official price) then remains. This may be seen with the aid of the two-period model which we used before. The price in the black market is p. Assume for the moment that the distribution $f(x)$ is unaffected by the existence of the black market. The problem may then be written as:

$$\max_{c_t,\, h_{t+1}} W = u(c_t) + v(t - h_t) + \delta\left[\int_0^{m_{t+1}} u(x + (m_{t+1} - x)/p)f(x)\,dx + \right.$$

$$\left. u(m_{t+1}) \int_{m_{t+1}}^{\infty} f(x)\,dx + v(t - h_{t+1}) \right]$$

subject to:

$$c_{ot} \leqslant x_t \tag{17}$$

$$c_{ot} + p(c_t - c_{ot}) \leqslant m_t \tag{18}$$

$$m_{t+1} = m_t - c_{ot} - p(c_t - c_{ot}) + h_{t+1} \tag{19}$$

$$c_{ot} \geqslant 0 \tag{20}$$

$$c_t - c_{ot} \geqslant 0 \tag{21}$$

$$0 \leqslant h_{t+1} \leqslant t. \tag{22}$$

In the first period, consumption (c_t) can exceed the amount bought at the official price (c_{ot}), the difference being acquired in the black market at price p. In this model the possibility of being availability-constrained is eliminated. As indicated by the first term within the square brackets in the maximand, if in the second period availability at the official price falls short of the amount of money available, then the amount of money left over after the maximum amount has been bought in the official market is used in the black market. Note that while availability is not risky and it is no longer possible to be availability-constrained, there is still risk: the peasant does not know how much he will be able to buy at the lower, official price.

The change in the incentive to hold money may be seen by differentiating the objective function with respect to m_{t+1}:

$$\frac{\partial W}{\partial m_{t+1}} = \delta\left[u'(m_{t+1}) \int_{m_{t+1}}^{\infty} f(x)\,dx + \right.$$

$$\left. \int_0^{m_{t+1}} u'(x + (m_{t+1} - x)/p)f(x)(1/p)\,dx \right] \tag{23}$$

The first term is the same as before: it indicates the incentive to build up money stocks for a situation in which the peasant would not want to use the black market anyway, because he is liquidity- rather than availability-constrained: the case $x_{t+1} > m_{t+1}$. The second term is new: it indicates that for $x_{t+1} < m_{t+1}$ excess money can be used in the black market. In this sense there is more reason to hold money under stochastic rationing with a black market than if only official purchases are possible. However, we must take into account that supply in the black market is at the expense of supply in the official market. This is equivalent to a reduction of $\bar{x}$ considered before. Hence the sign of this effect is ambiguous. However, for moderately severe rationing (i.e. for $\bar{x}$ higher than the value for which the maximum value of $E(m_t)$ is reached; cf. Fig. 3.2) the effect on money stocks is positive. In that case both effects work in the same direction. The presence of a black market then increases the demand for money.[9]

In another polar case all risk is reduced. Peasants who have been unusually lucky in the official market sell in the black market and vice versa. The role of risk is then eliminated and transactions demand is higher than in the case of effective price control only to the extent that the fraction s is sold at the higher black market price. In this case the black market eliminates the gain to the rest of the economy which is the result of the rent-seeking behaviour of peasants described in section 2.

Finally, it must be taken into account that peasants may not buy in black markets even if these exist.[10] This may be seen as follows. Assuming that rationing is effective (in the sense that it is optimal for the peasant to buy as much in the official market as he can get), the decision to buy in the black market involves a comparison of the utility of the extra quantity of consumer goods so acquired and the utility of the leisure forgone because financing the black market purchase requires extra farm work. Since the black market price must be higher than the official price, it is possible that a peasant will choose not to participate in the black market, preferring his leisure to the increase in consumption. Obviously, this depends on individual circumstances (income, preferences, and access at the official price). In the presence of a black market (and assuming that no one can attain an unrationed equilibrium) there are therefore two groups of peasants: those who do and those who do not participate in the black market. This distinction is important because the two groups respond differently to changes in prices or availability (see Table 3.1). Supply response is typically normal for the former group, but perverse for those who only buy officially (cash crop production falling in response to a producer price increase). Similarly, while the response of the former group to an improvement of availability is perverse, it is normal for those who do not buy in the black market.

However, the response of the aggregate is unaffected by the existence of the black market: it can be analysed as if the representative peasant does not buy in the black market. Abstracting from the monetary changes discussed above, there can be no improvement in the supply of cash crops. For, although the

---

[9] In the case of the log-normal examples used in the Appendix the multiplicative change in official availability is equivalent to a shift to the left of the normal distribution of $\ln(x)$. Hence the probability of x exceeding the value of the money stock is reduced. In terms of Fig. 3.2 mean availability has fallen while the log standard deviation is unaffected. This leads to an increase in money demand, provided we are on the negatively sloped part of the curve.

[10] The following argument is further developed in *Peasants and Governments*.

TABLE 3.1. *Supply response to changes in prices or availability in the case of rationing*

| | Increase in cash crop production in response to an increase in: | |
	producer price of cash crop	official availability
Peasants who only buy officially	perverse (−)	normal (+)
Peasants who also buy in the black market	normal (+)	perverse (−)
Total (all peasants)	perverse (−)	normal (+)

black market redistributes access, it cannot increase total supply to peasants. Hence, while the production of an individual peasant who buys in the black market is higher than it would be if price control were fully effective, aggregate supply cannot increase. It is therefore appropriate to model the representative peasant as if a black market did not exist. Indeed, as black marketeers derive an income from their activities, the aggregate supply of urban goods to peasants (and hence their cash crop production) is correspondingly lower. In this sense the earlier analysis is unaffected.

Black markets are not the only result of attempts to evade price controls. Foreign exchange control may make the illegal acquisition of foreign financial assets attractive. If exports can be smuggled out of the country this is an easy way to acquire foreign assets. A more complicated route to foreign-asset acquisition is overinvoicing. Overinvoicing is a response to price control in the market for foreign exchange, but is affected by controls in goods markets.

4.2. Overinvoicing and Price Controls

We now consider how import and price control systems affect the incentive to overcome foreign exchange controls by overinvoicing.

We compare the incentives for overinvoicing in four cases: without and with price control, and with imports controlled by volume or by value. We use the following notation:

$\bar{e}$ = the official exchange rate (domestic currency/$)
1 = (by choice of units) the price of imports (in $)
p_m = the price of imports in the overinvoicing case (in $)
q = the controlled (volume or value) level of imports
m = the mark-up rate in case of cost-plus price control
p_d = the domestic price (in domestic currency) in the absence of price control.

If domestic prices are not controlled then domestic profits on correctly invoiced imports are $q(p_d - \bar{e})$, irrespective of whether imports are controlled by volume or value. (The controls reflect an overvalued exchange rate, hence $p_d > \bar{e}$: the import activity is profitable.) If imports are controlled by volume then overinvoicing reduces domestic profits to $q(p_d - \bar{e}p_m)$, while the firm acquires $q(p_m - 1)$ in foreign exchange. Hence overinvoicing enables the firm to convert part of its domestic profits into foreign exchange. In fact, it is as if the firm acquires foreign exchange legally at the official exchange rate $\bar{e}$, since:

$$\bar{e}q(p_m - 1) + q(p_d - \bar{e}p_m) = q(p_d - \bar{e}). \qquad (24)$$

If imports are controlled by value then overinvoicing reduces the volume of imports to q/p_m. Hence $(q/p_m)(p_m - 1)$ is acquired in foreign exchange, and domestic profits are $(q/p_m)(p_d - \bar{e}p_m)$. This implies that the implicit exchange rate at which domestic profits can be converted into foreign exchange is p_d, since:

$$p_d(q/p_m)(p_m - 1) + (q/p_m)(p_d - \bar{e}p_m) = q(p_d - \bar{e}). \qquad (25)$$

Therefore, the incentive for overinvoicing is greater in the case of volume control: the implicit exchange rate is more favourable (since $p_d > \bar{e}$, by assumption).

Now suppose domestic prices are controlled. Then, if imports are correctly invoiced the domestic profits are $qm\bar{e}$. If imports are overinvoiced, then, if control is by value, the volume of imports falls to q/p_m and the domestic price rises to $p_m(1 + m)\bar{e}$, so that profits are unchanged at $qm\bar{e}$. The firm acquires, as before, $(q/p_m)(p_m - 1)$ in foreign exchange, but now this is (from the firm's point of view) acquired costlessly. Finally, if control is by volume, then domestic profits *rise* to $qp_m m\bar{e}$, while the overinvoicing firm acquires $q(p_m - 1)$ in foreign exchange.

Clearly, the four cases can be ranked, in terms of the incentive for overinvoicing, as shown in Table 3.2, for the implicit price of a unit of foreign exchange (in terms of a unit of domestic profits forgone) is negative in the first case, zero in the second case, $\bar{e}$ in the third case, and p_d in the fourth case.[11] Fig. 11 illustrates the welfare losses of overinvoicing. Here we consider an economy which produces one good (which is entirely exported) and consumes two goods. The first of these goods is the numeraire and is sold domestically at the world price (which is correctly invoiced). Export earnings are predetermined, so that the value of the total import bill (OA) is known. The indifference curves correspond to a social welfare function in which no weight is attached to illegally acquired foreign assets. If good 2 is correctly priced at p_2, then consumption will be at D on the budget line AG. However, if

[11] Since in Tanzania the second case is relevant (and sometimes the first), the incentive for overinvoicing is indeed very strong. In particular, it is stronger than in Kenya (which corresponds to rank 4), this difference having an important application in Chapter 6.

TABLE 3.2.   *Ranking of policies in terms of incentives for overinvoicing*

Import control	Price control (mark-up)	
	yes	no
Volume	1	3
Value	2	4

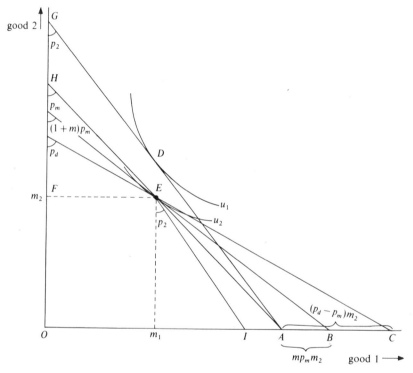

FIG. 3.11. *Welfare effects of overinvoicing*

good 2 is overinvoiced (say, at a price p_m), then the budget line rotates to AH and welfare obviously is reduced. If the volume of imports (of good 2) is constrained to be OF then consumption will be at E. At that point a quantity m_2 of good 2 is imported, for which the country pays IA too much (in terms of the numeraire, hence in terms of foreign exchange). IA therefore represents the amount of foreign exchange illegally acquired by the overinvoicers. Point E is compatible, as shown, with different systems of control. For example, if there is no price control, then the domestic price will rise to p_d. Importers then earn a rent $(p_d - p_m)m_2$, which is equal to AC in the diagram. Under price control, good 2 will be sold at the (lower) price $(1 + m)p_m$, demand for it is rationed, and excess demand spills over into the market for other, uncontrolled imports (good 1). Domestic profits in that case are equal to AB (as opposed to AC in the previous case). Since the final allocation is at E in either case, it does not seem to matter which system is chosen. This is misleading. First, as we have seen, the incentive for overinvoicing differs. If importers weigh this incentive against the probability of detection and the penalty involved, then they will choose a higher value of p_m when subject to price controls. Hence the budget line rotates further than it otherwise would and the welfare loss is therefore larger. Secondly, under price control there is rationing at E and this will lead to black market transactions. This implies a redistribution in favour of those with relatively better access to the rationed commodity. That group, of course, includes the overinvoicing importers themselves. Hence (domestic) real income is not only reduced, it is also likely to be less equally distributed. Finally, overinvoicing can have serious macro-economic consequences since it reduces the availability of consumer goods to peasants.

Overinvoicing affects not only flows but also stocks. There is a build-up of foreign financial assets (involuntary to the extent that there would be no incentive to acquire them in the absence of controls), the existence of which may be of crucial importance when controls are dismantled. If liberalization leads to the repatriation of these assets, they may be a substitute for aid (on which we concentrate in section 5) as a means of financing a liberalization policy.

Overinvoicing should not be considered as a matter of limited practical importance: the evidence, which we consider in Chapter 6, suggests that in Tanzania overinvoicing has been practised on a very large scale.

5. Dismantling Controls

Once the economy has arrived in a repressed inflation regime such as depicted in Fig. 3.9, the goods market does not clear, and secondly, government revenue from export crop taxation is sub-optimal. This differs from the repressed inflation regime in standard fix-price models. In our case peasants' demand for consumer goods is rationed, but the demand for the cash crop (a tradable good) is not rationed. The government could have obtained the cash crop at a more favourable rate of exchange (i.e. it has failed to use an 'optimal tariff' on its 'imports' from the peasant sector); however, the government's control over the producer price produces rationing not in that market, but (indirectly, through the effect of a lower volume of exports on the supply of consumer goods) in the markets for importables.

The design of liberalization policies has to take into account that the regime boundaries shown in the figure shift over time. A static analysis is therefore inappropriate. Three dynamic effects have to be taken into account: the effect, via the balance of payments, of export crop production on future goods availability; the adjustment of expectations in response to rationing experiences; and the adjustment over time of money balances.

Policies which aim at restoring equilibrium can, in principle, be grouped under two headings: policies which rely on changes in prices controlled by the government (i.e. c and g), including, at one extreme, the abolition of price control itself; and policies which aim at improving rural goods availability directly, including policies which have the effect of reducing the urban claim. We consider these in turn.

5.1. *Pricing Policies*

A policy which is of considerable practical interest (since countries with predominantly agricultural exports are often advised to raise producer prices of export crops) is an increase of c (i.e. a vertical move in Fig. 3.8). The analysis of section 2 indicates that such a policy is counter-productive if controls cannot be evaded. Since peasants will react to the price increase by reducing export crop production, the effect will be an outward shift of the G–E locus, hence an increase of the region of repressed inflation. Since the G–E locus is upward-sloping it is impossible, starting from a situation of repressed inflation, to eliminate goods market disequilibrium through an increase of the producer price. A policy of reducing c may be infeasible (if the initial point does not lie vertically above the G–E locus), and if feasible, has the drawback that agents would be given contradictory signals: the price reduction would have to be reversed later unless $c > c^*$ initially in order to reach full equilibrium at E.

A liberalization policy will have to take into account that point E cannot be reached through changes in c alone (since points vertically above or below E do not lie in the repressed inflation region). Changes in availability are considered in the next subsection; here we consider simultaneous changes of c and g.

Suppose that the economy has been in the repressed inflation zone for more than one period, so that a process as depicted in Fig. 3.9 has occurred. If pricing policies are the only instruments available to the government, then in some combination goods and crop prices must overshoot their long-run equilibrium levels, g^*, c^*. We consider three feasible reform sequences.

One sustainable sequence of reform is thus to increase prices to g^{**}, c^{**} in the present period, lowering them to c^*, g^* once expectations of goods market clearing have been re-established. However, this is not the only feasible sequence, and political considerations may well make it sub-optimal. In particular, the above sequence involves a reduction in the nominal price of crops, albeit offset by a greater proportionate reduction in the price of goods.

Next, consider an alternative which avoids any such subsequent reduction in crop prices yet still achieves goods market clearing. This involves setting prices in the present period at c^*, g^{***}, and then subsequently lowering goods prices to g^*. In addition to the avoidance of the need to reduce crop prices, this sequence has an important advantage over the achievement of full market clearing straight away, for goods prices do not have to overshoot as much, because g^{***} is unambiguously lower than g^{**}. The lower price of goods does not mean that peasants make a larger claim on them, because the effect of the lower nominal price is precisely offset by a higher relative price of goods to crops. That is: $g^{***}/c^* > g^{**}/c^{**}$.

Finally, if implosion has not proceeded far, the policy option of clearing the goods market without any overshooting of goods prices may exist. Fig. 3.12 depicts this case. The critical condition is that if goods prices are raised only to the long-run equilibrium level, g^*, and crop prices are reduced, the goods market clears at a crop price at or above c', the price at which government revenue is just sufficient to meet the urban claim. Such a point is shown in Fig. 3.12 by B. Starting from a repressed inflation point such as A, a feasible sequence is now to raise goods prices only to their long-run equilibrium level,

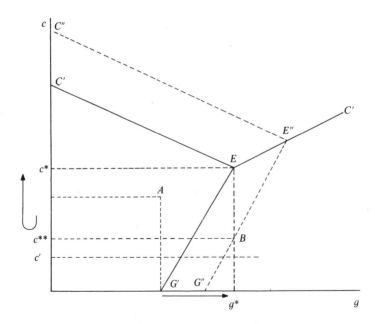

FIG. 3.12. *Compatible price reforms*

g^*, while crop prices undershoot, first being lowered to c^{**} and then being raised beyond their initial level to c^*. This sequence is dangerous, as noted previously, because *ex ante* it cannot be ascertained whether a point such as B, above c', exists, nor can the level of c' be known. Hence, the strategy of reducing the nominal price of crops might be infeasible, in which case it is steering the economy deeper into disequilibrium.

Pricing policies in general have two severe drawbacks: they often involve overshooting and they place an impossible information burden on the government. For the government has no way of knowing price levels such as c^{**} or g^{***}. These same objections apply to a policy of increasing the two prices in proportion, e.g. through a devaluation. When the initial relative crop price is too high relative to E (as in point A in Fig. 3.13) this implies a move towards the C–E locus, along AB. In this case the policy will fail to eliminate rationing. If the initial situation is at a point such as H (and it should be noted that the government is unlikely to be able to distinguish between the two cases) then a sufficiently large devaluation will (at F) eliminate rationing, but this involves overshooting, since the G'–G' locus will move back to G–E as crop production recovers. The policies can, however, be beneficial if the third dynamic effect is strong, that is if real balance effects are important.

In section 2 we emphasized the relation between uncertainty about goods availability and the size of money balances held by peasants. The probability that an agent will want to purchase more than is being supplied is an increasing function of his money stock. With the regime boundaries now

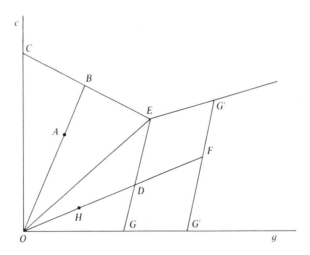

FIG. 3.13. *Devaluation*

suitably reinterpreted in this stochastic sense, the *G–E* locus becomes steeper (and hence the area of the repressed inflation regime larger) as money balances grow. Optimal money balances are homogeneous of degree one in prices. Hence a proportional increase of c and g triggers an adjustment process as peasants increase their production temporarily in order to rebuild real money balances. (This is strictly true only for non-rational expectations. For if expectations are rational then peasants will realize that availability is going to improve and this, it may be recalled from Fig. 3.2, reduces long-run optimal money balances under the conditions for the honeymoon result. The two effects then work in opposite directions.)

Abandoning price control for consumer goods (while maintaining the crop price c) moves the economy to a point on the *G–E* locus below *E*. In a static model this would be the best pricing policy since it requires no information about equilibrium prices and since it establishes goods market equilibrium instantaneously, a position from which *E* may be reached by trial and error (through variations in c). But in a dynamic model abandoning price control can be problematic. For example, if agents believe that market clearing is permanent they will attempt to eliminate their excess money holdings through a combination of working less and purchasing more. The expectation may then become self-defeating: the adjustment process involves a shift to the right of the *G–E* locus so that the economy is plunged back into the repressed inflation regime. We consider the effects of expectations of goods availability more fully in the next section.

Price policies, in summary, are sometimes infeasible (if the *G–E* locus cannot be reached or if the 'urban claim' cannot continue to be honoured), usually involve overshooting, and require information that is not available if full equilibrium is to be restored.

5.2. Changes in Goods Availability

The most common application of fix-price macroeconomic theory in developed economies is the analysis of the Keynesian zone, in which the goods market-clearing locus is shifted by the stimulation of demand. In its application to repressed inflation in developing countries, the analogous policy is again the shifting of the goods market-clearing locus, but by means of foreign aid augmenting goods supply. As depicted in Fig. 3.14, such an increase in goods supply reverses the endogenous implosion of the economy, reducing the size of the repressed inflation zone.

Aid alone cannot achieve a sustainable equilibrium unless it is permanent. However, in conjunction with price changes, temporary aid can greatly ease the path to such an equilibrium. The case for temporary aid is to avoid the policy overshoots which we have seen are otherwise likely to be necessary.

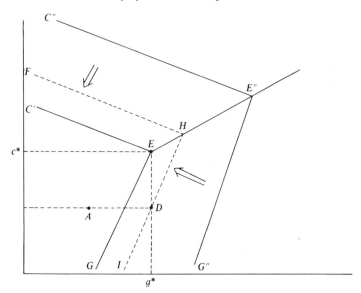

FIG. 3.14. *Compatible aid and price reforms*

The ideal deployment of aid, if there are sufficient funds, is to enable the economy to go straight to the long-run equilibrium prices, c^*, g^*. For this to be sustainable, aid must shift the market loci from C'', E'', G'' to the long-run loci C', E, G. An aid policy of this magnitude is thus compatible with pricing policies c^*, g^*.

If there is insufficient aid to enable the above strategy, aid might still enable the avoidance of price overshoots. Fig. 3.14 illustrates such a case. Aid is only sufficient to reduce the repressed inflation zone to the area bounded by FHI, so that the long-run equilibrium, E, remains in the interior of the zone. As before, initial prices are depicted by point A. If the temporary aid flow is combined with an increase in goods prices to g^*, crop prices being held constant, the goods market will clear at point D. Once the goods market has been clearing long enough for peasants to expect market clearing in the next period, the aid can be terminated in conjunction with an increase in crop prices to c^*, thereby reaching the long-run equilibrium, E, without the need to reverse price changes.

So far we have considered only adaptive expectations. As a characterization of how peasants interpret the unfolding evidence of the implosion phase this seems far more credible than rational expectations. However, as discussed in section 2, were peasants to have rational expectations of this process, the implosion would simply be more severe. Rational expectations are, however, a more credible characterization of the effects of foreign aid. A large increase in foreign aid to finance imports of consumer goods is a major public event constituting a change in regime of which peasants are quite likely to be aware. Indeed, since governments typically control information channels, it may well be a policy option for the government whether or not peasants are made aware that aid is increasing goods supply. Further, it may also be an option for the government to pre-announce such an event. We therefore consider the consequences of three distinct informational states of the world. In the first, peasants are unaware throughout that foreign aid is increasing goods supply, and they form their expectations adaptively on the basis of their individual experiences of goods availability. In the second, peasants are informed of the aid only at the start of the period in which the goods supply is increased by aid. In the third, they are informed one period in advance. Our analysis of this third case has some analogy with that of an anticipated change in monetary policy in a developed economy, as undertaken by Neary and Stiglitz (1983).

In the first case there may initially be no effect at all, for if rationing is stochastic there is no reason for an individual agent to interpret his experience as an improvement in availability: he may simply consider the amount on offer now as a lucky draw from an unchanged distribution. Sooner or later, however, he will recognize that the distribution itself has changed. This has a positive effect on production which, if the farmer believes the change to be permanent, is mitigated by the downward adjustment of money balances, a point to which we return. In the second case the peasant will, provided of course that he correctly estimates the effect of the aid programme on rural availability, immediately perceive how the distribution $f(x)$ of section 2 has changed. His response, an increase in production, shifts the G–E locus inward and therefore works exactly as the aid programme itself. Compared with the first case full liberalization can be achieved in a shorter period or with less aid (or a combination of the two). This is true *a fortiori* in the third case, provided the advance warning is indeed given exactly one period (agricultural season) ahead.[12] In this sense an announcement, and particularly an early announcement, is valuable. Note that this 'bootstrap effect' presupposes some form of rational expectations, for otherwise the announcement of the availability of aid would not need to be true to be effective. If peasants expected goods availability to improve, their expectation would become self-fulfilling, even if in fact no aid had been secured. Under rational expectations, since the ration available to an individual peasant is independent of his effort, the peasant realizes that an individual increase in effort makes no sense unless extra aid is indeed available.

As in the case of the abolition of price control, an aid policy can be undermined if agents react to it by running down money balances. This can

---

[12] The policy presupposes that the government is credible, a condition which may not be satisfied in all countries for which the analysis is relevant.

happen in the 'honeymoon case' only. Otherwise, peasants hold money stocks which, while higher than what they would want to hold in the absence of risk, are below the level corresponding to an unrationed equilibrium. In that case, therefore, the two effects on production, the direct effect of the perceived improvement in availability and the indirect effect via the adjustment of money stocks, work in the same direction. However, in the 'honeymoon case' peasants will want to reduce their money stocks. Since this would involve lower export crop production and an increased demand for tradables, an aid donor might be faced with the unnerving short-term response of soaring imports and falling exports. In the extreme case this outward shift of the G–G locus would more than offset the inward shift which is the policy's direct effect. The above distinction between the three informational states is again relevant, but now the 'bootstrap effect' is reversed. The adjustment of money balances cannot be avoided if full equilibrium is to be achieved,[13] but it can be delayed, and this will happen in the first case.

Any attempt at dismantling controls will have to confront the existence of rationing and the related monetary overhang. This overhang implies that the government must either offer something in return for the claims or default on them. In Chapter 6 we compare currency reconstruction and inflation as alternative mechanisms of default. One or other form of default will generally be necessary so as to prevent the monetary overhang from being unleashed while aid or some other policy temporarily increases the supply of consumer goods. The case for aid in this situatiion is not to bribe a recalcitrant government into making needed reforms but to avoid the need for policy changes which should be reversed once the economy is in unrationed equilibrium.

Appendix
Monte Carlo Experiments with the Two-Period Model

We have used the two-period simulation model described in Chapter 3, section 2.2, in Monte Carlo experiments; first, to test for ergodicity of the distribution of money stocks, and secondly, to test the effects of changes in availability or risk on the expected value of money stocks.

---

[13] Unless, of course, the equilibrium itself is shifted, as in the case of a devaluation.

1. *Solution Method*

We repeat the specificaion of the two-period problem:

$$\max_{c_t,\, h_{t+1}} u(c_t) + v(t - h_t) + \delta \left[\int_0^{m_{t+1}} u(x) f(x)\, dx + \right.$$

$$\left. u(m_{t+1}) \int_{m_{t+1}}^{\infty} f(x)\, dx + v(t - h_{t+1}) \right]$$

subject to

$$c_t \leqslant m_t \tag{1}$$

$$c_t \leqslant x_t \tag{2}$$

$$m_{t+1} = m_t - c_t + h_{t+1} \tag{3}$$

$$c_t \geqslant 0 \tag{4}$$

$$0 \leqslant h_{t+1} \leqslant t \tag{5}$$

and m_t, x_t, and h_t given and non-negative. We assume: $f(x) > 0$ for all $x > 0$; $u' > 0 > u''$ and $v' > 0 > v''$; $\delta \leqslant 1$; u', v' finite and

$$\lim_{h \to t} v'(t - h) = \infty. \tag{6}$$

It is convienent to define:

$$\bar{c}_t = \min(c_t, x_t) \tag{7}$$

$$\varphi(m) = u'(m) \int_m^{\infty} f(x)\, dx \tag{8}$$

$$\psi(c) = u'(c)/\delta. \tag{9}$$

Using these expressions the first-order conditions may be written as[1]

$$[\psi(c_t) - \varphi(m_{t+1})](c_t - \bar{c}_t) = 0 \qquad \psi(c_t) \geqslant \varphi(m_{t+1}); c_t \leqslant \bar{c}_t \tag{10}$$

$$[\varphi(m_{t+1}) - v'(t - h_{t+1})] h_{t+1} = 0 \qquad \varphi(m_{t+1}) \leqslant v'(t - h_{t+1}); h_{t+1} \geqslant 0 \tag{11}$$

It follows from (3), (8), and (9) that $\varphi(m_{t+1})$ is increasing, and that $v'(t - h_{t+1})$ is decreasing in h_{t+1}:

$$\frac{\partial \varphi(m_{t+1})}{\partial h_{t+1}} = u''(m_{t+1}) \int_{m_{t+1}}^{\infty} f(x)\, dx - u'(m_{t+1}) f(m_{t+1}) < 0 \tag{12}$$

$$\frac{\partial v'(t - h_{t+1})}{\partial h_{t+1}} = -v''(t - h_{t+1}) > 0. \tag{13}$$

---

[1] The constraint $c_t \geqslant 0$ can be dropped. For suppose $c_t = 0 < \bar{c}_t$ is optimal. Then $\psi(0) \leqslant \varphi(m_t + h_{t+1})$ must be satisfied and this is possible only for $\delta = 1$ and $m_t = h_{t+1} = 0$. But $m_t = 0$ contradicts $\bar{c}_t > 0$. Hence an optimum with $c_t = 0 < \bar{c}_t$ is impossible. Similarly, an optimum with $h_{t+1} = t$ contradicts (6). Hence the constraints $c_t \geqslant 0$ and $h_{t+1} \leqslant t$ can be ignored.

In Fig. 3A.1 $\varphi(m_{t+1}) = \varphi(m_t - c_t + h_{t+1})$ and $v'(t - h_{t+1})$ are shown as functions of h_{t+1}. There are four possible cases:

I $\qquad\qquad \varphi(m_t - \bar{c}_t) < \psi(\bar{c}_t) \qquad$ and $\qquad \varphi(m_t - \bar{c}_t) < v'(t)$

Since $h_{t+1} \geqslant 0$, $c_t \leqslant \bar{c}_t$, and $\psi(c_t)$ and $\varphi(m_t - c_t + h_{t+1})$ are both decreasing in c_t, the first inequality implies $c_t = \bar{c}_t$ and the second one $h_{t+1} = 0$.

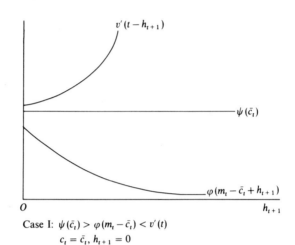

Case I: $\psi(\bar{c}_t) > \varphi(m_t - \bar{c}_t) < v'(t)$
$$c_t = \bar{c}_t, h_{t+1} = 0$$

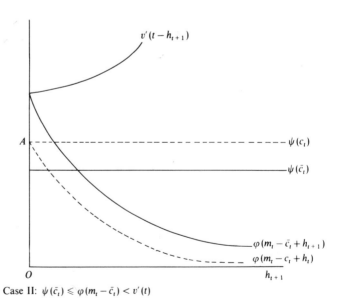

Case II: $\psi(\bar{c}_t) \leqslant \varphi(m_t - \bar{c}_t) < v'(t)$
$$c_t \leqslant \bar{c}_t, h_{t+1} = 0$$

FIG. 3A.1. *Optima in the two-period problem*

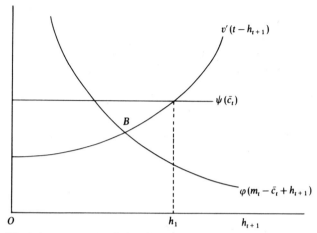

Case III: $v'(t) \leqslant \varphi(m_t - \bar{c}_t)$ and $v'(t - h_1) > \varphi(m_t - \bar{c}_t + h_1)$
$c_t = \bar{c}_t, h_{t+1} \geqslant 0$

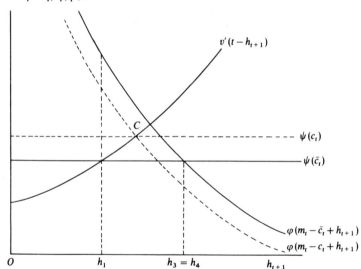

Case IV: $v'(t) \leqslant \varphi(m_t - \bar{c}_t)$ and $v'(t - h_1) \leqslant \varphi(m_t - \bar{c}_t + h_1)$
$c_t \leqslant \bar{c}_t, h_t \geqslant 0$

FIG. 3A.1. (*cont.*)

II $\qquad \varphi(m_t - \bar{c}_t) \geqslant \psi(\bar{c}_t) \qquad$ and $\qquad \varphi(m_t - \bar{c}_t) < v'(t)$

The first inequality implies $c_t \leqslant \bar{c}_t$, the second one $h_{t+1} = 0$, as before. The optimum (point A in the figure) may be found by solving c_t from:
$\psi(c_t) = \varphi(m_t - c_t + h_{t+1})$.

III $\qquad v'(t) \leqslant \varphi(m_t - \bar{c}_t) \qquad$ and $\qquad v'(t - h_1) > \varphi(m_t - \bar{c}_t + h_1)$

(where $h_1 = \max(0, h_2)$ and h_2 solves $\psi(\bar{c}_t) = v'(t - h_2)$). In this case at the optimum (point *B*) $\psi(c_t) > \varphi(m_{t+1})$, hence, from (10), $c_t = \bar{c}_t$.

IV $v'(t) \leqslant \varphi(m_t - \bar{c}_t)$ and $v'(t - h_1) \leqslant \varphi(m_t - \bar{c}_t + h_1)$

In this case at the optimum (point *C*) $\psi(c_t) = \varphi(m_{t+1})$, hence $c_t \leqslant \bar{c}_t$.

To find solutions satisfying the Kuhn–Tucker conditions (10) and (11) we make use of binary section. This method for finding the root (x^*) of a strictly increasing function $f(x)$ consists of the following steps:

1. choose $x_{\min}$ and $x_{\max}$ such that $f(x_{\min}) \leqslant 0 \leqslant f(x_{\max})$;
2. $x = (x_{\min} + x_{\max})/2$;
3. if $f(x) = 0$ or $(1 - x_{\min}/x_{\max}) < \varepsilon$ go to step 6;
4. if $f(x) > 0$ then $x_{\max} = x$; if $f(x) < 0$ then $x_{\min} = x$;
5. go to step 2;
6. $x^* = x$.

Our solution method proceeds as follows:

(a) Solve for h_1 and compare $\psi(\bar{c}_t)$, $\varphi(m_t - \bar{c}_t)$, $v'(t)$, $v'(t - h_1)$, and $\psi(m_t - \bar{c}_t + h_1)$ to determine whether the equilibrium is of type I, II, III, or IV.
(b) In case I the solution is $c_t = \bar{c}_t$, $h_{t+1} = 0$.
(c) In case II, $h_{t+1} = 0$ and c_t solves $f(x) = 0$ where $f(x) = \varphi(m_t - x) - \varphi(x)$ is strictly increasing. The root can be found using binary section with $x_{\min} = 0$ and $x_{\max} = \bar{c}_t$.
(d) In case III, $c_t = \bar{c}_t$ and h_{t+1} solves $f(x) = 0$ where $f(x) = v'(t - x) - \varphi(m_t - \bar{c}_t + x)$ is strictly increasing. The root can be found using binary section with $x_{\min} = 0$ and $x_{\max} = h_1$.
(e) In case IV define a function $c_t = \xi(h_{t+1})$ such that $\psi[\xi(h_{t+1})] = v'(t - h_{t+1})$. Then h_{t+1} solves $f(x) = 0$ where $f(x) = v'(t - x) - \varphi(m_t - \xi(x) + x)$ is strictly increasing. The root can be found using binary section with $x_{\min} = 0$ and $x_{\max} = h_3 = \min(t, h_4)$ where h_4 solves $\psi(\bar{c}_t) = \varphi(m_t - \bar{c}_t + h_4)$. Optimal consumption then follows from $c_t = \xi(h_{t+1})$.

It may be verified that this method yields a solution satisfying the Kuhn–Tucker conditions.

2. Design of the Experiments

We choose the following specification of the objective function:

$$u(c_t) + v(t - h_t) = \frac{c_t^{1-R}}{1 - R} + \frac{(t - h_t)^{1-\gamma}}{1 - \gamma}. \tag{14}$$

Hence the degree of relative risk aversion is constant and equal to R for consumption and γ for leisure. We assume that x is log-normally distributed:

$$\ln x \sim N(\mu, \sigma^2)$$

so that its expected value is given by

$$E(x) = \exp(\mu + \sigma^2/2). \tag{15}$$

We solve the two-period problem repeatedly. For a given value of the opening money balance (m_0) we solve for m_1 (which will of course depend on the value taken by the stochastic variable x_t). The problem then rolls forward, m_1 becoming the new starting value. This process is repeated T times and gives a single value of m_T, the money stock after T periods. This value will depend on:

(a) the values of the parameters m_0 (opening money balance), $E(x)$ (expected value of the ration), and σ (an indicator of the riskiness of availability: the standard deviation of $\ln x$);[2]
(b) the random variables $x_0, \ldots, x_{T+1}$. Obviously, m_T is a stochastic variable. In order to get an estimate of the distribution of m_T we repeat the process N times. These N experiments differ only in the random variables drawn.

We have chosen $T = 15$ and $N = 30$ so that a single run requires solving the two-period problem 450 times (each solution requiring on average about

TABLE 3A.1.   *Parameters in the simulation experiments*

Parameter		Value
Preferences		
Risk aversion (consumption)	R	2
Risk aversion (leisure)	γ	4
Discount rate	r	0
Discount factor ($1/(1+r)$)	δ	1
Available time	t	$10 + \sqrt{10}$
Starting volume		
Opening money balance	m_0	variable/10[a]
Availability distribution		
Expected value of x	$E(x)$	8/variable[b]
Standard deviation of $\ln x$	σ	0.5/variable[c]
Length of run		
Number of times the two-period problem is solved	T	15
Number of points on the distribution function of m_T generated	N	30

[a] Variable in ergodicity experiments (Table 3A.2), otherwise 10 (Table 3A.3).
[b] 8 in ergodicity experiments (Table 3A.2), otherwise variable (Table 3A.3).
[c] 0.5 in ergodicity experiments (Table 3A.2), otherwise variable (Table 3A.3).

[2] Note from Table 3A.1 that we do not vary the other parameters of the problem: the parameters of the objective function and the length of a run (T). The preference parameters imply that in stationary unrationed equilibrium $m = c = h = 10$.

ten binary section iterations). The end result of a run is a series of thirty values for m_T.

Table 3A.2 shows the results for four pairs of starting values: (10, 10), (9, 11), (8, 12) and (7, 13). Since 10 is the value of the money stock in unrationed equilibrium, the starting values are symmetric around this value and differ increasingly more from it.

For each pair the sixty calculated values of m_{15} are placed in increasing order. The variable d_i is given the value 1 if the ith value comes from the second series, and 0 otherwise. Define:

$$s_i = (\tfrac{1}{2}i - d_1 - d_2 - \ldots - d_i) \qquad (i = 1, 2, \ldots, 60) \qquad (16)$$

In order to apply the two-sample Kolmogorow–Smirnow test[3] we calculate the test statistic

$$t_{KS} = \max\{|s_1|, \ldots, |s_{60}|\}/\sqrt{15}. \qquad (17)$$

The probability $Q(\lambda)$ of finding a value of t_{KS} less than λ is approximately equal to

$$\sum_{j=-\infty}^{+\infty} (-1)^j e^{-2j^2\lambda^2}$$

and this sum is tabulated. In the table we show the test statistic t_{KS}. For a significance level of 5 per cent the critical value of t_{KS} is defined by

$$0.05 = 1 - Q(1.36) \qquad (18)$$

Hence for

$$t_{KS} < 1.36 \qquad (19)$$

we accept the hypothesis that the two samples come from the same population. The results in Table 3A.2 indicate that condition (19) is satisfied.

TABLE 3A.2.   *Ergodicity test*

m'_0	m''_0	t_{KS}
10	10	1.29
9	11	0.75
8	12	0.52
7	13	0.75

Note: For each value of m_0 the model is solved 30 times for a series of 15 periods. For each of the four pairs of starting values, the test statistic for the two-sample Kolmogorow–Smirnow test is calculated on the basis of the two series (of 30 values each) of m_{15} values. The critical value of t_{KS} for a 5% significance test is 1.36.

---

[3] See e.g. Hollander and Wolfe (1983). We are grateful to Herman Bierens for suggesting this way of testing ergodicity.

Hence we conclude that the distribution of m_t is ergodic for $T = 15$:[4] differences in starting values are (sufficiently) unimportant.

3. *Money Stock and Availability*

Next we consider changes in availability. In Table 3A.3 the results are shown for 15 runs. There are five levels for mean availability $\bar{x}$. Recall that in unrationed equilibrium $c = 10$. Hence $\bar{x}$ varies from extremely low values (only 40 per cent of the unrationed consumption level) to well above the unrationed level. For σ we use the values 0.2, 0.5, and 0.8. For $\sigma = 0.5$ the probability that x exceeds $0.5\bar{x}$, $\bar{x}$, and $1.5\bar{x}$ is respectively 0.87, 0.40, and 0.14.[5] Hence this is a case of moderate riskiness: there is a probability of 14 per cent that the stochastic outcome is more than 50 per cent above the mean and of 13 per cent that it falls more than 50 per cent below the mean. For $\sigma = 0.1$ these events are extremely unlikely, while $\sigma = 0.8$ is a case of very high risk: there is a probability of almost one-third that the outcome falls more than 50 per cent short of the mean.

The results are sketched in Fig. 3A.2. The simulation experiments confirm what was suggested in the body of the chapter: the expected value of money stocks, $E(m_T)$, initially increases as a function of the shortfall $(\bar{x} - c^*)$, where c^* is the unrationed consumption level, and eventually declines as availability

TABLE 3A.3. *Money stocks and availability changes*

(Mean value, over 30 trials, of money stocks after 15 periods, for different values of the mean, $\bar{x}$, and the log standard deviation, σ, of availability)

$\bar{x}$	σ		
	0.2	0.5	0.8
4	6.50	10.60	17.02
6	8.68	12.30	15.16
8	9.85	12.20	14.49
10	10.32	11.70	13.62
12	10.13	11.03	12.61

Note: Availability x_t is log normally distributed with log mean μ and log-standard deviation σ; $\bar{x}$ is given by $\exp(\mu + \sigma^2/2)$. In unrationed equilibrium $m = c = 10$.

[4] Obviously, the null hypothesis is strictly false since the observations are generated by processes with different starting values. However, what matters is if this dependence on starting values wears off sufficiently quickly for the distribution of m_{15} to be treated as ergodic. This we answer affirmatively.

[5] For $\sigma = 0.2$ these probabilities are 0.9996, 0.46, and 0.02, and for $\sigma = 0.8$ they are 0.68, 0.34, and 0.18.

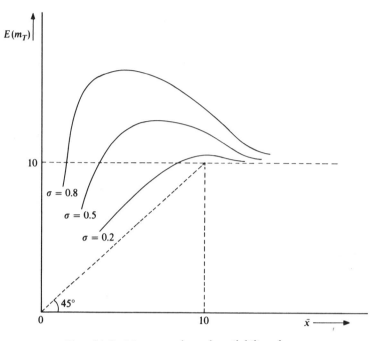

FIG. 3A.2. *Money stocks and availability changes*

approaches zero; for $\bar{x}$ above some critical level, $E(m_T) > c^*$, i.e. the honey-moon result; and finally, this critical level decreases if riskiness increases (note that for $\sigma = 0.8$ the honeymoon result applies everywhere, except for extremely low values of mean availability).

4

The Theory of a Temporary Windfall in a Controlled Economy

1. Introduction

In Chapter 2 we argued that for the analysis of changes in the control regime of an open developing economy the tradables/non-tradables disaggregation was inadequate: the endogeneity of trade controls required the further disaggregation of tradables into exportables and importables. Although some of our analysis was inter-temporal (notably that of the fiscal deficit), it was confined to steady states. We now develop the inter-temporal analysis, focusing upon the consequences of temporary export windfalls under a variety of control regimes. In the analysis of temporary shocks, the choice between consumption and investment plays a central role. Since we are concerned with open economies, the distinction between tradable and non-tradable goods also remains necessary. Analogously to Chapter 2, we argue that the tradables/non-tradables disaggregation is inadequate for the analysis of trade shocks: the endogeneity of investment requires a further disaggregation of non-tradables into capital and consumer goods. When combined, these distinctions identify a sector which has not previously received much analytic attention, namely the non-tradable capital goods sector, and this turns out to be the key sector for the analysis of temporary trade windfalls. The range of activities which fall into this sector will vary between economies, but one activity which is almost invariably so characterized is construction. For brevity, we shall refer to the non-tradable capital goods sector as 'construction' and to its output as 'buildings'.

Virtually all export windfalls will induce a temporary boom in the construction sector, and some control regimes can cause a costly exaggeration in such a boom. There are two routes by which a construction boom is induced, through a temporary increase in savings and through a permanent increase in consumption. The circumstances in which neither of these routes operates are quite special and illuminating. If agents correctly forecast export prices, and credit markets are perfect, then fluctuations in export prices have no consequences for any sector of the economy. Current income fluctuates around a known permanent income to which expenditure is continuously equated through changing financial assets and debts.

However, if credit markets are imperfect, then such fluctuations in saving will alter the availability or cost of domestic finance and hence give rise to fluctuations in domestic investment. Unless tradable and non-tradable capital are perfect substitutes in the production process (in which case the distinction is vacuous), these fluctuations in investment will cause fluctuations in demand for 'buildings'. Hence, perfect credit markets are a necessary, but by no means a sufficient, condition for the delinking of changes in export prices and construction booms.

Assume, for the present, that this condition is met. If price changes take agents by surprise (i.e. they are 'shocks'), they can affect the construction sector through a change in demand for consumer goods. This change in demand occurs because of a revision in permanent income, the magnitude of which depends upon the informational content of the shock. At one extreme a shock may have no informational content. The price change is only a shock in the sense that its magnitude and timing were previously unknown, and not in the sense that any revision is required in the agent's beliefs about the stochastic environment facing him. This may be either because the shock is believed to be unrepeatable and *sui generis*, or because it is regarded as an unsurprising though unpredicted realization of a familiar stochastic process. In the former case permanent income rises by the sustainable flow generated by saving the current windfall (since expectations of other future income are unaltered). In the latter case permanent income also rises (though by less): the timing of given income receipts is more favourable than anticipated and therefore the duration of the returns from savings is longer than anticipated. Only if, in addition to knowing the stochastic process, the agent correctly predicts the timing of the price increase is permanent income unaltered. But in this case the price increase is not in any sense a shock. At the other extreme a shock may lead to a wholesale revision of the agent's view of the world. A special case of this extreme is when the agent revises his forecast to the point expectation that the price shock will persist permanently. In this case, since permanent income is revised in line with current income, the shock will have no impact upon the savings rate. This is the implicit informational assumption underlying the existing theory of how economies respond to external shocks: Dutch Disease theory treats shocks as permanent.

Thus, with any information content a price shock leads to some revision of permanent income, and hence consumption. In consequence the demand for non-tradable consumer goods will normally increase. This increased demand must be met by domestic production. Unless the production process for non-tradable consumer goods happens not to use 'buildings', such extra production requires an increase in the stock of buildings in the sector. This increase can come either by redeploying buildings from the tradable sector of the economy or by temporarily increasing output of the construction sector. Since the costs of moving buildings between sectors are likely to be high (capital, once installed, is sector-specific), the price shock generates a construction boom.

These two routes by which a price windfall induces a construction boom, a temporary increase in savings and a permanent increase in consumption, will usually both operate to some extent. The latter is excluded only if the price increase is fully anticipated; the former, only if it generates point expectations of permanence. As noted, Dutch Disease theory implicitly assumes such point expectations, and so necessarily abstracts from the temporary savings route. As it happens, Dutch Disease theory has also abstracted from the consumption route to a construction boom. Capital is treated in one of three ways: either it is tradable, or it is in fixed supply to each sector, or it is fully mobile between sectors but in fixed supply to the economy. Clearly, each of these specifications excludes the construction sector. Our subsequent analysis concentrates primarily upon the temporary saving route; however, this route is of general importance. Recall that there are only two circumstances in which a trade windfall does not generate a construction boom via a temporary increase in savings. First, if credit markets are perfect and future prices known, there will be a temporary increase in savings but not in domestic investment. Second, if there are point expectations of permanence for the price shock, then there will be no temporary increase in savings. Neither of these special cases is of much practical relevance. Most developing countries face constraints in world capital markets, and in a world of uncertainty, even if agents regard permanence as the most likely outcome, they will attach some probability to transience. Hence, the circumstances in which a trade shock does not induce a construction boom through the temporary savings route can be dismissed as curiosa.

Once we abandon the special case of point expectations of permanence, the optimal response to a shock varies with its information content. We develop a taxonomy of how expectations might respond to a price change in section 2.6. In general, agents will neither hold point expectations about prices nor regard changes as permanent. Our formal analysis of optimal response relaxes the assumption of permanence but retains point expectations: agents are certain as to the duration of the price change, but this duration may be anything other than infinite. The extension to uncertainty would involve the weighting by probabilities of different durations. Even with this restriction, the theory is a generalization of Dutch Disease theory (the special case of point expectations of permanence). The abstraction from uncertainty yields the simplest framework in which the additional considerations raised by shocks of finite duration can be analysed. As it happens, the trade shock to which we apply the theory, the Kenyan coffee boom (Chapter 5), can be demonstrated to have had an informational content approximating quite closely to point expectations of a specific finite duration. However, all trade shocks (barring the curiosa discussed above) will to some extent generate the effects which we analyse by means of this abstraction.

Our analysis is confined to positive trade shocks. The pattern of price fluctuations of many primary commodities is that such peaks are more common than short, sharp troughs (see Deaton and Laroque, 1989). There are several important asymmetries which imply that the theory of booms developed here will not carry over to slumps merely by a reversal of sign. First, there may be asymmetries in the speed of price adjustment, prices rising in response to excess demand more rapidly than they fall in response to excess supply. Second, whereas with a boom it is always possible to accumulate assets in foreign financial markets and then run them down, during a slump it may not possible to borrow. Two further asymmetries arise once we relax the assumption of a perfect resale market in capital goods, so that, once installed, capital is sector-specific. Whereas during a boom it is always possible to add to the domestic capital stock through imports of capital goods, during a slump the rate of decumulation is constrained by the rate of depreciation. Finally, whereas a positive shock increases investment, a negative shock need not reduce it. This is clearest in the case of a permanent shock. Whether positive or negative, the shock changes the relative price of tradables to non-tradables and hence changes the optimal allocation of resources. Investment is the means by which capital can be added to the sector in which there is an incentive to expand output. Hence, any change in relative prices creates a premium upon mobility and thereby an incentive to increase investment. The less a given shock alters permanent income, the weaker is the incentive to reallocate resources. Thus, other than for point expectations of permanence, a positive shock stimulates investment both through this mobility premium effect and through the rise in savings. A negative shock has the mobility premium effect of stimulating investment, while transient dissaving reduces it so that the net effect is ambiguous.

The subsequent analysis is restricted to trade windfalls of known finite duration. It is thus only a component of the more general subject of trade shocks whose duration is uncertain, a subject for which there is as yet no adequate theory. As in previous chapters, our focus is the control regime. However, an analysis of how a control regime changes the consequences of temporary windfalls must be predicated upon their consequences in the absence of controls. Section 2 develops a theory of optimal responses in the absence of government. In section 3 government regulations in international trade, credit, and foreign exchange markets are progressively introduced, and the consequences of the optimizing behaviour of private agents are analysed. It is shown that such interventions can be expected both to reduce the efficiency with which private agents transform a windfall into productive investments, and to amplify the relative price changes which occur in the absence of regulations.

2. A Temporary Windfall in an Uncontrolled Economy

2.1. *Optimal Responses in the Absence of Government*

When an economy benefits from an exogenous change, such as a favourable movement in its terms of trade, some adjustment is necessary. The enhanced income implies increased domestic demand for both tradable and non-tradable goods and this requires a rise in the price of non-tradables relative to tradables, an expansion of non-tradable production, and a contraction of tradable production. This type of effect has been extensively analysed in a static framework, under the general description of 'Dutch Disease'.

The present chapter addresses exactly this issue and is concerned to trace these relative price effects. But we also wish to focus on the time dimension. Given that the windfall is perceived to be temporary, beneficiaries will wish to devote a large proportion of it to asset accumulation. In the normal case, to which we restrict attention, the price of non-tradable capital goods will therefore be driven up further than those of non-tradables in general. The allocation of these capital goods between productive sectors will in turn influence relative prices by altering the conditions of supply.

The effect of a permanent windfall is depicted in Fig. 4.1, which portrays the production possibility set for non-tradables, N, and for tradables other than the booming commodity, T. The case shown is that in which the booming commodity is not consumed domestically while only sector-specific factors are used in its production. Under these conditions exports (and hence the value of imports) are exogenous. In the figure this is the vertical distance $A'C$: consumption of non-booming tradables can exceed production by this amount, at pre-boom world prices. The windfall of AB shifts the production possibility set vertically, raising it from AA' to BB'. If the relative price of

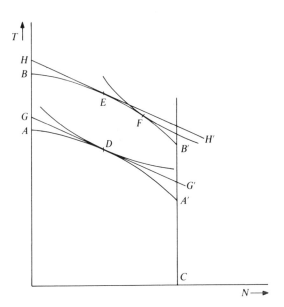

Key: N = non-tradables; T = tradables (other than the booming commodity)

FIG. 4.1. *Effect of a permanent windfall*

non-tradables were to remain unchanged, then the production point would shift vertically, from *D* to *E*. However, at the new production point (*E*) the budget line (*HH'*, parallel to the old budget line *GG'*) is not tangent to an indifference curve. The consumption point would lie to the right of the production point and there would therefore be excess demand for non-tradables. The relative price of non-tradables will have to increase until, at *F*, the production and consumption points coincide.[1]

The effect of a temporary windfall is depicted in Fig. 4.2. Non-tradables must now be disaggregated into capital, *K*, and consumer, *C*, goods, and two independent relative prices, p_K/p_T and p_C/p_T, define the space for the figure. *K–K* and *C–C* are the pre-windfall equilibrium price loci for the two non-tradables, *E* being the initial equilibrium. A permanent windfall, in which demand for these two goods expanded proportionately, would leave p_K/p_C unaffected (unless supply elasticities differed), shifting the equilibrium to *E'*. A temporary windfall, in which the investment rate rises, raises the *K–K* locus proportionately more than the *C–C* locus, shifting the equilibrium to a point such as *E''*. Hence p_K/p_T rises by more than p_C/p_T. These relative price

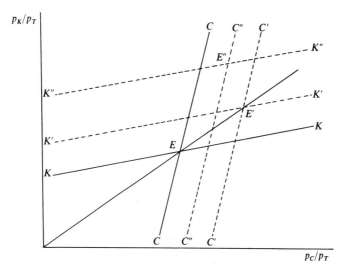

Key: *C*=consumer goods, non-tradable; *K*=capital goods, non-tradable; *T*=tradables (other than the booming commodity); p_C=price of consumer goods, non-tradable; p_K=price of capital goods, non-tradable; p_T=price of tradables.

FIG. 4.2. *Effect of a temporary windfall*

[1] In the one-agent case real appreciation (an increase in the relative price of non-tradables) will occur if both goods are substitutes and normal (recall that the third good, the exportable, is not consumed domestically, by assumption). In the many-agent case a real depreciation is possible; cf. Gunning (1987).

changes are likely to have two important effects besides the usual ones on supply and demand. First, they will have significant distributional consequences, as part of the initial incremental spending accrues as rents to suppliers of non-tradable goods. That is, part of the windfall is transferred to other agents within the economy. An important consequence of these transfers is the shift in the incidence of gains between the rural and urban sectors of the economy. The relative price changes will markedly reduce the proportion of the windfall which is invested, and raise the proportion consumed.[2] This involves two mechanisms. The first is the direct effect, with the high relative price of capital reducing the quantity demanded. At the first round, this induces both a substitution effect and a reinforcing income effect, since the purchasing power of the windfall in the hands of the initial recipients is reduced. The second mechanism is the income transfer already noted. To the extent that the rise in the price of non-tradables is fully accounted for by rents, these will in turn be spent and there is no economy-wide income effect; in aggregate the diversion of the windfall from asset accumulation reflects only the substitution effect. To the extent that the rise in price reflects a rise in resource costs, there will in addition be some residual income effect. Whatever the reasons for the supply curve of non-tradables to be upward-sloping, they are likely to operate more powerfully in the short than in the long run. This suggests that an attempt to absorb the windfall resources into the domestic economy quickly may be very costly. This raises three questions. First, what proportion of the windfall should be invested? Second, how much should be utilized for domestic capital formation? Third, how should this investment be phased? Each question is considered in turn.

2.2. *The Consumption–Investment Choice*

We may distinguish two cases. In the first, a household's current consumption is constrained by liquidity rather than by net worth. It then appears likely that part or all of a windfall may be consumed directly, with the residue being invested to provide an increment to permanent consumption. In the second, consumption is not constrained by liquidity, and the whole windfall will be invested, with consumption rising in line with the income from this investment. Peasants are typically credit-constrained, with on-farm investment limited by the level of household savings. An income windfall would permit both higher consumption and higher investment; in the textbook case of declining marginal product of capital, the optimal consumption path would then jump to a higher, flatter path, as in Fig. 4.3.

This argument suggests that the first case is the relevant one. However, it leaves out of account the nature of the investment choices facing the farmer.

---

[2] There may also be distributional effects on the average savings rate. This possibility is taken into account in Chapter 5 but is not considered here.

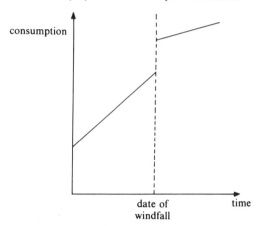

FIG. 4.3. *The consumption path with a credit constraint*

These frequently involve choices between relatively safe, low-return strategies and relatively risky, high-return ones. If relative risk aversion falls as
income rises, as is commonly supposed, or if there are economies of scale in
high-yield strategies, then a windfall income gain may permit or induce a
switch from low to high-return investments. In this case the windfall induces
investment in excess of its own value, and consumption temporarily drops.
This possibility is illustrated in Fig. 4.4.

To summarize, it appears that even in the credit-constrained case private
agents are likely to attempt to save a high proportion of the windfall. This
conclusion is confirmed by the calculations reported in our Kenyan
application.

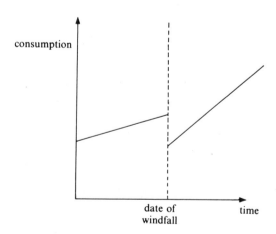

FIG. 4.4. *The consumption path with risk aversion and economies of scale*

2.3. *Investment in Domestic Capital*

Under perfect international capital markets, and in the presence of imper-
fectly correlated risk, part of the increased asset holding would be in the form
of domestic real assets, and part in the form of foreign financial assets.
However, international capital markets are not perfect. Many countries can
lend but not borrow at the world interest rate. The borrowing rate is higher,
country-specific, and upward-sloping. If the domestic capital market is
reasonably efficient, the domestic rate of return will be equated to the
borrowing rate if the country is a net debtor, to the lending rate if it is a
creditor, and otherwise lie between the two. For a capital-short economy, the
domestic rate of return will always lie above the lending rate, so additional
assets should always be held in the form of domestic real capital, once
adequate working reserves of foreign exchange have been acquired.

It might be objected that the discrepancy between borrowing and lending
rates is a risk premium and that the appropriate comparison is between
equivalent riskless rates. However, the risk premium embodied in the borrowing rate is appropriate to the risks faced by, or perceived by, the international financial community, and these need bear little relation to the risks
faced by the country's own nationals.

2.4. *Phasing of Investment*

It was noted earlier than an attempt to invest the windfall domestically might
prove very costly if carried out too quickly. This is because the supply of non-
tradable goods is likely to be less elastic in the short run than in the long,
because there are lags in the production process, and because there are
administrative difficulties in absorbing and managing rapid changes. These
are the familiar reasons for supposing that the marginal efficiency of investment schedule will slope down more steeply than the marginal efficiency of
capital schedule.

At the same time, too slow a rate of investment will also prove costly. This
is because the part of the windfall earmarked for investment but not yet
invested in domestic capital must be held in the form of foreign financial
assets, and these yield only the relatively low lending rate of interest.

The stages involved in this process are analysed in detail below, but an
overview is first provided using the usual schedules of investment theory. In
Fig. 4.5 the pre-windfall cost of funds schedule (MCF) is made up of three
sections; a flat portion denoting domestic savings at their opportunity cost,
which is the world depositing rate of interest; a vertical portion, which is the
spread charged by foreign banks before they will consider lending to domestic agents; and a steeply sloping portion, denoting how this spread would
widen as agents attempted in aggregate to borrow more. The marginal
efficiency of investment (MEI) schedule is shown as passing through the

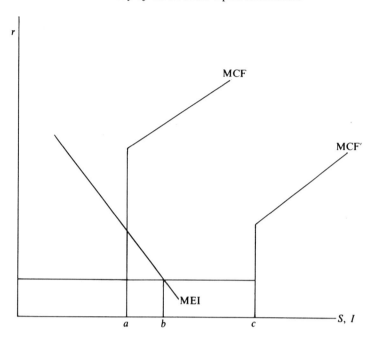

FIG. 4.5. *The effect on the marginal efficiency of investment*

vertical portion of the MCF schedule. The temporary windfall shifts the MCF to the right to (MCF′) and may also reduce bank spreads as perceived country credit worthiness improves. The effect is to augment domestic investment by the amount $a–b$, and to induce a temporary accumulation of foreign financial assets to the amount $b–c$.

The above model is now disaggregated so as to introduce the differential effects within the tradable and non-tradable sectors discussed previously. Fig. 4.6 illustrates the pre-windfall and adjustment phases. In the pre-boom equilibrium domestic financial intermediation is assumed to have equalized marginal returns to investment in the two sectors at a level r_0, above the world deposit rate of interest. The windfall augments savings by the amount $S–S'$. During the temporary adjustment phase, investment in the non-tradable sector increases, both because of the price increase of non-tradable goods (the shifts out in the MEI_N curve from MEI_N^0 to MEI_N^1) and because of the lower opportunity cost of finance at the margin (a movement down the MEI_N^1 curve to I_N^1). Investment in the tradable sector is ambiguously affected because the previously discussed shift back in the MEI_T curve to MEI_T^1 is offset by this movement down the curve.

We now consider the problem of the phasing of investment in more detail, using a very simple dynamic optimization model. In this model we drop the distinction between exportables and importables: substitution between the

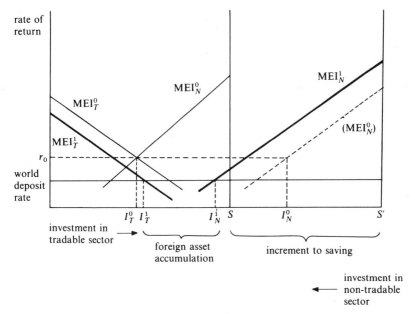

FIG. 4.6. *The allocation of windfall savings between domestic and foreign assets*

two (either in production or in demand) is not essential for our present purposes. Since this aggregation over tradables rules out a terms of trade change we model a boom as a transfer of tradables. In this section we ignore trade policy and do not distinguish between the private and the public sector.

We will consider a sequence of three models. There are two assets: a foreign financial asset which pays a fixed interest rate and domestic equity. In all three models the country faces a borrowing constraint: it can deposit savings abroad (at an interest rate which is lower than the discount rate) but it cannot issue external debt. This introduces an important difference from permanent income models in which the country is assumed to have access to a perfect world capital market. For in many of these models it is optimal to respond to a boom by raising consumption instantly by the increase in permanent income and investing the rest of windfall income in foreign assets. After the boom the level of foreign assets is kept constant and the return on these assets represents the permanent income increase. In our case, however, the international capital market is not perfect and it is optimal only to hold foreign assets temporarily.

Optimal dynamic adjustment to a temporary trade shock is affected by the irreversibility of investment in domestic real assets and by the non-tradability of some capital goods. Our sequence of models is designed to illustrate these two aspects.

In the first model the economy produces only one good, a tradable which can be used both for consumption and investment. In this model the optimal response to a boom involves both domestic investment and foreign asset acquisition in the boom period, followed by a phase of disinvestment as the economy returns to its pre-boom equilibrium.

The second model is different in only one respect: domestic investment is irreversible. As in the first model foreign assets are initially built up and then drawn down in response to the shock, but in this model the boom-induced increase in the domestic capital stock is necessarily permanent. In this model the price of capital goods is constant (as in the first model) when investment is positive but it becomes endogenous when the irreversibility constraint binds.

In the third model the economy has two sectors, one producing tradable consumer goods, the other producing non-tradable capital goods. In the capital goods sector all factors are fixed except for labour. Since capital goods are non-tradable their relative price is endogenous even if investment is positive. This price jumps up at the beginning of the boom and then declines. The decline of the price of capital goods provides an incentive to postpone investment. In this model foreign assets may be used to stretch the investment boom: some windfall savings are temporarily held as foreign assets. After the boom is over investment may continue, financed by drawing down the foreign assets acquired in the boom period.

A boom may lead to investment in two different ways: by lowering the cost of funds or by raising the marginal value productivity of capital in a sector. By construction, this second route does not apply in our three models. For only tradables are consumed so that a boom-induced increase in consumption does not affect relative prices. In addition, in the first model investment is reversible and capital goods are tradable so that their price is unaffected by the boom. In the other two models the boom does affect the price of capital goods, but in neither case does this induce investment. For in the second model the price is endogenous only if investment would be reversed if this were possible. In the third model an increase in the price of capital goods does not induce investment since labour is the only variable factor in the sector. This leaves the *transient income effect*: to the extent the boom is recognized as temporary, agents will want to save part of it and (except to the extent these windfall savings are invested abroad) this stimulates domestic investment by lowering the cost of funds. This is the effect which we emphasize.

In all three models there are two competitive, representative agents in the economy, a consumer and a producer.

The consumer's problem at time t is:

$$\max_{c} \int_{t}^{\infty} u(c)\ e^{\delta(t-\tau)}d\tau \tag{1}$$

subject to the flow budget constraint:[3]

$$\dot{a}(\tau) + \dot{e}(\tau) = r_d a(\tau) + r(\tau)e(\tau) + y(\tau) - c(\tau), \tag{2}$$

[3] A dot over a variable denotes a derivative with respect to time.

the condition that foreign assets cannot be negative

$$a \geq 0, \tag{3}$$

the intertemporal budget constraint (which at any moment restricts the present value of future differences between consumption and income to current wealth) and the initial conditions: the values $a(t)$ and $e(t)$ are given. Here δ is the discount rate (pure rate of time preference), r_d is the given interest rate on foreign deposits, r the equity return,[4] y non-asset income, c consumption, a the value of foreign assets, and e the value of domestic assets (equity). Labour supply $\bar{l}$ is exogenous and non-asset income y consists of wage income $y^* = w\bar{l}$ and (in case of a positive trade shock) of transfers received from abroad (in the form of tradables).

The consumer takes the time paths of prices (w, r) and non-asset income (y) as given. Preferences are time-separable and the utility function u is assumed to be unit-elastic:

$$u(c) = \log c.$$

In the initial equilibrium $a = 0$ and $r = \delta > r_d$. Hence it would be optimal to borrow at the foreign interest rate r_d but this is not possible.

Necessary conditions for an optimum include:

$$\dot{\lambda} = -r\lambda \tag{4}$$

$$\dot{\lambda} = -r_d\lambda + \mu \tag{5}$$

$$e^{-\delta\tau}/c = \lambda \tag{6}$$

where λ and μ are the dual variables corresponding to the equation of motion (2) and the non-negativity constraint (3) respectively. When this constraint is slack $(a > 0)$ $\mu = 0$. Hence (4) and (5) imply that $r = r_d$ whenever $a > 0$: when the country holds foreign assets the equity return r equals the interest rate on foreign deposits, r_d.

From (4) and (6):

$$\dot{c}/c = r - \delta. \tag{7}$$

Hence consumption decreases whenever the discount rate exceeds the interest rate.

The producer maximizes the value of the firm (v), the present value of dividends (profits net of investment expenditure).[5] Dividends are discounted at the shareholders' opportunity cost which is the equity return r. (The competitive producer takes the path of r as given.)

Now consider the first model. The producer's problem may be written as:

$$\max_{i, l} v(t) = \int_t^\infty \{f(k, l) - wl - i\} e^{-\int_t^\tau r(s)ds} d\tau \tag{8}$$

---

[4] This comprises both dividends and changes in the valuation of equity.
[5] Since there is only one consumer and one producer in the model the value of the firm is equal to the value of equity held by the consumer: $e = v$.

subject to

$$\dot{k} = i. \tag{9}$$

Here the function f is a concave, constant-returns-to-scale production function in capital and labour; investment requires only tradables and the wage rate w and the equity return r are taken as given by the firm. Since investment is reversible we obtain the first order condition:[6]

$$f_k(k, l) = r. \tag{10}$$

The model is closed by an equilibrium condition for the labour market ($l = \bar{l}$) and by the condition that domestic savings are equal to investment.

The initial value $k(0) = k^*$ satisfies:

$$f_k(k^*, \bar{l}) = \delta. \tag{11}$$

Hence the pre-boom equilibrium is a steady state in which there is no investment since the return to capital is equal to the discount rate and the country cannot borrow at the lower rate r_d.

Model I is illustrated in Fig. 4.7. Assets remain constant along the upward sloping $\dot{a} + \dot{k} = 0$ locus which is given by $c = f(k, \bar{l})$. Along this locus $a = 0$

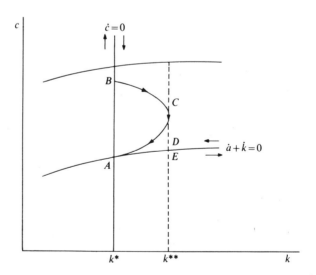

FIG. 4.7. *Adjustment to a boom in Models I and II*

---

[6] Subscripts k and l denote the marginal products of capital and labour. Note that since f is linear homogeneous $f - wl - i = f_k k + f_l l - wl - i = rk - \dot{k}$ at an optimum. Substituting this in (8) gives $v = k$: in this model (as in the second model) the value of the firm is equal to the value of the capital stock. The term re in the consumer's budget constraint is then equal to current profits: $re = rk = f - wl$.

hence there is no foreign interest income: income consists only of the value of output $f(k, \bar{l})$ and this is entirely consumed. Investment is positive below, and negative above this locus. From (7), (10), and (11) $\dot{c} = 0$ for $f_k(k, \bar{l}) = \delta$, i.e. for $k = k^*$. This defines the vertical $\dot{c} = 0$ locus. Consumption increases (decreases) to the left (right) of this locus.

The initial equilibrium is at point A. The boom raises income by a fixed amount and therefore shifts the $\dot{a} + \dot{k} = 0$ locus upwards. Point A then lies below this new locus and this triggers investment. At the beginning of the boom (at $t = 0$) there is an instantaneous increase in the level of consumption: the economy shifts from A to B. This is followed by a gradual adjustment process from B to C. Along this path consumption falls, domestic investment is positive and $r > r_d$. Hence there is no acquisition of foreign assets: all investment is domestic investment since the domestic rate of return exceeds the foreign interest rate.

When point C is reached r has fallen to the level of the foreign interest rate r_d (the level k^{**} is defined by $f_k(k^{**}, \bar{l}) = r_d$).[7] Hence for the remainder of the boom period investment is in foreign assets. During this second phase the level of consumption continues to fall and since k remains constant this involves a vertical move down from C in the figure.

When the boom is over the $\dot{a} + \dot{k} = 0$ locus shifts back. (Since income now consists not only of $f(k, \bar{l})$ but also of interest on foreign assets $r_d a$, the locus remains above its original position as long as a is positive.) This induces disinvestment. Initially the domestic capital stock remains constant as foreign assets are repatriated: in the diagram the economy remains on the vertical segment below C, shifting down towards D. (This reduces foreign interest income and therefore further lowers the $\dot{a} + \dot{k} = 0$ locus.) Eventually (at point D) $a = 0$ again and domestic investment is reversed along the path from D to the original equilibrium A.

Hence in this model adjustment involves four phases: domestic investment, foreign asset acquisition, repatriation of foreign assets and, finally, negative domestic investment.

In Model II domestic investment is irreversible. Hence we add the constraint $i \geq 0$ to the producer's problem. As a result the condition $f_k = r$ applies only for $i > 0$. In terms of Fig. 4.7 this implies that the $\dot{c} = 0$ locus shifts to the right with investment. As before, there is investment in both assets in the boom period. But after the boom k cannot fall below k^{**}. Hence in the post-boom period the domestic capital stock remains constant while consumption is smoothed by drawing down foreign assets. In the long run point E instead of the original equilibrium A is approached. However, this point will not be approached via B and C. Domestic investment is less

---

[7] We assume that the size of the windfall is such that it is optimal to invest up to this point. Obviously, for a small boom it may not be optimal to invest that much. In that case $a = 0$ throughout.

attractive as a response to the boom than in the first model: irreversibility makes the smoothing of consumption more costly. Therefore less will be saved: adjustment will start at a point above B with a higher level of consumption. Hence we may continue to assume that in both models k reaches k^{**} eventually, but the path of k will differ.

In Model III the tradable sector competes for labour with the capital goods sector. Output in that sector is given by $g(l-l_T)$ where l_T is employment in the tradable sector and $g(0) = 0$. We assume that the function g is concave and that the marginal productivity of labour $g_l(0)$ is finite. The producer takes the path of the price of capital goods p as given. Hence in this model the producer's problem is:[8]

$$\max_{i,l,l_T} v(t) = \int_t^\infty \{f(k,l_T) + pg(l-l_T) - wl - pi\} e^{-\int_t^\tau r(s)ds} d\tau \tag{12}$$

subject to

$$\dot{k} = i \tag{13}$$

and

$$i \geq 0. \tag{14}$$

This gives the conditions:[9]

$$f_l = pg_l = w \tag{15}$$

$$\dot{\pi} = r\pi - f_k \tag{16}$$

$$\pi \leq p \perp i \geq 0 \tag{17}$$

where π is the dual variable associated with (13). Since capital goods are non-tradable equilibrium requires $i = g(l - l_T)$.

The producer's problem is illustrated in Fig. 4.8. From $g = 0$ and the condition $f_l = pg_l$ we derive the upward sloping $\dot{k} = 0$ locus, given by $p = f_l(k,\bar{l})/g_l(0)$. Above this locus labour is drawn into the capital goods sector so that investment is positive and k increases. Note that if investment is positive $\pi = p$ and hence from (16):

$$f_k = rp - \dot{p}. \tag{18}$$

This implies that if the price of capital goods is constant investment proceeds until $f_k = rp$. However, if the price of capital goods is known to be falling ($\dot{p} < 0$) then f_k will be higher: it then is optimal to postpone investment.

---

[8] The value of the firm now consists of the discounted value of dividends of the tradable sector (as before) plus the discounted value of rents in the capital goods sector. In the absence of the non-negativity constraint (14) the first component can be shown to equal pk: the value of equity in tradables is equal to the replacement value of the capital stock in that sector. In that case the term re in the consumer's budget constraint is equal to profits plus a valuation change $(f - wl) + \dot{p}k$.

[9] The symbol $\perp$ denotes complementary slackness: in (17) one constraint is slack when the other one is binding.

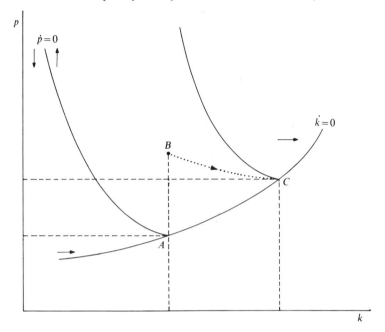

FIG. 4.8. *Adjustment to a boom in Model III*

From equation (18) we derive the downward sloping $\dot{p} = 0$ locus given by $p = f_k/r$. The price of capital goods increases (decreases) above (below) this locus. Since investment is irreversible this locus shifts to the right as investment proceeds.

The initial equilibrium is at A. As before, consumers react to the boom by saving. This lowers the equity return r which the producer takes as given. Hence the $\dot{p} = 0$ locus shifts upward. (The new locus shown in the figure, ending in C, is given by $p = f_k/r_d$. This is the relevant locus once $r = r_d$.) Adjustment then starts at point B:[10] the boom causes an instantaneous increase in p, the price of capital goods. Subsequently adjustment is along the path from B to C.

We have seen from (18) that there is a case for postponing investment if p declines. As a result it is possible in this model that investment continues after the boom. Consumers have then stopped saving but investment proceeds, financed by drawing down the foreign assets accumulated in the boom period.

In summary, in this model adjustment involves domestic investment, during the boom period and possibly also thereafter. The shock causes an

[10] Initially r may exceed r_d. In that case the $\dot{p} = 0$ locus has shifted outwards (and B lies below it) but not yet as far the locus shown through C. As investment proceeds the locus continues to shift to the right until $r = r_d$.

instantaneous increase in the price of capital goods. This price subsequently falls but it remains above its pre-boom level.

An essential element in all three models is the borrowing constraint, reflected in the initial gap between the domestic equity return and the interest rate on foreign deposits. Without such a gap windfall savings would all be invested abroad: it would not be optimal to invest domestically[11] since this would force the rate of return below what could be obtained abroad.

In general, the stronger the relative price effect, the longer foreign assets will be held along an optimal adjustment path. The temporary holding of foreign assets (to be converted later into domestic real capital) stretches the investment boom beyond the income boom.

The rationale for such a stretching process is to avoid the costs associated with short-run supply bottlenecks in the non-tradable capital goods sector. By deferring investment the cost of these capital goods is cheaper, so that the investment process is more efficient. However, the extra domestic investment is not indefinitely deferred, because offsetting this temporary reason for investing abroad is an underlying reason for investing at home, namely, that by assumption the economy achieves a rate of return above that available on the world capital market.

The above analysis is both normative and positive. It describes both what the path of the economy ought to be and that path which it would in fact take were private agents to be unrestricted and well informed. The informational requirements placed upon agents are to recognize that the windfall is temporary and to deduce from that that the investment boom they observe around them is also temporary, with its corollary for the price of investment goods; requirements which will often not be unreasonable.

2.5. The Demand for Domestic Financial Assets

Many agents are not in a position directly to diversify their asset accumulation into interest-bearing foreign financial assets. Instead, this activity is likely to be performed by specialized agents, in particular banks, against whom the majority of private agents acquire claims denominated in domestic currency. This implies that even in an unregulated open economy a temporary trade shock will have short-term monetary repercussions. The foreign financial assets trajectory discussed above will have as a counterpart a corresponding domestic money supply trajectory. If the banks are subject to a cash-to-deposits ratio (to be discussed in more detail below), then there will be a consequent increase in the demand for currency. The supply of currency is automatically increased initially by the extent of the windfall as agents convert foreign exchange into domestic currency through the exchange equalization account. Once portfolio choices have been implemented, that

[11] Except in response to induced price changes, an effect we have assumed away in this section.

part of asset acquisition which is financial will be held as follows. If private agents wish directly to hold financial assets only denominated in domestic currency, they will hold bank deposits. The banks will hold two types of asset as the counterpart to these liabilities. To support the increase in deposits they will hold domestic currency, which is a claim on the government, and beyond this they will hold foreign financial assets. The latter will show up in the balance of payments as a private capital outflow. The former represents a liability incurred by the government. As a counterpart to this it will itself acquire foreign financial assets which will appear in the reserves of the central bank. The government is thus a custodian of a fraction of the foreign financial assets temporarily and indirectly accumulated by private agents, the fraction being determined by the cash-to-deposits ratio.

So far only relative price determination has been discussed, nominal values being unspecified. To determine nominal values we introduce a monetary authority, and a demand for money function.

The demand for money by non-bank agents can be thought to comprise two elements. First, there is a conventional transactions demand which is a function of expenditure. As in the basic model developed in Chapter 2 we assume that exportable goods are not consumed domestically, so we shall represent expenditure as comprising only importables (M) and non-traded gooda (N). The transactions demand for money, D, can thus be characterized as:

$$D = a(p_N N + p_M M) \qquad (19)$$

where

p_N = the price of non-tradable goods
p_M = the price of importable goods
N = quantity of non-tradable goods
M = quantity of importables purchased.

Second, again as in the core model, we assume that there are no financial securities markets. Private agents cannot hold domestic currency bonds or equity and so their only financial assets (in the absence of government regulations) would be domestic money and foreign financial assets. Since only the latter offer a positive yield we may assume that the asset demand for domestic money would be negligible. The demand for foreign financial assets (which is itself likely to be small if the country is a net debtor) can readily be introduced into a simple model.

In the absence of a windfall let the proportion saved out of income (Y) be s and let the proportion of asset accumulation which is financial (rather than being directly channelled into real assets) be q. Then (foreign) financial asset accumulation is qsY. Expenditure (E) is identified from (19) as:

$$(1-qs)Y = E = p_N N + p_M M. \qquad (20)$$

Finally, let the capital output ratio be v.

Then with v, q, s and a all constant the ratio of the demand for financial assets, A, to the transactions demand for money is constant:

$$\frac{A}{D} = \frac{vq/(1-q)}{a(1-qs)} \tag{21}$$

The supply of money is made up of fiat money (c) and bank lending, the banks being constrained by a cash ratio, β_b, and by private agents choosing a cash-to-deposits ratio of β_p. Hence,

$$c = c_p + c_b \tag{22}$$

where subscripts denote non-bank (p) and bank (b) agents. Since

$$c_p = \beta_p d$$

and

$$c_b = \beta_b d$$

so

$$c = (\beta_p + \beta_b)d$$

and

$$d = \frac{c}{\beta_p + \beta_b}$$

so that money supplied to non-bank agents is:

$$d + c_p = \frac{(1+\beta_p)c}{\beta_p + \beta_b} = kc = (1+\beta_p)d. \tag{23}$$

The pre-boom monetary equilibrium thus requires:

$$a(p_N N + p_M M) = kc. \tag{24}$$

The process by which the domestic supply of fiat money is altered depends upon whether the exchange rate is freely floating or managed. If it is freely floating, and there are no large holdings of the national currency outside the country, the only mechanism for increasing the supply of fiat money is the fiscal deficit. If, however, the government maintains the exchange rate at a target level then it must be prepared to supply either foreign exchange or domestic currency depending upon which side of the market is short. The supply of fiat money is then the sum of the fiscal deficit and the payments surplus. Here we confine our analysis to the case of a freely floating exchange rate, the consequences of a fixed exchange rate being considered as part of our discussion of the control regime adopted by the government.

During the windfall the demand for money rises for two distinct reasons. First, as discussed previously, the demand for foreign financial assets is likely to be indirect: most private agents will hold claims on local banks denominated in domestic currency, with the banks holding foreign assets together with the extra fiat money entailed by the cash ratio. We shall term this the 'asset effect'. The second component of the increase in the demand for money is the increase in real expenditure, which, since it reflects the increase in permanent income, is discrete and sustained, this being termed the 'liquidity effect' by Neary (1985).

Combining the two components, the demand for money jumps at the onset of the windfall, then rises further as a result of the build-up of financial assets, and subsequently declines. Whether these changes are accommodated by changes in the money supply or by offsetting changes in other components of money demand depends upon the fiscal policy adopted.

Here we wish to abstract from monetary policy and so in some sense keep it neutral. One bench-mark of neutrality is a constant money supply. An alternative is to define a neutral monetary policy as that which produces no change in the price level. These are alternatives because, as we have seen, as a result of the windfall there is a permanent increase in real expenditure so that at constant prices there is a permanent increase in the demand for money, which with a floating exchange rate can only be accommodated by a budget deficit. Hence, defining neutrality in terms of budget balance implies a permanent fall in the price level. However, defining neutrality in terms of a continuously constant price level is also unattractive because, as we have seen, there is also a temporary increase in the demand for money which, to keep prices constant, would require an additional temporary deficit. Thus, requiring a continuously constant price level imposes a particular, and curious, pattern on fiscal policy. Hence, neither of these positions by itself seems attractive and we adopt a hybrid. We shall assume that fiscal policy is adjusted in such a way that the windfall has no permanent effect upon the price level. This implies that at some stage there is a deficit. However, we assume that during the windfall there is fiscal balance, so that the above changes in the demand for money must be accommodated by offsetting changes in other components of the demand.

A further alternative monetary policy is that which minimizes inflation, subject to the constraint that no nominal prices should be required to fall. This would be an appropriate policy if there were considerable downwards inflexibility in nominal prices. This policy involves maintaining the nominal exchange rate constant, and so the analysis of its consequences can be subsumed under our discussion of such an exchange rate policy in section 3.3.

With these assumptions the short-term changes in the demand for money which occur during the windfall are not accommodated by supply and so must be offset, whereas the long-term change is accommodated. Thus in the short term there must be an offsetting decline in the remaining transactions demand. This is achieved by an appreciation in the currency, which lowers the domestic price of tradable goods, and is an automatic response to excess demand in the currency market. In the long term, because by assumption there is no change in the price level, the exchange rate reverts to its initial level.

The effects of the windfall on nominal and relative prices can be depicted in a simple diagram due to Neary (1985) (Fig. 4.9). Non-tradables are treated as a single aggregate, the N–N schedule depicting the locus of effective equilibria in that market. It is flatter than a ray through the origin because, for a given money supply, an increase in the price level increases hoarding at the expense of goods demand. The D–D locus depicts monetary equilibrium, again for the given money supply. The 'asset' and 'liquidity' effects of the windfall shift the D–D locus to D'–D', whereas the increased demand for non-tradables shifts the N–N locus to N'–N'. With continuous clearing in both markets the exchange rate appreciates from e_0 to e_1. Recall that because the boom is temporary there is additionally a relative price change within the non-tradables, as described in Fig. 4.2. The path of the relative price of non-tradable capital goods has been analysed above, namely a jump followed by a gradual fall. The price of non-tradable consumer goods should behave in the same fashion but for different reasons. The initial jump reflects the permanent increase in demand commensurate with the increase in permanent income, but this is gradually accommodated by increased supply as investment is attracted into the sector, driving prices back down. Hence, in both of the non-tradable sectors relative prices jump and then gradually revert to their initial levels, in the capital goods sector because demand recedes and in the consumer goods sector because supply is augmented.

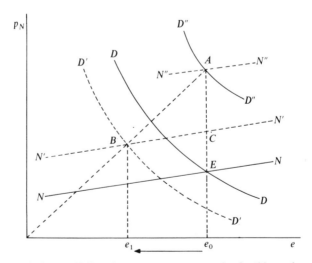

FIG. 4.9. *Effects of a windfall with constant money supply, flexible exchange rate, and constant tariffs*

   The time path of the exchange rate reflects the time path of the demand for domestic currency: there is a temporary appreciation followed by a depreciation of the same magnitude. The asset and liquidity effects cause a jump in the exchange rate at the onset of the windfall. As foreign financial assets are depleted, so the asset demand for domestic money derived from them falls. This decline in the demand for money is offset by exchange rate depreciation. Hence, the nominal exchange rate jumps at the onset of the windfall and declines during asset decumulation, eventually reverting to its initial level.

   This trajectory of the exchange rate has implications for the interest rate available on foreign financial assets. Since the exchange rate depreciates after its instantaneous appreciation upon 'news' of the windfall, this represents a domestic currency loss which must be deducted from the nominal interest rate available on the world capital market before determining the nominal interest rate on domestic currency bank deposits which can be afforded by the local banks. This assumes that banks do not make systematic errors in their forecasts of the exchange rate.

   The path of the exchange rate and the domestic interest rate consequent upon a trade windfall is shown in Fig. 4.10. To simplify, the interest rate available to the country on the world capital market is treated as a constant, r_w (although our previous discussion emphasizes that it is likely, in fact, to be a variable). The temporary increase in the domestic interest rate, r_d, coincides with a rising nominal price of tradable goods, p_T, consequent upon the depreciating exchange rate:

$$r_d - r_w = \dot{e} = \dot{p}_T. \tag{25}$$

Hence, in units of tradable goods the domestic interest rate remains equal to the (constant) world interest rate. Since this was the concept of the real interest rate used in our analysis of section 2.4, the above path of the nominal interest rate does not qualify the results reached there.[12]

2.6. *Optimal Tax and Expenditure Policies in the Uncontrolled Economy*

The part played by government in determining the overall response to the trade shock is considered in this section from three distinct perspectives. The first (2.6.1) examines what tax and expenditure choices may be appropriate when the shock initially accrues to the private sector and when the private sector is itself capable of responding optimally. The second (2.6.2) poses the same question, but relaxes the assumption of optimal private response. The third (2.6.3) is concerned with public responses in the case where a windfall accrues directly to the government.

---

[12] Between the onset of the boom and the acquisition of foreign financial assets there may be a phase during which all asset acquisition is domestic. During such a phase there would be a gradual decline in the domestic interest rate to r_w.

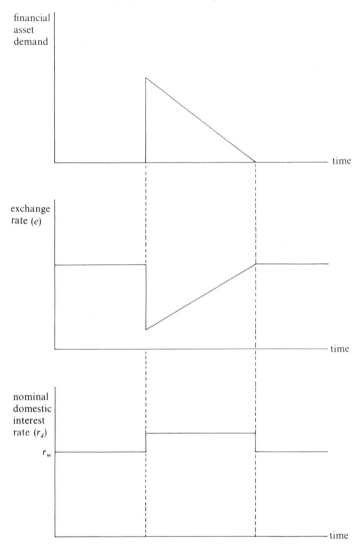

FIG. 4.10. *The path of the nominal exchange rate and domestic interest rate*

2.6.1. *Government taxation and spending in response to a private windfall*

Since a well-managed windfall requires no custodial intervention from government, it might appear that a relatively passive or *laissez-faire* public response would be appropriate. Matters are more complicated than this, however, for three different sets of reasons. These involve, respectively, the long-run level of public expenditure and taxation, the marginal cost of public funds, and the nature and composition of public expenditure. The first relates to the new long-run equilibrium following adjustments to the shock, the others tend to affect the trajectory of adjustment to this equilibrium. Each is considered in turn.

Permanent national income is higher following the boom, and so tax revenue will rise at existing tax rates. There is no equivalent mechanism ensuring an automatic rise in public expenditure, so a passive response will generate an arbitrary fall in the public sector deficit. However, it is plausible to assume that the elasticity of desired public expenditure with respect to permanent national income is positive, and so there should be discretionary increases in planned public expenditure. If this elasticity differs from the corresponding elasticity of tax revenue at existing rates, some change in the level and/or structure of tax rates will also be necessary. In effect, the size and shape of the public sector will automatically change, but there is no reason to suppose that these automatic changes will correspond to what is wanted.

We do not consider this question of long-run design further here. The properties of the short-run adjustment path will be compounded from the changes required to implement the new long-run equilibrium and those of a purely transitional nature. In the rest of this section we concentrate on the latter.

One reason for supposing that the appropriate short-run fiscal response should differ from the long-run response is that the marginal cost of public funds may temporarily drop during the boom (see, e.g. the round table discussion in Neary and Van Wijnbergen, 1986). The usual argument is that the windfall is rather like an economic rent, so that it can be taxed away with minimal incentive effects. Whether this is so depends on the type of income instability involved, and the informational content attributed to the increment in income.

When income is in any case volatile, the increment may carry no informational content at all. This is to say, it is perceived as being generated by a known stochastic process, and does not cause individuals to revise their perceptions of that process. This we have called unrevised inclusive expectations. Second, the increment may be viewed as generated by a special one-off event, not allowed for in the prior perception of the underlying stochastic process, and not relevant to later perceptions in view of its unrepeatable singularity. This we have called unrevised exclusive expectations. Finally, the increment may be viewed as not only generated by the underlying stochastic process, but throwing some light on that process. In other words, individuals have incomplete knowledge of this process, or believe that it is non-stationary, and so revise their expectations in the light of events. This we have called revised inclusive expectations.

These three cases provide a full characterization of the possibilities.[13] In each case perceptions may or may not be rational, in the sense that the

---

[13] The taxonomy might suggest a fourth possibility, that of revised exclusive expectations. But this is an 'empty box', since if the increment was believed to be a unique event (exclusive) it could not sensibly be held to induce a revision of opinion about the 'normal' stochastic process.

revision—or lack of it—is appropriate to the underlying process. Such marginal or incremental expectations may be rational without necessarily requiring that expectations are rational on average. They have different implications for the marginal cost of public funds.

The principal determinant of the marginal cost of public funds is the deadweight cost of the tax system, reflecting disincentive effects. The marginal cost will be low when these disincentive effects are small because the relevant private substitution elasticities are low. The question, therefore, is whether these elasticities are likely to be low in respect of incremental income. For the unrevised exclusive case, this does appear to be likely. The increment is truly a windfall in this case; it was anticipated neither in fact nor probabilistically; and it has no implications for future supply decisions. If the windfall could be gathered with no increase in current labour supply, it would then be pure profit or rental income, and taxation of it would have no incentive effects.

Now suppose that one of the inclusive cases holds. Taxation of the incremental income at an enhanced rate now lowers mean expected net income, unless it is accompanied by correspondingly reduced taxation during periods of low income. No general conclusions can be drawn about the implications of either approach for the level of the marginal cost of public funds. In principle this could rise or fall, depending on the nature of preferences, the form of the distribution, and the structure of taxes. Hence there does not appear to be any general presumption in favour of a high effective tax rate on the increment in cases where this is perceived to be part of the normal ups and downs of economic life.

This discussion may be summarized as follows. If a windfall is commonly perceived as both temporary and once for all, then there are powerful arguments that a high proportion of the incremental income should be taxed at source. If it is perceived as unusual, but part of the normal pattern, these arguments do not go through.

Finally, appropriate fiscal response may be influenced by the nature and composition of public expenditure, particularly by the allocation between tradable and non-tradable goods on the one hand, and that between capital and consumption goods on the other. The sharp movement in the relative price of non-tradable goods will imply some shift in the optimal allocation of public expenditure between tradable and non-tradable goods, more markedly in the short run than in the long run.

It may also have implications for the level of government spending, as opposed to its allocation. For example, if the major part of public services is non-tradable, these will become relatively more expensive during the windfall and contraction of public expenditure might be desirable. Expenditure on non-tradable goods during this period will be relatively inefficient from the government's point of view. In the worst case the rise in non-tradable prices reflects real increases in resource costs, so there is a social loss arising from excessively bunched spending. But even if the price rises constitute pure transfers to factor owners, there is no reason to suppose that the government would value these unintended transfers high enough to match the marginal cost of public funds.

The flow of current government services can be sustained in two quite different ways. The government may simply purchase part of current final output and then supply this in the form of public services. Alternatively, it may create and operate capital facilities which generate output directly (as with government-owned factories) or in co-operation with privately owned factors (as with much infrastructure).

Assume, for simplicity, that the government wishes to increase the flow of public services in line with changes in permanent national income. Then if public services constitute only purchases of final output, public expenditure will also rise in line with permanent national income. However, to the extent that public services are provided by public capital, the actual pattern of incremental expenditure will exhibit an early peak followed by a decline. As a polar case, suppose that the government's main activity was building in-frastructure with very low maintenance costs and depreciation rates. Then virtually all the incremental government expenditure would occur as a short surge of capital expenditure very soon after the windfall.

While inter-temporal considerations indicate that a stable deficit is un-likely to be optimal during a windfall, this discussion demonstrates that even the direction of change is ambiguous. Consider the following polar cases. In the first, the windfall is external to expectations, so it is optimal for the government to obtain a large share of it as incremental revenue. Meanwhile, public expenditure exclusively takes the form of purchases of final output. In these circumstances, expenditure rises in line with government permanent income, which increases relative to permanent national income following the boom. During the boom, the government runs a large surplus and has the task of lending this to the private sector and attempting to ensure that it is all invested in private capital.

In the second polar case, the windfall is internal to expectations, so the government's revenue rises only proportionately. Meanwhile, public ex-penditure exclusively takes the form of infrastructure investment (non-tradable goods are ignored). Public services are planned to rise proportion-ately to permanent national income. Hence the government undertakes a massive capital expenditure programme equal to the sum of its windfall tax income and the present value of taxes on incremental permanent national income. In consequence, the budget goes heavily into deficit during the boom.

A realistic pattern would lie somewhere between these extremes; but it does not appear possible to sign the transitional budget changes.

2.6.2. *Stabilizing taxation*

So far, we have assumed that the private sector responds optimally. Deferring consideration of the control regime itself, there are two principal reasons why this may not hold. The first involves market imperfections that constrain private choices, the second involves faulty private perceptions of events.

If private sector agents' spending decisions are constrained not by their permanent income but by—for example—their marketable assets and current income, then the government has to correct for these contraints. Its fiscal stance must be chosen in such a way that the paths of private sector current assets and disposable income permit spending decisions which are appropriate to the underlying permanent incomes. This problem is likely to be acute in the case of a long-lived windfall, for example the discovery of oil reserves. It may then be necessary for the government to run a large deficit to generate a sufficient relaxation of private sector current contraints to enable the sector to increase spending appropriately. In the case of a very short-lived windfall, this complication is likely to be much less serious, and will be ignored here.

Both public and private sectors may misunderstand what is happening during the windfall. For example, either or both may get the duration of the windfall, and hence its magnitude, wrong. For concreteness, suppose that the government gets it right, while the private sector is over-optimistic. Then the private sector is likely to attempt to consume too high a proportion of the windfall, and the government must attempt to prevent this. Ideally the government would raise a forced loan, returning the money when the windfall was clearly over, or equivalently, temporarily raise taxes, subsequently to lower them. However, all this is predicated on two assumptions: that the government has more accurate perceptions than the private sector of the underlying instability, and that it is capable of exercising the required custodial function. Even if the first assumption holds, the obvious response is to disseminate the superior information rather than to act on the assumed ignorance of private agents. In any case, the second assumption requires substantiation.

2.6.3. *Public windfalls*

Sometimes trade booms automatically accrue to the government without any tax decision because it owns the asset (e.g. oil). In principle, this raises exactly the same issues as when the windfall accrues to the private sector. The government again has to decide how to share the windfall between public and private sectors. If lump sum taxes and transfers were available, and if the windfall were of the unrevised exclusive type, it would be a matter of indifference whether the windfall accrued to the government, to the private sector, or partly to both. In each case, the ultimate distribution of the gain and the real impact on the economy would be the same.

In the realistic case where taxes and transfers are distortionary, this is no longer so. To the extent that taxing a private windfall inhibits supply, a smaller transfer to the public sector is appropriate. To the extent that subsidizing the private sector also results in deadweight losses, a smaller share of a public windfall should be distributed to the private sector. Hence it is likely to be optimal for the public sector to retain a larger share of a public windfall than the share it would appropriate of a private windfall.

The transfer of part of a public windfall also poses difficult problems of timing, partly because of the relative price effects, and partly because the visibility of the windfall may constrain the government's ability to transform it into an equivalent permanent income transfer. This may be important, since the danger of false expectations is now compounded, requiring private sector agents to predict the time paths of transfers, taxes, and subsidies, rather than simply of the initiating event.

3. The Effect of Government Controls

3.1. *Introduction*

The behaviour, private and public, described above hardly characterizes what actually takes place when developing countries experience temporary windfalls. The reason for this is partly that we have not yet appropriately characterized the choice-set facing private agents, and partly that we have not appropriately characterized government behaviour. In this section we revise the choice-set of private agents to take into account constraints imposed by a variety of government controls which commonly exist before a boom.

3.2. *Foreign Exchange Controls*

Probably the most significant control is on the holding of foreign exchange. In many countries private citizens cannot hold either foreign currency or foreign assets. This drastically changes behaviour, for private agents are now compelled to accumulate, and then decumulate, domestic assets. In the absence of a bond market the only domestic financial asset is money. The opportunity cost of using funds for a proposed investment project is therefore whichever is the greater of the return on the best other project available and the return on money (which we shall take to be zero in nominal terms). In Fig. 4.11 the NPV_0 schedule shows the pre-boom net present value (NPV) of projects discounted at the opportunity cost of funds over the life of the project. As drawn, in the presence of exchange controls the boom is assumed so to increase desired savings that during the boom phase there are not enough domestic projects with a positive NPV to absorb them, the balance being an asset demand for money. Since the return on this is zero it indicates that the discount rate used to generate the NPV is zero during this boom phase. Exchange controls cause this fall in the domestic interest rate during

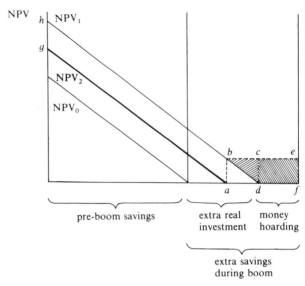

FIG. 4.11. *The deadweight loss from foreign exchange controls*

the boom, and this is one reason for the upward shift in the schedule to NPV_1.

The effect of this control is partly a deadweight loss in the form of a misallocation of investible resources. The schedule NPV_2 denotes the present values which would appertain during the boom were citizens free to hold interest-bearing foreign securities. Since the discount rate would be higher, the NPV schedule is likely to be shifted downwards relative to that with exchange controls. The controls, by lowering the discount rate during the boom, induce a quantity $a-d$ of investment, which yields a NPV $b-c-d$ less than foreign securities. Additionally, there is a transfer $a-d-h-g$ from domestic lenders to domestic borrowers, and a transfer $d-c-e-f$ from holders of money as an asset to the monetary authority. The latter occurs because the authority now accumulates foreign exchange equivalent to $d-f$, which it holds on behalf of private citizens. It is itself free to purchase foreign financial assets with this foreign currency.

An increase in the supply of fiat money to private agents can accrue through either a budget deficit or a balance-of-payments surplus. Via the latter there is thus an increase in fiat money equal to the extra money which is desired as a temporary asset. Denoting windfall income as W and the propensity to accumulate temporary financial assets as h, this increase in fiat money is hW. Thus, if the banks are able to find borrowers (which since there are no further investments with positive NPVs must be for consumption), the money supply available to private agents can expand by an amount khW. Hence, $(k-1)hW$ represents an increase in the money supply relative to demand, which therefore raises the price level.

The impact effect of the boom given foreign exchange controls is therefore temporarily to raise the demand for money by an amount hW, in addition to the permanent increase discussed in section 2; temporarily to raise the money supply by khW; and for the monetary authority to acquire a temporary command over foreign exchange equal to hW. Supposing k to be sufficiently large, there is an increase in money supply relative to demand, which therefore raises the nominal price of tradable goods by an amount proportionate to the excess increase in the money supply, the nominal price of non-tradable goods rising so as to preserve the relative price. In turn this leads to a depreciation of the nominal exchange rate by the extent of the increase in the nominal price of tradable goods. Both of these effects are temporary, being reversed as monetary assets are converted into real assets.

However, the management of this trajectory poses two difficult judgements for the government. First, it must recognize that this part of its windfall increase in fiat money is, in contrast to that considered in section 2, only temporary. The government must distinguish between those extra liabilities which, since it will never be called upon to pay them back and which bear no interest, it can regard as assets, and those which it will shortly be called upon to repay. Second, if banks succeed in increasing their lending so that the money supply expands not by hW but by khW, then despite the increase in the demand for money discussed in section 2, there might be excess supply of money at the initial price level. In this eventuality, even though foreign exchange reserves are accumulating, a possible second-best response is for the government to depreciate the nominal exchange rate, so that the price level rises uniformly without disturbing the relative price of tradable and non-tradable goods.

3.3. *A Managed Exchange Rate*

In most developing countries the government intervenes directly in exchange rate determination, selecting a target rate, or path, which it maintains by means of reserve accumulation and decumulation. With such an intervention, there are two ways in which a temporary windfall can generate a divergence between the actual exchange rate and that which would prevail in a freely floating market. First, the government might simply maintain the initial exchange rate fixed. In this case the divergence is identical to the path taken by the floating rate as analysed in section 2.5. Alternatively, given the policy rule which the government uses to determine the exchange rate, the windfall might trigger a change in the rate. The divergence then depends upon differences between the policy rule and the determination of the floating rate. In each of these cases the divergence in the exchange rate has consequences for the price level and the real economy.

First, consider the case in which the government maintains the exchange rate fixed at its initial level throughout the boom. Recall from section 2.5 that the windfall changes two components of the demand for money, which in a freely floating regime are accommodated by means of a fall in the price of tradable goods consequent upon exchange rate appreciation. With the exchange rate fixed, these increases in the demand for money cannot be accommodated by a reduction in the price of tradable goods, for these prices are also fixed. Instead, the supply of money is increased. From (40), an increase in the money supply held by private non-bank agents of Δd requires an increase in fiat money, of $\Delta d/k$. This increase in fiat money is achieved as private agents in aggregate exchange foreign currency for domestic currency, the counterpart being reserve accumulation on the part of the government. Hence, whereas in a floating-rate regime all the increase in foreign financial assets is held by private agents (typically banks), with a fixed rate, e, the government acquires a part of these holdings equal to $e(\Delta d/k)$. The increased demand for money is partly transient (the asset demand), and partly permanent (the transactions demand generated by higher permanent income). Hence, part of the increase in reserves represents a temporary loan from private agents and part is resources permanently available to the government. In the case of a floating exchange rate, on our previous assumption of an eventual reversion to the initial price level the government also eventually acquires resources as a result of the permanent increase in the transactions demand for money. Here, because of the fixed exchange rate, this resource transfer occurs in the early stages of the windfall rather than at whatever future phase the government chooses to run a fiscal deficit, and the government becomes a custodian of part of the foreign financial assets temporarily accumulated by private agents.

Conceptually, four components of government foreign exchange reserves can be distinguished.

First, there is foreign currency acquired by the government directly or indirectly through taxation. There are no liabilities to offset against these holdings. Second, there is foreign currency acquired in exchange for domestic currency which will be held permanently by private agents for domestic transactions. The government in this case has only a notional liability. Third, there is foreign currency borrowed from foreign agents. The government has a known and clear liability which can be dated, subject to uncertainties about rollovers. Finally, there is foreign currency acquired in exchange for domestic currency which will only be held temporarily by private agents. Corresponding to this the government has a liability which it will only know about and be able to date if it understands the intentions behind the current money demand of private agents.

The information problem facing the government is therefore to interpret changes in reserves by attributing them to temporary and permanent changes in the private sector and to temporary and permanent changes in the budget deficit and trade controls. This problem is considerable, both because, as we have seen, private sector responses are complex, involving overshoots in both the relative price of tradable to non-tradable goods and in money demand,

and because that part of the government which sets the exchange rate will at best only discover changes in trade controls and the budget deficit after a lag.

If the government misinterprets the accumulation of reserves it may spend them, pre-empting resources which would otherwise be spent by the private sector on capital accumulation.

A second consequence of a fixed exchange rate is that the price level rises during the boom, whereas with a floating exchange rate it falls. This occurs because, with the price of tradables fixed, any increase in the prices of non-tradables raises the price level. This might seem to imply that the price level jumps at the onset of the boom and subsequently declines, since in our non-monetary analysis this was the path of non-tradables prices. However, this would be to ignore the path of the money supply. The only mechanism for an increase in the money supply is via a payments surplus. Unlike the effect of a floating exchange rate, which makes a discrete jump and hence instantan-eously reduces money demand, the accumulation of a payments surplus is a flow adjustment. Since the rise in the transactions demand for money is immediate, the impact effect of the windfall is to create an excess demand for domestic currency. This will, in turn, have a moderating effect upon the rise in the price of non-tradables (and the increased quantity of imports). This effect is gradually eroded as the payments surplus leads to monetary accumulation, equilibrium being restored once the surplus has accumulated in excess of the desired trajectory of temporary foreign financial assets by the extent of the increase in the transactions demand for money. It is therefore possible that the prices of non-tradable goods, and hence the price level, continue to rise for some time after their initial jump. This second consequence is illustrated in Fig. 4.9. The impact effect of the windfall is to shift the economy from E to C, at which the non-tradables market clears. Note that because of the excess demand for money this is at a lower relative price of non-tradable goods than at B, the flexible exchange rate equilibrium. At C there is a payments surplus and so the money supply is increasing. This increase shifts upwards both the $N–N$ and $D–D$ loci until real money balances reach the same level as at B. This occurs at A, at which the relative price of non-tradables is the same as at B.

The third consequence is that, because the exchange rate is fixed, local banks can pay an interest rate on domestic bank deposits equal to the world interest rate, instead of making allowance for a depreciating exchange rate. This effect in isolation restores our preliminary analysis of the effects of the windfall on interest rates as set out in section 2.4. The rate of interest in units of tradable goods is, however, the same in both cases.

Hence, the fixed exchange rate implies, first, that the government auto-matically acquires a custodial role for temporary holdings of windfall foreign exchange. Secondly, there is a higher price level during the windfall, and a smaller initial increase in the relative prices of the non-tradable goods. Third, there is a lower nominal domestic interest rate.

Finally, if the exchange rate is managed but not fixed, the accumulation of reserves might trigger a revaluation of the exchange rate. That is, the policy rule which determines the rate is likely to be related to reserve levels. Since an appreciation of the rate would occur automatically in a floating-rate regime, such a revaluation would in itself reduce the divergence implied by a fixed-rate regime. However, the government policy rule might involve an asymmetry of response to reserve accumulation and decumulation. The political costs of devaluation are so high in some countries that the latter might be met by import controls. Hence, if the government misinterprets temporary reserve accumulation and believes that a permanently higher exchange rate is sustainable, the long-term legacy of the windfall can be an overvalued exchange rate.

3.4. *Import Controls with a Fixed Exchange Rate*

In section 3.3 we considered the effects of a fixed exchange rate abstracting from trade policy but implicitly in the context of free trade. We now introduce import controls and so revert to the analytic framework of such a control regime developed in Chapter 2. Fig. 4.12 incorporates a terms-of-trade windfall into the basic diagram.

We first introduce a second locus of non-tradable goods market equilibria. Corresponding to N–N, which was derived on constant world prices by varying import controls, is N^W–N^W, which is derived on varying world prices but constant import controls. Recall from Fig. 2.1 that in our derivation of N–N, B is characterized by excess supply in the non-tradables sector and H by excess demand, A and C being equilibria. However, if the reduction in the relative price of exportables to importables is due not to an increase in import restrictions but to a change in world prices, if A is an equilibrium c must be characterized by excess supply. This is because, although the resource shifts between A and C are independent of the cause of the relative price change to which producers respond, consumption of non-tradable goods must now be lower, owing to the loss of income consequent upon terms-of-trade deterioration. Hence, the N^W–N^W locus through A must be flatter than the N–N locus (it may or may not be shallower than the ray through the origin). Recalling that at A world prices coincide with domestic prices, N^W–N^W is the locus of free trade equilibria for varying world prices. Similarly, there is a locus for each rate of import restrictions. Fig. 4.12 depicts an increase in the world price of exports from p_X^* to $p_X^{*\prime}$. The N–N locus shifts to N'–N', the free trade equilibrium in the non-tradables sector shifting from A to A' (both lying on N^W–N^W) and the equilibrium with import restrictions of t_q shifting from E to E' (both lying on N^{Wt}–N^{Wt}). If the money supply is maintained constant then the impact effect, r, at which both p_N and p_M are unaltered, must be characterized by an excess demand for money. As discussed previously, the demand for money rises with the increase in expenditure consequent upon the

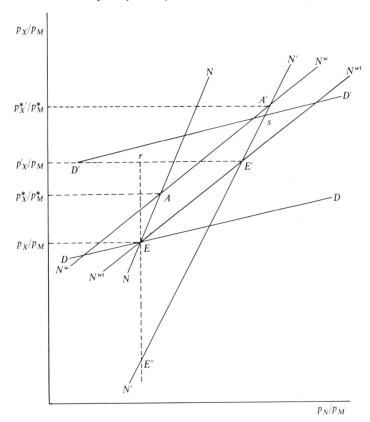

FIG. 4.12. *The relative price effects of a trade shock*

'liquidity effect' and the 'asset effect'. Thus the locus of monetary equilibria shifts to $D'-D'$, passing above r. At r there is an excess demand for non-tradables, which, given t_q, is only alleviated at E', a point of excess demand for money. Hence, the terms-of-trade improvement disrupts the original equilibrium, E, and requires either some combination of an increase in the money supply and (or) an appreciation in the exchange rate, which would validate E', or a reduction in import restrictions which would validate s, these strategies implying, of course, different equilibrium relative prices.

Whereas E' keeps import restrictions constant as measured by the implicit tariff rate, if controls take the form of quotas a passive policy which maintains them will cause the implicit tariff rate to increase. Because importables are now non-tradable at the margin, their supply is constrained in a way similar to that of non-tradables. *A priori* the domestic price of such quota-constrained importables could rise or fall relative to non-tradables. The figure depicts the case in which there is no relative price change between importables and non-tradables, and the economy achieves a new equilibrium at E''.

With binding quotas, despite the rise at world prices in the relative price of exports, at domestic prices exports cheapen relative to both non-tradables and importables. Since this is a powerful consequence of quota controls which appears not to have received attention in the literature, a simplified version of the same result is shown in Fig. 4.13. The figure abstracts from non-tradables. The ray OF depicts the initial terms of trade, the economy being at point A (on the home offer curve OAH), at which the quantity of imports is $\bar{Q}$. Although there is an import quota constraining import volumes to not more than $\bar{Q}$, this is assumed to be not quite binding (an 'auxiliary constraint'). Hence, domestic relative prices coincide with world prices. Now there is a terms-of-trade improvement as the foreign offer curve shifts to OF'. The quota now binds, constraining the economy to B (on the home offer curve depicted by the dashed line OB). The change in domestic relative prices can be inferred from the slopes of the trade indifference curves through A and B. As long as imports are not inferior goods, the slope must be steeper at B than at A. Thus, although at world prices imports become cheaper relative to exports, at domestic prices they become dearer.

Now consider how boom-induced savings are used in a quota-constrained economy. The only way in which the foreign assets can be spent is by a reduction in the size of the export sector, so that with a given volume of imports the country runs a current account deficit made up by income from and depletion of foreign assets. Hence, instead of deriving a permanent income from foreign financial assets, these resources can only be realized as domestic factors are redeployed from the export sector into the importables and non-tradables sector. In the case of a permanent trade shock the incentive for such a resource shift is indeed signalled by the decrease in the domestic relative price of the export goods described above. However, during a temporary boom, the domestic relative price of the export good can rise.

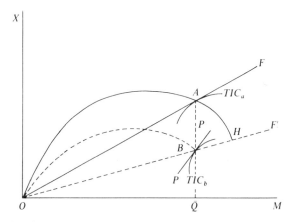

FIG. 4.13. *The effect of a windfall on export prices with an import quota*

Since a given rise in the world export price translates into a smaller increase in permanent income, the price increase for importables and non-tradables is smaller the briefer the boom. Thus, unless private agents hold sophisticated (rational) expectations the contraction in the export sector necessary to utilize the accumulating foreign assets is likely to be delayed. Indeed, agents might well direct resources towards the export sector because of the short-run price incentive. Hence, if there is no relaxation of QRs private agents' expectations must be sophisticated and financial intermediation efficient for a second-best outcome to be attained.

However, if the government relaxes QRs it faces a difficult calculation. First, recall that given foreign exchange controls the reserves of the monetary authority would in response to optimal private behaviour follow a trajectory. Until QRs are relaxed, imports cannot increase so reserves would accumulate yet more rapidly than this trajectory. Second, the existence of QRs implies some prior repressed demand for imports which in turn sustains a real exchange rate above the level at which the foreign exchange market would clear in the absence of QRs. Incremental imports permitted by a partial relaxation of quotas will be sought not only by agents wishing to convert the new foreign assets into domestic capital accumulation, but by agents wishing to satisfy more of their existing repressed demand for consumer imports. To the extent that the latter gain access to incremental imports some of the foreign exchange reserves are pre-empted.

Taking the two above points together, it is easy for the rapid initial accumulation of reserves to prompt more substantial trade liberalization at the existing real exchange rate than is in fact justified. This may come about either because the monetary authority itself misinterprets information, or because the growth of reserves changes the balance of bargaining power among policy makers. The consumption of importables can only be increased at a sustained level by an amount equal to the eventual increase in the output of the tradables sector. This may be quite modest and is certainly only a small fraction of the increase in foreign exchange receipts. Hence, the existence of foreign exchange and QR controls may generate signals which mislead the government into excessive trade liberalization. This may be reinforced by a misinterpretation of the counsel of foreign advisers such as the World Bank and the IMF which urge liberalization on efficiency grounds. However, these agencies advocate only permanent liberalization and this, to be sustainable, requires the acceptance of a lower exchange rate.

Suppose then that lagging the windfall the government liberalizes or even abolishes QRs without lowering the exchange rate. Rational private agents will recognize that they are now presented with a temporary opportunity to satisfy not just current but also future repressed demands of consumer imports. Future repressed import demand for non-durable consumer goods cannot efficiently be satisfied by current consumption, but future durables consumption can be advanced to the present if agents can finance such an increase in expenditure relative to income. This behaviour creates an increase in the demand for consumption loans. Banks are able to meet these requests because, as discussed above, owing to foreign exchange controls an extra quantity of fiat money has entered the economy equal to the payments surplus. This surplus is made up of hW, the previously described counterpart of domestic currency held as a temporary asset before conversion into real domestic assets which in the absence of exchange controls would be held as foreign bonds, and jW, the repressed desired increase in imports for consumption. This increase in fiat money sustains a total increase in money held by private non-bank agents of $k(h+j)W$. Recalling the cash-to-deposits ratio, β_p, of private agents, and the cash ratio of banks, β_b, bank deposits rise by

$$\frac{1}{\beta_b + \beta_p}(h+j)W$$

of which the proportion β_b is backed by cash held by the banks, so that bank loans can increase by

$$\left(\frac{1-\beta_b}{\beta_b + \beta_p}\right)(h+j)W.$$

If QRs are relaxed there are thus two demands for imported consumer goods which pre-empt the foreign exchange requirements of future investment. The first is the previously repressed import demand generated by pre-boom incomes and the second is the loan-financed increase in imported durables demand. Note that neither of these corresponds to jW, the initially repressed desired expenditure of incremental (boom) income on consumer imports, for jW alone could be financed without pre-empting the investment demand hW. The reason why these two demands pre-empt rather than compete with the investment demand is that hW is the counterpart of domestic currency accumulated because investors have reached the current limit of projects with positive NPVs. Investors wish to delay real investment because of the temporary rise in the price of domestic capital goods, but during this delay consumer demands for foreign exchange are satisfied.

To conclude our discussion of the problems introduced by import controls, if QRs are never relaxed the private sector is liable to pursue an inefficient and slow route to the deployment of the windfall so as to generate a sustained increase in consumption by means of a contraction in exports. However, if QRs are relaxed without a simultaneous sustainable trade liberalization package (which is perceived as such), foreign exchange will be pre-empted by consumption. Even a modest and sustainable relaxation will be initially pre-empted by the claims of originally repressed (pre-boom) import demand, and once investment projects have been devised only a fraction of them will succeed in competing with this consumption demand. But if QRs are relaxed further to an extent which is unsustainable without a depreciation of the exchange rate (which would accommodate sustainable trade liberalization), a large new consumption demand is generated which can be expected to pre-empt still more of the foreign exchange windfall.

Finally, we have argued that because of the rapid accumulation of foreign exchange reserves induced by both exchange and trade controls it is easy for the government to become over-confident in its relaxation of QRs.

3.5. *Monetary Control*

The monetary authority regulates the banking system through two types of intervention, a minimum cash-to-deposits ratio and a maximum nominal loan interest rate.

The control of the cash-to-deposits ratio enables the authority to control the money supply over and above its control of fiat money. In some countries such regulation has at times encompassed either or both of a cash ratio and a liquidity ratio. However, in essence the difference between these ratios is primarily that the latter includes Treasury Bills. In effect, Treasury Bills are fiat money which bears interest. Regulation of either ratio can achieve the same money supply objective so at least one must always be slack or auxiliary. We will confine our discussion to the cash ratio, recognizing that this generalizes to the liquidity ratio.

The ability to control the cash ratio can be viewed either as conferring the freedom to choose the price level given some predetermined change in fiat money through the balance of payments and the budget deficit, or equivalently, as the ability to choose the budget deficit given the balance of payments and a predetermined price level objective. Regarded in the latter way, that is as conferring a resource-pre-empting facility on the government, it might appear that the optimal cash-to-deposits ratio would be 100 per cent, thereby ensuring that all money holdings were in the form of government-issued fiat money. With a ratio less than this, banks acquire for their own use some of the never-to-be-claimed liabilities which money holdings constitute. In a monopoly bank this accrues as extra profit; in a competitive banking system it accrues to borrowers and lenders. However, the social cost of setting such a cash ratio would be that by closing down the banking system the gains of financial intermediation would be lost. These gains, if financial intermediation were perfect, and banks the only such intermediaries, would be the efficient allocation of investment resources to the highest-yielding opportunities, as compared with the direction of savings by the savers into opportunities directly available to them. In many developing countries the banks are virtually the only intermediaries, so that the costs of closing or restricting their financial intermediation are likely to be large. Recall that the banks, in addition to lending on the base of the transactions demand for deposits, also operate as a surrogate securities market through their lending backed by the asset demand for deposits.

The control of interest rates similarly generates financial repression. Additionally, it biases the composition of bank-financed investment towards low-risk, low-return projects, an effect now well understood. Finally, an interest rate ceiling produces a transfer from savers to borrowers, successful borrowers acquiring a rent which may be dissipated by rent-seeking investment composition effects noted above.

These controls both influence and are influenced by a terms-of-trade windfall. They influence the use made of windfall savings by inhibiting the allocative efficiency role of financial intermediation. We should expect that in a financially repressed economy relatively little savings would be reallocated from savers to investors in different enterprises. Further, even those resources directed into investment by banks would tend to go into low-return activities, since the banks have accumulated expertise only in the minimization of risk.

The controls are influenced by the windfall via the effect on the money supply. A sufficiently large increase in the money supply held as an asset relaxes financial repression, both directly and by lowering the equilibrium interest rate towards the official ceiling, enabling a larger proportion of savings to be allocated by financial intermediaries. The resulting financial liberalization is gradually eroded after the windfall as the equilibrium interest rate rises and the initial ratio of asset to transactions holdings of money is restored.

Such a temporary liberalization could be avoided by a temporary increase in the minimum cash (or liquidity) ratio to:

$$\beta'_b = \frac{\beta_b kc + (h+j)W}{kc + (h+j)W} \tag{26}$$

This could prevent the increase in fiat money consequent upon the initial balance-of-payments surplus from increasing holdings of inside money. It is ambiguous whether such an intervention would be desirable. On the one hand, by preventing an increase in inside money the authorities would curb the undesirable pre-emption of foreign exchange by loan-financed purchases of imported consumer durables discussed above, and reduce inflationary pressure. On the other hand, temporary liberalization does enable financial intermediaries to reallocate investment resources during the phase in which these resources are atypically large. However, the ability of banks to identify the best investment opportunities may be severely curtailed by their previous expertise acquired under financial repression.

We must conclude that, starting from control-induced financial repression, it is difficult *a priori* to identify the optimal second-best use of controls during the windfall. The appearance of liberalization which results temporarily, merely from leaving the controls unaltered, may well be worse than the maintenance of repression, even though permanent liberalization in conjunction with permanent trade liberalization would be superior to permanent repression.

3.6. *Fiscal Policy in the Presence of Controls*

Section 2.6 discussed optimal fiscal policy in the uncontrolled case. There seems little point in discussing the more onerous optimization of policy in the presence of controls, since the controls are themselves so clearly inoptimal. The same difficulty arises with cost-benefit analysis, where sophisticated second-best optimization exercises are routinely set against a background of inoptimal policies; but in that case, it can be plausibly argued that different departments of government are involved. It is also clear from Chapter 2 that even the comparative dynamics of arbitrary controlled fiscal regimes are dauntingly complex. An adequate analysis of the disequilibrium dynamics of such regimes could only be attempted using an appropriate computable model.

The purpose of this section is simply to illustrate how confusing fiscal management of a temporary shock may be in the controlled case. We use the model of Chapter 2, section 3, and suppress all disequilibrium dynamic complications by solving the model in each period for fiscal instruments set in response to the outcome of the previous period.

We consider the possible sequence of events when the economy is disturbed from a free trade equilibrium by a temporary favourable external shock. Tables 4.1 and 4.2 illustrate two possible sequences in the badly behaved case of Table 2.4.

TABLE 4.1. *Government response to a favourable external shock: increased spending on the non-tradable*

	Period						Equilibrium
	0	1	2	3	4	5	
g_m	0.2	0.2	0.2	0.2	0.2	0.2	0.2
g_n	0.5	0.5	0.7073	0.7073	0.7073	0.7073	0.7073
t	0.2857	0.2857	0.2857	0.2857	0.3500	0.3600	0.3393
z	0	−0.0341	0	0.0697	0	0	0
l_q	0	0	0	0	0.3391	0.7310	0
Q_M	1	0.5901	0.5850	0.9840	1.1560	1.2902	0.9890
Q_N	1.5811	1.2570	1.2972	1.6306	1.7840	1.9008	1.6152
Q_X	4	4.7209	4.6797	3.9360	3.4530	2.9815	3.9562
Import volume	4	9.1305	9.4	4.2309	3.4530	2.9815	3.9562
National income	7.5	12.7096	12.8211	7.6221	8.6878	10.0621	7.5829

The period 0 column in Table 4.1 replicates the equilibrium of column (1) of Table 2.4A. The economy is in free trade equilibrium with an expenditure tax rate of 0.2857, and with relative government expenditure rates $g_m = 0.2$, $g_n = 0.5$. In period 1, the price of the exportable doubles: the government acts passively, maintaining the tax and expenditure rates at their previous *ad valorem* values. In consequence, a budget surplus emerges, and this is translated into a balance-of-payments surplus ($z = -0.0341$, so there is a capital outflow).

In period 2, the government responds by raising its expenditure rate on non-tradables from 0.5 to 0.7073 and this re-establishes a free trade equilibrium with balanced current account at the new terms of trade.

In period 3, the exportable price falls back to its original level. Once again the government maintains the (new) fiscal structure, and the consequence is a deficit on the current account equal to 4 per cent of national income at factor cost ($(4.2309 - 3.9360)/7.6221$).

In period 4, the government decides to maintain the new spending pattern, and to resolve the consequent budgetary and balance-of-payments problems by raising the tax rate and adopting import controls. It decides to raise the tax rate to 0.35, since this gives a revenue share in national income of 26 per cent (0.35/1.35) compared with the present share of 22 per cent (0.2857/1.2857), which should suffice to close the budgetary gap. However, as the final column of the table shows, the equilibrium value of the tax rate, given the terms of trade and spending pattern, is 0.3393. Hence the fiscal retrenchment of column 4 is an overshoot, but because the fiscal structure is badly behaved, the import controls are effective, import volume falls dramatically, and the implicit tariff rate associated with the quota is 0.3391.

In period 5, the government concludes that the fiscal retrenchment was insufficiently severe, and raises the tax rate to 0.36 in an attempt at liberalization. This exacerbates the decline in import availability, and the implicit tariff rate rises to 0.7310. The government concludes that the fiscal problem is unmanageable in a free trade setting, and settles for a quota-ridden equilibrium.

A similar pattern unfolds in Table 4.2. Periods 0 and 1 are the same as for Table 4.1, so they are not repeated. In period 2, the difference is that the government raises its spending rate on the importable (from 0.2 to 0.2385), leaving that on the non-tradable at its prior level. In period 3, when the exportable price reverts to its old value, a current account deficit again emerges, at 2 per cent of national income ($(4.1604 - 4)/7.5$). The government decides to maintain the new spending pattern, and to raise the tax rate to 0.32 accordingly, giving an increase in revenue share of 2 per cent ($0.32/1.32 - 0.2857/1.2857$). This is again higher than the equilibrium rate, given as 0.3141 in the final column. If retrenchment is carried out within a framework of quotas, they will again be effective ($t_q = 0.3217$), and this will be reinforced by further retrenchment. For example, column 5 has tax rate 0.33 associated with $t_q = 1.1628$.

TABLE 4.2.   *Government response to a favourable external shock: increased spending on the tradable*

	Period				Equilibrium
	2	3	4	5	
g_m	0.2385	0.2385	0.2385	0.2385	0.2385
g_n	0.5	0.5	0.5	0.5	0.5
t	0.2857	0.2857	0.32	0.33	0.3141
z	0	0.0385	0	0	0
t_q	0	0	0.3217	1.1628	0
Q_M	0.5901	1	1.1679	1.4213	1.0026
Q_N	1.2570	1.5811	1.7356	1.9372	1.5727
Q_X	4.7209	4	3.5347	2.6286	4.0104
Import volume	9.4417	4.1604	3.5347	2.6286	4.0105
National income	12.7096	7.5	8.4872	11.4133	7.4804

This again underlines the earlier conclusion, namely that correct diagnosis may be far from trivial, and that it is likely to be extraordinarily difficult within a controlled economy to get fiscal policy right, to respond to changed circumstances, or to pursue liberalization effectively.

4. Conclusion

In this chapter, we have extended the apparatus developed in Chapter 2 to permit analysis of temporary trade shocks. This involved two additional steps. The first was a further disaggregation of non-tradables into capital and consumer goods, which focuses attention on the central role of the non-tradable capital goods sector in the adjustment process. The second was to take explicitly into account the perceptions of agents, both public and private, concerning the nature of the shock and, particularly, its likely duration. The central point here is that, except in the extreme case of point perceptions that the shock will be permanent, all shocks will be perceived as effectively temporary. It follows that the representative shock is indeed temporary, and that the permanent shocks which have hitherto been the principal focus of analysis are no more than polar special cases.

Within this context, the chapter first analysed public and private responses in an uncontrolled economy. It emerged that optimal private responses were of a pattern familiar from the theory of permanent income, but that optimal public responses were rather more complicated, depending on the detailed structure of government activities, even when there was no custodial role for government.

Section 3 of the chapter introduced a variety of government controls. These were shown to have powerful consequences in making both private and public responses to a shock sub-optimal. This was due to two types of cause. First, the linkage between the private and social consequences of actions was disrupted, so that rational private responses ceased to induce desirable aggregate outcomes. Second, the informational requirement, and degree of analytic sophistication, demanded of government if it was to manage events successfully appeared altogether excessive. In other words, even a combination of well-informed and well-intentioned public and private agents would find it impossible to manage a trade shock successfully if they were trapped in an inherited system of economic controls.

II
Two African Applications

5

An Application to the Kenyan Coffee Boom
of 1975–1983

1. Introduction

In Kenya the coffee boom amounted to a terms-of-trade gain of K£256 million (in 1975 prices) in the period 1976–9, a gain equivalent to 24 per cent of 1975 GDP. While in Tanzania the price increase was largely taxed away, in Kenya the producer price of coffee rose almost as much as the world price, so that coffee producers (predominantly smallholders) were the initial beneficiaries of the boom. However, we are concerned to trace the shock through the economy. In section 2 estimates are made of relative price changes, private investment expenditure, and real changes in assets, using standard National Accounts data. In section 3 this analysis is supplemented by a general equilibrium analysis using a simulation model. This enables us, in particular, to estimate the extent to which farmers lost their initial gains through transfers to urban groups. Section 4 uses the model to simulate the effects of stabilizing taxation and of the dismantling of the control regime.

2. An Analysis of National Accounts Data

2.1. *The Nature of the Shock*

The coffee boom was a large, short trade shock caused by frost in Brazil. It was recognized at the time both as temporary and as exceptional. The price Kenya received for its coffee exports more than quadrupled between 1975 and the peak of the boom in 1977, this directly constituting a 38 per cent improvement in the barter terms of trade.[1] However, the boom which Kenya enjoyed in this period was much larger: the coffee boom triggered a substantial increase in tea prices and there were other terms-of-trade improvements, the total increase in the barter terms of trade being 54 per cent.[2] As shown in Fig. 5.1, by 1980 the terms of trade had virtually returned to their

---

[1] Import prices rose by 25% between 1975 and 1977 and coffee accounted for 16.4% of the value of exports in 1975.

[2] Although coffee thus accounted for only 70% of the 1977 gain, we shall refer to the entire terms-of-trade gain as the coffee boom.

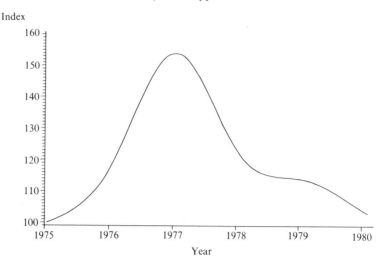

Source: Government of Kenya, *Statistical Abstract*, 1981, p. 57, and corresponding tables for other years.

Fig. 5.1. *The barter terms of trade, 1975–1980*

1975 level. Thus the boom lasted for four years, with much of the gains accruing in 1977.

To construct a counterfactual for the 1976–9 period we assume that without the boom the barter terms of trade would have remained constant at the 1975 level. We also take the actual export volumes as given. In fact, in 1977 coffee exports were over 20 per cent greater in volume than in 1975, and this was no doubt largely a response to the price increase: labour input on coffee rose, partly at the expense of other crops and partly at the expense of leisure. However, to count the increase in coffee output entirely as a windfall gain of the boom would be to ignore that it was achieved at a cost. Since we cannot estimate the net effect, we make the conservative assumption that the trade shock had no effect on export volumes. Hence in Table 5.1, the counterfactual value of exports is obtained by dividing the actual value by the barter terms-of-trade index (the ratio of export and import prices). We then calculate the windfall as the difference between the actual and the counter-factual values of exports. This gives the windfall series shown in column (5) of Table 5.1. Deflating this by the import price index we obtain the real value of the boom at 1975 prices: £37 million in 1976, £135 million in 1977, £53 million in 1978, and £30 million in 1979. This gives an (undiscounted) total of £256 million, equivalent to almost a quarter (24 per cent) of 1975 GDP (at factor cost).

To convert this windfall into the gain in permanent income had it been fully invested we need to know the rate of return on domestic capital

TABLE 5.1. *Magnitude of the coffee boom*

Year	Value of exports[a]	Price indices[b]		Counterfactual exports[c]	Windfall at:	
		Exports	Imports		Current prices[d]	1975 prices
	(1)	(2)	(3)	(4)	(5)	(6)
1975	230.4	100	100	230.4	—	—
1976	335.4	136	116	286.1	49.3	37
1977	480.3	193	125	311.1	169.2	135
1978	370.0	163	132	299.6	70.4	53
1979	385.5	174	153	339.0	46.5	30
TOTAL	1976–9				335.4	256

[a] £m. (current prices), derived from Government of Kenya, *Statistical Abstract, 1981*, p. 66.
[b] From *Statistical Abstract, 1979*, p. 83 (for 1975–6) and ibid. *1981*, p. 81 (for 1977–9).
[c] Col. (1) times col. (3), divided by col. (2).
[d] Col. (1) minus col. (4).

formation. Since there is no reliable estimate we shall use 10 per cent to discount the real annual gains (considering 5 per cent and 15 per cent as alternatives). This gives the present value of the boom in 1976 as £227 million. Again using 10 per cent, this implies a permanent income increase of £23 million, equivalent to 2.1 per cent of 1975 GDP.[3]

After a short period of uncertainty about the extent of the damage to the Brazilian coffee trees, the boom's temporariness was widely known and accepted. The Kenyan government knew it to be temporary, stating: 'Coffee prices cannot be expected to indefinitely remain at present high levels'.[4] The government took steps to convey this information to coffee farmers through the co-operatives and extension services.

As discussed in Chapter 4, shocks may be classified on the basis of their effects on expectations. Using this taxonomy for Kenyan coffee farmers we rule out the inclusive case. Coffee was fairly recently established as a small holder crop in Kenya. Within the period that smallholders had been growing the crop they had experienced no price change like the 1976–9 boom. It seems highly unlikely that in their subjective probability distributions they allowed for such an event. We therefore consider the shock as exclusive. This leaves the revised and unrevised exclusive cases. In the unrevised case the frost would have been interpreted as an event which did not make future price increases more likely, so there would be no need to revise permanent coffee

[3] In relative terms this estimate is quite sensitive to the choice of discount rate: the permanent income gain is 1.1% of GDP for a 5% discount rate and 3.0% of GDP for a 15% discount rate. However, in all three cases the permanent income gain is small relative to GDP.
[4] Government of Kenya (Economic Survey 1977: p 8).

income estimates. Alternatively, agents could have allowed for the reoc-currence of a large boom, and revised their expectations. However, taking into account the low probability of such an event (occurring, say, once every thirty years), the resulting increase in permanent income would be small, so that in fact there is little difference between the two cases. We therefore concentrate on the unrevised exclusive case: the shock was truly unexpected and was considered a pure windfall, not calling for any revision of expecta-tions; permanent income rose only to the extent the windfall was invested.

2.2. *Behaviour of the Representative Agent and of the Economy as a Whole*

2.2.1. *Asset changes and savings rates*

We now estimate the savings rate from windfall income and for this we must define a counterfactual to the observed changes in assets. For this we must specify counterfactual income and counterfactual propensities to acquire assets (domestic and foreign) out of income. First consider the propensity to acquire domestic assets in the form of capital formation (GFKF). The actual propensity to acquire GFKF out of income (at current factor cost prices) is shown in the first column of Table 5.2. To convert expenditure on GFKF into real terms these propensities are applied to a series of real income.[5] Were there no terms-of-trade shock, the real income series would simply be GDP at constant (1975) prices. However, this omits the windfall. We can regard windfall imports as like the discovery of a resource which augments GDP in those years and whose quantities valued at 1975 prices are set out in the final column of Table 5.1. Hence, real income is the sum of GDP at constant 1975 prices plus this windfall resource: it is shown in the second column of Table 5.2. The value of GFKF at 1975 prices is then the propensity times real income, and is shown in column (3).

We now need counterfactual income and propensities. In 1975 and 1976 counterfactual income would have been actual GDP at constant prices.[6] In subsequent years it is actual GDP at constant prices minus the assumed 10 per cent return upon windfall investment. The latter is calculated as the difference between actual and counterfactual investment. The propensity to acquire GFKF out of income was higher in 1972 and 1973 than during the oil-shock period of 1974–5. We assume that in the absence of the boom there would have been a gradual reversion to the average of the 1972–3 period by 1978. The counterfactual propensity is then linearly interpolated between the actual 1975 value and this posited 1978 value. The resulting series for windfall

---

[5] Note that the resulting series does not show the volume of GFKF, since it does not allow for changes in the relative price of capital goods to GDP. Rather, it shows the value of expenditure on GFKF in units of GDP at 1975 prices.

[6] We assume a one-year gestation lag between investment and its returns. Since windfall investment can only start in 1976, income from it can only begin in 1977.

TABLE 5.2. *Counterfactual growth and capital formation*

	Actuals			Counterfactuals			Windfall GFKF		
	GFKF/income[a] (%)	Real income[b]	GFKF[c]	Real income[d]	GFKF/income[e] (%)	GFKF[f]	Annual[g]	Cum.[h]	Return at 10%[i]
	(1)	(2)	(3)	(4)	(5)	(6)	(7)	(8)	(9)
1972	25.1								
1973	24.6								
1974	21.7								
1975	22.9	1,054.4	241.9	1,054.4	22.9	241.9	0		
1976	22.8	1,138.2	259.1	1,101.2	23.5	258.8	0.3	0.3	0.0
1977	23.9	1,332.1	317.8	1,197.1	24.2	289.7	28.1	28.4	2.8
1978	28.9	1,328.8	383.7	1,273.0	24.8	315.7	68.0	96.4	9.6
1979	27.3	1,360.2	371.8	1,320.6	24.8	327.5	44.3	140.7	14.1

[a] At current prices (Factor cost)
[b] GDP at 1975 prices plus windfall imports.
[c] Col. (1) times col. (2).
[d] In 1975 and 1976 actual GDP at 1975 prices; in 1977–9 also corrected for returns on windfall investment as shown in col. (9), lagged one year.
[e] Linear reversion to 1972–3 average by 1978.
[f] Col. (4) times col. (5).
[g] Col. (3) minus col. (6).
[h] Col. (7) summed.
[i] Col. (8) times 0.1 (10% return on capital).

Sources: Col. (1): Government of Kenya, *Statistical Abstract, 1987*, table 37(b) and corresponding tables for earlier years; col. (2): *Statistical Abstract, 1984*, table 37(b) and corresponding tables for earlier years for GDP at 1976 prices, converted to 1975 prices by the factor 0.864 (from *Statistical Abstract, 1983*, tables 37(a) and (b)). plus windfall at 1975 prices from Table 5.1 above.

investment (column 7) can be checked by its implication for behaviour in 1976 and 1977. Since investment out of unplanned income is likely to be lagged, the propensity to invest in 1976 out of 1976 windfall income should be negligible. This is indeed what the counterfactual implies. Windfall income is £37 million (Table 5.1) but windfall investment is only £0.3 million. Similarly, in 1977 cumulative windfall income is £172 million but windfall investment is only £28.1 million. Hence, the present counterfactual yields credible implications.[7] Overall, the counterfactual implies that during the period windfall GFKF was £140.7 million at 1975 prices.

The analysis is now repeated for the propensity to accumulate foreign debt. Foreign savings at 1975 prices (deflated by the imports deflator) as a proportion of real income at 1975 prices are shown in the first column of Table 5.3. As might be expected, the period 1974–5 was atypical because of the oil shock: indebtedness was increased far more rapidly than during 1972–3. Again we assume a gradual adjustment process to the 1972–3 average reached by 1978. As before, the counterfactual propensity for 1976–7 is a

TABLE 5.3.   *Actual and counterfactual foreign savings*

	Foreign savings propensity (%)		Foreign savings (£m. at 1975 prices)		
	Actual[a]	Counterfactual[b]	Actual[c]	Counterfactual[d]	Windfall[e]
	(1)	(2)	(3)	(4)	(5)
1972	3.49				
1973	2.02				
1974	8.70				
1975	5.32				
1976		4.47	−8.7	49.2	−57.9
1977		3.61	−50.1	43.2	−93.3
1978		2.76	151.4	35.1	116.3
1979		2.76	89.2	36.4	52.8

[a] Source as col. (1) of Table 5.2
[b] See text.
[c] Source as col. (1) of Table 5.2, deflated by the imports deflator.
[d] Col. (2) times counterfactual income as given in col. (4) of Table 5.2
[e] Col. (3) minus col. (4).

[7] Since it would be implausible that windfall income in 1976 actually reduced investment, this places a bound upon the speed of recovery of the GFKF propensity to its 1972–3 average. Were we to assume a faster recovery (restoration by 1977 instead of 1978), then implied windfall GFKF in 1976 would be negative. A slower recovery than we have assumed would increase the estimate of windfall GFKF. Hence, our estimate of the windfall savings propensity is a lower bound.

linear interpolation between the actual 1975 figure and this posited 1978 value.

Counterfactual foreign savings are then derived as this counterfactual propensity times the counterfactual income derived in Table 5.2. Cumulated over the period this constitutes a net increase in indebtedness of £17.9 million as a result of the windfall. This implies that the increase in income as a result of the coffee boom increased the perceived debt capacity of the economy.

Bringing the two counterfactuals together, windfall assets amounted to £122.8 million. We shall show later that these estimates mask large differences in savings rates between the private and the public sector.

To derive savings rates out of transient income we must relate the above estimate of savings to an estimate of windfall income. Recall that our estimate of the terms-of-trade change itself, discounted at 10 per cent, is £227 million. Now reconsider the change in savings. Two modifications must be made for comparability with this estimate of windfall income. That part of savings generated by extra permanent income must be deducted and the resulting stream of savings discounted. Our estimate of counterfactual savings is the GFKF propensity minus the foreign indebtedness propensity. Saving out of permanent income is thus calculated at this rate. For example, in 1979 the sum of the two propensities is 22.0 per cent and income from windfall GFKF £9.6 million (Table 5.2). Hence, such savings amount to £2.1 million. The net present value of these savings over the period is £1.7 million. The other two components of the savings calculation are the discounted present value of windfall GFKF, which is £115.3 million, and the discounted present value of the changes in foreign indebtedness, which is −£6.9 million[8]. Windfall savings out of windfall income is then £120.5 million. The propensity to save out of windfall income is thus windfall savings (£120.5 million) divided by windfall income (£227 million), which is 53.1 per cent of windfall income. We conclude that in aggregate a high fraction of the windfall was saved.[9]

This high aggregate saving propensity conflates two effects. First, as we will show from survey evidence, those agents who were direct recipients of windfall income changed their savings behaviour, saving a far higher proportion of windfall income than of other income. Second, as we will show from our CGE model, the boom gave rise to powerful income redistributions both within the private sector and between the private and public sectors. Within the private sector there was a large transfer from peasants other than coffee-growers to the urban economy. Since the savings rate of peasants is normally much lower than that of urban-based firms, such a transfer raised the aggregate private sector savings rate during the windfall. Potentially, if the

---

[8] That is, although undiscounted there is a rise in indebtedness of £17.9m. because this occurs late in the period, the discounted present value of the changes is negative.

[9] This result is insensitive to the discount rate. Repeating the calculation with discount rates of 5% or 15% we find windfall savings rates of 49.9% and 56.4% respectively.

transfer is large relative to the windfall, the measured aggregate propensity to save out of windfall income can exceed 100%. We will see that underlying the measured savings rate of 53.1% are low public and high private rates, the latter in turn being a composite of high transient savings rates by windfall recipients and transfers from low to high savers.

2.2.2. Goods markets

We now turn to the impact of the boom in goods markets. An unanticipated gain in permanent income will normally lead to a rise in demand for non-tradables and hence an increase in their relative price. A transient windfall which leaves permanent income unaltered will normally lead to a 'construction boom': a rise in demand for non-tradable capital goods. So far we have suggested that the information set available to Kenyan agents was sufficient for them to recognize the increase in the coffee price as temporary, though this increase was outside their previous experience and hence likely to be exclusive to their prior expectations. We have seen that initially savings behaviour was consistent with what optimizing agents with such information sets would tend to do. For rational, far-sighted agents, any increase in consumption as a result of the windfall was therefore something of a second-order effect arising from one of three possibilities:

1. the increase in permanent income arising from the anticipated return upon windfall savings;
2. the increase in permanent income arising from any upwards revision of expected coffee prices: that is, if expectations were revised;
3. the effect of a temporary slackening of credit constraints.

The first question we address is whether there were Dutch Disease effects, of which a necessary symptom is a rise in the relative price of non-tradable consumer goods. This can be induced by a terms-of-trade improvement through both the *spending effect* and a *resource movement effect* (Corden, 1984). The former occurs if there is an increase in consumer demand consequent upon the income gain. The latter occurs if resources are attracted to the boom sector(s) of the economy, thereby shifting back the supply curve of the consumer non-tradables sector.

To determine whether consumption (private plus public) increased as a result of the windfall requires the specification of a counterfactual. We have already constructed a counterfactual for GDP by deducting from actual GDP growth that part due to windfall investment. Consumption in real terms would have grown in line with this GDP counterfactual (col. (1) of Table 5.4) had the domestic savings rate been constant at its 1975 level. We have already implicitly almost fully specified the path of the counterfactual domestic savings propensity by specifying the GFKF and foreign savings propensities. Column (2) of Table 5.4 shows what these imply for the consumption counterfactual. The final component of domestic savings to be

TABLE 5.4. *Actual and counterfactual consumption (1975 = 100)*

	Counterfactual GDP	Counterfactual Consumption	Consumption	Actual consumption	Difference between actual and counterfactual
		(see note a)	(see note b)		
	(1)	(2)	(3)	(4)	(5)
1975	100	100	100	100	0
1976	104.4	102.6	99.9	100.3	+0.4
1977	113.5	109.4	103.1	103.1	0
1978	120.7	114.3	105.0	109.6	+1.6
1979	125.1	118.5	118.0	116.4	−4.6

ᵃ (1) modified by the GFKF and foreign savings propensities.
ᵇ (2) modified by changes in inventory accumulation.

Sources: Actual from National Accounts. Private consumption deflated by 'Lower Income' CPI; public consumption has its own deflator. Counterfactual from Table 5.2. Inventories from Government of Kenya, *Statistical Abstracts, 1983*, table 37(b) and corresponding tables for earlier years.

specified is changes in inventories. There were, in fact, substantial changes in the rate of accumulation of inventories: in 1975 there was rapid destocking, which was reversed in subsequent years. Since destocking is clearly unsustainable, it must be supposed that this turn-around would have occurred even without the coffee boom, and so our non-boom counterfactual should allow for it. The unsustainable destocking in 1975 has as a counterpart in that year either an unsustainably high level of capital formation or an unsustainably high level of consumption or both. If capital formation was unsustainably high in 1975 then by using it as our counterfactual we have underestimated windfall-induced investment. We have already seen in Table 5.2 that capital formation in 1975 was atypically low. Hence, it seems more likely that consumption in 1975 was unsustainably high. Column (3) of Table 5.4 corrects counterfactual consumption for the change in inventory accumulation. For example, in 1976 inventories increased by £3.3 million (at 1975 prices) whereas in 1975 they fell by £24.8 million. The turn-around of £28.1 million is therefore deducted from counterfactual 1976 consumption.

The resulting series of counterfactual consumption (what would have happened had consumption risen in line with counterfactual GDP except for deviations due to the changing propensity to save) can then be compared with actual consumption, the difference being attributed to windfall consumption. As shown in the final column of Table 5.4, on this basis consumption rose as a result of the windfall in 1976 and 1978, but was reduced in 1979. The net effect (undiscounted) is that consumption during the windfall period (1976–9) averages only 1.6 per cent more than had the boom not happened.

Had all the windfall been spent on consumption it would have augmented counterfactual consumption expenditure by 6.2 per cent during the period 1976–9. In section 2.2.1 we derived the actual propensity to consume out of the windfall as 46.9 per cent. Hence, we would have expected the windfall to augment consumption expenditure by 2.9 per cent (0.469 × 6.2%), whereas our counterfactual implies that it only augmented consumption in real terms by 1.6 per cent. For consumption in real terms to rise by less than windfall expenditure on consumption there must have been a small rise in the relative price of consumer goods. This would indeed be implied by the resource movement and spending effects in the market for non-tradable consumer goods. Although in an economy without import controls such a price rise would be confined to non-tradables, in Kenya, as we shall argue in section 2.6, because of widespread import quotas much of consumption is non-tradable at the margin. Hence, we should not necessarily expect the price of fully non-tradable consumer goods to rise relative to that of importables. In Fig. 5.2 we use sector-specific GDP deflators as proxies for this relative price. Such a proxy is far from ideal, partly because for consumption the prices of final output rather than value added are appropriate. However, it indeed suggests that there was a modest rise in the price of non-tradable consumer goods, especially in the later years in which windfall expenditure took place.

Now consider capital goods and in particular the construction sector. As shown in Fig. 5.3, the income boom was rapidly transmitted into higher demand for traded capital goods. Already in 1977 volume was far higher than any plausible counterfactual. However, the boom in demand for non-tradable capital goods was both markedly smaller and lagged the income windfall by some two years. This is probably because of differential implementation lags. First, windfall savings must be translated into investment plans, this lag being common to tradable and non-tradable capital goods. Second, these plans must be realized. It is easier to increase purchases of traded capital goods rapidly (since these can be imported) than non-traded capital (since typically land must be purchased and buildings designed and then gradually constructed). Evidence that this differential implementation lag fully accounts for the delay in the non-tradable capital goods boom comes from building plans approved by Municipal Councils. As shown in Fig. 5.3, the constant price value of approved plans jumped in 1977 and 1978. Indeed, in these years planned purchases of non-tradable capital track actual purchases of traded capital very closely.

The construction boom thus took place during 1978–81 rather than 1976–9. Fig. 5.4 shows that with 1977 as a base, there was a substantial shift in relative output into the sector during the following four years. During this period output increased at its peak by 14 per cent relative to GDP.

Fig. 5.2 brings together the construction sector and Dutch Disease. The central prediction of construction boom theory is borne out: comparing non-

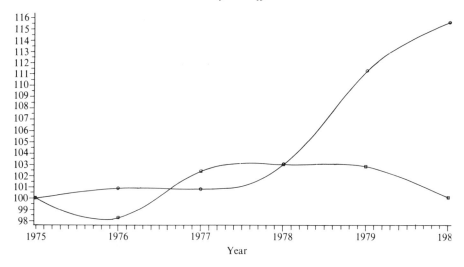

□ = Relative price non-tradable consumer goods to import substitutes
○ = Relative price non-tradable capital goods to import substitutes

Note: Relative prices are based on the value-added deflators from the National Accounts. Import substitutes are proxied by the manufacturing sector, non-tradable capital goods by the construction sector, and non-tradable consumer goods by the sum of the following: electricity and water; wholesale and retail trade, restaurants and hotels; transport, storage, and communications; finance, insurance, real estate, and business services; other services in the monetary sector; and domestic services purchased by private household sectors. The source for each year is the most recent edition of the *Statistical Abstract* in which that year is included.

FIG. 5.2. *Prices of non-tradable capital and consumer goods relative to import substitutes*

tradable capital goods with non-tradable consumer goods, the price of the former rises substantially relative to the latter. Further, the path of the relative price is consistent with the different consumption and investment lags. At the peak of the income boom, 1977, there had been time for consumer expenditure to rise but not for that on non-tradable capital goods. In that year non-tradable consumer goods prices rise relative to those of non-tradable capital; thereafter they rapidly fall. To conclude, as a result of the temporary terms-of-trade gain there were two boom sectors; the beneficiary of the primary price increase (the coffee- and tea-growing sector) and the beneficiary of the induced price increase in non-tradable capital goods (the construction sector). These two boom sectors presumably therefore attracted resources from other sectors (the 'resource movement effect'). We now consider these reallocations of factors.

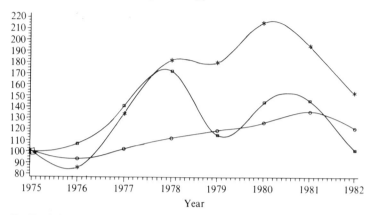

□ = Traded capital
○ = Non-traded capital
∗ = Approved municipal building plans

Sources: Economic Survey and Statistical Abstract, various issues.
FIG. 5.3. *Traded and non-traded capital goods at constant prices*

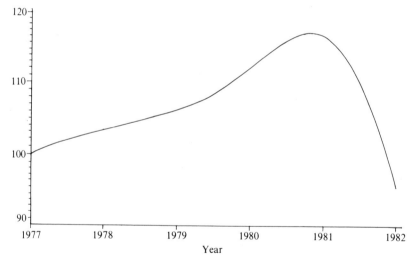

Sources: National Accounts; Government of Kenya, *Statistical Abstract* (various issues).

FIG. 5.4. *Output of non-traded capital goods relative to GDP, 1977–1981 (1977 = 100)*

2.2.3. *Factor markets*

The resource movement effect in the Dutch Disease literature is normally dismissed as negligible. The boom sector is usually oil production, which is very capital-intensive. The only internally mobile factor is assumed to be labour, since capital is *ex post* sector-specific and a permanent boom does not give rise to windfall investment out of transient income. Hence, the factor which can move, labour, is not needed in the boom sector. There are three reasons to regard the resource movement effect as more important in the context of a temporary windfall. First, as we have seen, there are two boom sectors instead of one. Second, in Kenya both of these sectors were labour-intensive. Third, because so much of the windfall was saved, capital became inter-sectorally mobile as a result of the investment boom (investment being mobile even though the existing capital stock is not).

Substantial factor movements into the two boom sectors start to take place in 1977 (Table 5.5 refers). The construction sector has an enormous increase in relative investment and employment. Between 1976 and 1978 (the peak) its investment relative to national investment rises by 84 per cent. Employment relative to the national labour force peaks in 1979 with an increase of 19 per cent. Since nationally both employment and investment were rising rapidly, these relative increases implied large absolute increases. At the onset of the boom the sector which attracts the largest increase in labour is the coffee and tea plantations. Between 1976 and 1977 the labour force increased by 9 per cent relative to the national labour force. Investment also grew rapidly, though even in this period by less than that in the construction sector. This pattern of factor movements is consistent with what rational, far-sighted agents would have been likely to do. Agents who correctly anticipate that the construction boom will last longer than the beverage boom will shift reversible factors (labour) into the plantations and irreversible factors (capital) into construction.

To summarize, the windfall was treated as though it were temporary. Overall there was a very high savings rate in the early stages of the windfall. There was a modest Dutch Disease effect: the relative price of non-traded consumer goods rose slightly, so that consumption in real terms rose by less than windfall consumption expenditure. There was a far stronger construction boom. Output of non-tradable capital goods rose substantially relative to GDP, as did their relative price. Evidence from the allocation of labour and capital bears out this picture. The primary boom sector (coffee and tea) attracted the reversible factor, labour, but not the irreversible factor. The construction sector attracted both a massive increase in investment and a large increase in its labour force. The rising payments for value added must have in part accrued as windfall profits. To the extent that there was a transfer to profits this may help to account for the high savings rate in the economy. However, this is a matter for the next section, in which we disaggregate by type of agent.

2.3. *Public Sector Response to the Kenyan Coffee Boom*

Detailed budget breakdowns are available on a number of organizing principles for a variety of governmental definitions. It is necessary to choose a

TABLE 5.5. *Wage Employment and investment by sector, 1975–1981 (1977 = 100)*

A. *Level relative to level in 1977*

	Coffee and tea plantations		Manufacturing		Construction		Consumer non-tradables		Whole economy	
	Emp[a]	Inv[b]	Emp	Inv	Emp	Inv	Emp	Inv	Emp	Inv
1975	88	77	85	73	83	75	89	86	94	83
1976	89	77	92	82	96	71	95	84	97	83
1977	100	100	100	100	100	100	100	100	100	100
1978	97	95	110	116	112	183	103	117	103	117
1979	101	98	117	112	126	131	109	106	107	109
1980	100	103	120	88	128	156	112	111	111	112
1981	100	92	124	88	126	131	113	122	115	117

B. *Share in economy relative to share in 1977*

	Coffee and tea plantations		Manufacturing		Construction		Consumer non-tradables		Whole economy	
	Emp	Inv	Emp	Inv	Emp	Inv	Emp	Inv	Emp	Inv
1975	94	93	90	88	88	90	95	104	100	100
1976	92	93	95	99	99	85	98	101	100	100
1977	100	100	100	100	100	100	100	100	100	100
1978	94	81	107	99	109	156	100	100	100	100
1979	94	90	109	103	118	120	102	97	100	100
1980	90	92	108	79	115	139	101	99	100	100
1981	88	79	109	75	111	112	99	104	100	100

[a] Emp = employment.
[b] Inv = investment.

Sources: For investment, coffee and tea plantations are proxied by 'land improvement and plantations', Government of Kenya, *Statistical Abstract, 1987*, table 44(b) and corresponding tables for earlier years. Formal sector employment from *Statistical Abstract, 1984*, table 213.

coherent organizing approach that keeps track of government's own spending while also providing some measure of its impact on private spending. The calculations reported below are restricted to central government operations for reasons of data availability and reliability. However, these account for over 90 per cent of spending by general government and the results would not be much affected if the more comprehensive definition were used.

The budget concepts used are defined below:

Total revenue is the sum of current revenue (principally direct and indirect taxation) and the external grant component of capital revenue. It is the aggregate of all[10] non-repayable receipts of the central government.

Total exhaustive expenditure is the sum of government consumption expenditure (current expenditure on goods and services plus wages and salaries) and gross fixed capital formation (GFKF) by government.[11]

Exhaustive surplus is the excess of total revenue over total exhaustive expenditure.

Total transfers are the sum of unrequited transfers (e.g. grants to persons), interest on domestic debt, and interest on foreign debt.

Net domestic borrowing is a broader concept than that normally adopted. It is defined here so as to provide an estimate of the fall in the domestic financial component of the government's net worth. Accordingly, it consists of domestic borrowing by government (long-term and short-term) minus amortization; minus the change in government cash balance; minus the 'investment' category of the development budget, net of loans repaid to the government.[12]

Net foreign borrowing is simply foreign borrowing net of amortization. The budget identity then requires that the exhaustive surplus plus net domestic and foreign borrowing should equal total transfer payments.

This framework has the desired features of enabling us to track exhaustive expenditures and transfers separately while also providing a measure of foreign indebtedness and one relevant to domestic crowding-out. As with any framework constructed from accounting identities, no causal propositions can be derived without further assumptions. The rationale for the framework adopted here is the assumption that exhaustive expenditures (such as civil service salaries) have some claim to autonomy, because they are relatively hard to adjust; transfers then play, to some extent, an accommodating role,

---

[10] Strictly, these would also include receipts from sales of capital assets, but this has been a negligible category in Kenya over the period reviewed.

[11] There is no information on government stock appreciation, so this is ignored.

[12] The investment component consists primarily of loans and purchases of equity in parastatals. The treatment here is to assume that these loans duly 'perform' and that the equity purchases are worth their purchase price. If, instead, the investment component does not result in acquisition of assets of equivalent value, the shortfall must be thought of as a transfer. In that case, an accurate treatment would require that both unrequited (and total) transfers and net domestic borrowing be raised by that amount.

and fiscal rectification ultimately requires the government to achieve an appropriate relationship between revenue and exhaustive expenditure. The gap between these two is termed the exhaustive deficit; it is this which, given the rate of interest, and the path of unrequited transfers, determines the evolution of public indebtedness. Exhaustive expenditures are also of special interest because, in the absence of a substantial social security system, they are the principal vehicle for government directly to influence the composition and distribution of goods and services to the economy.

Table 5.6 shows the time path of these budget concepts over the period 1970–83,[13] with the data presented as percentages of gross domestic product at factor cost.

The first thing to note is that the relative size of the budget (measured by exhaustive expenditure as a percentage of GDP) increased after 1977. Hence, the coffee boom was followed by a rapid expansion in government spending. In addition the decline in the early 1980s suggests that the levels attained at the turn of the decade were perceived as an overshooting of what was appropriate or desirable, and official documents (such as the report of the Ndegwa Commission of 1982) support this view.

It should also be noted from Table 5.6 that the exhaustive surplus was consistently small. Over the period 1975–83 it never exceeded 1 per cent of GDP and its average value was about one tenth per cent. Hence, government revenue (inclusive of external capital grants) was just sufficient to finance government exhaustive expenditure on consumption and capital formation. In consequence, the entire transfer component of the budget was consistently financed by borrowing. A similar pattern, though somewhat less marked, held in the earlier period 1970–4, when the exhaustive surplus was never sufficient fully to cover unrequited transfers, let alone contribute to covering interest payments. It follows that the fiscal pattern shown in the table was never sustainable in the long run, but would sooner or later have required correction in the form of a rise in the exhaustive surplus to cover at least a large proportion of total transfers (all of unrequited transfers and some fraction at least of interest payments[14]) if the debt/income ratio was to be stabilized. The longer this correction was delayed, the larger in absolute magnitude it would have to be. Despite some progressive improvement between 1981 and 1983, it is clear that most of the correction still remained to be done in 1983.

Three further points may be noted. First, despite the intention of the government to raise capital formation following the boom, and its initial success in raising the development component of the budget relative to the

---

[13] Since the fiscal year in Kenya runs from 1 July, the data have been put onto a calendar year basis by simple averaging. This introduces some distortions, but leaves the overall trend unaffected.

[14] This assumes that the growth rate of GDP is less than the interest rate on public debt in the long run.

TABLE 5.6. *Fiscal pattern as percentage of GDP at factor cost, 1970–1983*

	Total revenue	Consumption	GFKF	Total exhaustive expenditure[a]	Exhaustive surplus[b]	Unrequited transfers	Domestic interest	Foreign interest	Total transfers[c]	Overall deficit[d]	Net domestic borrowing	Net foreign borrowing
	(1)	(2)	(3)	(4)	(5)	(6)	(7)	(8)	(9)	(10)	(11)	(12)
1970	20.8	13.5	4.7	18.2	2.6	3.3	0.7	0.6	4.6	2.0	0.4	1.7
1971	22.8	15.6	5.7	21.2	1.6	2.8	0.8	0.6	4.2	2.6	1.2	1.4
1972	21.1	15.3	5.6	20.8	0.2	2.3	0.7	0.7	3.7	3.5	1.4	2.1
1973	21.6	15.1	5.3	20.5	1.1	2.4	0.8	0.7	3.8	2.7	0.8	2.0
1974	22.6	15.8	5.0	20.8	1.8	2.6	0.8	0.6	4.0	2.2	0.7	1.5
1975	23.8	18.3	5.0	23.3	0.5	2.0	1.0	0.6	3.7	3.1	0.8	2.3
1976	23.4	18.4	5.0	23.4	0.0	1.1	1.1	0.6	2.8	2.8	0.7	2.2
1977	24.1	18.1	5.0	23.1	1.0	1.0	1.1	0.6	2.8	1.8	0.3	1.4
1978	27.5	21.4	5.6	27.0	0.5	1.4	1.4	0.7	3.6	3.1	0.8	2.2
1979	28.7	22.4	6.3	28.8	-0.1	1.5	1.4	0.9	3.8	3.8	0.8	3.0
1980	29.9	23.0	6.9	30.0	-0.1	1.8	1.4	1.2	4.4	4.5	1.0	3.5
1981	28.6	24.0	5.6	29.6	-1.0	2.0	2.0	1.6	5.6	6.6	2.8	3.8
1982	27.4	23.3	4.4	27.7	-0.3	1.6	2.7	1.8	6.1	6.4	3.1	3.3
1983	26.9	21.8	3.4	26.2	0.7	1.8	3.0	2.0	6.7	6.0	2.3	3.7

[a] Col. (2) plus col. (3).
[b] Col. (1) minus col. (4).
[c] Col. (6) plus col. (7) plus col. (8).
[d] Col. (9) minus col. (5); equals col. (11) plus col. (12).

Sources: Government of Kenya, *Statistical Abstract* (various issues), Public Finance Tables.

recurrent component, the bulk of the increased spending was in the form of consumption. By the end of the period, government capital formation had a smaller share of GDP than in 1975, while consumption was several percentage points higher.

Secondly, the bulk of the government's net borrowing was foreign throughout the period.[15] This implies that the government's failure to balance its budget largely took a deferred form, building up future debt-servicing problems, rather than immediately crowding out private domestic capital formation.

Thirdly, it may be noted (but is not shown in the table) that the contribution of direct taxation to revenue was very stable throughout the period, varying between 7 and 8 per cent of GDP; the rise of revenue was primarily due to indirect taxation, which rose from 12.3 per cent of GDP in 1975 to peak at 17.0 per cent in 1981. The main increases took place in the period 1978–80, when sales taxes and some import duties were raised in order to finance the raised levels of expenditure which had been triggered by the boom.

In order to determine whether the fiscal changes shown in Table 5.6 can be attributed to the boom we construct a counterfactual case. We use the counterfactual GDP series from Table 5.2 and assume that the 1975 fiscal pattern of revenue and exhaustive expenditures would have been maintained in the counterfactual,[16] but that unrequited transfers would have followed the same path as they actually did.

The 1975 fiscal pattern is then applied to the counterfactual GDP series to generate counterfactual time series of fiscal aggregates. These series are subtracted from the actual values of the fiscal aggregates. The differences may be considered as fiscal changes due to the boom and are shown in Table 5.7. This shows the powerful ratchet effect of the boom. The government does not merely spend out of its windfall income plus any continuing income accruing from windfall investment; what would be a temporary increase is transformed into a permanent (or at least long-lived) increase because of the relative irreversibility of government expenditure. This sustained rise in turn forces accommodating increases in taxation or borrowing or both.

The original rise in spending reflected partly the planned response of the central authorities to the rise in revenue, and partly a change in the relative bargaining power of the central authorities *vis-à-vis* the spending departments of the government. It is evidently much harder for the Ministry of Finance to exercise effective control of spending when revenue is known to be

[15] This reflects the consolidation of borrowing and 'investment' discussed earlier: on the conventional definition, domestic borrowing is of a similar magnitude to foreign.

[16] It is worth noting here that over the period 1975–80 the ratio of government expenditure to GDP was stationary for LDCs as a whole, and fell quite steeply (by 3%) for Africa (IMF, *Government Finance Statistics Yearbook*, 9 (1985), 70). In 1975, the Kenyan ratio was similar to the African average; it appears as easily conceivable that it would have fallen in the counterfactual case as risen.

TABLE 5.7.   *Fiscal changes due to the boom, 1976–1983* (K£m. in 1975 prices)

	Total revenue	Consumption	GFKF	Total exhaustive expenditure[a]	Exhaustive surplus
	(1)	(2)	(3)	(4)	(5)
1976	4.2	8.1	1.5	9.5	− 5.3
1977	36.6	22.7	6.1	28.9	7.7
1978	48.4	41.1	7.4	48.5	0.0
1979	76.8	63.7	20.2	84.1	− 7.3
1980	86.7	67.5	27.4	94.9	− 8.2
1981	72.9	85.5	9.3	94.7	− 21.8
1982	57.6	77.5	− 8.1	69.4	− 11.8
1983	52.7	58.2	− 9.1	49.2	3.4

[a] Col. (2) plus col. (3).
[b] Col. (1) minus col. (4).

Sources: Table 5.6, and computations described in the text.

rising rapidly. The second feature, the relative irreversibility of the rise in public spending, is a familiar phenomenon in many countries, regardless of the original cause of the rise.[17] In the Kenyan case it was accompanied by a refusal of some spending ministries to prioritize their programmes, making these much harder for the Ministry of Finance to cut.

From column (5) it emerges that revenue was not raised sufficiently to match the boom-induced increase in expenditure. The cumulative deterioration in the exhaustive surplus over the period was K£43.3 million.

While caution must be exercised in interpreting any counterfactual, the implications are quite striking. Despite the lack of any serious effort directly to tax the windfall, government revenue rose over the period 1976–9 (relative to the counterfactual) by nearly 65 per cent of the undiscounted value of the windfall.[18] This very high level of the government's share reflects the energy with which the authorities set out to increase discretionary revenue during the later years of the boom.

The direct positive impact of the government on capital formation was concentrated in 1979 and 1980, with a moderate negative contribution in the last two years of the period. The cumulative rise in government capital formation over the period was K£54.7 million. When this is set against the deterioration in the exhaustive surplus, it is clear that less than a fifth of it was

[17] For example, the rise in public expenditure associated with an outbreak of war is typically reversed only partly in the subsequent peace.

[18] By £166.0m. This was skewed towards the end of the boom. In 1976 windfall revenue was only 11% of the windfall to the economy and in 1977 only 27%.

financed by increased government saving, with the remainder being financed
by increased borrowing. What is more, these cumulative figures conceal a
marked deterioration between the boom period proper, 1976–9, and the post-
boom period, 1980–3. In the earlier sub-period, increased capital formation of
K£35.2 million was associated with a deterioration in the surplus of £4.9 million: virtually all (86 per cent) of the financing came from increased saving. In
the later sub-period, increased capital formation of K£19.5 million was
associated with a deterioration in the surplus of K£38.4 million: government
saving actually fell by about K£19 million relative to the counterfactual.

In consequence, the overall impact of the government on capital formation
is ambiguous. It certainly contributed to the sharp rise in non-tradable
capital goods prices in 1979–81, and the deficit increased sharply in 1981–2.
These two effects would probably have induced substantial crowding out of
private capital formation, a possibility we consider further in the following
section.

The above calculations yield two main conclusions. First, even though the
boom was perceived to be short-lived, it induced an increase in government
spending of much longer duration. Second, the government's impact on
capital formation was probably perverse in both timing and direction, raising
it sharply when the capital goods sector was least able to accommodate the
increased demand, but possibly lowering it overall.

We now disaggregate these changes in government revenue into tradables
and non-tradables. In Kenya, the proportion of indirect taxation which falls
on non-tradables or exportables appears to be negligible: to a first approximation, all indirect taxes (mainly excises, sales taxes on manufactures, and
import duties) fall on importables. The rest of central government revenue
consists of direct taxes on personal and company income, and income from
property (mainly profits from financial enterprises). Table 5.8 gives the contribution of these three categories to total revenue (now excluding external

TABLE 5.8. *Revenue composition, 1975–1983* (% of GDP)

	1975	Average change from 1975 pattern	
		1976–9	1980–3
Indirect taxes	12.3	1.3	4.1
Direct taxes	7.9	0.1	−0.3
Property income	3.0	0.6	0.4
Total revenue	23.2	2.0	4.2

Source: Government of Kenya, *Statistical Abstract* (various issues),
Public Finance Tables.

grants) in 1975, as shares of GDP, and the average changes in these shares over 1976–9 and 1980–3.

If we assume that property income and direct taxes are both neutral to the tradable/non-tradable balance of the economy, and can be aggregated together, then they contribute about one third (0.7 in 2.0 points) to the rise in revenue share in the first sub-period, but play a negligible role (0.1 in 4.2 points) in the second sub-period. Allowing for the increase in all tax revenue at existing rates caused by the boom, during 1976–9 perhaps 60 per cent of increased revenue fell on tradables (about K£100 million at 1975 prices on the basis of the calculations of Table 5.8). During 1980–3 the entire increase of nearly K£270 million fell on the tradable sector.

We have already decomposed government revenue into tradables and non-tradables; we now undertake a parallel disaggregation of expenditure. In Fig. 5.5, government capital formation, government current expenditure on goods, and private capital formation are split between tradables and non-tradables. There is no straightforward procedure for decomposing private consumption expenditure since this is computed in the National Accounts as a residual, rather than being built up from its constituent categories.

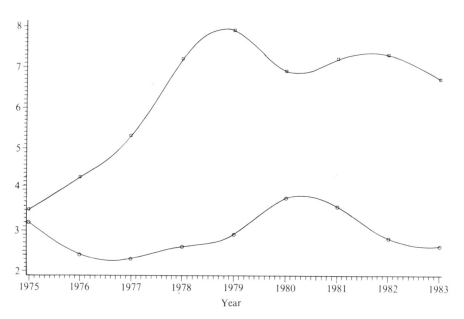

□ = Central government consumption, tradables
○ = Central government consumption, non-tradables

Source: Government of Kenya, *Statistical Abstract* (various issues), Public Finance Tables.

FIG. 5.5. *Expenditure decomposition (% of GDP)*

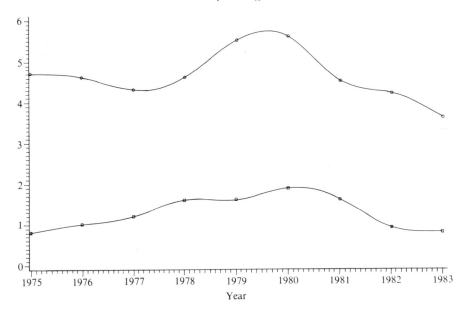

□ = Central government GFKF, tradables
○ = Central government GFKF, non-tradables

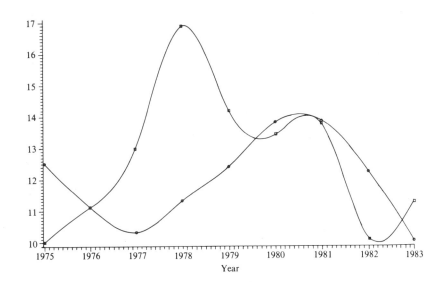

□ = Private sector GFKF, tradables
○ = Private sector GFKF, non-tradables

FIG. 5.5. (*cont.*)

The most noticeable feature of the decompositions is the very rapid rise in 1978 of tradables for government consumption and private capital formation, the former stabilizing at the higher level but the latter being short-lived. Nevertheless, there is also a temporary rise in all three non-tradable series during this period. During the three years of the construction boom, 1978–81, the government contributed a substantial share in the first two years but probably very little in the third. The other interesting feature in the figure is that the familiar ratchet effect of the boom on government expenditures appears to have been restricted to the consumption of tradables.

The discussion so far has been restricted to the field of aggregate public expenditure, and has concentrated on the associated problems of financing and fiscal management. Total expenditure rose dramatically, and this naturally raises the question of whether a similar movement took place in those components of expenditure which were likely to be socially productive.

The relevant criterion for an expenditure category to be selected for study is that it should have a relatively direct impact on households. The impact may be on output, as where public expenditure provides complementary inputs in the production process, or it may be directly on consumption, as where the public expenditure produces goods which enter preferences. These considerations exclude general administration, defence, and a wide range of economic services. The most important categories remaining are health, education, agricultural services, and roads. Table 5.9 gives time-series data for each of these, expressed as percentages of GDP at market prices. It also shows the share of total public expenditure represented by these categories taken together. Data on Tanzania are provided for purposes of comparison.

The data on which the table is based are not very reliable, particularly in the Tanzanian case, so conclusions must be provisional at best. The main points are as follows. While total exhaustive public expenditure is a consistently larger proportion of GDP in Tanzania than in Kenya, this does not hold for the subtotal of interest. Up to the fiscal year 1979, this ran at much the same, rather stable, level (about 11 per cent of GDP) in both countries;[19] thereafter it rose temporarily in Kenya but not in Tanzania. In consequence there does not appear to be any evidence that the coffee boom led to a relative expansion in relevant services in Tanzania.

As regards Kenya, there was a marked increase in the relative size of the subtotal, but this did not really take place until fiscal year 1981. In that year, it again reached the share in total public expenditure it had held in fiscal 1977. In other words, increased expenditure within the subtotal was heavily lagged on the general increase in public spending. As a consequence, its share in total public expenditure fell dramatically from 60 per cent in 1974–5 to about 47 per cent in the immediate post-boom period, 1978–80.

[19] There is evidently something wrong with the Tanzanian 1975 figures: probably the GDP estimate itself.

TABLE 5.9. *Time paths of selected government expenditure categories as percentage of GDP* (fiscal years)

A. *Kenya*

	1974	1975	1976	1977	1978	1979	1980	1981	1982	1983
Total exhaustive expenditure	17.8	19.2	10.8	19.4	22.3	24.3	25.0	25.7	25.2	22.6
Health	1.5	1.8	1.8	1.8	1.9	2.0	2.2	2.3	2.2	1.9
Education	4.8	5.5	5.3	4.8	4.8	4.9	5.4	6.1	6.0	5.7
Agricultural services	1.7	1.7	2.4	2.2	2.2	2.3	2.3	3.3	2.7	2.8
Roads	2.8	2.3	2.0	1.8	1.7	2.0	2.3	2.0	2.4	1.8
Subtotal	10.7	11.4	11.6	10.5	10.5	11.3	12.2	13.7	13.3	12.3
Subtotal as % of total exhaustive expenditure	60.1	59.5	55.7	54.3	47.2	46.3	48.8	53.3	52.9	54.3

B. *Tanzania*

	1974	1975	1976	1977	1978	1979	1980	1981
Total exhaustive expenditure	21.7	26.8	21.2	23.5	26.4	34.0	27.2	24.6
Health	1.8	2.2	1.9	1.9	2.2	2.1	1.8	1.7
Of which hospitals, clinics	(1.6)	(1.6)	(1.4)	(1.6)	(1.7)	(1.6)	(1.4)	(1.5)
Education	3.4	4.0	3.7	3.7	4.3	4.6	4.1	3.7
Of which schools	(1.8)	(1.7)	(2.4)	(2.0)	(2.5)	(2.2)	(2.3)	(2.2)
Agricultural services	3.3	5.0	3.7	3.2	2.8	2.7	3.3	3.1
Roads	1.3	1.1	1.3	1.6	1.4	1.4	1.6	1.7
Subtotal	9.9	12.4	10.4	10.4	10.7	10.8	10.8	10.2
Subtotal as % of total exhaustive expenditure	45.4	46.1	49.2	44.1	40.4	31.9	39.6	41.4

Sources: IMF, *Government Finance Statistics Yearbook*; Government of Kenya, *Statistical Abstract*; Government of Tanzania, *National Accounts of Tanzania* (all various years).

This raises the question whether such a heavily lagged increase had anything to do with the windfall income of the coffee boom. A major part of the increase was within the education sector, and this probably reflected the impact of the Presidential directive of 1979 which abolished all kinds of levies charged directly to parents and generated a marked increase in enrolment. At the same time a programme of free school milk was instituted. These changes are probably best interpreted as having rather little to do with the coffee boom, for two reasons. First, they represented a continuation of a process begun in the early 1970s to improve educational provision, particularly at the primary level. The 1979 directive can probably best be seen as a renewed attempt to achieve the objectives of the earlier Presidential directive of 1974. Second, the decisions leading to these second-round increases were taken after it had become clear that the coffee boom was history. It is hard to see them as part of a more or less involuntary loss of control.

If our interpretation is accepted, the categories of expenditure isolated here did not follow a very different path from the one that would have obtained in the absence of the boom. The principal beneficiaries of the expenditure increases were general administration and defence, not those categories of utility or productive consequence to households.

A more formal analysis supports these somewhat casual inferences. Table 5.10 presents selected regression results for Kenyan public expenditure. The logarithms of total expenditure (LTEXP) and expenditure on education (LEDUC), health (LHEAL), agricultural services (LAGS), and roads (LROAD) were

TABLE 5.10.   *Public expenditure and the boom: Kenya*

Dependent variable	Constant	LGDP	TIME	D78/81	F-Statistic	Durbin–Watson
LTEXP	−3.141 (1.00)	1.243 (2.43)	−0.003 (0.04)	—	$F(2, 10) = 602.6$	1.39
LTEXP	1.70 (0.63)	0.449 (1.05)	0.108 (1.67)	0.134 (3.25)	$F(3, 9) = 789.4$	2.33
LEDUC	7.34 (2.28)	−0.178 (0.35)	0.193 (2.58)	—	$F(2, 7) = 297.7$	1.73
LEDUC	8.21 (1,89)	−0.315 (0.46)	0.213 (2.14)	0.019 (0.33)	$F(3, 6) = 173.2$	1.74
LHEAL	−4.55 (1.03)	1.526 (2.19)	−0.045 (0.44)	—	$F(2, 7) = 184.4$	1.50
LHEAL	−0.667 (0.12)	0.912 (1.06)	0.041 (0.33)	0.083 (1.18)	$F(3, 6) = 130.1$	1.74
LAGS	−2.51 (0.39)	1.198 (1.18)	0.028 (0.19)	—	$F(2, 7) = 112.4$	2.48
LAGS	−1.85 (0.21)	1.094 (0.79)	0.043 (0.21)	0.013 (0.12)	$F(3, 6) = 64.4$	2.43
LROAD	12.77 (1.95)	−1.136 (1.10)	0.300 (1.96)	—	$F(2, 7) = 45.5$	1.77
LROAD	16.88 (1.99)	−1.786 (1.33)	0.391 (2.00)	0.088 (0.79)	$F(3, 6) = 28.9$	2.36

each regressed on the logarithm of gross domestic product (LGDP), time (TIME), and a dummy variable for the effects of the boom. A variety of specifications were used, including a simple lag and a quadratic equation, and a dummy variable for the years 1978–81 (D78/81) gave broadly the best results. Absolute values of *t*-ratios are given in parentheses. The equations were fitted by ordinary least squares.

The interesting feature of these five pairs of equations is that the dummy variable on the years 1978–81 is highly significant in the equation for total expenditure and markedly improves the fit of that equation, whereas the converse is true for each of the four sub-components.

Since these sub-components appear to have been unaffected, it might seem that no further discussion of public expenditure would be required in analysing the boom. However, it is certainly interesting to examine the alternative policy responses that were available to the governments, rather than restricting ourselves to an analysis of what actually happened. For this type of exercise, it is necessary to discover how public spending is distributed, to form a view as to how useful or productive it is, and to estimate the consequences of increasing it. This analysis is carried out by the present authors in *Peasants and Governments*.

In the present, macroeconomic, context, it suffices to note that the rapid expansion of public expenditure following the boom probably had very restricted beneficial effects on households other than on civil servants themselves.

2.4. *The Transmission of the Public Expenditure Boom onto Private Incomes*

In Kenya the principal transmission mechanism between public and private agents was clearly from the latter to the former by means of windfall government tax revenue. However, the public expenditure boom which this induced, in turn, transferred windfall income back to the private sector through various mechanisms. Here we consider such mechanisms, though it should be stressed that in the context of the Kenyan boom they are only of a second order of importance.

In addition to any direct benefits of public expenditure (which we have suggested were modest in this instance), there are three mechanisms which can potentially transfer windfall income to private agents as a result of a public expenditure boom. The first involves rents in the public sector labour market. If there is a wage differential in favour of the public sector, and public sector employment increases as part of windfall expenditure, the rents from public sector employment will increase. To estimate the changes in such rents thus requires two components: quantifying the public sector wage premium, and quantifying counterfactual public sector employment growth in order to identify boom-induced increases in employment. The specification of a counterfactual is always problematic. One specification is to assume that the public sector wage bill would have grown in line with our GDP counterfactual. Below we argue that to a first approximation the boom did not alter real wages in the public sector. Hence, public employment would have grown by the rate of growth in the counterfactual wage bill less any growth in actual real wages. While this counterfactual is *a priori* reasonable, it yields the unreasonable conclusion (given that there was an induced public expenditure boom) that public sector employment fell because of the windfall. An alternative simple counterfactual is to assume that any boom-related change in public sector employment had been nullified by 1986 (our most recent data point). The path of actual public sector employment can then be compared with that which would have occurred had the growth rate which applied for the end-points of the period 1976–86 also applied in each year. Between 1976 and 1986 public sector employment grew at an annual rate of 5.3 per cent. However, during the boom years growth was noticeably more rapid, the differential being shown in Table 5.11.

Such a counterfactual has two offsetting biases. First, if indeed public employment rises as a result of the expenditure boom, even if there is a ratchet effect so that it is permanently higher, a trajectory will be generated by the method. However, this trajectory will underestimate boom-induced employment expansion. Such long-term effects are quite likely, given the difficulty of reducing the public sector payroll. Second, however, in the early 1980s the economy was suffering from the second oil shock so that, even without the coffee boom, there would have been some deceleration in the growth of employment during the 1980s compared with the late 1970s. Our

TABLE 5.11. *Public sector employment rents, 1976–1986*

	Extra employment ('000)	Rents if wage premium 16% (K£m., current prices)
1976	—	—
1977	1.0	—
1978	5.5	0.6
1979	8.2	0.9
1980	32.6	3.7
1981	21.7	3.9
1982	18.5	2.7
1983	14.7	2.3
1984	1.0	—
1985	5.2	—
1986	—	—

Source: Government of Kenya, *Statistical Abstract, 1987*, table 211 and corresponding table in earlier years.

method misinterprets such an oil-induced deceleration in the 1980s as a boom-induced expansion in the 1970s. Although the counterfactual is therefore tenuous, the pattern of windfall employment which it yields is quite credible: the first signs of employment expansion are in 1978 and this persists until 1983 with a peak in 1980.

However, there are strong grounds for regarding this transmission mechanism as unimportant, because any wage premium in favour of the public sector was small. There is good evidence for this from surveys of the wage labour force in 1971 (Johnson, 1971), 1977/8 (Bigsten, 1984), and 1980 (Knight and Sabot, 1989). All three concluded that there was no significant premium for the public sector as a whole, although there might be a small premium for the uneducated. Johnson, for example, found a 16 per cent premium for the non-unionized unskilled. As an upper bound we adopt this 16 per cent premium for the whole of the public sector, though it should be recognized that a more defensible figure would be zero. Table 5.11 then shows the rents which such a premium would imply, given the magnitude of boom-induced employment expansion. The main point to note about these figures is that they are small even at their (real) peak in 1980. We have already estimated that windfall public revenue in 1980 was K£141 million at current prices,[20] so that even at its peak this mechanism was transferring only 3 per cent of the public revenue windfall back to the private sector as labour market rents.

The second transfer mechanism also works through the labour market. If wages rise as a result of the boom then existing public sector wage earners receive a boom-induced windfall. Prima facie, however, there is no boom-attributable rise in public sector wages. From 1976 onwards there is a fairly steady fall. The counterfactual is particularly problematic in this case. First, Collier and Lal (1986) show that real wages had been falling since the late 1960s and that this can be interpreted as a gradual movement to equilibrium which still had some way to go as of the mid-1970s. Second, the oil shock sharply reduced the equilibrium wage. The former effect would imply that the counterfactual is for wages to fall more rapidly in the late 1970s than in the early 1980s, the latter would imply the reverse. In fact, wages fell fairly continuously. In the peak expenditure year of 1980 they were a little below their long-run trend 1976–85. Therefore, there seems no basis for attributing a wage increase to the coffee boom.

The final possible transmission mechanism works through the commodity market. Any boom-induced rise in the price of non-tradable goods will increase the cost of government purchases. Recall that for both consumer non-tradables and non-tradable capital goods there was a boom-induced price increase. The former (see Fig. 5.2) applies to the period 1977–9, the latter, owing to the lag and longer duration of the non-tradable capital boom,

---

[20] Table 5.7 gives incremental revenue in 1980 as K£86.7m. at 1975 prices, and the implicit GDP deflator for 1980 is 162.9, based to 1975.

applies to 1978–81. The rents resulting from the rise in the price of non-tradable consumer goods sold to the government were only £2.8 million[21] Again this estimate is an upper bound since it attributes all the rise in the price to the boom. The construction boom effects were, however, more powerful. Applying the same procedure yields the estimate of Table 5.12. At its peak in 1980 one-sixth of government windfall revenue was transferred back to the private sector in the form of rents on the sale of non-tradable capital goods to the public sector.

TABLE 5.12. *Transfers via the non-tradable capital goods market, 1977–1981*

	Price of non-tradable cap./price of imp. sub. (1975 = 100)	Govt. expenditure on non-tradable cap. (K£m. current prices)	Transfer[a] (K£m.)
	(1)	(2)	(3)
1977	101	70.2	0.7
1978	103	81.0	2.4
1979	111	108.9	12.0
1980	116	125.2	20.0
1981	116	117.9	18.9

Note: Parastatals are excluded from the public sector.

    [a] $[((1)/100) - 1] \times (2)$.

Sources: Col. (1): as Fig. 5.22. col. (2): Government expenditure on non-tradable capital was assumed to comprise the categories 'residential buildings', 'non-residential buildings', 'construction and works', and 'land'.

Taken together, the three mechanisms imply that by 1980 possibly about a fifth of the public revenue boom was transferred back to the private sector in the form of rents. Since this transfer peaked well after the primary private sector windfall, it had the effect of somewhat stretching the private income boom beyond the income windfall to the economy, shifting private windfall income from the coffee boom years to the public expenditure boom years.

2.5. *Public and Private Use of the Windfall Compared*

2.5.1. *Assets*

The relative contributions of public and private sectors to fixed capital formation may be assessed by bringing together the counterfactual exercises of Tables 5.2, 5.3, and 5.7 in Table 5.13.

---

[21] These are derived as the change in the relative price of consumer non-tradables to import substitutes from its 1975 level times government expenditure on consumer non-tradables.

TABLE 5.13. *Boom-induced capital formation, 1975* (K£m.)

	Total	Of which, govt.	Govt. share (%)
1976	0.3	1.5	500.0
1977	28.1	6.1	21.7
1978	68.0	7.4	10.9
1979	44.3	20.2	45.6
Cumulative			
1976–9	140.7	35.2	25.0
1980		27.4	
1981		9.3	

Overall, these calculations attribute nearly a quarter of induced capital formation during the sub-period to the central government. The government contributed materially to causing the construction boom of 1979–81, shown in Figs. 5.2 and 5.4, both incremental government capital formation and the relative price of construction peaking in 1980.

Offsetting this cumulative capital formation of K£35.2 million was the small cumulative deterioration in the primary surplus attributed to the boom in Table 5.7 of K£4.9 million at 1975 prices. Putting all this together, public assets rose by K£30.3 million (35.2 − 4.9), private assets by K£92.5 million ((140.7 − 35.2)+4.9 − 17.9). The total value of the windfall was K£268.5 million,[22] of which K£166.0 million or 62 per cent accrued to government in increased revenues.[23] While the overall savings rate out of transient income was 49 per cent in the boom period,[24] that of the government emerges from these calculations as 18.3 per cent (30.3/166.0), and that of the private sector as 90.2 per cent (92.5/102.5). While this private rate is exceptionally high, as an order of magnitude it is not implausible, for three reasons. First, the original windfall was perceived to be transitory; second, the limited relaxation of foreign exchange controls inhibited any large increase in private consumption; third, and partly in consequence, there was redistribution of income in favour of profits.

---

[22] Undiscounted, at 1975 prices, including the return on windfall investment accruing during the period, from Table 5.1, i.e. 256.1 + 12.4.

[23] See Table 5.7.

[24] Note that this differs from the 53% figure of section 2.2.1 for two reasons. First, that figure involved discounting at 10% whereas the present figure is undiscounted. Second, that figure excluded the permanent income from windfall investment and the savings which it generated whereas the present does not.

For an important sub-set of private agents, peasant coffee farmers, we have direct evidence that the windfall savings propensity was indeed high, our results being reported in detail in *Peasants and Governments*. In the first year of the boom, coffee farmers saved about 45 per cent of windfall income in bank deposits. These savings were subsequently spent. During the boom years the mean coffee farmer in our sample received windfall income of sh.6,330. Over the period 1975–82 these farmers invested over four times as much in equipment and buildings as did farmers not growing coffee, while having permanent incomes only 20 per cent higher. The excess of their investment over that of other farmers (correcting for their higher permanent income) was sh.3,070, implying a propensity to invest in this form out of windfall income of 49 per cent. Coffee farmers were also significantly more likely to adopt improved livestock than other farmers during this period, and undertook substantial extra coffee planting, the two together constituting a 17 per cent investment rate out of windfall income. Between them these identified forms of investment (which are by no means comprehensive) yield a 66 per cent investment rate out of the windfall.

2.6. *The 'Control Regime' and its Consequences*

The government operated a wide-ranging control regime which had been put in place during the preceding decade. Some of these controls were a façade, others were binding. Price and wage controls were very largely a façade. A price commission notionally regulated consumer prices since the government needed to be seen to be 'doing something' about inflation. However, it did not attempt to hold prices below market-clearing levels. Wages were controlled in both directions: minimum wage laws held wages above the supply price of labour for unskilled recruits; annual wage guidelines attempted to reduce wages in real terms. The minimum wage had tended to distort the wage structure, while the incomes policy has been shown to be slack: real wages were falling because of market forces by more than required under the policy (see Collier and Lal, 1986).

Nominal interest rate ceilings were imposed so that real interest rates were negative. The banks were also constrained by a minimum cash-to-deposits ratio requirement set by the Central Bank. As a result of these controls there was financial repression: on the eve of the boom only about 15 per cent of private sector capital formation was financed through the banking system. The government attempted to allocate bank loans to favoured sectors, but these allocations were not enforced.

The exchange rate was fixed to the SDR and was not seen as a policy instrument to be used actively. Exchange controls applied to capital movements. Although it was possible to bypass these controls through the black market or overinvoicing, penalties could be severe and the controls were vigorously enforced.

Finally, there were extensive controls over imports, usually in the form of quantitative restrictions. These had built up rapidly in response to the balance-of-payments crisis of 1972 and the oil crisis of 1974. Quantitative trade restrictions had become endogenous to the macroeconomic environment, accommodating monetary and exchange rate decisions. Phelps and Waswo (1972) had found that as of 1971 over 40 per cent of consumer goods industries in the manufacturing sector had negative value-added at world prices. Between 1970 and 1976 the final output price of manufactures rose by a further 18 per cent relative to their world prices. Hence, on the eve of the boom Kenya had a heavily protected manufacturing sector. We now consider the consequences of four of these controls in some detail.

2.6.1. *Foreign exchange controls*

As a result of foreign exchange controls private agents in aggregate faced a restricted choice as to which assets they might acquire with their remarkably high savings rates out of windfall income. In particular, they were denied access to foreign financial assets either as direct holders or, more likely, as indirect holders via the banking system.[25] The case for temporarily holding financial assets is that the investment boom is thereby stretched beyond the income and savings boom, enabling investment to take place when non-tradable capital goods prices are lower and returns (net of capital losses) higher. Since the private sector cannot, in aggregate, increase net financial claims against itself, the prohibition on foreign assets precludes it from acquiring financial assets unless the government permits an increase in fiat money. Hence, foreign exchange controls raise two issues. First, what would have been the rate of return on deferring investment by means of temporary foreign savings? Second, to what extent did the government permit private agents to acquire alternatives in the form of domestic financial assets? We consider these questions in turn.

The most attractive financial asset which private agents in aggregate could acquire was a claim on the government in the form of Treasury Bills. The relevant interest rate on these is the rediscount rate which the Central Bank will pay to commercial banks if they are cashed. On the world market, equivalent short-term financial assets were 6-month Eurocurrency deposits. Since the Kenyan currency was pegged to the SDR until 1981, the risk-minimizing strategy, had private agents been free to hold such deposits, would have been to hold them in a basket of currencies corresponding to the Eurodollar basket. We compare the return on Kenyan Treasury Bills with that on such a basket.[26] First, consider windfall savings earned at the start of

---

[25] That is, farmers, for example, might have had claims on banks denominated in domestic currency, which the banks could have used to acquire foreign currency assets.

[26] Until 1981 the SDR basket was a highly complex and varying basket of many currencies, for some of which there was no Eurocurrency market. In 1981 a simplified basket of five major currencies was adopted. Throughout, our calculations are based upon this latter basket.

the boom (January 1976) and held in financial assets until the end of 1982. In Kenyan Treasury Bills the compound interest would have been 57 per cent, whereas converted into foreign exchange, held in the Eurocurrency market, and finally reconverted, compound interest would have been 183 per cent. The large difference between these returns represents a tax levied by the government on financial asset holding achieved by foreign exchange controls. A private agent who saved through Treasury Bills enabled the government to earn 183 per cent interest and received 57 per cent. This is equivalent to the government permitting private agents to hold foreign assets but taxing their cash-in value at 45 per cent.[27] Such a high rate of implicit taxation presumably discouraged the acquisition of financial assets out of windfall income. One consequence is that the overall private savings rate out of the windfall would have been even higher in the absence of exchange controls, the other is an accelerated acquisition of capital goods, the effect of which we now quantify.

Recall that most of windfall income accrued in 1977. Compare the return on saving income received at the end of 1977 with and without the constraint of exchange controls, if in both cases it ends up invested in non-traded capital goods. With controls it is probably best to make purchases of capital goods as soon as possible after the receipt of windfall income, subject to the lags imposed by planning, purchase, and construction. We will take as an example the case in which such lags amount to two years. £100 held in Treasury Bills for two years would have accumulated to £111.7 by end-1979. Without controls, shrewd private agents might have chosen to defer purchases of non-tradable capital goods until after the peak of the construction boom. From Fig. 5.3, the boom was rapidly fading in the two years following its peak in 1980. Hence, we consider a strategy in which savings are held abroad until end-1982 and then switched into non-tradable capital goods. By this time the £100 initially saved would have accumulated to £251.3. Because non-tradable capital goods prices rose in nominal terms between end-1979 and end-1982 by 38 per cent, this would have bought only £182.6 worth of non-tradable capital goods at end-1979 prices. However, this is substantially more than the £111.7 of such goods bought when exchange controls prevail. By using foreign financial assets to defer investment for three years the shrewd unconstrained investor ends up with 63 per cent more capital goods. Hence, the annual real rate of return on investment which the constrained investor must earn during those three years in order to match this performance is 17.8 per cent. This seems implausibly high, even as a long-term rate of return on capital in Kenya. Further, during 1980–2 because of the investment boom firms were presumably being forced to accept atypically low returns.

To conclude, exchange controls had effects equivalent to the government levying a 45 per cent tax on the value of financial assets held abroad. This

[27] $1 - (1.57/2.83)$

discouraged private agents from deferring their investment, a strategy which would have had a real annual rate of return of 17.8 per cent between end-1979 and end-1982. Thus, exchange controls constituted a powerful disincentive to a strategy which would have yielded a very high real social rate of return.

Now consider the extent to which the government allowed private agents in aggregate to acquire financial assets. As we have seen, the government did permit such an increase in claims upon it, partly through running a payments surplus and partly through a budget deficit. However, of this increase in the money supply much was to meet a transactions demand rather than an asset demand. To calculate how much went to the latter we compare actual private sector money holdings (deposits and non-bank holdings of currency) with a counterfactual. The counterfactual is that the velocity of circulation with respect to private monetary expenditure would have stayed constant at its 1975 level. On this counterfactual, asset holdings of money increased as shown in Table 5.14.

There is a clear trajectory of asset holdings of money, the peak year for adding to such holdings occurring right at the start of the boom in 1977, and the peak of money holdings being in 1979. By 1981 they are largely run down. However, not all of this build-up in asset holdings of money was in the form of claims on the government. In 1977 the sum of the budget deficit and the payments surplus exceeded the increase in asset holdings of money, so that this asset build-up of private agents was net as well as gross. But in 1978 the entire increase was attributable to private money creation, so there was no net accumulation by private agents. The expansion in private credit was aided by the government actually reducing the minimum required cash ratio at this time. Hence, the trajectory overstates the extent to which investment could be deferred by means of financial savings. Further, although money matched by a budget deficit constituted a net claim of the private sector on the government, this was not a claim that could be honoured except by the

TABLE 5.14. *Sources of the change in money supply, 1976–1981* (K£m., current prices)

	Change in money supply	Change in asset holdings of money		Sources of change (%)		
		Annual	Cumulative	Net foreign assets	Public sector deficit	Private creation
1976	98.9	−4.6	−4.6	40	23	37
1977	195.0	73.7	69.1	56	3	41
1978	84.9	35.1	104.2	−88	47	141
1979	151.1	37.5	141.7	48	23	29
1980	22.0	−78.3	63.4	−301	−50	451
1981	90.8	−8.4	55.0	−108	138	70

Source: IMF, *International Financial Statistics*, various issues.

government running a budget surplus, which was unlikely and did not occur. The only part of the monetary build-up by the private sector which constituted claims on the government and which it retained the resources to honour were those matched by a payments surplus.

Even this is a very generous treatment of the backing for private money holdings since it assumes that all the increase in net foreign assets was potentially available for meeting private claims. In fact, some of this build-up in reserves was required for the finance of a higher foreign currency value of imports, this being the government counterpart transactions demand for foreign currency to the private transactions demand for money. At its peak in 1979 the private sector had built up asset holdings of money by K£141.7 million. By 1981 it had succeeded in running these down by K£86.7 million. Further reduction could not be matched by foreign currency since the cupboard was already bare: the government had already spent all the foreign exchange reserves accumulated earlier. Because of financial repression, the figure of K£141.7 million must be below the amount of financial assets the private sector would have liked to acquire in the absence of foreign exchange controls, since interest rates were depressed (see below). With convertibility, this larger sum could all have been deferred investment. As it was, only K£86.7 million was so deferred.

2.6.2. *Financial repression*

In an initially credit-constrained economy such as Kenya's, many private agents wished to borrow more than was available before the boom. One side-effect of the foreign exchange controls was that the increased asset demand for domestic money gave rise to a temporary financial liberalization. There were two possible routes by which this could come about, depending upon the initial cause of financial repression. The government used two instru-

TABLE 5.15. *Money holding and foreign asset backing, 1976–1981* (K£m.)

	Annual change		Cumulative change	
	Net foreign assets	Asset holdings of money	Net foreign assets	Asset holdings of money
1976	39.4	−4.6	39.4	−4.6
1977	108.8	73.7	148.2	69.1
1978	−74.8	35.1	73.4	104.2
1979	73.0	37.5	146.4	141.7
1980	−66.2	−78.3	80.2	63.4
1981	−98.2	−8.4	−18.0	55.0

Source: IMF, *International Financial Statistics*, various issues.

ments to control the banking system; the cash-to-deposits ratio and interest rate ceilings. The latter reduced the flow of savings deposits to the banks, the former restricted their capacity to make loans, given their deposit flow. As we have seen, the government permitted an increase in fiat money, so that for a given cash ratio and savings behaviour, more could be lent. Additionally, as we have seen, the savings propensity rose sharply: those agents who received windfall income and wished to save it could lend it to initially rationed agents. This build-up of financial savings was disproportionately held in the form of bank deposits. The combined result was a substantial increase in the liquid assets of the banking system: more money could be lent (see Fig 5.6).

The control regime included both maximum and minimum interest rates on bank loans: in 1975 these were 10 per cent and 8 per cent respectively.[28] The maximum rate was maintained constant throughout the boom[29] but the capacity of the banks to lend expanded so substantially that this regulation rapidly ceased to be a binding constraint. The minimum interest rate regulation would have become binding but was suspended from 1977 onwards.[30] Reviewing the banking system during 1977 the government commented that 'lending was a problem for some financial institutions and particularly in the middle of the year some reserves available for short term borrowing could not find lending outlets even at near-zero rates of interest'.[31] The liquidity ratio, the minimum for which was set at 18 per cent, rose from 19 per cent at the end of 1975 (when it was presumably binding) to a peak of 37 per cent through the third quarter of 1977 (see Fig. 5.6). Even by the end of 1979 it had only fallen to 23 per cent.[32] Thus, between 1976 and 1980 the maximum lending rate temporarily ceased to bind and credit was readily available at low nominal rates of interest. As we have seen in section 2.2.3, the sector which undertook the dominant share of windfall investment was manufacturing industry, and we now consider the real interest rates which it faced during this period. Between 1976 and 1980 the rate of inflation for value-added in the manufacturing sector averaged 8.6 per cent. Although there are no data as to the average interest rate paid on advances, the fact that the 8 per cent minimum requirement had to be abandoned between 1976 and 1980, together with the government's comment concerning 'near-zero rates of interest', suggests that in real terms interest rates were significantly negative.

Since the commercial banks were unable to lend out all their available funds even at these rates, it suggests that had firms drawn up additional investment plans with positive real returns they would have been able to finance them at a profit. That firms did not do this presumably implies that such opportunities were already being exhausted by the investment boom. A

---

[28] Central Bank of Kenya, *Quarterly Economic Review*, Apr. 1988. table 1.8.2.
[29] In 1980 it was raised to 11%.
[30] It was briefly reintroduced in 1980.
[31] Government of Kenya, *Economic Survey* (1978), 36.
[32] The statutory minimum was briefly raised to 20% in 1978.

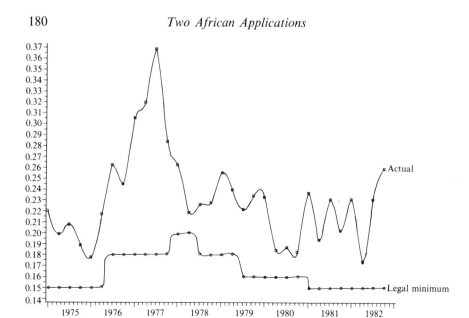

Liquidity ratios: actual and legal minimum

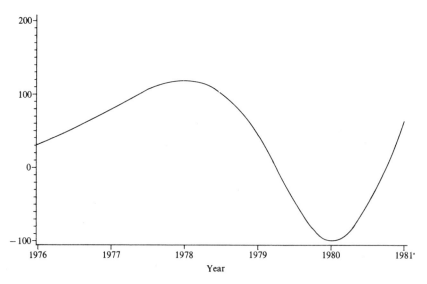

Money creation

Sources: IMF, *International Financial Statistics*, and Central Bank of Kenya, *Quarterly Economic Review*, table 1.6.3 (both various issues).

FIG. 5.6. *Liquidity ratios of banks and money creation*

crucial implication of this is that the real (private) *ex ante* rate of return upon the marginal investment project undertaken during the period was probably very low, and may well have been zero or even negative.

The temporary financial liberalization permitted an increase in financial intermediation for investment. This can be quantified through Central Bank data on advances, which are classified partly by sector and partly by use. From this we have constructed proxies for advances used to finance capital formation in the enterprise sector.[33]

Loans outstanding at the end of each year are then deflated by the manufacturing GDP deflator[34] to 1975 constant prices. The annual change in the real value of these loans, which is the proxy for new lending to enterprises for investment, is shown in Fig. 5.7.

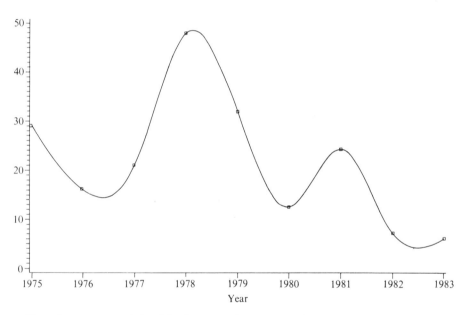

Note: Loans are as defined in the text. Figures are deflated by the manufacturing GDP deflator to 1975 prices.

Sources: Government of Kenya, *Statistical Abstract*, 1986, tables 132(d) and 142 and corresponding tables for earlier years.

FIG. 5.7. *New Advances to the private sector for investment (£m. at constant 1975 prices)*

---

[33] Our proxy is: commercial bank loans to enterprises in agriculture, mining, manufacturing, construction, electricity and water, and transport, and non-bank financial intermediary loans to agriculture, manufacturing, and construction.

[34] This deflator is chosen since manufacturing was the dominant sector to which loans were made.

Although the series is rather volatile, it is evident that there was a major expansion of credit during 1978 and 1979 followed by a credit squeeze in 1982–3. Indeed, so substantial was the expansion at its peak in 1978 that despite the investment boom an increased proportion of investment was financed through the banking system: 20 per cent as opposed to only 15 per cent during 1975–6.[35]

Financial liberalization also enabled previously credit-constrained agents to borrow for consumption. Had this been widespread, it would have been possible for recipients of the windfall to have had a very high savings rate (as they did) while the private sector as a whole had no increase in savings. Although it is not possible to construct an adequate proxy for bank advances to finance consumption, the fact that net savings rose so substantially suggests that this effect was relatively minor.

Potentially, the temporary financial liberalization was highly beneficial. Financial intermediation should improve the efficiency of investment allocation. By being synchronized with the investment boom, this improvement in efficiency occurred when it was of most use. However, this inference must be somewhat qualified. The banking system had been repressed for about a decade by the time of the temporary liberalization. It may well not have had the knowledge base with which to identify appropriate borrowers. During the period of liberalization a secondary banking fringe developed rapidly. This mainly borrowed from the deposit-taking banks and probably lent to finance construction (much as in the British financial liberalization of 1973). It cannot be assumed that private investment during the boom occurred in an allocatively efficient way.

2.6.3. *Import controls*

In Kenya trade restrictions were pervasive and largely took the form of binding quotas. Faced with an influx of foreign exchange, the government had the choice of maintaining these controls or relaxing them partially or completely. The two extremes, maintenance or abolition, would each have caused severe problems. If quotas are kept constant then the only way the private sector can benefit from an improvement in the terms of trade is for export production to fall, releasing resources to the import substitute sector. This is brought about as follows. With fixed quotas importables behave as non-tradables at the margin. Increased demand drives up their price until it has risen relative to the export good, for only then will resources be induced to reallocate into the sector, enabling the extra demand to be met. This is obviously highly inefficient, especially since the economy should use the period of high prices to increase export production. At the other extreme, had

---

[35] New loans in 1975 were £29.1 m. and in 1976 were £16.1 m. Converting the latter figure to current prices gives £18.5 m. Hence, at current prices new loans totalled £47.6 m. Private GFKF at current prices in those years was £309.8 m., so 15% of GFKF was loan-financed. In 1978 new advances were £48.0 m. at constant prices, £64.3 m. at current prices, and GFKF was £320.6 m., so 20% of GFKF was loan-financed.

controls been abolished, private agents would rationally have interpreted this as a temporary event associated with the boom. They would have used the temporary financial liberalization to borrow in order to import consumer durables in anticipation of subsequent controls. There would therefore have been an inflated demand for consumer imports unrelated to the sustainable increase in consumption. Foreign exchange reserves built up as a counterpart to the domestic financial asset accumulation of those agents who wished to make subsequent real investments would have been pre-empted by this increased demand for consumer durables.

Partial relaxation of quotas must navigate between this Scylla and Charybdis. What is worse, optimal public response will indeed involve an overshooting of liberalization, so that rational private agents will expect some of the liberalization to be temporary. It is optimal to overshoot for two reasons. First, resources are thereby released to the construction sector, which needs them temporarily. Without extra consumer imports the construction boom will require consumption to fall temporarily. Second, since permanent income will be higher as a result of boom savings, consumption can rise now in anticipation. However, until the non-tradable consumer sector is expanded by investment, this extra consumption can only be met by imports.

We now investigate what actually happened to trade policy. Changes in the trade regime cannot be inferred directly from tariff schedules or tariff revenue because of the prevalence of quotas. Instead, we use two distinct measures. The first is the ratio of total private consumption to household consumption of imports. As can be seen from Fig. 5.8, this ratio changes very substantially over the decade. Changes in the volume of consumer imports relative to the volume of total private consumption should reflect changes in the domestic price of importable consumer goods to non-tradable consumer goods. Between 1975 and 1980 the exchange rate was maintained constant against SDR, so that the principal cause of these large alterations can only be changes in trade policy. Fig. 5.8 then compares this with a second measure of trade policy, the ratio of an index of the c.i.f. price of imports to an index of the final output price of domestic manufactures (using as weights the share in manufacturing output). The two should be correlated for the constant exchange rate period. Although the period is too short for statistical testing, it is evident from Fig. 5.8 that they are closely related. We may therefore be confident that Fig. 5.8 provides a good indicator of trade policy.

Quite clearly, trade policy changed with the windfall. In 1976–8 there was a continuous liberalization, which was reversed in 1979 as the windfall receded.[36] We refer to this as an endogenous trade policy: that is, trade policy is

---

[36] The subsequent resumption of liberalization in 1980 was also boom-related. Recall that a high proportion of boom-induced investment took place in the import-substitute sector. By 1980 this investment had raised output sufficiently for the demand for imports to decline. This would have reduced the implicit tariff rate even had quotas been held constant. In fact, there was a temporary liberalization of quotas in 1980, so that the two effects combined to reduce the implicit tariff rate.

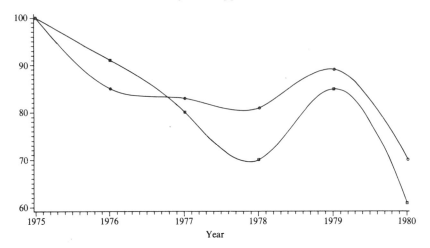

□ = Domestic price/world price of import-substitutes
○ = Volume of private consumption/volume of household imports

Sources: Private consumption at current prices from Government of Kenya, *Statistical Abstract, 1984*, table 37(a) (and corresponding tables for other years), deflated by the lower income consumer price index for constant series. Household consumer imports at current c.i.f. prices from *Statistical Abstract, 1985*, table 70(b), deflated by a weighted average of the c.i.f. price indices from table 66. Index of protection based on tables 66, 99(a), and 99(b). Detailed calculations are available from the authors.

FIG. 5.8. *Two measures of trade policy*

used as a macroeconomic policy instrument. It suggests that it might be important to disaggregate within the set of tradable goods beyond the obvious distinction between boom and non-boom tradables proposed by the theory of Dutch Disease.

Although import quotas were liberalized, this may, as discussed above, have been either excessive or inadequate. Again counterfactuals are required. Table 5.16 shows exports and final consumer imports (public plus private) during the boom at constant 1975 domestic prices and compares them with counterfactuals. We assume that without the boom exports would have risen in line with GDP. We therefore apply the GDP counterfactual constructed in Table 5.2. This is quite a conservative counterfactual for exports since consumption grew less rapidly than GDP, leaving room for exports to grow more rapidly.[37] We assume that without the boom consumer imports would have grown in line with counterfactual consumption, previously estimated in Table 5.4.

It is evident that actual export performance is well short of this counterfactual. Indeed, by 1981 export volumes are lower in absolute terms than in

[37] See Table 5.4.

TABLE 5.16. *Actual and counterfactual exports and consumer imports, 1975–1979*

	Exports			Consumer imports		
	Actual	Counterf.	Diff.	Actual	Counterf.	Diff.
1975	230.4	230.4	0	95.3	95.3	0
1976	245.1	235.9	9.2	108.5	95.2	13.3
1977	250.0	252.1	−2.1	106.3	98.3	8.0
1978	235.3	273.9	−38.6	119.3	100.1	19.2
1979	230.4	269.3	−38.9	120.0	112.5	7.5

Notes

Exports: Quantum series for 'all exports' times 1975 value for 'total exports', Government of Kenya, *Statistical Abstract, 1983*. Domestic prices assumed to equal world prices.

Imports: Consumer imports for households at 1975 world prices from *Statistical Abstract, 1987*, table 68(b), 'final consumption of households: retained imports', deflated by the non-oil imports deflator from table 64; and corresponding tables for earlier years. In 1975 there were extensive quota restrictions on these goods. Between 1975 and 1985, a period of major trade liberalization, the ratio of world to domestic prices for manufactured consumer imports rose by a factor of 2.27. This is a lower bound to the divergence in 1975. Hence the value of consumer imports at world prices is multiplied by 2.27 to get to domestic prices. Consumer imports for government at 1975 prices are from *Statistical Abstract*. The two series are then summed.

1975 despite a 35 per cent growth in GDP. At first sight this decline in exports might appear to be an instance of Dutch Disease, perhaps as a by-product of a decline in the volume of non-boom tradables output. However, as we have seen, there was substantial investment into the non-boom tradables sector and output rose as a result relative to GDP. The decline in export volumes therefore occurred despite rather than because of a change in the output of non-boom tradables.

A possible explanation for the decline in export volumes comes from the changes in imports of final consumer goods (private and public). Although such imports increased relative to their counterfactual, during the coffee boom period these increases were modest, averaging £12.0 million during 1976–9. This permitted an increase in consumption relative to its 1975 level of only 1.2 per cent.[38] Against this modest addition to the capacity to meet the demand for windfall consumption, there were losses due to the resource movement effects into the two boom sectors, tree crops and construction. For the formal part of the construction sector this can be quantified. Table 5.5B shows employment in the sector relative to the national labour force. Taking as our counterfactual that this would have been constant at its 1975 level yields boom-induced construction employment. Multiplying this by mean

[38] This makes no allowance for intermediate imports. Such imports are hard to assign, but in any case were below their 1975 level for the entire period of the boom. Hence, it would be difficult to argue that extra imports of intermediates for the consumer sector enabled the economy to meet the demands for windfall consumption.

earnings in construction and deflating to 1975 prices gives an estimate of the value of labour withdrawn from other sectors into construction. Finally, the 1976 input–output table shows that for the consumption sector the average ratio of output to value-added was 2.2. Hence, the loss of value-added in the form of labour is multiplied by 2.2 for an estimate of the loss of output which this withdrawal of labour induced. During the boom period 1976–9 this averaged £8.1 million. Thus the extra consumer imports were barely sufficient merely to compensate for the resource movement effect of labour into the formal part of the construction sector. The total resource movement effect must have been far larger than this. First, there was a large increase in informal construction, notably the upgrading of residential property in rural areas.[39] Second, there was a large increase in resources devoted to coffee and tea growing, particularly in the smallholder sector. Although these cannot be quantified, it is evident that imports were not sufficiently liberalized to compensate for the combined resource movement effects into the boom sectors. Being constrained by quotas from offsetting the resource movement effect through extra imports, the only remaining avenue was to offset them through reducing exports. Had exports stayed on their counterfactual, consumption would therefore necessarily have fallen as a result of the boom. The decline in exports is therefore explicable as a diversion of resources to meet domestic consumption. Note that this was not a diversion of resources from non-boom tradables to the consumer non-tradables sector as implied by Dutch Disease. Manufactures (a sector which before the boom was producing mainly import substitutes but also exports) rose much more rapidly than GDP: by 1979 output was 38 per cent above its 1975 level against only 24 per cent for GDP. Rather, therefore, it was a switch within tradable goods from exports to import substitutes.

Even though imports were not liberalized enough to prevent exports from falling, there may still have been pre-emptive imports of consumer durables to take advantage of their selective temporary liberalization. There is much anecdotal evidence for this, such as multiple imports of Mercedes which were then garaged. A direct way of investigating whether the perception of temporariness induced pre-emptive importing of consumer durables is to look at the composition of consumer imports. Fig. 5.9 compares total consumer imports (at constant prices) with imports of cars plus televisions, the closest proxy for imports of private consumer durables. There is indeed an enormous increase in such imports: during the peak liberalization years of 1978 and 1980 (as measured by the indicators in Fig. 5.8) the volume of imports of these durables more than doubles relative to 1975. However, this increase is open to two interpretations. Even were there no import controls we would expect some increase in the consumption of durables as part of the

---

[39] This is one of the major investments made by coffee farmers out of windfall income identified in the survey discussed above.

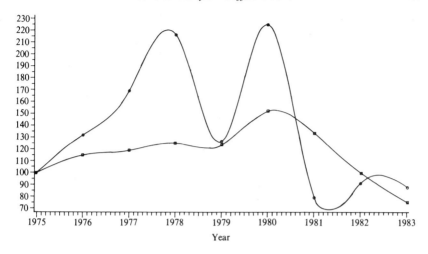

☐ = Private consumer imports at constant prices
○ = Imports of cars and TVs at constant prices

Sources: Cars and TVs from Government of Kenya, *Statistical Abstract, 1986*, table 85(b), and ibid., *1981*, table 61(a) and 61(b), weighted at 1975 import c.i.f. values. Total consumer imports derived as for FIG. 5.8.

FIG. 5.9. *Imports of consumer durables*

response to high transient income. We have already seen that the private sector recognized boom income as transient, since it had such high savings and investment rates. Durables are merely the capital goods of the household sector. There is, however, one feature which cautions against this as the sole interpretation. The peak year for durables imports was 1980. By then the private sector income windfall was over, except for the relatively small transmission from the public expenditure boom, and so transient income had largely ended. By contrast, rational agents might well have concluded by 1980 that the party was nearly over as far as access to imports was concerned. Recall from Tables 5.14 and 5.15 that in 1980 there was a large private credit creation of about K£100 million and the foreign exchange reserves built up as part of the rise in the private asset demand for money were depleted. Possibly, then, it was during 1980 that some private agents were able to use the last stage of the temporary financial liberalization in order to borrow to take advantage of the last stage of the trade liberalization, thereby pre-empting the foreign exchange that other private agents had planned to use to finance investment. However, such an inference can only be speculative.

2.6.4. *Fixed nominal exchange rate*

The government fixed the exchange rate in units of SDRs. Immediately before the coffee boom, in September 1975, it had devalued the currency by 14 per cent.[40] Thereafter, the nominal exchange rate was held constant throughout the boom period.

If the exchange rate is allowed to float, the increase in real expenditure consequent upon the boom will tend to lead to an increase in the demand for domestic currency and hence an appreciation in its value. A corollary of this would be that the extra transactions demand for real money balances would be accommodated, at least partly, by a fall in the price of tradable goods (relative to the counterfactual). Hence, the implication is that this control of the exchange rate caused more inflation than had the exchange rate floated.

This proposition is difficult to test because the key step is not the inflation counterfactual but the exchange rate counterfactual. Rather than construct such a counterfactual, which would inevitably be contrived, a more robust guide, at least qualitatively, to what would have happened is to observe that part of the foreign exchange market which was freely floating, namely the black market. The black market rate stood at a small premium to the official rate. Since the latter was fixed (in terms of the SDR), the movement in the premium is an indicator of the direction in which a freely floating exchange rate would probably have moved. The course of the premium is shown in Fig. 5.10.

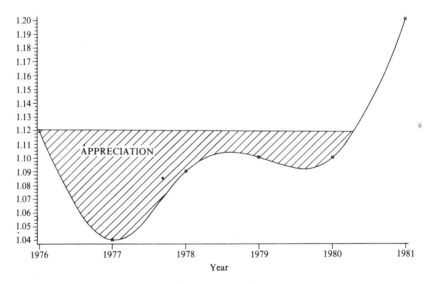

Source: *World Currency Yearbook* (various issues).

FIG. 5.10. *Black market/official exchange rate*

---

[40] The resulting credit squeeze as the demand for money increased explains two phenomena we have noted at the start of the boom: banks were constrained by the minimum liquidity ratio rule, and there was substantial destocking during 1975.

At the peak of the boom, in 1977, the black market exchange rate appreciated by 7 per cent (in units of SDRs) and in 1978 it was still 3 per cent above its 1976 value. Hence, the black market rate supports the hypothesis that the fixed exchange rate control was inflationary.

2.7. *Assessment*

2.7.1. *The Dutch Disease critique: construction booms and endogenous trade policy*

The theory of how a trade shock might affect relative prices (and hence resource allocation) developed in Chapter 4 emphasized two departures from the Dutch Disease model. First, if the windfall is perceived as to some extent transient, there will be a disproportionate increase in demand for non-tradable capital goods and so their price is likely to rise relative to that of non-tradable consumer goods: a phenomenon we refer to as a *construction boom*. Second, if trade restrictions are used as a macroeconomic policy instrument, a windfall is likely to induce a trade liberalization: a phenomenon we refer to as an *endogenous trade policy*. The former implies that non-tradables must be disaggregated (into capital and consumer goods), the latter implies that tradables should be disaggregated (into protected and un-protected). Each of these propositions has found support in our analysis of the Kenyan coffee boom. Construction boom theory and its application to Kenya are illustrated in Fig. 5.11. The left-hand panel, based on Fig. 4.2, depicts the likely comparative statics of an exclusive unrevised favourable trade shock: because demand for capital goods rises by more than that for consumer goods, the non-tradable capital equilibrium locus (K–K) shifts by more than the non-tradable consumption locus (C–C). The right-hand panel shows how relative prices changed in Kenya during the period 1975–80: the change is both substantial and in the predicted direction.

Endogenous trade policy theory and application to Kenya are illustrated in Fig. 5.12. The left-hand panel, based on Fig. 2.1, depicts the likely comparative statics of a favourable trade shock. The increase in demand for non-tradables (both consumer and capital goods) shifts the non-tradables equilibrium locus (N–N) to the right. The increase in expenditure raises the transactions demand for money and windfall saving raises the asset demand for money, both effects shifting the money equilibrium locus (D–D) upwards. The right-hand panel shows how relative prices changed in Kenya during the period 1975–80. Again, the change is both substantial and in the predicted direction.

Finally, compare these models with that of Dutch Disease, which predicts a rise in the price of non-tradables relative to non-boom tradables. This is, in fact, measured by the horizontal axis in Fig. 5.12. It is evident that although there is indeed a price change in the predicted direction, it is negligible.

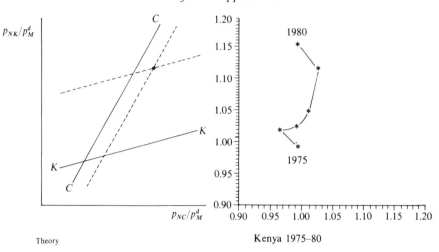

P_{NK} = price of non-tradable capital goods
P_{NC} = price of non-tradable consumer goods
P_M^d = domestic price of importables

Note: All prices are for value-added using sector-specific GDP deflators.

FIG. 5.11. *A construction boom: theory and application*

Hence, using the Dutch Disease disaggregation into tradables and non-tradables in the case of the Kenyan coffee boom adds nothing significant to working with a single-aggregate model of the economy, while missing powerful effects which become apparent only with further disaggregation.

2.7.2. *Government policy*

The government correctly assessed the nature of the shock and elected to allow the benefits to accrue to producers. Even so, it received a substantial lagged share of the proceeds through the operation of the existing tax system and the temporary liberalization of imports which the boom made possible and which we have argued was a rational response by government. Given the nature of the shock, it would probably have been optimal to save the bulk of this revenue gain: the long-run addition to permanent national income and hence the desirable increase in the size of the public sector was bound to be small. Hence it was probably a mistake to attempt a rapid increase in public capital formation, even disregarding the danger of thereby inducing long-run increases in current expenditure, as proved to be the case. In addition, the presence of foreign exchange controls tended to exacerbate the construction boom which the windfall would in any case have induced. In these circumstances, the decision to invest was a mistake, albeit a very natural one. The failure to save sufficiently to cover this incremental investment, and hence the increase in the overall deficit, was also inadvisable, even within the boom

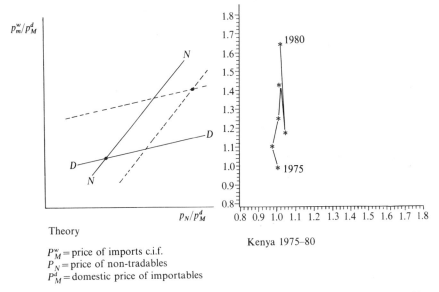

Theory

Kenya 1975–80

P_M^w = price of imports c.i.f.
P_N = price of non-tradables
P_M^d = domestic price of importables

Note: The relative price on the horizontal axis is for value-added using sector-specific GDP deflators. The relative price on the vertical axis, which measures trade policy, is for final output, using c.i.f. and domestic ex-factory prices. Non-tradables here include both capital consumer goods and are proxied by adding the construction sector to our previous proxy for non-tradable consumption.

FIG. 5.12. *Endogenous trade policy: theory and application*

period itself, 1976–9. In the later period, 1980–3, public performance deteriorated still further, with capital investment only a little up overall (and declining through time) but saving markedly down, and a widening deficit. Thus the relatively small increase in saving in the first sub-period was wholly reversed in the second, and the entire increase in public capital formation over the period was ultimately financed by borrowing. To caricature the situation, the government should have saved but not invested: instead, it invested but did not save.

Before the boom the government had enacted a wide-ranging control regime. During the boom two aspects of this regime deserve emphasis: first, it had powerful repercussions on the capacity of private agents to utilize the windfall, and second, the government made relatively little attempt to modify the controls during the course of the boom. To take the latter point first, the fixed exchange rate was held constant, exchange controls were maintained constant, and nominal interest rate ceilings were maintained constant. There were small modifications to the cash ratio requirement on banks and there were some relaxations of import quotas.

We have established reasonable grounds for concluding that this regulatory framework reduced the private windfall savings rate, accelerated the conversion of savings into local investment, thereby inefficiently amplifying the construction boom, reduced exports, induced a surge in imports of consumer durables, and increased the price level. Foreign exchange controls operated like a 45 per cent tax on the cash-in value of savings temporarily held in foreign assets. As such, they must surely have discouraged the saving of windfall income and induced a more rapid transformation of that part which was saved into real investment. We have shown that without exchange controls, had private agents taken advantage of foreign financial assets to defer investment by three years, they and the economy would have achieved about an 18 per cent annual real return on savings so utilized. Exchange controls forced private agents into accepting returns which were probably very much lower than this. We have shown that there are good grounds for regarding the real rate of return on domestic investment as being zero at the margin during the boom period. Exchange controls thus seriously impaired the capacity of the economy to convert a temporary windfall into permanent income. Since a disproportionately large amount of an economy's savings take place during favourable temporary shocks, this effect can be important even if such shocks are rare. Import controls were relaxed, but not sufficiently to prevent exports falling as production was diverted from the non-boom export sector to the home market: by 1981 export volumes were actually lower than in 1975, despite a 35 per cent growth of GDP. The temporary liberalization of import controls on consumer durables probably induced hoarding in anticipation of subsequent retightening: between 1979 and 1980 such imports increased by 80 per cent, whereas by 1981 they had fallen 40 per cent below their 1979 level. The hoarding of imported consumer durables is hardly a socially efficient form of saving. Finally, the fixed nominal exchange rate prevented what might otherwise have been a modest appreciation: on the black market the currency appreciated by 7 per cent. It seems likely that such an appreciation would have reduced the price level.

In summary, it is hard to avoid the conclusion that if private agents could be trusted to recognize windfall income as transient, the Kenyan government was operating a control regime quite unsuited to a country prone to temporary favourable external shocks.

Quite clearly, private agents did recognize windfall income as transient. Our estimates for the entire private sector imply that the private savings rate out of windfall income was about 90 per cent. Such a high savings rate probably compounds two effects: not only was there conscious saving out of income perceived as transient, but there was a redistribution in favour of profits. However, the latter effect is certainly not the sole explanation: survey evidence shows coffee farmers to have had a windfall savings rate in excess of 66 per cent. The private sector translated these savings into investment, disproportionately skewed towards the tradable sector of the economy, and in particular import-substitute manufacturing. Inadvertently, this investment contributed towards a powerful trade liberalization in the early 1980s as the demand for imports fell even more rapidly than import volumes were reduced.

This leads to a paradox. Given the lack of faulty perceptions or apparently irrational behaviour in the private sector, the main argument for custodial intervention by the public sector rests on the existence of controls operated by the public sector, which interfere with private responses. However, the major weapon for such intervention would be compensatory taxation, and the track record of the government in handling the non-discretionary increase in revenues does not generate confidence that it would have handled a discretionary increase much better. Indeed, if discretionary changes had led to incremental expenditure consequences similar to non-discretionary ones, then government intervention would probably have worsened the situation, notwithstanding the presence of controls. We now explore this and other policy counterfactuals using the more sophisticated methodology of a computable general equilibrium model.

3. A General Equilibrium Analysis

3.1. *Introduction*

In this section we use a general equilibrium model to analyse the effects of the boom. The use of a model has two advantages. First, it allows us to separate the effects of the coffee boom itself from the consequences of several other shocks which affected the Kenyan economy in the period 1975–83. Shortly after coffee prices peaked (in 1977), both public expenditure and external borrowing rose enormously. Also, at the end of the period, the economy suffered a double terms-of-trade loss: coffee (and tea) prices fell and oil prices rose. We need a model to disentangle the effects of all these various shocks. Secondly, the model allows us to widen the scope of the analysis compared with what we could do in section 2. In addition to changes induced by the boom in asset formation, relative prices, and resource allocation, we shall consider the question of who benefited from the boom.

In Chapter 4 we suggested that a temporary windfall would cause large changes in relative prices, and some of these have already been identified in section 2. The model enables us to trace the distributional effects of these price changes. The results of the simulations performed with the model indicate that the boom led to large transfers of income between various groups in the Kenyan economy (in particular between rural and urban groups). The boom's distributional effects, both in the short run and in the long run, are powerfully affected by these transfers.

3.2. *Simulation Experiments*

The model is a fairly disaggregated general equilibrium model.[41] There are thirty-six commodities (goods and non-factor services), which fall into four categories: *exportables* (largely agricultural commodities, in particular coffee and tea), which are traded at given world prices; *food commodities*, which are subject to tariffs but not to quantitative restrictions; *non-food importables*, which are subject to import controls; and *non-tradables* (services). For each of these commodities the market must clear, either through changes in quantities (e.g. excess demand for food at given domestic prices being met through imports) or through changes in relative prices (e.g. the price of non-food manufactured products rising until domestic supply plus the controlled level of imports is equal to domestic demand).

There are forty-eight groups of peasants in the model. They are distinguished by the size and the location of their holding, location being an indicator of the crops which can be grown, the possibilities for non-agricultural activities (e.g. formal sector wage employment), and land quality. Peasants earn their incomes from crops, from livestock, from wage employment (partly on other smallholdings or on large farms, partly outside agriculture), and from non-farm enterprises (e.g. trading). The producer prices which they receive for their crops and livestock products are set by the government. Their consumption consists partly of own-produced items (in particular food), partly of goods (e.g. clothing) which are imported or produced domestically by urban firms. The combination of the endogeneity of the consumer prices paid by peasants and the exogeneity of the producer prices they receive is the main reason why changes in relative prices strongly affect the real income of peasants.

There are eight groups of urban households, distinguished by their endowments (e.g. educational qualifications), which determine their access to formal sector wage employment and high-income self-employment. Real wages in the formal sector are given at a level at which there is excess supply. As a result, an important mechanism in the model is that output can expand (at given real wage rates) without investment or change in prices, since urban workers can be drawn into formal sector employment, out of unemployment or low-income self-employment in the informal sector.

The government receives its revenue from direct and indirect taxes and tariffs. It uses this revenue partly for public consumption (which implies a demand for goods and for labour, but which does not add directly to anyone's utility)[42] and partly for investment. Utility maximization determines the composition of the household's consumption, but private saving is

[41] The model is described in detail in Appendix 2 to this chapter, to which we shall occasionally refer. Data sources and estimation results are given in Gunning (1983).

[42] In this book we are not concerned with the productive effects of public expenditures. We consider these in *Peasants and Governments*.

not determined by inter-temporal optimization. Each household saves a fixed proportion out of its (non-transient) income. These savings rates differ between household groups, being very low for peasants and much higher for urban households. Rural–urban transfers therefore affect the rate of investment. All households save a large part of the income they consider transient (the increase in household income due to the boom being so classified). In section 2 we showed that coffee farmers had a savings propensity out of transient income of 0.66. Here we make the more conservative assumption of 0.6.

The capital inflow from abroad (i.e. the value of the resource deficit, or the concept of foreign savings used in the National Accounts) is given, in terms of world prices. Hence an increase in the value of exports (such as occurred during the coffee boom) is automatically matched by an equal increase in the value of total imports. This means that changes in the external environment are fully and instantaneously passed on to the domestic economy. A temporary sterilization, for example a build-up of foreign exchange resources in response to a terms-of-trade gain, would have to be modelled explicitly. This we shall do when, in some of the counterfactual policy simulation experiments, we explore the effects of various stabilization policies. For the moment, however, we assume instantaneous adjustment.

In the model, savings determine investment rather than vice versa: the given amount of foreign savings is added to the endogenously determined amount of private and public savings and this gives the total value of investment. As we shall see, prices of capital goods vary enormously (partly because of import controls), so that an increase in the value of investment may be eroded to a large extent by relative price changes. This, of course, was one of the effects of the boom which we emphasized in Chapter 4. The allocation of investment between sectors is given exogenously. As a result, rates of return are not equalized and, without modelling the microeconomic distortions in the investment process in detail, the model incorporates the bias in investment against agriculture and in favour of manufacturing.

The model is solved for the years 1975 through 1983. In this section we describe the results of four simulation experiments, which differ in the assumptions on coffee and tea prices, foreign capital flows, public consumption, and oil prices (Table 5.17). In the simulation experiments we introduce a cumulative set of changes. The first run is a counterfactual in which the economy is not exposed to any shocks. In the second run we introduce the coffee boom itself and the associated rise in tea prices. In this run public expenditure remains under control, in the sense that public consumption rises in absolute terms but remains constant as a share of GDP. External borrowing in this run is the same as in the counterfactual. In the third run we relax those two assumptions, imposing the actual value of public consumption and external borrowing. This implies a contraction of public expenditure (compared with the second run) in the first two years of the

TABLE 5.17. *Design of the simulation experiments*

Run	Coffee and tea prices	Public consumption	External borrowing	Oil prices	Real wages
1. Counterfactual	A	C	E	G	I
2. Boom run	B	C	E	G	I
3. Public expenditures	B	D	F	G	J
4. Oil shock	B	D	F	H	J

Key

A: In 1976–80 world prices and domestic producer prices of coffee and tea increase at the same rate as non-oil-import prices. Actual prices are used for 1981–83 (cf. Table 5.19).

B: World prices and producer prices for coffee and tea have their actual values in all years (cf. Table 5.19).

C: The share of public consumption in GDP remains constant.

D: Actual values are imposed for public consumption, implying an increase in its share in GDP (cf. Table 5.27).

E: External borrowing (the value of the resource deficit in dollars) grows at a constant rate (cf. Table 5.27)

F: Actual values of the resource deficit are imposed. This gives the same total capital inflow (1976–83) as in the first two runs, but much higher values in 1978–81 and much lower values in 1976, 1977, 1982, and 1983 (cf. Table 5.27).

G: Import and export prices of oil increase, after 1979, at the same rate as non-oil-import prices (cf. Table 5.30).

H: Actual oil prices are imposed (cf. Table 5.30).

I: Mean formal sector real wages are constant (in 1974 prices) throughout the period 1975–83.

J: Real wages are constant for 1975–81, but fall to 92.1% of the 1975 level in 1982 and to 85.6% in 1983 (cf. Table 5.18).

simulation period, a sharp rise in the period 1978–81, and a sharp contraction at the very end of the period, in 1982 and 1983. In the fourth run we introduce the final shock, the second oil price increase. This implies a large terms-of-trade loss in the years 1980–3.

Finally, runs differ in what is assumed about real wages in the formal sector. Actual wages are shown in Table 5.18. These data indicate that real wages were remarkably stable in the period 1975–81 and, in particular, that the coffee boom (and the resulting investment boom in 1978 and subsequent years) did not lead to a rise in real wages. In fact, one would have expected wages to rise in this period even in the absence of the coffee boom: even in our counterfactual run labour demand rises sharply, partly as a result of the economy's recovery from the 1975 recession caused by the first oil-price increase and the 1974/5 drought. That they did not reflects, in our view, the effect of a very sluggish adjustment to the large excess supply of urban labour in the pre-1975 period. We do not attempt to model the effects on real wages of shifts in labour demand and supply explicitly, assuming instead that real wages are constant in 1975–81 in all runs. For the first two runs we extend this assumption to the last two years, since in these runs the economy is in 1982 and 1983 fairly close to a steady growth path. However, for runs 3 and 4 (in which growth stagnates at the end of the simulation period, largely

TABLE 5.18. *Formal sector wages*

	Real wages[a]	Index[b]
1975	368	100.0
1976	388	105.4
1977	372	101.1
1978	367	99.7
1979	370	100.5
1980	374	101.6
1981	378	102.7
1982	339	92.1
1983	315	85.6

[a] Average current earnings in K£ per employee, deflated by consumer price indices based on January–June 1975.

[b] 1975 = 100.

Sources: Government of Kenya, *Economic Survey, 1978* (p. 59, for 1975 and 1976), *1981* (p. 62, for 1977), *1982* (p. 50, for 1978 and 1979), and *1984* (p. 55, for 1980–3).

because of the sharp decline in the capital inflow from abroad), we impose the actual fall of real wages: 7.9 per cent in 1982 and 14.4 per cent in 1983.

All other assumptions are common to all runs. This applies, for example, to all world prices, other than those for coffee, tea, and oil. Two of these common assumptions deserve to be emphasized. First, in all runs all domestic food prices (both producer prices and consumer prices) increase over time in proportion to world prices. This implies that the coffee boom is a relative price change for farmers, giving them an incentive to shift resources from food crops to coffee and tea. It also implies, less obviously, that as prices of urban goods rise during the boom, product wages fall. Urban real wages are fixed in terms of a consumer price index in which food prices have a heavy weight. Hence, as the price of manufactured products rises, for example, the product wage in that sector falls, and this, of course, induces factor substitution. Secondly, the assumption on trade policy regarding non-food manufactured products is common to all runs. For these goods, the controlled level of imports of consumer goods and of capital goods is given as a percentage of domestic consumption and investment demand. When this constraint is effective, domestic prices must adjust to clear the market, as in the case of non-tradables. However, we allow for an endogenous change in regime. Trade is liberalized if domestic prices reach a predetermined ceiling. The protection afforded to domestic producers is then increased no further: the equivalent tariff rate[43] is kept constant, the market being cleared through imports over and above the controlled level. As a result of this assumption,

---

[43] The government receives tariffs on all imports at fixed rates. The tariff equivalent of quantitative restrictions accrues, however, to domestic producers, as rents.

the extent of trade liberalization differs between runs. After 1980, however, import controls are effective in all runs.

As may be seen from Table 5.17, our last run describes reality, in the sense that it incorporates the actual values for all variables which differ between runs. Starting from the hypothetical case of our counterfactual,[44] we introduce the shocks in sequence. In the next section we consider the coffee boom itself, in section 3.4 the changes in public expenditure, and, finally, in section 3.5 the oil shock.

3.3. *The Coffee Boom*

The coffee boom consisted of an enormous, but short-lived, rise in the world prices of coffee and (since consumers substituted tea for coffee) tea. In 1977 world prices were 3.3 and 1.8 times higher, respectively, than in our counterfactual (Table 5.19).

We begin by looking at the magnitude of the boom at the aggregate level. In the simple model of the previous section we suppressed all output responses because they were very difficult to incorporate within that framework. The CGE model gives us a means of introducing these effects and we pay particular attention to two of them. The first involves increased output of the coffee and tea sectors in response to the price rises. The second can be regarded as a multiplier process from the boom sector on to other sectors, with the extra employment in expanding modern sector activities reducing output in other sectors by much less than the modern sector wage. In both cases this is because the extra labour can come from reduced leisure (the welfare cost of which is not counted in GDP). Additionally, extra modern sector labour can be supplied from lower-earning labour in other sectors. In the CGE model these induced gains generate savings in just the same way as the direct terms of trade gain. In consequence we would expect the CGE model to estimate a larger real income gain from the coffee boom than the simple model and this is indeed the case. In the simple model the coffee boom raised real income by 5.5% during the boom period whereas in the CGE model it raises it by 10.1%.

An illustrative reconciliation of this difference is set out below:

	CGE model	Simple model
Terms of trade gain	5.2	5.2
Coffee and tea response	1.8	0.0
Multiplier process	2.4	0.0
Investment return	0.7	0.3
Total	10.1	5.5

[44] It should be noted that this counterfactual differs from that used in the previous section. There we had to assume that, in the absence of the boom, the economy would have remained on a trend path. The model allows us to construct a more sophisticated counterfactual, in which the various shocks are assumed away, but all other assumptions are maintained.

TABLE 5.19. *Coffee and tea prices* (indices, in domestic currency, 1975 = 100)

	Coffee prices				Tea prices			
	Producer		World		Producer		World	
	Run 1	Runs 2–4	Run 1	Runs 2–4	Run 1	Runs 2–4	Run 1	Runs 2–4
1975	100	100	100	100	100	100	100	100
1976	116	236	116	237	116	131	116	123
1977	127	372	127	416	127	266	127	234
1978	138	264	138	281	138	196	138	170
1979	153	265	153	275	153	168	153	154
1980	183	246	183	260	183	197	183	178
1981	211	211	244	244	219	219	186	186
1982	260	260	275	275	240	240	222	222
1983	326	326	340	340	270	270	284	284

Notes: Prices differ between runs only for the period 1976–80: actual prices are used for 1981–3 in all runs.

In terms of domestic currency, the index of non-oil-import prices (1975 = 100) stood at 116, 127, 138, 153, and 183 respectively in the years 1976–80; this series is used in runs 1 and 2, both for producer prices and for world prices.

The terms of trade gain, as previously calculated, was K£256 m at 1975 prices, or 5.2% of counterfactual GDP during the boom period.[45] In the CGE model the supply response during the boom period raises coffee and tea output by K£115 m at 1975 prices. Since the costs of this extra output were largely foregone leisure, most of the extra output was a net addition to GDP: perhaps of the order of K£90 m, or 1.8% of counterfactual GDP. The multiplier effects are somewhat larger, at 2.4%. Since these effects are working on both the direct terms of trade gain and the coffee and tea response, this implies a value of the multiplier of 0.34 (2.4/7.0). Such a value appears plausible, especially in view of the much higher value found in a similar context by Bell *et al.* (1982). In the pure coffee boom run of the CGE model the rate of return on investment turns out to be 16.3%, considerably higher than the 10% assumed in the simple model. This partly explains the difference in investment returns during the boom period, 0.7% as opposed to 0.3% of counterfactual GDP, the remainder reflecting higher savings arising from the induced output changes.

Similar arguments can be used in connection with the comparable differences between the models in their estimates of long run GDP. However, we do not attempt any reconciliation here since the long run can only be approximated in the simple model by a stationary permanent income calculation and it would not be appropriate to simulate the CGE model over the length of horizon required for a comparison.

[45] See Table 5.2.

Recall that the assumptions used for the first two runs differ only with regard to coffee and tea prices. The differences between these runs can therefore be considered as measures of the effects of the boom, in the special sense that, for the moment, we abstract from induced changes in, for example, public expenditures.

We begin by comparing the results for smallholders. They constitute the largest group of the poor in Kenya and are significant producers of coffee and tea (accounting, in 1975, for 48 per cent and 28 per cent respectively of total production), and they might therefore be expected to have benefited enormously from the Kenyan government's policy of passing the increase in world prices on to farmers. Peasant incomes increased by 20.8 per cent (Table 5.20) as a result of the boom: 16.7 per cent as a result of the price rise itself, the rest as a result of indirect effects. These indirect effects include: a substantial rise in coffee and tea production (more labour is allocated to these crops, partly at the expense of other crops, partly at the expense of leisure); increases in remittances received by peasants from urban households; and finally, a rise in income from non-farm enterprises and (both agricultural and non-agricultural) wage employment.

The most important thing to note about Table 5.20, however, is not the composition of the 21 per cent increase in peasant incomes, but the fact that it

TABLE 5.20. *Effects of the Coffee Boom on Peasants, 1977*

(Results of the boom run)

	Absolute value	As % of counterfactual result
Coffee		
Production	282.4[a]	125.6
Producer price	371.3[b]	292.8
Value of output	1,050.0[c]	367.6
Tea		
Production	98.9[a]	124.4
Producer price	266.0[b]	209.4
Value of output	263.2[c]	260.7
Value of production		
(all crops and livestock)	4,740.2[c]	117.7
Other income components	1,955.9[c]	128.8
Total income	6,696.1[c]	120.8
Consumer prices	208.0[d]	108.7
Real income	3,220.0[e]	111.2

[a] Mean value in shillings per household, in 1975 prices.
[b] Index, 1975 = 100.
[c] Mean value in shillings per household, in current prices.
[d] Index, 1974 = 100.
[e] Mean value in shillings per household, in 1974 prices.

is, to a considerable extent (more than 40 per cent), offset by adverse relative price changes. Rural consumer prices rise so much that the *real* income gain of peasants is reduced to 11.2 per cent.

Before we attempt to explain this result it should be stressed how surprising it is, given what we know about the composition of peasants' consumption expenditure. They have a high marginal propensity to consume food (0.7) and food commodities are modelled as tradables which are not subject to any quantitative restrictions. In the extreme case—if coffee and tea were only grown by peasants, if they had not adjusted their production, and if they had spent all of the additional income on food—very little would have changed outside the peasant sector, since domestic food prices are tied to world prices and the market is cleared through changes in imports. Food consumption and imports would both have increased by the amount of the terms-of-trade gain and the balance of trade would have been preserved without any other change in real variables. This mental experiment is not completely unrealistic: given the absence of quantitative restrictions on food imports, peasants' high marginal propensity to consume food does tend to isolate the rest of the economy to a considerable extent from changes in peasant incomes. But, of course, part of the extra income is saved, part of it is used to increase non-food consumption, all of the extra spending requires trade and transportation activities, coffee and tea are also produced on large farms, and, finally, input–output linkages and the government's spending of its extra tariff and tax revenue spread the effects to other sectors. This increased demand for urban commodities requires, in the case of non-tradables, increases in domestic production. But in the short run (with a given capital stock) supply elasticities are very low: the output increases are accompanied by substantially higher prices, as predicted by the theory. At the peak of the boom, in 1977, gross output prices for non-tradables are (in run 2) 50 per cent higher than in the counterfactual,[46] with particularly large price increases in trade and construction.

To what extent extra spending also increases demand for importables depends critically on trade policy. Since only non-food imports are subject to quantitative restrictions, food prices are unaffected by the boom: extra demand is not reflected in price rises but in extra food imports. But non-food imports are subject to restrictions, and hence, if controls are maintained, the relative price of non-food importables will rise as a result of the boom, just as for non-tradables. Kenya did, however, relax import controls, during the boom and, as noted before, trade liberalization is endogenous in the model.[47] Demand for imports in excess of the controlled level is choked off by price rises until a ceiling is reached and (extra) imports are allowed to clear the

[46] This is a relative price increase, since the price of non-oil imports is the same in the two runs.

[47] The details of changes in import quotas during the boom are discussed in Appendix 1 to this chapter. In the model we simplify enormously by aggregating over all the different quotas which were in force: we pretend that all controlled imports are covered by a single quota.

market. This specification has a powerful effect on the results. In 1978, for example, import controls are effective in the counterfactual run, but in the boom run the price ceiling[48] is reached and extra imports account for 43 per cent of total imports in that year. Clearly, if trade liberalization were not to go quite this far, then domestic prices of non-food manufactured consumer goods would be higher and the income gains of peasants would be further eroded.

In Table 5.20 we have aggregated over all peasant households. These results mask the differences between coffee and tea growers and other peasants. It is often argued that the boom benefited only the former group and therefore led to a large increase in rural inequality. Peasants who did not grow coffee or tea were, however, in several ways affected by the boom. First, there is a 'trickle-down' effect operating through the rural labour market: they benefit from coffee and tea growers' increased demand for hired labour. As Table 5.21 shows, total labour use on smallholdings increased by over 20 per cent on average and wages in the peasant sector in 1977 are 29 per cent higher than in the counterfactual. Since those peasants who did not benefit directly from the boom were, in aggregate, net suppliers of hired labour, they experienced a terms-of-trade gain, realizing a substantial increase in their wage incomes. Secondly, the spending of coffee and tea growers raises the income from non-farm enterprises accruing to other peasants. Thirdly, their

TABLE 5.21. *Interprovincial differences, 1977*

(Results of the boom run as % of the counterfactual)

Province	Total labour use on smallholdings	Wage rate on smallholdings	Real household income (peasants)
Central	125.8	151.5	119.3
Coast	97.6	111.8	103.6
Eastern	142.6	136.2	120.9
Nyanza	112.2	116.9	133.8
Rift valley	105.5	107.9	97.5
Western	100.8	109.9	100.7
TOTAL	120.4	128.6	111.2

[48] The ceiling price is defined in terms of the tariff equivalent of the controls: the maximum equivalent tariff rate is set equal to the rate in 1976 in the counterfactual run. Hence the government is modelled as being unwilling to let the boom lead to an increase in protection of domestic producers. If one were to relax this assumption, non-food importables would behave more like non-tradables and the model would then generate even higher estimates of the distributional effects of the boom. It is worth stressing that changes in trade policy affect imports in two ways. First, there is a composition effect: trade liberalization implies an increase of imports of manufactured consumer goods at the expense of imports not subject to QRs. Secondly, changes in QRs affect the volume of exports (and hence the volume of total imports) through induced relative price changes.

income from remittances increases with boom-induced urban income rises. Finally, there is a negative effect: all peasants are affected by the rise in rural consumer prices which is due to the boom. Table 5.21 shows that income gains are not restricted to peasants in Central and Eastern provinces, where coffee growing is concentrated. Peasants in Coast and Nyanza provinces also benefit. Only in Rift Valley and Western provinces is the change in income negligible or even negative. In these two provinces the first two effects are very weak and, since peasants in Rift and Western do not maintain strong urban ties (as those in e.g. Central Province do), the third effect, the one which operates through remittances from urban to rural households, is also weak. The rise in consumer prices therefore dominates the other three effects.

Rural inequality increases slightly: for example, the income share of the bottom 40 per cent of peasants falls from 31 per cent to 29 per cent. But the boom reduces absolute poverty: the number of peasant households below the poverty line used in the model falls by 11 per cent.

In Tables 5.20 and 5.21 we show the results of the model for only one year, 1977. After this peak year the differences between the two runs become progressively smaller, until at the very end of the simulation period (1983) the difference in real income is reduced to 3.1 per cent.

During the boom coffee growers invested quite heavily in land, coffee trees, livestock, housing, water supply, education, and financial assets. Using our survey data, we analyse the details of these decisions (and their consequences for peasants' permanent income) in *Peasants and Governments*. Here we treat peasants as if they invested only in coffee and in financial assets, our concern being the extent to which savings are eroded by price changes.[49]

Using the marginal savings rate of private agents out of the extra income generated by the boom of 0.6 as previously discussed, the model generates the savings amounts shown in the first column of Table 5.22: out of their transient income peasants save a total of K£128.3 million (excluding investment in coffee) in the period of the boom. Part of this (19 per cent) is withdrawn in the first four years after the boom, but peasants leave the bulk of their savings (K£103.9 million) deposited with the banking system after 1983. Much of this consists of claims on crop authorities and of demand deposits, so that the rate of return on these assets is close to zero: transaction costs (which, in the case of time deposits, are very high for peasants) and long delays in payments for crops effectively preclude investment in financial assets with a positive return. Hence the assets acquired during the boom do not add to peasants' permanent income.[50] Nevertheless, their income in 1983

---

[49] Note that, in any case, some of the investment which took place (but which we ignore in the model) transfers assets between farmers (this would be the case for investment in land or, to a lesser extent, in livestock) and, to that extent, does not affect the permanent income of smallholders as a group.

[50] Note that, in any case, the real rate of return on financial assets would have to be very high (8.7%) by Kenyan standards to give even a modest 1% increase in permanent income $(0.01(901.1)/103.9 = 0.087)$.

TABLE 5.22. *Private savings out of transient income* (K£ million at current prices)

	Peasant households	Urban households
1976	17.0	48.0
1977	54.1	215.4
1978	33.3	135.7
1979	24.0	81.1
TOTAL	128.3	480.2
Savings left deposited after 1983	103.9	480.2
Consumption loans taken out in the boom period	—	91.2
Household incomes in 1983	901.1	1,207.5

is 3 per cent higher in the boom run than in the counterfactual (Table 5.23). This may seem modest, but even if peasants had invested 100 per cent of the extra income in the boom period in (real or financial) assets yielding 12 per cent per annum, they would not have realized a permanent income increase of 3 per cent.

Hence, what the simulation experiments demonstrate is that the indirect effects of a commodity boom can be very strong. There are two such effects. First, peasants benefit (in the form of remittances and higher incomes from non-agricultural activities) from boom-induced urban growth (which is, it should be noted, partly financed out of peasants' savings). This accounts for about half of the 3 per cent permanent income gain. The other half is due to relative price changes, which now favour peasants: the adverse short-run effect which we discussed earlier is reversed in the long run. This is because in

TABLE 5.23. *Impact and long-run effects of the boom on peasants*

(Results of the boom run as % of the counterfactual)

	1977	1983
Coffee production[a]	125.6	105.3
Producer price	292.8	100.0
Value of coffee output[a]	367.6	105.2
Value of production (all crops plus livestock)[a]	117.7	100.2
Other income components[a]	128.8	107.3
Total income[a]	120.8	101.4
Real income[b]	111.2	103.1
Consumer prices	108.7	98.4
Formal wages	119.9	94.1
Informal wages	128.6	101.6

[a] Mean value per household.
[b] Deflated by consumer prices.

the post-boom period domestic demand drops but the supply curves of urban goods have shifted to the right as a result of investment. Table 5.23 indicates the importance of the resulting differences between the two runs in relative prices: they account for a 1.6 per cent increase of the real income of peasants, more than half of their total income gain in the final year.

For urban households the real income gain is about 15 per cent increase in the short run and 8 per cent in the long run (Table 5.24). Since urban incomes are much higher than those of peasants, these figures imply a massive redistribution of income from rural to urban groups. Measured in current prices, total transient household income (the difference between runs 2 and 1 in incomes of rural and urban households in the boom period, 1976–9) amounts to K£1019.3 million, and of this total K£804.4 (more than three-quarters) accrues to urban households. Hence, in spite of the decision of the Kenyan government to pass the coffee prices intact on to farmers the bulk of the income gain does not accrue to them. More than 75 per cent of the boom income eventually ends up in the hands of urban households, a group which forms a small proportion of the population.

There are two reasons for this surprising result, a static and a dynamic one. In a static model, the boom would have the familiar Dutch Disease effects of increases in the relative price of importables (to the extent that they are not subject to import controls) and of non-tradables. Peasants do not produce these commodities and hence the benefits of these price changes accrue (as higher wage and profit income) entirely to other groups. Secondly, the boom leads to a very large increase in the level of investment: gross fixed capital formation is (in constant prices) in the boom period 48 per cent higher than in the counterfactual case. In Kenya the allocation of investment was already strongly biased towards the urban sector before the boom and, as we saw in section 2, this bias increased during the boom. Hence the benefits of the boom

TABLE 5.24. *Urban incomes, employment, and prices*

(Results of the boom run as % of the counterfactual)

	1977	1983
Employment: labour force members who are:		
wage-employed	119.0	107.6
self-employed in the informal sector	87.5	101.1
unemployed	79.7	76.7
Household incomes (in current prices)	136.0	103.5
Real incomes (in 1974 prices) of:		∗
wage earners	100.0	100.0
self-employed in the informal sector	119.7	116.8
all urban households	114.9	107.8
Consumer prices	118.3	96.0

ended up largely in urban hands, in part because of the relative price changes discussed before, but also because of the way in which investment was allocated. Table 5.24 shows that even in 1977 urban groups benefited more from the boom than peasants. Urban household incomes in that year are in the boom run 36 per cent higher than in the counterfactual case, as opposed to the 21 per cent income gain for peasants. Urban consumer prices in that year are 18.3 per cent higher than in the counterfactual,[51] so that price changes offset about half of the income gain, leaving a real income gain of 14.9 per cent.

Since wage employees form about three-quarters of the urban labour force, this income gain is largely explained by the increase (19 per cent in 1977) in formal sector wage employment.[52] As discussed previously, the spending of the proceeds of the boom (whether on consumption or on investment) requires increased output from the urban sector.[53] Since the capital stock is given in the short run, this requires increased employment: unemployed and self-employed are drawn into formal sector wage employment. This process is reflected in income changes: as fewer people are left to compete in the informal sector, incomes there rise considerably, by 20 per cent in real terms. Hence urban inequality is reduced: first, because more people gain access to (high-income) wage employment and, secondly, because the lowest incomes (those in the informal sector) rise.

The investment boom leaves the urban economy with a larger capital stock at the end of the simulation period. In addition, while in the short run product wages fall so that labour is substituted for capital, in the long run prices differ but little between runs, so that the labour intensity of the urban sectors falls back to what it would have been in the absence of the boom. The result is a permanent increase (of 7.6 per cent) in formal sector wage employment. Mainly because of this, the income of urban households in 1983 is, in the boom run, still about 8 per cent higher in real terms than in the counterfactual. Hence, in the long run too, urban households gain much more from the boom than peasants.[54]

Finally we consider the boom's effect on National Accounts variables (Table 5.25). Note that the boom increases GDP at factor cost by 4.4 per cent

[51] Recall from Table 5.23 that rural consumer prices are 8.7% higher. The main reason for the difference is that food prices are the same in the two runs and peasants consume relatively more food than urban households.

[52] Note that, since real wages are the same in the two runs, the increase in wage income is entirely a quantity change.

[53] An increase in output may seem inconsistent with profit maximization, since the capital stock is given in the short run and real wages are constant. The paradox is easily resolved. The real wage is defined in terms of urban consumer prices, which (since food prices are unaffected by the boom) rise much less than the output prices of the urban sectors. Hence product wages fall and this induces profit-maximizing firms to increase employment and hence output.

[54] Recall that for peasants the real income gain in 1983 was 3.1% (Table 5.23). Since the growth of formal wage employment attracts rural-to-urban migrants, the beneficiaries are not just the existing urban households but also the migrants. However, migration is very small relative to the urban labour force.

TABLE 5.25. *National Accounts (1972 prices)*

(Results of the boom run as % of the counterfactual)

	1977	1983
GDP at factor cost	104.4	106.8
Of which:		
agriculture	102.8	100.3
industry	92.4	115.7
other	108.0	107.2
GDP at market prices	105.4	106.6
Private consumption	100.5	104.3
Public consumption	105.4	106.6
Investment	178.1	113.4
Exports	105.3	107.9
Imports	137.4	106.8
Domestic savings	124.4	114.7

in the short run and by almost 7 per cent in the long run.[55] Output growth is increasingly concentrated in the industrial sector, largely because of the way investment is allocated. The second part of the table illustrates the investment boom to which we have traced many of the income effects of the terms of trade gain. At its peak in 1977 investment is 78 per cent higher than in the counterfactual case. At the end of the period investment is still 13 per cent higher, partly as a result of multiplier effects, partly because the boom redistributes income to urban groups, which save a much larger fraction out of non-boom income than rural groups.

In Table 5.26 we present the model's analogue of the price and quantity changes discussed in section 2. In the early years of the boom food production is adversely affected by the boom, which leads to a huge increase in food imports in 1977. By 1978, however, production of all four groups of commodities is higher in the boom run, the difference being largest for non-food importables, closely followed by non-tradables. These two sectors benefit most from the increase in investment demand. Investment demand is also reflected in the relative price changes. For non-tradables, prices increase by over 20 per cent in 1978 as a result of the boom. For non-food importables the price rise is much less pronounced (7 per cent), since in this case much of the investment demand is met through imports of capital goods. As we stressed before, these relative price changes are reversed in the long run: heavy investment in manufacturing (largely non-food importables) and in services (i.e. non-tradables) in the boom run is reflected in their prices, which are, in 1983, 10 and 6 per cent lower respectively than in the counterfactual. This, again, is the reason why relative price changes (which offset much of the

[55] Use of resources (C + G + I) increases by much more: since GDP is measured in constant relative prices it does not capture the terms-of-trade gain.

TABLE 5.26.   *Effects of the boom on prices and quantities of domestically produced*
commodities

(Results of the boom run as % of the counterfactual)

Commodities[a]	Quantities		Prices	
	1978	1983	1978	1983
A. Exportables	111	102	144	100
B. Importables: food	104[b]	114	100[c]	100[c]
C. Importables: non-food	114	113	107[d]	90
D. Non-tradables	112	108	121	94

[a] Cf. Table 5A2.1. Groups A–D cover commodities 1–18; they exclude the production of the informal sector.

[b] For the beginning of the boom we find a negative effect: for 1976 and 1977 the results are 97 and 93 respectively.

[c] Domestic food prices are tied to world prices and are therefore identical in the two runs.

[d] Trade liberalization prevents a further increase: in the boom run the price of non-food importables reaches the price ceiling.

gains of peasants in the short run) benefit farmers long after the boom has passed.

Now we summarize our main conclusions from these two runs.[56]

(i) *Relative prices.* First, the boom led to large changes in relative prices. In Kenya the 'normal', boom-induced rise in the price of non-tradables was accompanied by price rises for tradables because of the import controls policy.

(ii) *Asset acquisition.* Secondly, the boom led to a very large increase in savings. This would be true for any economy which experienced a large terms-of-trade gain as long as the government kept public consumption under control (investing most of its additional revenue) and private agents saved most of their extra income (considering it as transient). But in Kenya there were special factors. Private agents did not have the opportunity of accumulating foreign assets and hence had to acquire domestic assets more quickly than would otherwise have been the case. In addition the boom led to

[56] It should be emphasized that our conclusions are based entirely on a comparison of two simulation experiments. To avoid cumbersome formulations, we have used shorthand expressions such as 'the boom led to an increase in investment'. This simply means that investment is higher in the 'boom run' that in the 'counterfactual run' (for which the assumptions are identical except that the rise in coffee and tea prices is assumed away). Also, at this stage we are concerned only with the effects of the boom itself, narrowly interpreted as the rise in coffee and tea prices. In the following subsections we shall consider other changes, including some (e.g. the rise in public expenditure) which might well be considered as having been caused by the boom. Hence our 'boom run' is not designed to show what actually happened, and, secondly, phrases such as 'farmers gained as a result of the boom' should be understood as applying to the direct effects of the boom only. At the end of this section (in Table 5.32) we decompose changes in the key variables over the period 1975–83 into changes due to three different shocks, including the coffee boom (narrowly defined).

transfers of income (from rural to urban groups, and between urban groups, from those without to those with access to rents), which increased savings because the beneficiaries tended to be richer groups which saved a larger fraction of their non-transient income. The rise in savings was not fully reflected in growth of the domestic capital stock: the boom pushed up the relative price of capital goods and this eroded the long-run effect of the rise in savings. Finally, the investment boom itself led to new changes in relative prices, making non-tradable and manufactured goods relatively cheaper in the long run.

(iii) *Distributional effects.* One of the model's most interesting results is that the boom had very strong distributional effects. In fact our general equilibrium analysis suggests an unorthodox interpretation of the effects of a commodity boom in an economy such as the Kenyan one. Conventional wisdom would imply that most of the benefits would accrue to coffee growers, since the Kenyan government chose to pass the rise in world prices on to farmers. However, the direct effect is likely to be offset to a considerable extent by the relative price changes and the rise in investment which accompany a commodity boom. This is true *a fortiori* in the Kenyan case because of import controls and because of the way investment was allocated. As a result we find that most of the gains end up in urban rather than in rural hands.

(iv) *Timing.* Finally, our results indicate that short-run and long-run effects of a boom can be very different. Indeed, the very distortions which diminish the income gains of peasants in the short run account for reversals in relative price changes in the long run, which significantly increase their permanent income.

3.4. *The Time Path of Public Expenditures*

In our third simulation experiment we take into account that the boom induced changes in public expenditures and in external borrowing. First, while in the first two runs the share of public consumption in GDP was assumed to remain constant, we now impose the actual values for public consumption. Similarly, while we assumed that external borrowing (more precisely: the value of the resource deficit, i.e. net factor service income, capital imports, and use of reserves) would grow at a constant rate (in terms of constant world prices), we now impose the actual values. As may be seen from Table 5.27, the time path of the resource deficit in run 3 is dramatically different from the steady growth which we assumed for runs 1 and 2: external borrowing is negative in 1976 and 1977 (when there was a large build-up of reserves), reaches very high levels in 1978–81, and then falls back to a very low level: in 1983 the value of the resource deficit is only two-thirds of the value in 1975 (in current dollars). Since the total capital inflow is the same in the two cases ($2.5 billion), this amounts to inter-temporal shifts in external borrowing: the inflow is considerably higher (compared with runs 1 and 2) in 1978–81, at the expense of borrowing in the first two and the last two years of

TABLE 5.27. *Public consumption and external borrowing: differences between runs*

| | Public consumption (K£ million at 1972 prices) | | Net foreign capital inflow | | |
| | | | ($ million at current prices) | | (K£ million at 1972 prices) |
	Coffee and public expenditure boom (run 3)[a]	Effect of public expenditure boom (increase over run 2)[b]	No boom and pure coffee boom (runs 1, 2)[c]	Coffee boom and public expenditure boom (run 3)[d]	Effect of public expenditure boom (increase over runs 1,2)[e]
1976	154.8	−7.8	166.3	−24.1	−30.8
1977	173.7	6.0	196.9	−151.3	−52.9
1978	199.3	18.9	244.9	516.6	35.0
1979	196.9	9.5	300.3	365.2	7.1
TOTAL	724.7	26.6	908.4	706.4	−41.6
1980	206.0	15.4	387.0	807.0	37.8
1981	202.9	8.7	400.6	601.3	18.5
1982	197.5	−1.2	401.0	290.1	−10.9
1983	206.0	−5.6	407.9	100.2	−31.7
TOTAL	812.4	17.3	1,596.5	1,798.6	−13.7
TOTAL 1976–83	1,537.1	43.9	2,505.0	2,505.0	−27.9

[a] Actual values.

[b] In runs 1 and 2 the share of public consumption in GDP is kept constant, hence the increase is the difference between the exogenous value in run 3 and the endogenous value in run 2.

[c] This series is obtained by letting the net foreign capital inflow grow, from a 1975 base of $152.8m. (the actual value), at a constant rate (6.94%) in terms of constant dollar prices for non-oil imports; this ensures that (in terms of current dollars) the total for the period 1976–83 is the same in all runs.

[d] Actual values.

[e] Difference between the two preceding columns, converted at current exchange rates and deflated by the import prices of run 2.

the period. Since import prices are not constant, these shifts of nominal amounts are not neutral in terms of the real value of the resource deficit: as the last column in Table 5.27 shows, the total, in terms of constant import prices, is reduced by K£28 million.

For the interpretation of the results of our third run it is important to realize how changes in public expenditures and external borrowing work in the model. First, public savings are calculated as the difference between government revenue (which is endogenously determined in the model) and public consumption (which is exogenous). Hence, the direct effect of an increase in public consumption is a reduction in public savings by the same amount. Total investment will then also fall by that amount. There are, of course, indirect effects: government revenue and private savings will be affected and to that extent the effect of an increase in public consumption can be very different from the initial, pound-for-pound reduction in investment. Secondly, in the model we are not concerned with the distinction between private and public investment. The flow of funds is very simplified: private, public, and foreign savings are added to arrive at the total amount of investment, a total which is then distributed over sectors, irrespective of the savings source. Thirdly, this implies that while in fact public consumption and public investment both rose, we need to consider only the former, for an increase in public expenditure can be financed in two ways. Either it implies a rise in public savings, hence (for given government revenue) an equivalent reduction in public consumption; or, it is financed through external borrowing. Since changes in public consumption and external borrowing are explicitly considered in run 3, we do not need to consider changes in public investment separately. Fourthly, if the government tried to affect the economy's growth by increasing public investment without changes in public consumption and external borrowing, it would have to increase its revenue and it would therefore partly crowd out private investment. However, it is reasonable to assume that the government attempted to prevent this crowding-out by financing the increase in public investment from foreign savings. This is why in this run we consider changes in public consumption and external borrowing simultaneously: to the extent that the increased borrowing does not simply reflect loss of control we consider it as a deliberate attempt to raise total investment in the boom period.

Before we consider the results of the model, it is useful to get a rough idea of the magnitude of the shock introduced in run 3. We subtract the increase in public consumption (given in the second column of Table 5.27) from the increase in external borrowing (in the last column). For 1978, for example, this gives $35.0 - 18.9 = K£16.1$ million. The rationale for this calculation is that *ceteris paribus* (i.e. abstracting from induced changes in government revenue and private savings), investment would fall by that amount, since total investment equals private savings plus government revenue minus public consumption plus external borrowing and other foreign savings.

Hence this calculation suggests that the changes in public expenditure and external borrowing would reduce total investment by K£68.2 million ($=41.6+26.6$) in the period of the boom (1976–9) and by K£71.8 million ($=27.9+43.9$) in the whole period 1976–83. Taking into account that in 1975 total investment was K£131 million (in 1972 prices), it is already clear that the changes in public expenditure must have had a substantial negative effect.

In the previous section we saw, however, that such calculations are likely to be misleading. The effect of the coffee boom on total use of resources was much larger than the terms-of-trade gain itself, as a consequence of the induced changes in relative prices, in production, in private savings, and in trade policy. Since the terms-of-trade gain in 1976–9 (K£127.3 million) is to a large extent (K£68.2 million) offset by the public expenditure changes, we would expect about 55 per cent of the effect of the boom to be wiped out. Table 5.28 shows that the offsetting effect is in fact even stronger: of the increase in investment in the boom period only 30 per cent remains and in 1979 only a third of the GDP gain remains.[57] Indirect effects are so strong for three reasons. First, since private agents save almost 60 per cent out of transient income, there is, in the coffee boom run, a strong multiplier effect: investment creates rents, which are largely saved, thereby further adding to investment. That process is now reversed. Secondly, the timing of public expenditure changes is unfortunate. Investment is shifted (compared with the boom run), partly to 1978, but largely to the first two years after the boom, 1980 and 1981, when external borrowing *doubles*. The investment boom is thereby shifted to periods when multiplier effects are weakest. A rise in rent

TABLE 5.28. *The effects of the pure coffee boom and of changes in public expenditure compared*

(Results of runs 2 and 3 as % of run 1)

	Pure coffee boom	Coffee and public expenditure booms
GDP 1979[a]	108.2	102.8
Investment 1976–9[b]	147.9	114.3
Urban incomes 1979[c]	106.8	104.7
Rural incomes 1979[d]	110.5	105.7
GDP 1983[a]	106.6	100.5
Investment 1980–3[b]	114.7	109.4
Urban incomes 1983[c]	107.8	91.8
Rural incomes 1983[d]	103.1	101.0

[a] GDP at 1972 market prices.
[b] Total investment in the four-year period, at 1972 prices.
[c] Mean urban household income, at 1974 prices.
[d] Mean rural household income, at 1975 prices.

[57] $14.3/47.9=0.299$ and $2.8/8.2=0.341$.

income in 1978 is checked by trade liberalization: as a result there is a temporary surge in imports of consumer goods rather than in private savings. In the post-boom years multiplier effects are also weak, but for a different reason. We assume that after the boom all rural and urban households consider their incomes as permanent, saving at 'normal' (pre-boom) rates. Hence, to the extent that the government's reactions to the boom shift the rise in investment beyond the boom period, multiplier effects are weaker.

This brings out the importance of private agents' expectations. It seems reasonable to assume, as we have done, that private agents consider their income gains in the boom period as transient. They therefore save a large part of these gains. However, it does not seem sensible to extend this assumption to the post-boom period. We would then be saying that private agents realized that their incomes in that period were inflated by the government's borrowing abroad at a level which could not be maintained permanently. This would seem to push the idea of rational expectations too far. It seems more realistic to assume, as in fact we have done, that private agents considered their incomes as permanent once the boom was over. What matters in the present context is only that savings rates fall as a result, so that multiplier effects become weaker than in the boom period. But our argument about changes in expectations has a wider implication: it means that the effects of government policies in response to a boom depend critically on whether the induced income changes are perceived as transient or permanent by private agents. In this case the effectiveness of a policy is reduced because it shifts income gains to a period in which private agents are unlikely to recognize them as transient.

Thirdly, the smoother the time path of investment, the less its real value is eroded by relative price changes. As we saw in the previous section the investment boom is associated with sharp increases in the relative price of capital goods. In the present run, where the public expenditure changes make investment still more unstable, this is true *a fortiori*. This is illustrated in Table 5.29: in the period 1978–81, capital goods prices are much higher than in the coffee boom run.

It might be thought that the public expenditure changes would have little effect in the post-boom period. After all, they amount (for the period 1980–3)

TABLE 5.29. *The effects of the public expenditure boom on capital goods prices, 1976–1983*

(Prices in run 3 as % of run 2)

1976	83.6	1980	153.5
1977	70.0	1981	121.9
1978	113.0	1982	98.8
1979	118.7	1983	90.7

to a decrease in savings of only K£3.6 million.[58] The bottom half of Table 5.28 shows that this is not the case. The first reason for this is that the difference between runs in investment in the boom period continues to exert its influence: in run 3 the post-boom period starts with a much lower capital stock than in run 2. Secondly, and more importantly, the need to repay the earlier borrowing implies a very sharp contraction of the foreign capital inflow at the end of the period. In 1983 the resource deficit amounts (in run 3) to only $100 million, two-thirds (as we noted before) of what it was in 1975 and only one-quarter of its 1983 value in the coffee boom run. Hence, the productivity of capital falls as demand growth stagnates at the end of the period.

In 1983 urban households are most seriously affected. They benefit from lower prices but they lose much more from a fall in wages and in formal sector employment. The net result is that, while in the short run (in 1977) the public expenditure changes reduce their real income gain from the boom to about 70 per cent of what it would have been otherwise, in the long run not only is their gain eliminated, but they actually end up with substantially lower real income (8 per cent) than in the absence of the boom. For rural incomes the change is less dramatic but still very strong: the real income gain in 1979 is reduced from 10.5 per cent to 5.7 per cent and in 1983 from 3 per cent to 1 per cent.[59]

It will be clear that these effects are exaggerated, since public consumption is essentially modelled as waste. For example, if the increase in public expenditure is used for road repair, the effect of this on production is ignored in the model. But the purpose of the simulation experiment is not to estimate all the microeconomic repercussions of public expenditures. What we want to emphasize is the importance of the phasing of public expenditure. In a controlled economy such as the Kenyan one, where rents are an important source of savings and where trade controls make relative prices very sensitive to changes in investment, concentrating investment in a short period erodes its real value dramatically. While the coffee boom itself had this effect and the government's reaction might have been aimed at preventing this, the results suggest that the cure was worse than the disease. Rather than smoothing the process of acquisition of real assets, the sharp changes in public expenditure destabilized the investment path. As a result, much of the long-run gain which might have been realized from the coffee boom was lost.

3.5. The Second Oil Shock

Whereas in the first three runs we abstracted from the second oil price increase (assuming that in the period 1980–3 oil prices would rise at the same rate as prices of non-oil imports), we now introduce this final shock, using actual oil prices not just for 1975–9 but also for 1980–3. This implies that in

[58] Namely, the increase in external borrowing of 13.7 minus the increase in public consumption of 17.3 (Table 5.25).

[59] Note from Table 5.28 that in 1983 urban real incomes in run 3 are only 91.8 per cent of what they are in run 1.

each of those last four years oil prices are, on average, 66 per cent higher than in the three runs we have considered so far. The last column of Table 5.30 shows the ratio of oil prices in run 4 and in the first three runs. For 1980–3 this ratio is 1.42, 1.74. 1.82, and 1.62 respectively. The average ratio is 1.66.

If we deflate the published data on the value of oil imports and exports in 1980 by the price index in the second column of Table 5.30, we obtain an estimate of net oil imports in that year of K£73.8 million in 1976 prices. On this basis the terms-of-trade loss may be estimated as equivalent to about 3 per cent of GDP.[60] For comparison, if we calculate the effect of the rise of coffee and tea prices in 1976–7 in the same way we find an average annual terms-of-trade gain in that period equivalent to 4.6 per cent of GDP. Hence the oil price increase is a very large shock indeed: even if we take into account that Kenya's net oil imports are only about half of its gross imports, the terms-of-trade loss is equal to two-thirds of the gain of the coffee boom.

This is reflected in the model's results. The oil shock lowers total consumption and investment initially in 1979, by about 3.5 per cent, but multiplier effects are, again, strong and in the final year the difference has become 8 per cent.[61]

TABLE 5.30. *Oil prices, 1975–1983* (index of c.i.f. oil import prices, in Kenyan currency, 1976 = 100)

	Runs 1–3[a]	Run 4[b]	Ratio
1975	85	85	1.00
1976	100	100	1.00
1977	108	108	1.00
1978	106	106	1.00
1979	130	130	1.00
1980	155	220	1.42
1981	183	319	1.74
1982	207	376	1.82
1983	240	393	1.64

[a] Actual values are used for 1975–9; thereafter the index is assumed to grow at the same rate as the price index of non-oil imports.

[b] Actual values for all years, from Government of Kenya, *Statistical Abstract, 1984*, p. 78.

[60] The *Statistical Abstract, 1984* gives the value of oil imports ('mineral fuels, lubricants and related minerals') as K£325.1m. (p. 67) and the value of oil exports ('petroleum products' and 'petroleum by-products') as K£162.7m. (p. 55). Using the price index of 220 this gives net oil imports as $(325.1-162.7)/2.2 = K£73.8m.$ (in 1976 prices). GDP at factor cost (in 1976 prices) was K£1,590.7m. (p. 34). Using the average price increase we estimate the annual terms-of-trade loss in the period 1980–3 as $(0.66) (73.8)/(1590.7) = 0.031.$

[61] The model may overestimate the impact of the price increase because it does not allow for substitution: oil imports are treated as complementary intermediate inputs. The published data, however, suggest significant substitution: the volume of oil imports falls by 25% between 1979 and 1983, while both industrial and total GDP increase by 17%.

Investment falls sharply and output of the non-agricultural sectors now stagnates at the end of the period. Value added in manufacturing is in 1983, for example, 9 per cent lower than in the third run and in services the difference is 6 per cent. As one would expect, urban households suffer most from the oil shock: their real incomes are reduced by 9 per cent, mainly as a result of a fall in formal sector wage employment (Table 5.31).

3.6. *Three Runs Compared*

Since our last run incorporates all shocks it can in principle (unlike e.g. the coffee boom run) be compared with actual data. Unfortunately this is less straightforward than it seems. For example, National Accounts data for the early years of the simulation period are in 1972 prices. The model is based on those data but the 1972 series has been replaced by a series in 1976 prices. Most seriously, the published data are frequently revised and the revisions are often so large that it is not at all clear what a comparison with 'actuals' would mean.[62] Nevertheless, it is important to have some indication of how well the model tracks. We consider two indicators central to the coffee boom.

First, according to the model (in run 4) coffee production increased between 1975 and 1983 by 55 per cent. According to the *Statistical Abstract* actual growth was 45 per cent, so that the model's result is within 7 per cent of the actual. Secondly, we consider gross fixed capital formation. Total investment (in 1972 prices) in the period 1976–83 was K£1,317 million.[63] The model's result is K£1,124 million (14.7 per cent too low). Considering the

TABLE 5.31.   *Long-run effects of the oil shock*

(Results of run 4 in 1983 as % of run 3)

GDP at factor cost (1972 prices)	95
Of which:	
agriculture	100
industry	91
services	94
Investment	76
Private consumption	93
Formal sector employment	90
Real urban household incomes	91
Price of non-food importables	115
Price of non-tradables	97
Real peasant incomes	98

[62] For example, if we compare the National Accounts data for 1975 in the *Statistical Abstracts* of 1977 and 1979 we find that GDP at factor cost was increased by 24%, private consumption by 28% and exports by 21%.

[63] This number is obtained by multiplying the investment data in 1976 prices by the ratio of 131.4 and 290.4 (1976 investment in 1972 and 1976 prices).

TABLE 5.32. *Three shocks compared*

(Results of runs 2–4 as % of the counterfactual)

	Coffee boom	Public expenditure	Oil shock
Quantities (1983)			
Exportables	102.4	107.0	107.2
Importables (food)	113.8	108.7	103.0
Importables (non-food)	113.1	102.6	93.0
Non-tradables	108.1	99.9	92.5
Value added in agriculture	100.3	102.7	102.7
Value added in industry	115.7	105.1	95.6
Value added in services	107.2	99.7	93.9
Total value added	106.8	101.3	96.4
Prices (1983)			
Prices of exportables	100.0	100.0	100.0
Prices of importables (food)	100.0	100.0	100.0
Prices of importables (non-food)	90.5	83.8	96.7
Prices of non-tradables	93.9	76.4	76.2
Rural consumer prices	98.4	96.6	98.1
Urban consumer prices	96.0	85.5	83.0
Real mean household income (1983)			
Peasant households	103.1	101.0	98.5
Urban households	107.8	91.8	83.8
Asset accumulation (1976–83)			
Total investment	129.9	111.7	101.5

length of the simulation period and the fact that (as we have seen) investment is an extremely sensitive variable in the model, this is very encouraging.

Our results are summarized in Table 5.32, where the three shocks are compared. At the end of section 3.3 we emphasized that the long-run effects of the coffee boom itself consist mainly of a substantial addition to the urban capital stock. Output increases substantially in industry and services, but very little in agriculture. Partly because of unfavourable relative price changes and partly because of the restricted choice of assets available to them, incomes of peasants increase in the long run by 3 per cent, while urban groups gain much more.

The government's reaction to the boom led to large increases in public expenditure and in external borrowing. This may be seen partly as a loss of control, partly as an attempt to increase the long-run benefits of the boom by stabilizing the process whereby the terms-of-trade gain was converted into domestic real assets. As such it failed, since, if we impose the actual time path of public expenditure in the model, most of the economy's long-run gains

from the boom are eliminated. There are two reasons for this. First, as we
have seen, the timing of investment is very important, since the real value of
an investment boom is eroded by relative price changes if it takes place in a
very short period. In this respect the government's reaction to the coffee
boom actually made matters worse, since it made the time path of investment
even less stable than it otherwise would have been. Secondly, the external
debt accumulated in the years following the boom had to be repaid later. As a
result investment fell sharply in the early 1980s and the consequent stagnation very much reduced the long-run benefits derived from the capital stock
built up during the period 1976–80. Finally, this recessionary effect was
reinforced by an event beyond the government's control: the second oil price
increase.

Two points emerge very clearly from Table 5.32. First, that in the period
1975–83 the Kenyan economy was subjected to two shocks other than the
coffee boom itself, the magnitude of which was comparable to that of the
boom. The second shock, for example, which we have modelled as changes in
public expenditures and external borrowing, was sufficiently large to reduce
the long-run GDP increase from 6.8 per cent (the effect of the boom itself) to
only 1.3 per cent. Secondly, while the coffee boom benefited (as we have
stressed) urban groups to a surprising extent, urban households lost much
more as a result of the other two shocks than farmers did: the boom
redistributed income from rural to urban groups, but the other two shocks
reversed that process.

4. Counterfactual Policies: Stabilizing Taxation and the Dismantling of Controls

In section 3 we described our general equilibrium model and used it to
estimate effects of the coffee boom itself, of the related second shock (the
increase in public expenditure and foreign borrowing triggered by the boom),
and, finally, of the 1979/80 oil shock. In this section we use the model for
eleven counterfactual experiments. In the following subsections we consider,
first, taxation and stabilization measures (runs 5–9), then trade policy (runs
10–13), next financial liberalization (run 14), and finally a policy package
(run 15).

4.1. *Taxation and Stabilization*

We begin by considering the most obvious counterfactual policy question:
what would have happened if Kenya had reacted to the boom as Tanzania
did, by imposing an export tax on coffee?

In Tanzania coffee was in the period 1977–80 taxed at a rate of, on average,
29 per cent. In three of our simulation experiments (runs 5, 6, and 7) we

TABLE 5.33. *Taxation and stabilization policies: design of the simulation experiments*

Run	Comparison run	Coffee tax	Income tax	Public consumption	Public investment	External borrowing
5	2	A	C	E	H	J
6	3	A	C	F	H	K
7	3	A	C	G	H	L
8	3	B	D	F	H	M
9	3	B	C	F	I	N

Key

A: Coffee production is taxed in 1977–80 at the average rate of the Tanzanian coffee tax in that period (29%).

B: No coffee tax imposed: coffee producer price proportional to world price throughout the period 1975–83 (as in runs 2–4 of section 3).

C: Income tax rates unchanged (as in the runs of section 3).

D: Surcharge of 5% on urban incomes imposed in 1978 and maintained thereafter.

E: The share of public consumption in GDP remains constant (as in runs 1 and 2 of section 3).

F: Actual values are imposed for public consumption, implying an increase in its share in GDP (as in runs 3 and 4).

G: Coffee tax revenues add to public consumption with an elasticity of 1.35 (over and above the actual levels of case F).

H: For given values of external borrowing and public consumption, the difference between government revenue and public consumption adds to domestic investment (as in runs 1–4 of section 3).

I: The budget is used in 1976–80 to stabilize investment at a trend growth rate of 5% in real terms, the government increasing or decreasing its holding of foreign assets if total investment would otherwise deviate too much from this trend.

J: External borrowing (the value of the resource deficit in dollars) is equal to its trend value (the steady growth paths assumed for runs 1 and 2; cf. Table 5.27) minus the proceeds of the coffee tax (in 1977–80), which are assumed to be entirely invested abroad. In 1981–3 the foreign assets thus accumulated are repatriated: in 1981 a third of the amount then outstanding (including interest earned), in 1982 a half of the balance, and in 1983 the remainder.

K: External borrowing is equal to its actual value (as in runs 3 and 4; cf. Table 5.27) minus the excess (if any) of the coffee tax proceeds over the increase in public consumption (the difference between cases E and F). In 1981–3 foreign assets are used as in case J.

L: External borrowing is equal to its actual value (as in runs 3 and 4 of section 3): there is no foreign asset accumulation.

M: External borrowing is equal to its actual value (as in runs 3 and 4; cf. Table 5.27) minus the proceeds of the income tax surcharge. Those proceeds are invested entirely abroad (in 1978–80) and are used in 1981–3 as in case J.

N: The changes in public investment defined under I are invested abroad in 1976–80. Thereafter foreign assets are used as in case J.

impose this tax rate for Kenya.[64] The three runs differ in what use we assume the government would have made of the revenues generated by the coffee tax.

In the first case (run 5) we portray a 'super-virtuous' government: external borrowing follows a trend path, public consumption remains constant as a

[64] The design of the simulation experiments discussed in this section is summarized in Table 5.33.

share of GDP,[65] and the proceeds of the coffee tax are entirely invested abroad. Hence, in the period 1977–80 there is a build-up of foreign assets and these assets are used, we assume, in the remainder of the simulation period (1981–3). In run 5 the coffee tax generates $366 million in revenue. Hence the foreign capital inflow is reduced by this amount in 1977–80 and increased by this amount, plus the accrued interest, in the period 1981–3.[66] This inter-temporal transfer is equivalent to 15 per cent of the value of the total foreign capital inflow in 1976–83.

The results are shown in Table 5.35. In the short run (1977) the adverse effect for peasants is fairly small: the policy reduces their real incomes by only 4.4 per cent. The difference is small for two reasons. First, as we noted before, coffee accounts for only a small part of the income of peasants; while their coffee income falls by a third, their total income is reduced by only 6.7 per cent. Secondly, as we have now come to expect, about one-third of the fall is offset by relative price changes which, this time, favour peasants: the increase in domestic demand is reduced by the coffee tax and, as a result, prices rise less than in the boom run of section 3.

TABLE 5.34. *Interest and exchange rates*
applicable to foreign assets, 1975–1983

	Interest rate[a]	Exchange rates[b]	
		sh./$	$/£
1975	(11.20)	7.34	2.22
1976	(12.23)	8.37	1.81
1977	(8.45)	8.28	1.75
1978	11.23	7.73	1.72
1979	13.55	7.48	2.12
1980	15.77	7.42	2.33
1981	14.28	9.05	2.03
1982	12.60	10.92	1.75
1983	10.26	13.31	1.52

[a] London Interbank Rates on six-month sterling deposits are used as interest rate for 1978–83. For that period that series is on average 10% higher than the UK Treasury Bill Rate; LIBOR series is extended backwards by increasing the Treasury Bill Rate by 10%.
[b] Averages for the year.

[65] Hence public expenditure remains under control in the same sense as in run 2 of section 3. Recall that if we impose the actual values for public consumption and external borrowing (as in run 3) the gains from the boom are largely eliminated.

[66] Since interest rates are high in the earlier period (Table 5.34), the amount of extra capital available in 1983 ($524m.) is (in terms of dollars) substantially higher than the amount invested, in spite of an unfavourable exchange rate movement.

TABLE 5.35.   *Coffee tax and foreign asset accumulation: I*

(Results of run 5 as % of run 2)

	1977	1983
Coffee: producer price[a]	71.0	100.0
Coffee: production[b]	92.6	98.2
Peasant incomes[c]	93.3	100.3
Rural consumer prices[d]	97.4	101.3
Real peasant incomes[e]	95.6	99.6
Urban wage employment	94.9	102.3
Urban household incomes[c]	91.0	107.0
Urban consumer prices[f]	95.2	105.1
Real urban incomes[g]	95.6	101.8
GDP (factor cost)[b]		100.4
GDP (market prices)[b]		100.6
Private consumption[b]		101.9
Public consumption[b]		100.8
Investment[b]		108.9
Exports[b]		97.5
Imports[b]		105.3

	1976–9	1980–3
Total investment[b]	88.9	103.9

	1977–80
Foreign asset acquisition[h]	$366m.

[a] The coffee tax is reflected in the producer price being 29% lower in 1977; since the tax is imposed only in 1977–80, there is no difference in the producer price for 1983.

[b] In 1972 prices.

[c] In current prices.

[d] 1974-based.

[e] In 1974 prices.

[f] 1975-based.

[g] In 1975 prices.

[h] In millions of dollars, current prices (absolute value: in the comparison run there is no foreign asset acquisition).

The investment boom which transferred so much of the gains of the coffee boom to the urban population in run 2 is now much less pronounced. In 1977, for example, investment is 13 per cent lower in real terms (compared to run 2). This is reflected in lower urban employment and incomes. The results for 1983 in Table 5.35 show that at the end of the simulation period there is little difference between the two runs, in spite of the fact that we have reallocated savings from high-yield domestic capital formation to low-yield foreign asset acquisition.[67] This is remarkable, because in run 5 less is invested. Investing the coffee tax proceeds abroad has the effect of reducing the rents which we identified in section 2 as an important source of domestic savings. The stabilization policy also has the effect of transferring income from the boom period (when households consider these income gains as transient and therefore have high marginal savings rates) to the post-boom period. For these two reasons, total investment in the 1976–83 period is reduced. The corollary, of course, is that since investment is stabilized the real value of savings is not eroded by relative price changes to the same extent as in run 2 and, in addition, that the policy transfers income to the end of the period so that savings are invested in sectors which then face a higher demand. Hence a lower amount of domestic savings leads to (practically) the same increase in output, because capital goods prices rise less in the boom period and because demand growth in the post-boom period permanently affects the efficiency of investment.[68]

Hence, what the experiment illustrates is that the adverse effects of the relative price changes induced by the investment boom are so strong that stabilizing the investment path through an export tax means no long-run loss of income, even if the proceeds are held in the form of foreign financial assets with a low yield (compared with domestic real assets). Note that in the long run the negative effect of the policy on peasants disappears: their real incomes in 1983 are virtually the same as in run 2 (Table 5.35). But for urban households there is a substantial real income gain. For them the long-run effect of the boom on their real incomes now is an increase of 9.6 instead of 7.7 per cent. Secondly, we may conclude that coffee growers are much less affected by a coffee tax than a partial equilibrium approach would suggest, since the tax reduces the boom-induced rise in consumer prices.

Whether a coffee tax really would have been so successful depends, of course, on how far the government would have deviated from the 'super-virtuous' ideal in its use of the proceeds. We consider, in runs 6 and 7, two alternatives to the assumption that the proceeds would have been used only for foreign asset acquisition. In run 6 we let public consumption increase to the levels it in fact reached (as in run 3 of section 3) but use the coffee tax proceeds when possible to finance this increase. The coffee tax revenues are invested abroad only to the extent that they exceed the value of the increase in public consumption. As it turns out, this happens only in 1977 (when coffee

---

[67] The data in Table 5.34 imply that sh.100 invested in sterling in 1977 would have grown to sh.140 in 1980 because of the shilling's depreciation in terms of sterling and to sh.289 if, in addition, we take the interest earned into account. If we deflate this by non-oil-import prices (which increased by 123% over the period 1977–83) the investment would have grown to only sh.130 (in terms of constant 1977 non-oil-import prices). Hence foreign assets have a positive real rate of return, but one which is low compared with that of domestic real assets.

[68] Measured in 1972 prices, the efficiency of investment increases by about 5%.

prices peak), and even then the amount invested abroad is very small—only $46 million. In 1978–80 the coffee tax does not yield enough to finance the increase in public expenditure and in 1981–3 (since so little was invested abroad in 1977) the use of foreign assets increases the level of investment but little. Hence in this scenario the coffee tax fails as a stabilization device: the time path of foreign savings differs very little from that in run 3 (the only difference being the inter-temporal transfer of the $46 million plus interest, from 1977 to 1981–3). Nevertheless, one would expect the policy to have a positive effect on capital accumulation. The coffee tax, after all, transfers income from farmers, who save about 60 per cent out of transient income during the boom, to the government, which is now modelled as having a marginal savings rate of 100 per cent. This partial equilibrium argument turns out to be false. We saw in section 3 that the investment boom was largely financed by savings of urban households out of rents which were created by the spending by farmers of the coffee boom income on non-tradables (or tradables subject to import controls). Taxing the income of the initial beneficiaries of the boom, the coffee growers, reduces these rents and this more than offsets the positive effect on investment of the transfer of income to a group (the government) with a higher marginal propensity to save. Hence, comparing runs 3 and 6 we find very little difference (Table 5.36). Rural (and, to a lesser extent, urban) households lose in the short run from the tax. At the end of the simulation period, however, the differences between the two runs are infinitesimally small.

While in run 6 the revenue of the coffee tax is to a large extent used to increase public consumption expenditure rather than to build up foreign assets (as in run 5), the government is still modelled as being in control to an unrealistic extent: the actual level of public consumption which we imposed in run 5 was after all reached without an increase in taxation. It is probably more realistic to assume that the government would have adjusted its consumption expenditure to the coffee tax revenue in the same way as it reacted to the actual increase in revenue. In the boom period consumption expenditure increased 1.35 times as fast as revenue. This elasticity we use in run 7, assuming that public consumption, above its actual level, is related to the revenue from the coffee tax by the 1.35 elasticity. Thus there is no build-up of foreign assets, since the budget deficit increases (unlike runs 5 and 6), thereby reducing public investment. Hence, while run 5 depicted the best use of the coffee tax, in this run we show the worst case.

While it may be pedantic to use a general equilibrium model to illustrate what should be obvious, namely that under these assumptions the coffee tax policy is disastrous, it is worth stressing the point. The results shown for run 7 in Table 5.36 suggest that if the government had reacted in this way to the increase in its revenue it would have reduced real domestic investment in the boom period by almost a quarter. Since public consumption is very labour intensive, urban households would have benefited considerably from an

TABLE 5.36. *Coffee tax and foreign asset accumulation: II*

(Results of runs 6 and 7 as % of run 3)

	Run 6		Run 7	
	1977	1983	1977	1983
Coffee: producer price[a]	71.0	100.0	71.0	100.0
Coffee: production[b]	91.8	99.2	92.0	99.5
Peasant income[c]	94.9	99.7	99.7	99.7
Rural consumer prices[d]	99.6	100.3	100.0	102.1
Real peasant incomes[e]	95.3	99.4	99.8	97.6
Urban wage employment	98.1	100.4	107.0	96.8
Urban household incomes[c]	97.1	102.0	106.4	102.6
Urban consumer prices[f]	99.0	101.1	101.9	106.3
Real urban incomes[g]	98.1	99.9	104.3	96.5
GDP (factor cost)[b]		100.1		96.4
GDP (market prices)[b]		100.2		96.4
Private consumption[b]		100.0		96.8
Public consumption[b]		103.6		100.0
Investment[b]		103.6		88.2
Exports[b]		99.6		96.7
Imports[b]		100.8		97.1
	1976–9	1980–3	1976–9	1980–3
Total investment[b]	96.7	100.7	77.2	82.7
	1977–80		1977–80	
Foreign asset acquisition[h]	$46m.		—	

[a] The coffee tax is reflected in the producer price being 29% lower in 1977; since the tax is imposed only in 1977–80, there is no difference in the producer price for 1983.

[b] In 1972 prices.

[c] In current prices.

[d] 1974-based.

[e] In 1974 prices.

[f] 1975-based.

[g] In 1975 prices.

[h] In millions of dollars, current prices (absolute value: in the comparison run there is no foreign asset acquisition).

increase in employment opportunities.[69] Increases in wage employment and in urban-to-rural remittances would compensate farmers for the reduction in their income from coffee growing. However, the shift from investment to consumption in the boom period leaves the economy with a smaller capital

[69] Note that in 1977 urban wage employment would be considerably higher.

stock at the end of the simulation period. Hence in 1983 real household incomes (both urban and rural), GDP, wage employment, and total investment are all considerably lower.

Again, run 7 is presented here only as a cautionary tale. In other runs we shall assume that the government resists the temptation to use for public consumption the proceeds of taxes introduced to stabilize the economy. How critical this assumption is should then be borne in mind.

Since we found in section 3 that the coffee boom benefited urban households, paradoxically, much more than peasants, it is worthwhile to explore the effect of an increase in urban income taxation instead of the imposition of a coffee tax. This is done in run 8. Here an additional tax on urban incomes of 5 per cent is imposed and the proceeds of this tax are invested abroad in 1977–80 (as in the 'super-virtuous' coffee tax variant of run 5) and used in 1981–3. This amounts to a considerable inter-temporal transfer of foreign savings: foreign assets of almost $500 million are built up in the first period.

The results in Table 5.37 indicate, again, that a stabilization policy can be very beneficial: as in the case of run 5 we find that, while considerably less is invested in the 1976–83 period than in the comparison run, real household incomes and GDP reach very much the same levels as in the comparison run, in spite of the low yield on foreign assets. It is interesting to note that, while one would expect the use of an urban income tax instead of the coffee tax to have favourable distributional effects, this is not the case. Peasants actually lose from the policy: the favourable effect on their incomes of increased remittances and improved formal sector employment opportunities is more than offset by price rises. Since investment is now very much higher in 1983 than in run 3, the slump in urban prices from which peasants benefited in that run does not now occur.

Comparing the effects of the coffee tax (the difference between runs 2 and 5 in Table 5.35) and the income tax (the difference between runs 3 and 8 in Table 5.37) it turns out that the results are surprisingly close.[70] Peasants are, contrary to what partial equilibrium analysis would suggest, better off under the coffee tax policy. (The reason is that under the income tax policy the high investment levels at the end of the period involve relative price changes which are unfavourable for peasants.)

In the final simulation experiment, run 9, we do not impose new taxes. We postulate a trend growth path of total investment of 5 per cent per annum (in real terms). In the period 1976–80, savings are invested abroad if investment rises above this trend (and, similarly, foreign assets are repatriated in the case of a shortfall). As in the other four experiments, the foreign assets thus accumulated are used at the end of the period, in 1981–3. There are two ways

---

[70] The most striking difference is for investment in the final year. The increase of investment is much larger under the income tax policy because a larger amount ($486m. instead of $366m.) is invested abroad.

TABLE 5.37. *Income taxes, public investment, and foreign asset accumulation*
(Results of runs 8 and 9 as % of run 3)

	Run 8 (income taxes)		Run 9 (public investment)	
	1977[a]	1983	1977	1983
Peasant incomes[b]	100.0	100.8	100.7	100.0
Rural consumer prices[c]	100.0	102.1	100.9	99.6
Real peasant incomes[d]	100.0	98.7	99.8	100.5
Urban wage employment	100.0	101.1	106.1	100.4
Urban household incomes[b]	100.0	110.4	106.1	98.9
Urban consumer prices[e]	100.0	111.1	101.8	98.8
Real urban incomes[f]	100.0	99.4	104.2	100.1
GDP (factor cost)[g]		100.3		100.3
GDP (market prices)[g]		100.6		100.3
Private consumption[g]		99.7		100.3
Public consumption[g]		100.0		100.0
Investment[g]		127.7		106.7
Exports[g]		98.8		98.0
Imports[g]		107.8		100.3
	1976–9	1980–3	1976–9	1980–3
Total investment[g]	86.0	105.4	104.7	100.6
	1977–80		1977–80	
Foreign asset acquisition[h]	$486m.		$231m.	

    [a] Since the income tax is imposed in 1978, the results for 1977 are identical.
    [b] In current prices.
    [c] 1974-based.
    [d] In 1974 prices.
    [e] 1975-based.
    [f] In 1975 prices.
    [g] In 1972 prices.
    [h] In millions of dollars, current prices (absolute value: in the comparison run there is no foreign asset acquisition).

of interpreting this somewhat artificial design of the simulation experiment. First (and this is the interpretation we used in Tables 5.33 and 5.37), we might assume that the government changes the allocation of public savings between domestic and foreign investment in such a way that total domestic investment is stabilized. Alternatively, private agents might be allowed to hold foreign assets. As we discussed in Chapter 4, it would be optimal for private agents to accumulate foreign assets during the boom and to convert these into domestic real assets later.

Table 5.37 indicates that in this case real rural and urban incomes are both higher in 1983 (unlike any of the other four runs in this section). The difference is small (only 0.5 per cent for peasants and virtually nothing for urban households), but it should be mentioned again that a substantial loss would have been a more likely outcome, since the return on foreign assets is low relative to that on domestic assets. Hence the run illustrates the benefits of stabilization (in terms of avoiding the adverse relative price changes of section 3). We consider the runs as no more than illustrative, however, especially on the first interpretation, since the government would, after all, have to be uncharacteristically flexible in changing public investment in response to changes in private sector behaviour for the implicit assumptions of this run to be fulfilled. It seems more realistic to assume a tax policy for stabilization purposes. In the policy package to be discussed below we shall do this, including the urban income tax in the package.[71]

4.2. *Trade Policy*

In this section we consider two alternative ways of changing trade policy in response to the commodity boom: imposing additional controls on imports, and the opposite extreme, trade liberalization.[72]

It is sometimes argued that under free trade a commodity boom will be 'wasted' on imports of consumer goods and that the appropriate policy response is therefore to control these imports. This advice is clearly absurd, since if foreign savings are given and the volume of imports cannot increase because of quantitative restrictions, then external equilibrium implies that the terms-of-trade gain is offset by a reduction in the volume of exports. In the Kenyan context it would mean that domestic food prices would rise (as a result of import controls), thereby inducing farmers to switch from export crops to food crops. Such a policy is modelled in run 10, where, starting in 1977, all competitive imports are controlled at their 1976 level.[73] Table 5.39 shows the results for 1977. Since exports consist largely of two crops (coffee and tea) with low supply elasticities, very large price increases for importables and non-tradables are required to effect the necessary export reduction. For food importables and for non-tradables prices increase by almost 60 per cent (compared with run 3); for non-food manufacturing the price increases almost 150 per cent. Hence in agriculture relative prices change in favour of food: food production increases and the volume of export crop production falls. In

---

[71] The difference from run 9 is that we there assume that interest is paid on foreign assets.

[72] The design of the four runs discussed in this section is summarised in Table 5.38.

[73] Recall that in section 3 food imports were not subject to controls, while in the case of non-food imports controls were relaxed endogenously if domestic prices reached a ceiling (as they did in run 3 in 1977).

TABLE 5.38. *Trade policies: design of the simulation experiments*

Run	Comparison run	Tariffs	Quantitative restrictions	Public consumption	Price regime manufacturing
10	3	A	D	F	I
11	3	B	E	F	J
12	3	B	E	G	J
13	3	C	E	H	J

Key

A: Tariff rates remain constant throughout the simulation period (as in the runs discussed in section 3).

B: In 1977 tariffs are raised by the equivalent of the removed QRs on non-food manufactured goods imports (hence in that year the domestic price of those goods is the same as in run 3); the higher tariff rates remain in force after 1977.

C: QRs are converted to tariffs as in case B; after 1979 they are gradually reduced.

D: Imports are controlled at the 1976 level both for non-food manufactured goods (for which controls were relaxed during the boom in run 3) and for food imports (which in run 3 were not subject to QRs).

E: QRs on the imports of non-food manufactured goods are replaced by equivalent tariffs in 1977.

F: Actual values are imposed for public consumption (as in run 3).

G: Tariff proceeds are partly spent: the extra revenue of the tariff equivalent of the extra protection generated by the boom adds to public consumption (i.e. when QRs are converted to tariffs, only that part of the revenue is spent which corresponds to the boom-induced increase in the equivalent tariff rate).

H: As in case F for 1977–9, but thereafter public consumption is cut as tariffs are reduced.

I: The domestic price of non-food manufacturing is market-clearing; there is no regime switch (trade liberalization if a price ceiling is reached, as there was in run 3).

J: Starting in 1977 imports clear the market for non-food manufactured goods, the domestic price being equal to the c.i.f. price plus the tariff.

TABLE 5.39. *Controlling imports during a boom*

(Results of run 10 for 1977 as % of run 3)

Volume of domestic production	
Exportables	91.6
Importables: food	116.8
Importables: non-food	116.7
Non-tradables	103.6
Domestic prices	
Exportables	100.0
Importables: food	159.6
Importables: non-food	248.9
Non-tradables	155.3
Real household incomes	
Rural	89.0
Urban	109.3

the non-agricultural sector relative price increases favour the production of importables, at the expenses of non-tradables.

That the imposition of import controls is Pareto inefficient is obvious. What the simulation experiment illustrates is that such a policy would exacerbate the two problematic effects of the boom which we emphasized in section 3: the change in the distribution of income in favour of urban groups and the erosion of the real value of savings by relative price increases. The use of import controls in run 10 reduces the real income of peasants by 11 per cent and increases the real income of urban households by 9.3 per cent. Further, in 1977 the price of capital goods is more than twice as high as in run 3. Hence the value of savings in terms of domestic capital formation is indeed very seriously affected by import controls.

In runs 11, 12, and 13 the government reacts to the boom with trade liberalization. The idea, of course, is that groups benefiting from trade controls will resist trade liberalization less if this takes place at a time when their incomes are rising anyway: a boom may make liberalization politically feasible. The conventional policy advice advocates a two-stage procedure, first replacing quantitative restrictions by equivalent tariffs and then lowering the tariffs. Run 11 incorporates the first phase: we assume that in 1977 the import controls are lifted and that tariff rates are raised sufficiently to give domestic producers the same degree of protection. In the short run this only transfers income: the domestic price of the protected sector is, by definition, unaffected, but the income which previously accrued to private agents in the form of rents now goes to the government as tariff revenue. If the government saves this income (and this we assume in run 11: public consumption is exogenous so the tariff proceeds are entirely saved) then one would expect the policy to have a positive effect on the rate of investment. Income would be transferred from private agents (with a marginal savings rate of about 60 per cent during the boom) to the government (with a savings rate of 100 per cent). This is why Table 5.40 shows a real increase of 10 per cent (in 1979) for the level of investment. This is the only substantial macroeconomic change. Household incomes are negatively affected since urban households lose the rents generated by the import controls and rural households suffer a terms-of-trade loss.[74]

The effect of the substitution of tariffs for import controls depends, of course, on the use the government makes of the tariff proceeds. Run 11 assumes that the government is 'virtuous' in the sense that the extra revenue is not used to increase public consumption: it is entirely saved and hence adds to (domestic) investment.[75] This assumption is relaxed for run 12, where part

[74] The loss amounts, however, only to about 1% in the case of peasants. The loss would have been larger had it not been that the increase in investment pushes up the price of non-tradables (e.g. transport) as before (and this implies a terms-of-trade loss for peasants), but now, since import controls are abolished, it does not push up the price of non-food manufactured goods.
[75] The difference from the 'super-virtuous' case of run 5 is that there the revenue from the coffee tax was not only saved but was entirely invested abroad.

TABLE 5.40. *Short-run effects of replacing import controls by tariffs*

(Results of runs 11 and 12 for 1979 as % of run 3)

	Run 11 (tariff proceeds entirely saved)	Run 12 (tariff proceeds partly spent)
National Accounts (1972 prices)		
GDP (market prices)	101.1	99.3
Private consumption	98.3	97.1
Public consumption	100.0	108.1
Investment	110.2	95.4
Exports	100.8	98.2
Imports	101.0	98.9
Real incomes		
Peasants	99.1	100.6
Urban households	95.3	92.4

of the tariff revenue is used to increase public consumption.[76] This is only a modest relaxation, since the revenue involved amounts to what would have been generated by a 9 per cent tariff; the tariff equivalent of import controls is very much higher. Nevertheless, this change in government behaviour makes a substantial difference, as may be seen by comparing the two columns of Table 5.40. Investment is now reduced by 4.6 per cent. As a result, prices of non-tradables fall (compared with run 3) and this benefits peasants, while it increases the income loss of urban households.

The two runs do not incorporate the second phase of a liberalization programme: the reduction of tariff rates. Tariffs are set in the peak year of the boom at the high levels which are then equivalent to the import controls. Maintaining these rates means that the benefits of liberalization are forgone, but might well be thought to be harmless otherwise. The model suggests that, on the contrary, it would exacerbate the redistribution of income from peasants to urban householders, as may be seen from Table 5.41, in which runs 3 and 12 are compared for 1983. The reason is that in runs 11 and 12, with tariff rates fixed, the price of non-food manufactured goods rises in proportion to the c.i.f. prices, i.e. by 55 per cent between 1980 and 1983 (in terms of domestic currency). In run 3, however, with import controls maintained, the domestic price falls continuously in this period, relative to the world price.[77] Maintaining a fixed tariff rate may seem harmless (and our

[76] Since the policy change is implemented in 1977, we assume that the government bases its decision on what happens in 1976. The value of the protection afforded by the import controls increases in that year (because of the boom), hence the equivalent tariff increases. We assume that what the government uses to increase its current expenditure is only the income corresponding to this increase in the equivalent tariff rates.

[77] Recall from section 3 that this relative price decline in the model's results can be observed: the price of manufacturing in 1983 was 24% lower than it would have been if it had (since 1975) increased in line with the world price of non-oil imports.

TABLE 5.41.   Long-run effects of replacing import controls by tariffs

(Results of run 12 in 1983 as % of run 3)

National Accounts (1972 prices)	
GDP (market prices)	107.4
Private consumption	105.4
Public consumption	103.3
Investment	124.4
Exports	103.2
Imports	100.6
Real incomes	
Peasants	92.3
Urban households	111.6

results therefore counter-intuitive), because the rate of protection then does not change. What matters, however, is not the change in the level of protection over time but between runs. Replacing import controls by fixed tariff rates amounts to an increase, indeed to a substantial increase, in protection because domestic prices would otherwise have fallen relative to world prices. The obvious reason for this is that when the coffee boom is over, the protective value of the import controls declines. The less obvious reason is that investment in a sector protected by import controls diminishes the protective value of these controls, a theoretical point discussed in Chapter 4. The second-best argument used there implied that, given import controls, the economy gains from concentrating investment in manufacturing. Hence the substitution of tariffs for import controls is, paradoxically, equivalent to increasing protectionism, because if import controls had been maintained then investment in manufacturing would have reduced the difference between domestic and world prices, just as if trade policy had been liberalized.

This explains why peasants suffer a terms-of-trade loss, so that their real income is reduced by 7.7 per cent in 1983; and why, conversely, the policy raises the real income of urban households substantially (11.6 per cent). It does not, however, explain why GDP and the level of investment are so much higher at the end of the period. The reason for this lies in the difference between savings rates of urban households and the government. As we emphasized above, the transfer of income from the former to the latter raises domestic savings, but not by very much, since in the boom period the marginal savings rate of urban households is very high anyway. After the boom period, however, private agents do not consider changes in their income as transient. Their marginal savings rates therefore fall, and as a result (even though the government continues to use part of the tariff income for current expenditure), maintaining the high tariff rates after the boom increases the economy's savings rate substantially. In fact, what happens is very similar to increasing the urban income tax and almost entirely saving the proceeds. Clearly, the favourable results shown in Table 5.41 are contingent on the assumed 'virtuous' government behaviour. If the government had spent the entire tariff revenue (or even enough of it to equate its marginal savings rate to that of private agents) then the policy would be immiserizing, because, to repeat, it would amount to a substantial increase in protectionism.

Our last trade policy experiment, run 13, does include a second phase of the liberalization programme, involving reductions in tariffs. For 1975–9 the run is identical to run 11: controls are converted to tariffs in 1977, tariff rates then remain constant, and public consumption is unaffected so that all of the extra tariff revenue is saved. Starting in 1980, however, tariff rates are reduced. For this to amount to trade liberalization the reductions must be substantial, since, as we noted above, without a change in trade policy industrial investment would reduce the domestic price of manufactured goods considerably (relative to world prices). We assume that in 1980–3 tariff rates are lowered each year by the same percentage, bringing the domestic price in 1983 just below its level in run 3 (cf. Fig. 5.13). The results are shown in Table 5.42. Since protection is reduced there is an efficiency effect. But this effect is small, since, as we emphasized above, protection would have been reduced substantially even without a change in trade policy.[78] This weak effect is completely swamped by the policy's negative effect on savings: the redistribution of income from the government to private households (which, under our assumption of government 'virtue', save a much smaller fraction of the transferred income) reduces total savings substantially. Total investment in 1980–3 is one-third lower (in real terms) than in run 3. This far outweighs the efficiency gain. In the final year the real income of peasants is about the same, that of urban households is almost 10 per cent higher, but GDP and investment are substantially reduced. The point is, of course, not that trade liberalization is undesirable, but rather that the effect depends critically on how the government spends tariff income. Obviously, if in the absence of liberalization the government had reacted to the increase in its revenue (as a result of the conversion of QRs into tariffs) by an equal increase in its current expenditure, then the efficiency effect of liberalization would have been reinforced by its positive effect on savings.

4.3. Financial Liberalization

So far we have considered taxation, stabilization, and trade policies. Our next experiment, run 14, is concerned with financial liberalization. While the sectoral allocation of investment has been exogenous in the runs discussed so far, in run 14 the allocation depends (starting in 1977) on differentials in the

---

[78] Note that the price of non-food manufacturing is (as in Fig. 5.13) only slightly below its value in run 3 in the final year.

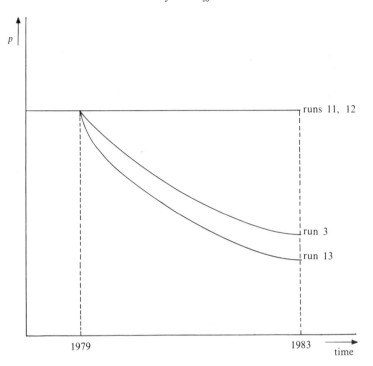

Note: Protection (*p*) is measured along the vertical axis as the ratio of the domestic and the c.i.f. prices of non-food manufactured goods. When import controls are maintained (run 3), protection declines because of industrial investment. In runs 11 and 12 import controls are replaced by equivalent tariffs in the boom period. Hence, after the boom, protection remains constant over time but increases relative to run 3. In run 13 tariff rates are cut in the post-boom period.

FIG. 5.13. *Protection of manufacturing under various trade policy assumptions*

rate of return on capital.[79] In the model this has the effect of increasing investment in manufacturing and in 'other services', at the expense of investment in construction, transport, and trade. In run 3 investment in these five sectors in 1977–83 (in 1972 prices) is allocated between the first two and the last three in the ratio 44:56. In run 14 these shares become 67 per cent and 33 per cent. Table 5.43 shows that this reallocation has substantial effects. For example, in 1983 GDP is 7.5 per cent higher; real incomes of peasants are

---

[79] The five sectors involved in this experiment are manufacturing, trade, transport, construction, and 'other services' (which excludes housing and government services). We model a partial adjustment process. If, for example, a sector's current rate of return is 40% and the average for the five sectors 15%, we increase its share in investment by 2.5 percentage points, i.e. one-tenth of the rate of return differential. This severe damping is adopted, first, because rates of return differ markedly in 1976, and secondly, because they vary over time.

TABLE 5.42. *Effects of tariff reductions,*
1980–1983

(Results of run 13 for 1983 as % of run 3)

National Accounts (1972 prices)	
GDP (market prices)	94.5
Private consumption	107.8
Public consumption	80.4
Investment	50.4
Exports	98.6
Imports	96.4
Total investment, 1980–3 (1972 prices)	68.2
Real incomes	
Peasants	99.5
Urban households	109.9
Domestic prices	
Importables: non-food	98.2
Non-tradables	106.7

TABLE 5.43. *Financial liberalization: investment allocation*
responsive to rate-of-return differentials

(Results of run 14 for 1983 as % of run 3)

National Accounts (1972 prices)	
GDP (market prices)	107.5
Private consumption	110.6
Public consumption	100.0
Investment	107.5
Exports	106.6
Imports	106.3
Domestic prices	
Exportables	100.0
Importables: food	100.0
Importables: non-food	91.0
Non-tradables	108.2
Real incomes	
Peasants	102.0
Urban households	113.6
Investment 1977–83 in:	
manufacturing and 'other services'	154.4
trade, transport, and construction	59.0

higher (largely because prices of manufactured goods are lower); and the real income of urban households is 13.6 per cent higher than in run 3. If we measure the efficiency of investment as the ratio of the increase in GDP at factor cost from 1975 to 1983 and total investment from 1975 to 1982, we find a 27 per cent improvement in efficiency. This suggests that financial liberalization (which usually receives much less emphasis than trade policy reform in liberalization programmes) can have very large efficiency effects.

4.4. *A Policy Package*

In our final experiment, run 15, we combine policies discussed in the preceding sections. Compared with run 3, it involves three changes in policy:

(a) taxation and stabilization: an extra tax of 5 per cent on urban incomes is introduced in 1978, and the proceeds are invested in foreign assets and repatriated in 1981–3, together with the accumulated interest;

(b) trade policy: quantitative restrictions are replaced by equivalent tariffs, and after 1979 tariffs are gradually reduced (as in run 13; cf. Tables 5.38 and 5.42);

(c) financial liberalization: the allocation of investment between sectors becomes responsive to rate-of-return differentials (as in run 14; cf. Table 5.43).

These assumptions lead to the results shown in Table 5.44. In this experiment peasants benefit, but the improvement in their real incomes is small (only 0.9 per cent). This seems to be a general result: the real incomes of peasants are insensitive to the sort of policy changes we have considered. Policies (except, of course, for the coffee tax) affect peasants only indirectly, through changes in formal sector employment, urban remittances, and non-agricultural prices. In most experiments these effects offset each other so that the net effect on peasants is weak. An increase in the rate of investment, for example, benefits them through increased remittances and improved

TABLE 5.44. *Income taxation, stabilization, trade and financial liberalization combined*

(Results of run 15 for 1983 as % of run 3)

National Accounts (1972 prices)	
GDP (market prices)	103.7
Private consumption	120.7
Public consumption	79.6
Investment	85.0
Exports	104.2
Imports	113.2
Real incomes	
Peasants	100.9
Urban households	127.1
Total investment, 1976–83	95.0
Efficiency of investment, 1975–82	113.2

Note: The efficiency of investment is measured as the ratio of the increase in GDP at factor cost (in 1972 prices) from 1975 to 1983 and total investment in the period 1975–82.

opportunities for formal sector employment, but is offset by increases in non-agricultural prices.

Urban incomes, on the other hand, are very sensitive to policy changes. In this run real urban incomes increase by more than a quarter. This is because the package combines financial liberalization and trade liberalization, and these policies, if introduced in isolation, already raise urban incomes by 14 and 10 per cent respectively (Tables 5.43 and 5.42).

Investment is reduced in this run, but by much less than in run 13 (where, it will be recalled, trade liberalization reduced savings by transferring tariff income from a government assumed to be 'virtuous' to urban households). The offsetting factor is the stabilization policy: urban incomes continue to be taxed (after the boom) and, in addition, post-boom savings are supplemented by the repatriation of $537 million in foreign assets. In spite of lower investment, GDP is higher in the long run. This is because financial liberalization leads (as in run 14) to a very large improvement (13 per cent) in the efficiency of investment.

5. Conclusion

In section 2.5 of this chapter we considered private responses to the windfall of the coffee boom. We found that the private savings rate must have risen during the boom from 20 per cent to over 60 per cent. This large increase reflects the controls which were in force, as a result of which the spending of the boom income generated large rents. Much of the investment went into the production of import substitutes, which increased by over 50 per cent over the period 1975–83. Private agents foresaw that the trade liberalization during the boom would be temporary and therefore increased their imports of consumer goods beyond that which would be sustainable (given the way investment was allocated between tradable and non-tradable goods).

In section 2.3 we saw that the boom led to large increases in public spending. The government lost control in the sense that the growth in spending exceeded what would have been sustainable. While this was partly corrected between 1981 and 1983, most of the necessary corrections still remained to be done in 1983.

In section 3 we used a general equilibrium model, in part to disentangle the effects of the three shocks to which the Kenyan economy was exposed in 1975–83: the boom itself, the government's response to it, and the second oil price increase. The results indicated that, in spite of the government's policy of passing the price increases on to farmers, urban groups benefited (partly in the form of rents) much more from the boom than farmers. We also saw that the loss of fiscal control documented in section 2.3 had disastrous consequences. By 1983 it had wiped out most of the gains from the coffee boom, with further retrenchments still to be made.

With the benefit of hindsight it is easy to say that it would have been better if the government had remained passive. We would like to distinguish, however, between the government's loss of fiscal control and its lack of success in using controls optimally when confronted with the boom. The government can of course be blamed for the former, but its culpability with regard to the latter is much less clear.

We have already noted in Chapter 2 that once one has a set of controls such as the Kenyan ones in force, it is exceedingly difficult to design changes in policy instruments which are compatible and which add up to an optimal response to a windfall. That conclusion is reinforced by the result of the simulation experiments, which showed that the permanent effects of a boom are very sensitive to the timing of investment. For the government to have phased its own actions optimally it would have needed to determine (*ex ante*) both the extent and the phasing of private investment out of boom income and the large changes in relative prices (e.g. of capital goods) induced by the boom itself, by the responses of private agents, and by its own actions.

The difficulty of devising an optimal response to a shock in a controlled economy may be an important argument against the controls. But given the control regime, it seems fairer to say that the government was faced with an impossible task than that it wasted a unique opportunity.

We simulated alternative responses to the boom and the dismantling of the control regime in section 4. What do we learn from these simulation experiments? First, that the efficacy of stabilization policy is critically dependent upon how the government uses the revenue. 'Super-virtue' (temporarily acquiring foreign assets) dominates 'virtue' (acquiring only domestic assets), and fecklessness (increasing recurrent expenditure) is a disaster. Secondly, either 'super-virtuous' stabilization policies or, alternatively, allowing private agents to acquire foreign assets during the boom would be particularly beneficial. This is so because the fundamental argument in favour of stabilization (discussed in Chapter 4) is reinforced by the effect a commodity boom in a controlled economy has on rents. Thirdly, there is a case for taxing boom income not in the first round (as through a coffee tax) but in a subsequent round of spending (as through an urban income tax). Fourthly, the efficiency effects of the traditional trade liberalization programme (first converting import controls to equivalent tariffs and subsequently reducing those tariffs) can be swamped by the effect of the implied transfer of income between the government and private agents, depending upon how the government treats its tariff income. Fifthly, since the protective effect of quantitative import controls would have been reduced substantially over time as a result of import-substituting investment, converting the controls into tariffs which are then slowly lowered may, paradoxically, leave the manufacturing sector more protected by the end of the period than unchanged trade policies. Finally, if the boom is seen as an opportunity for liberalization measures, then (permanent) financial liberalization would be particularly effective.

Appendix 1
A Narrative of Macroeconomic Events

> We can record it down firmly that this stage in our country's history
> should not be lost sight of without learning a few lessons. Kenya should
> take advantage of good years to build an adequate precautionary reserve
> of foreign currencies.
>
> (D.N. Ndegwa, Governor, Central Bank of Kenya, 1981)

1. *Introduction*

With the benefit of hindsight, Kenyan policy makers came to regard the
coffee boom as a major missed opportunity. This appendix provides a
narrative of macroeconomic events and policy changes in order to convey a
sense of how the boom was perceived by policy makers and commentators at
the time. We therefore use official data rather than the re-estimations
constructed in the main body of the chapter. We set the scene with an account
of the macroeconomy before the boom.

2. *The period up to 1975*

Kenya became independent in 1963. During the first years of independence,
efforts were concentrated on Africanization, primarily of the civil service but
also in the private sector. The official strategy was set out in Sessional Paper
no. 10 of 1965 on *African Socialism and its Application to Planning.* In spite of
its name it was essentially a conventional strategy which emphasized growth,
though it was stressed that the gains would be shared by broad segments of
the population. The private sector was encouraged, and Kenya pursued a
fairly open policy *vis-à-vis* foreign enterprises. At the same time, however,
there was a rapid expansion of the public sector and increased government
intervention. Industrial development was supported through an import
substitution policy.

Fiscal and monetary policies were generally cautious, and the budgetary
situation was perceived by commentators as sound (Killick, 1984; p. 166).
Even though the government rapidly expanded public services and increased
investment, it managed to improve the budget balance. There was little
deficit-financing, and the exchange rate was stable. In 1971 for the first time
Kenya experienced a balance-of-payments problem caused by expansionary
budgets in 1970 and 1971. In responding to this problem, policy makers had
recourse not to monetary policy but to import controls. However, these were
not very restrictive, and external debts were still almost non-existent. The
Ministry of Finance pursued a more restrictive budgetary policy in the period
1972 to 1974, when it widened the tax base and used very little bank

borrowing. Kenya thus remained an open economy by African standards, and the balance of payments had by 1973 been brought under a measure of control. The first decade of independence was a very successful period economically. The rate of inflation fluctuated between 0 and 3 per cent, GDP grew on average at $6\frac{1}{2}$ per cent per year (in real terms), and most households experienced considerable improvements in living standards.

In the Second Development Plan (1970–4) rural development played a larger role than in the first plan (1966–70), owing to a concern for urban–rural imbalance. Inequalities were brought to the forefront of the discussion in Kenya with the ILO report of 1972, and the ideas launched there came to feature prominently in the Third Development Plan (1974–8). However, although employment and equity objectives were emphasized, there was in fact not much change in overall policy and little specific action to bring about a more equitable income distribution.

The plan was written before Kenya was hit by the oil shock with a quadrupling of oil prices and a 30 per cent increase in other import prices, and was therefore already obsolete before it was published. The oil shock created a balance-of-payments crisis in 1974, the current account deficit doubling and the basic balance going from zero to a deficit of 3.9 per cent of GDP. The government borrowed heavily from the IMF, for example under the oil facility, but in spite of this, foreign reserves at the end of 1974 were reduced to 2.7 months of imports from 5.1 months of imports a year before. With rapid increases in both import prices and the money supply, inflation became a serious problem. The government reacted by curtailing credit to the private sector, extending the 15 per cent liquidity ratio to non-bank financial institutions, increasing interest rates, and encouraging companies to borrow money abroad. The government also attempted to stimulate export production by an export subsidy of 10 per cent. However, the criteria of eligibility made the procedure cumbersome, and so the facility was little used. Refunds of import duties were also introduced, but these measures meant little relative to the fact that the currency was becoming overvalued.

Even if the set-back in 1974 was mainly the effect of the oil price shock, there was also an underlying trend which was worrying. Since 1970 exports had grown at a slower rate than GDP, and there had been little success with attempts at export diversification. Only about 8 per cent of manufacturing output was exported, and manufacturing was heavily reliant on imports of intermediate goods and capital equipment. Domestic terms of trade had turned against agriculture, and since 1970 agricultural output had not kept pace with the growth of population. The oil shock was not the only adverse change: in 1974 Kenya was also hit by a drought.

3. *The Economic Situation in 1975*

The rate of growth of the Kenyan economy up to the oil crisis had been high, but the impact of the oil price increase was dramatic. The barter terms of

240   *Two African Applications*

trade worsened by 23 per cent between 1972 and 1975 (see Table 5A1.1), and the trade balance was by 1975 in considerable deficit. This was in part compensated by positive service and transfer balances as well as a large net inflow of long-term capital, but in spite of this the basic balance deficit was 2.2 per cent of GDP (see Table 5A1.2).

In this difficult economic situation the government rethought its economic strategy, the result being Sessional Paper no. 4 of 1975, *On Economic Prospects and Policies.* The major points in the proposed programme were: more emphasis on agricultural development through higher producer prices and increased government expenditures directed to this sector, reduced dependence on imported intermediate inputs in the manufacturing sector, reduced inflation through wage restraint, and the active use of fiscal policy in the stabilization effort. This last intention, presumably sincere, is ironic in view of the macroeconomic débâcle of the next eight years.

TABLE 5A1.1. *Kenyan terms of trade, 1972–1983* (1975 = 100)

1972	130	1979	113
1975	100	1980	103
1976	116	1981	90
1977	152	1982	85
1978	122	1983	91

Source: Government of Kenya, *Statistical Abstract*, various issues.

TABLE 5A1.2. *The balance of payments, 1975–1983* (K£ million)

	Trade balance	Service balance	Transfer balance	Balance on current account	Net long-term capital balance	Basic balance	Basic balance as % of GDP
1975	−125.0	22.6	18.5	−83.9	57.4	−26.5	−2.2
1976	−77.3	19.3	6.1	−51.9	90.7	38.8	+2.7
1977	−61.3	45.2	27.5	11.4	83.9	95.3	+5.1
1978	−355.5	65.0	35.2	−255.3	168.0	−87.3	−4.3
1979	−299.4	79.0	34.1	−186.3	189.5	3.2	0.1
1980	−526.6	143.2	54.7	−328.7	186.1	−142.6	−5.4
1981	−497.0	118.0	42.9	−336.1	162.7	−173.5	−5.7
1982	−430.4	140.2	36.8	−253.4	139.0	−114.4	−3.4
1983	−335.6	143.5	76.5	−115.6	116.3	0.7	0.0

Source: Government of Kenya, *Statistical Abstract*, various issues; Annual Reports from the Central Bank.

Wage guidelines had been made stricter in January, but in the aftermath of the Kariuki affair (the murder of a popular MP) they were somewhat relaxed again in April. The budget for 1975/6, which was published a few months later, reflected the ambition to stabilize the economy. However, many of the ideas in the document were not fully implemented. A major reason for this was that by 1976 the coffee boom took the pressure off the government.

A number of policy initiatives were taken during 1975 to improve the external balance. In July the government reached an agreement with the IMF about an extended facility to support the programme outlined in Sessional Paper no. 4. In October the shilling was devalued by 12 per cent against the SDR, and the import control system was made progressively more restrictive. The IMF facility was payable in six instalments with most scheduled for 1976 and 1977, payments being subject to six-monthly reviews of progress on the basis of established performance criteria. Only the first instalment of sh.74 million was drawn, the government being unwilling or unable to keep borrowing under the agreed ceiling. During the second half of 1975 coffee prices started to increase, which made it less urgent for the government to stand by the IMF agreement.

By this time the import control system had become a maze of restrictive licensing procedures consisting of, for example, import bans, firm-specific import quotas, and 'No-Objection Certificates' requirements from specific firms or government officials. They also included a series of foreign exchange allocation procedures operated in a discretionary, firm-by-firm manner by the Foreign Exchange Allocation Committee and the Central Bank. These policies increased domestic prices and were a source of economic rent. This was tapped both by the producers and by officials engaged in the allocation of licences.

The economy stagnated in 1975, the aggregate growth rate being 0.9 per cent. Only public services continued to expand (at 7.5 per cent), while there was no growth in either agriculture or industry (see Tables 5A1.3 and 5A1.4).

One result of the foreign deficit was that, although domestic credit expanded rapidly, domestic money supply did not expand as fast as monetary GDP at current prices. There was thus a monetary contraction. Other factors which contributed to the stagnation of real output were the world recession and the drought, which held back agricultural production in 1974 and 1975. However, the decline in growth was also due to changes on the supply side. As the external balance weakened, imports of intermediate goods were curtailed and this had a negative effect on production.

With the continued expansion of public services coupled with stagnation in the rest of the economy, the total deficit of the government (the budgetary financing requirement) increased to 6.0 per cent in 1974/5 and 7.3 per cent[1] in

---

[1] The presentation in this appendix is based on the official estimates of the aggregate deficit, which differ somewhat from the estimate used in the main body of the chapter. There we construct an alternative measure which is conceptually more appropriate, and which is a better guide to the true fiscal position.

TABLE 5A1.3. *Growth rates, 1975–1983* (%)

	GDP	GDP per capita	Agriculture	Manufacturing	Public services
1964–74	6.3	3.0	4.3	8.3	9.2
1975	0.9	− 2.4	0.3	− 0.2	7.5
1976	2.1	− 1.2	0.3	18.5	5.3
1977	9.4	6.1	10.2	15.9	5.1
1978	7.3	4.0	3.8	12.6	6.4
1979	3.9	0.6	− 0.8	7.1	7.1
1980	4.8	1.5	− 1.3	5.7	5.6
1981	3.9	0.6	6.2	6.0	5.3
1982	1.7	− 1.6	4.4	0.0	3.5
1983	3.8	0.5	4.1	4.5	4.2

Source: Government of Kenya, *Statistical Abstract*, various issues.

TABLE 5A.1.4. *Economic structure by sector, 1975–1983*(%)

	Production (current prices)			Modern sector employment		
	Agric.	Indust.	Services	Agric.	Indust.	Services
1975	37.6	18.0	44.4	29.8	17.2	53.0
1976	41.2	16.5	42.3	28.8	19.2	52.0
1977	45.1	15.8	39.1	29.2	19.6	51.2
1978	40.3	17.8	41.9	26.9	21.4	51.7
1979	38.0	18.7	43.3	26.4	21.6	52.0
1980	35.9	19.8	44.3	23.2	21.3	55.5
1981	35.6	19.6	44.8	23.2	21.3	55.5
1982	36.1	18.9	45.0	21.7	21.1	57.2
1983	36.8	17.9	45.3	21.5	20.7	57.8

Source: Government of Kenya, *Statistical Abstract*, various issues.

1975/6 (see Table 5A1.5). Owing to the large budget deficit, money supply increased rapidly, and inflation was around 18 per cent in 1975 (see Table 5A1.6).

By 1975 general government accounted for 15 per cent of GDP, but the shares of the public sector in capital formation and modern sector employment were considerably higher. The government activities outside the public service sector related mainly to electricity generation and distribution, oil refining, banking, and insurance, although there were also several parastatals outside these areas.

TABLE 5A1.5. *Total budget deficit at market prices 1974/5–1983/4* (%of GDP)

1974/5	6.0	1979/80	6.2
1975/6	7.3	1980/1	10.5
1976/7	4.8	1981/2	9.5
1977/8	5.6	1982/3	6.7
1978/9	8.2	1983/4	4.0

*Sources:*Government of Kenya, *Statistical Abstract*, various issues; Annual Reports from the Central Bank.

TABLE 5A1.6. *Monetary data, 1975–1983*

	Rate of change in lower income index of consumer prices (%)	Exchange rate Ksh/$US (end period)	Rate of growth of money supply (%)	
			M1[a]	M2[b]
1975	18.4	8.26	13.0	17.1
1976	9.1	8.31	25.0	24.1
1977	21.0	7.95	48.5	46.8
1978	13.7	7.40	10.4	13.7
1979	9.1	7.33	14.2	16.1
1980	13.1	7.57	−6.9	−1.1
1981	19.3	10.29	12.2	13.3
1982	13.3	12.73	20.2	16.1
1983	10.0	13.76	4.3	4.9

[a] M1: currency in circulation plus all demand deposits and 7-day time deposits, except those of central government and non-resident banks.
[b] M2: same as M1 plus all other deposits, except those of the central government and non-resident banks.
Source: Government of Kenya, *Statistical Abstract*, various issues.

To summarize, the economic situation in 1975 was difficult. The deficit in the basic balance was considerable at 2.2 per cent of GDP, and the domestic budget deficit reached a record level of over 7 per cent of GDP. The domestic savings rate had fallen to 17.7 per cent of GDP (see Table 5A1.7), and capital formation in real terms had declined by 2.1 per cent. The economy was thus suffering from severe imbalances, but the government had started to take action to halt the decline.

4. *The Boom, 1976–1978*

Although the situation at the beginning of 1976 was difficult, coffee prices were increasing, the real coffee price doubling between 1975 and 1976. The

TABLE 5A1.7. *Expenditure shares of GDP, 1975–1983* (current prices)

	Public sector consumption	Private consumption	Gross fixed capital formation	Export	Import	Export minus import[a]	Domestic savings as % of GDP
1975	18.4	68.1	20.3	29.9	34.6	−4.7	17.7
1976	17.5	61.5	20.0	32.5	31.8	+0.7	21.0
1977	17.4	55.5	21.0	35.1	31.7	+3.4	21.3
1978	19.4	60.5	25.1	28.9	38.7	−9.8	17.1
1979	19.7	63.6	23.8	26.4	32.4	−6.0	15.1
1980	20.3	61.1	23.6	28.6	40.0	−11.4	18.6
1981	19.0	61.7	23.9	25.5	34.4	−8.9	19.3
1982	19.0	63.1	19.7	24.9	29.6	−4.7	17.8
1983	19.6	61.1	19.7	25.4	27.2	−1.8	19.4

[a] Note that there is a difference between 'export minus import' in this table and the current account balance reported in Table 5A1.2. The latter concept is slightly broader, including factor service income and payments and current transfers.

Source: Government of Kenya, *Statistical Abstract*, various issues.

increased prices for coffee (and tea) implied a 16 per cent improvement in Kenyan terms of trade in 1976, and considerably improved Kenya's trade balance. The basic balance swung from a deficit of 2.2 per cent of GDP to a surplus of 2.7 per cent, helped by a large increase in the inflow of foreign capital. According to Killick (1981*a*: 64), for 1976 and 1977 the total balance-of-payments impact of the higher export prices was sh.5,280 million, the terms-of-trade improvements being equivalent to a 15 per cent increase in GDP (our own estimate is provided in the main body of the chapter).

Real GDP growth was resumed in 1976, although only at the rate of 2.1 per cent. Per capita income (unadjusted for terms-of-trade effects) thus continued to decline. Agricultural real output increased by just 0.3 per cent, but the share of agriculture at current prices increased significantly. Incomes were thus shifted towards the agricultural sector by the change in relative prices (although, as we have shown, this was largely offset by subsequent increases in non-agricultural prices). The manufacturing sector accelerated dramatically, growing by over 18 per cent. This was due partly to the easing of import controls, which made it possible to import needed inputs, partly to the more expansionary fiscal and monetary policy, and, largely, to the spending of the boom income. In 1977 the economy grew at 9.4 per cent in real terms, the highest rate on record. Real agricultural output increased rapidly at 10 per cent, owing to the improvement in the weather but also to increased efforts reflecting the increase in prices, coffee yields increasing dramatically. There was also a boom in investment, which increased by 21 per cent. To accommodate this, imports of capital goods increased rapidly.

The increased world market price of coffee was allowed to change the domestic price fully without interference by the government. The domestic price followed the export price closely (see Table 5A1.8). Kenya was unusual at the outset of the boom in that farmers received the full world price except for deductions for costs of marketing and processing (see Davis (1983), for an international comparison of taxation policies). There were no attempts to sterilize the coffee money by putting it in, for example, some form of stabilization fund, although both the Central Bank and the IMF argued for something along these lines. The government, however, refused to take any such action and decided to let all the gains be passed on to the farmers. It is said to have been a personal decision by President Kenyatta that the farmers should have the money, and Finance Minister Kibaki, facing difficult party elections, accepted the decision willingly (Killick, 1984: 179). Not until June 1977 did the government introduce an *ad valorem* export tax on coffee, but by then the boom had already peaked and the rates were so low that very little money was actually generated by this tax. In no year did it amount to more than 5 per cent of the export price.[2]

The budget of 1976/7 was fairly restrictive in an attempt to control the government deficit. There was some tightening of taxation during the period 1976 to 1978, mainly in the form of reductions of allowances, while the tax rates otherwise remained unchanged. Killick (1984: 190) interprets the budget as giving 'forewarning that the government was not serious in its statements of the use of fiscal policy for stabilization'. Even so, the overall deficit was reduced to under 5 per cent of GDP.

During 1976/7 there were no serious attempts at offsetting the monetary impulses of the coffee boom, although the liquidity ratio was raised to 18 per cent in mid-1976. At the same time, however, interest rates were lowered and there was a promotion of credit to the private sector. There was a very rapid increase in domestic credit, even though the net borrowing to the government from the banking system was reduced. The government decided to exceed the credit ceilings which it had agreed with the IMF, thereby forfeiting the extended facility negotiated in 1975.

Foreign trade policy was *de facto* liberalized. Although during 1976/7 there were no changes in the regulations, there was a more liberal interpretation of the rules.

Both coffee and tea prices continued to rise strongly well into 1977. The government now had an opportunity to restore a long-term sustainable development path by using the temporary windfall to strengthen the budget and to liberalize foreign trade. This would have required a less expansionary fiscal and monetary policy and sterilization of the coffee revenue. Finance Minister Kibaki was aware of the temporary nature of the boom, and noted that 'if we are not to dissipate, through inflation, the benefits of the present commodity boom, it is important that the main part of the higher money incomes now available should be saved, and utilized for investment while we

---

[2] In Tanzania the average rate of the coffee tax in the period of the boom was 29%.

TABLE 5A1.8. *Coffee statistics, 1975–1983 (1975 = 100)*

	Deflated export price (A)	Deflated producer price (B)	(B)/(A)	Producer's share of price[a] (%)	Export tax share (%)	Coffee's share in exports (%)	Deliveries	Exports
1975	100	100	1.00	—	0	16.4	100	100
1976	195	217	1.11	—	0	29.3	121	115
1977	323	282	0.87	—	2.0	42.5	147	139
1978	180	176	0.98	(75)	4.8	33.7	127	126
1979	155	162	1.05	(78)	4.4	28.7	115	114
1980	129	133	1.03	—	4.0	22.2	138	118
1981	93	96	1.03	—	3.4	21.3	137	127
1982	93	104	1.12	—	—	26.5	134	149
1983	104	119	1.14	—	—	25.4	144	134

[a] The estimates of producer's share in export price refer to co-operatives.

Sources: Government of Kenya, *Statistical Abstract*, various issues; Annual Reports from the Coffee Board. The estimates of producer's share in export prices are taken from Ministry of Cooperative Development, *Report on a Survey on Coffee Handled by Cooperatives during 1977/78 and 1978/79 Coffee Seasons*, mimeo (1982).

can afford it' (*Budget Speech, 1977/78*: 3). The government was not strong enough, however, to bring about a strict policy. Kibaki defended his 1977/8 budget (p. 11) by saying that he was gambling on there being 'sufficient unemployed resources in the country that can be put to work by higher government spending without causing serious inflation'. In reality the Treasury would probably have preferred a smaller deficit, but it could not hold back the claims from the ministries. There was also pressure from urban wage earners and in August 1977 the wage guidelines were relaxed.

The fact that the government control of expenditures was slipping reflected the political difficulty of holding back expenditures in an economy with many obvious needs, when it was widely known that the Treasury had access to extra money. In an attempt to make it more difficult for the Treasury to cut down their requests, spending ministries refused to rank projects in any priority. The Treasury therefore had to enforce spending ceilings on ministries with little guidance about the relative merits of proposals. Not only did many bad projects thus come to be retained, but the net effect was for the Treasury to err on the side of extravagance.

During the boom large sums were invested in the EAC corporations and the sugar industry, and the government decided to embark on a major expansion of its defence budget (there was concern about the Ogaden war). Military expenditures increased from sh.400 million in 1975/6 to over sh.2,300 million in 1977/8. Finance Minister Kibaki said (*Budget Speech, 1977/78*: 11) that he was 'taking a risk that Ministries will contain their expenditure within the increased provision made for them in the estimates without asking for more'. This was a vain hope: in 1977/8 recurrent expenditure was sh.2,000 million higher than budgeted. More than two-thirds of this related to increased defence expenditures, while the rest was related to the taking over of the EAC and supplementary expenditure. Even if some of this expenditure was inevitable, we can safely conclude that much of the net increase would not have come about without the boom money.

This rapid increase of expenditures suggests that the control of the Treasury over spending had broken down. Normal procedures were abandoned or pursued with less rigour, and ministries became accustomed to negotiating considerable increases in their allocation. Even though the coffee boom led to rapid and unanticipated increases in government revenue, (receipts in 1977/8 being 27 per cent above the original estimate), the budget deficit started to increase.

In 1977 the government actually stimulated the expansion of bank credit to the private sector. The banking system was by then very liquid, the interest rate on short-term money falling below one per cent. In April 1977 the limits on local lending to foreign-controlled companies were relaxed for a period of two years. Between the end of 1976 and the end of 1978 the foreign assets of the banking system increased by around 50 per cent, while total domestic credit rose by 67 per cent.

As export income increased dramatically the overall balance improved. Long-term capital inflows almost doubled in 1977, consisting mainly of reinvestment of profits by foreign firms. The foreign reserves peaked in September 1977, when they were equivalent to over six months of imports, and then started to decline. There was a relaxation of import controls in early 1978, and imports continued to rise throughout 1978, by which time export income had already started to fall. Export income fell by sh.2,080 million in 1978, while imports increased by sh.3,760 million. In consequence, the current account deteriorated drastically. Long-term capital inflows increased by a further 40 per cent, but by the end of 1978 foreign reserves were down to under three months of imports.

During 1978 it gradually became clear that the boom was over and that this required policy changes. The terms of trade worsened by 20 per cent, so that per capita incomes adjusted for the terms-of-trade effect fell considerably (although the unadjusted figure showed an increase of 4 per cent). The Central Bank imposed a mild credit squeeze, which was made increasingly restrictive over the year. In January the liquidity ratio was increased to 20 per cent, in May interest rates were raised, and in July a cash ratio of 4 per cent was introduced, together with a limit to the rate of growth of bank advances of 1.5 per cent per month. (The liquidity ratio was at the same time lowered to 18 per cent.) Despite these measures there was a rapid increase in credit to the private sector. When the coffee boom receded the commercial banks were holding excess reserves and could therefore increase money supply independently of the growth in primary liquidity. The liquidity ratio of the commercial banks fell from a peak of 37 per cent in September 1977 to 22 per cent in June 1978, and so credit was not tight in this period. Capital formation was thus never constrained by reserve requirements, and in 1978 was at the record level of 25 per cent of GDP, the boom in terms of investment activity peaking after incomes had started to decline.

In May the Central Bank introduced administrative restraints on the approval of import licences, which were tightened in August. This was effective in reducing imports, but it was not sufficient to stop the decline of the foreign reserves. In December the government decided that the reserves were dangerously low and introduced a tax on foreign air travel and an import deposit scheme, under which importers had to place large deposits against the value of goods ordered. Once again the government thus chose to use direct administrative measures to reduce imports. Action had been delayed until the reserves were critically low. Devaluation was not considered, and monetary measures were too modest and too late. The balance-of-payments deficit reduced the rate of M1 growth to only 10 per cent in 1978 in spite of the large budget deficit. During a deficit banks run down their cash holdings, credit is restricted, and the resulting monetary squeeze reduces subsequent imports. This automatic mechanism has been more important than active government regulations. The expansion in money supply in 1977 at a rate close to 50 per cent, and the reverse impact in 1978, are clear instances of this passive policy stance.

Manufacturing continued to grow rapidly (12.6 per cent), while agricultural growth decelerated. Since relative prices also turned against it, the share of agriculture in GDP was considerably reduced. The growth of the public sector accelerated and increased further in 1979. The public sector aggregate deficit in 1978/9 reached a remarkable 8.2 per cent of GDP. The basic balance changed from a large surplus of 5.1 per cent of GDP in 1977 to a deficit of 4.3 per cent of GDP in 1978. Killick and Thorne (1981: 65) interpret what happened in 1978 as 'the 1974 crisis finally . . . coming home to roost'. Note that we have offered a rather different interpretation, namely that the coffee windfall itself rapidly destabilized the budget.

In the budget for 1978/9 current expenditures increased rapidly, and the current surplus showed a drastic decline. Government short-term borrowing increased rapidly. Part of the explanation for this may be poor government forecasting of expenditure because of budgetary procedures that led to considerable errors. The forecasts of revenue were also very imprecise. Finally, it must be acknowledged that the economic environment changed in a way which was difficult to predict.

The balance-of-payments problem was extensively discussed at the time, but no serious policy measures were proposed. The same is true of the Fourth Development Plan, for 1979–84. The passivity in policy-making as the boom drew to a close may in part be due to a period of political instability and uncertainty between the death of President Kenyatta in August 1978 and the elections in November 1979.

Many expenditure plans which were conceived during the height of the boom had their major impact when the boom had largely passed. The government sector thus acted as a destabilizer. During the boom revenue increased rapidly, and then expenditures followed. Development expenditures increased rapidly, but current expenditures also soared. The ratio between development expenditure and recurrent expenditure reached its peak in the 1977/8 budget, when it was 51 per cent. For 1978/9 it was down to 42 per cent. Thus, the public sector investment programme did not peak until 1978. There was an ambition to build up assets during the boom, but it turned out to be difficult to get the phasing right. Furthermore, the investments led to needs for recurrent expenditures, which in many instances could not be met. In consequence some investments could not be effectively used. One example of inefficiency is rural water supply: completed schemes were ceasing to operate at much the same rate as new ones were being introduced. Another example is that large amounts of money were spent on providing new beds at Kenyatta hospital in well-provided Nairobi, while at the same time rural dispensaries were running out of drugs.

5. *The Post-Boom Period*

Over the period 1978 to 1980 export prices fell to more normal levels, while import prices continued to rise sharply because of the second oil shock in 1979. Dick *et al.* (1984) have shown that Kenyan unit export costs are sensitive to oil price increases, since exports are highly oil-intensive and to a lesser extent intensive in other purchased intermediate inputs. Hence, the Kenyan trade balance was strongly affected by the higher oil prices. In addition, 1979 and 1980 were drought years and large quantities of food had to be imported. Both the budget and the balance of payments were therefore suddenly under intense pressure.

Let us consider for a moment the options before the government. One possibility was that necessity would be the mother of liberalization: faced with adversity the government could have decided that it could no longer afford the deadweight losses imposed by the control regime and so have dismantled it. This did not happen. Just as the government had not taken the opportunity provided by the windfall income to finance the adjustment costs of a sustainable liberalization on the ground that there was no necessity, so, come necessity, it baulked at the adjustment costs. Having rejected liberalization, the government still had other choices. The loss of revenue could be offset by tax increases or accommodated by expenditure reductions or inflation. The loss of foreign exchange could be offset by foreign borrowing or accommodated by tighter trade restrictions. However, large-scale foreign borrowing could only be unlocked by agreements with the IMF and the World Bank. The 'price' of such agreements would be some commitment to liberalization. Hence, the apparently softest option of borrowing from abroad would return the government to consideration of a persistently rejected option.

The preference of the government for this apparently softest option was duly revealed. During 1979 and 1980 there was an exceptionally large inflow of capital. In the second quarter of 1979 the government arranged balance-of-payments support from the IMF through the first, and nearly automatic, credit tranche. The government also signed agreements with the World Bank and several other donors for both stand-by credits and programme loans.

In August 1979 the government concluded an agreement with the IMF for a stand-by credit. The agreement consisted of a two-year programme which included:

(*a*) improvements in tax revenues;
(*b*) real reductions in government spending in 1979/80;
(*c*) 15 per cent expansion of bank credit to the private sector;
(*d*) a study of international adjustment;
(*e*) a policy of wage restraint (implying reductions in real wages);
(*f*) careful control over public debt.

The performance criteria included:

(*a*) ceilings on the net domestic assets of the Central Bank;
(*b*) ceilings on government borrowing from the banking system;
(*c*) an understanding to be reached with the Fund on exchange rate policy;
(*d*) another understanding about an early elimination of the import deposit scheme of 1978.

The course of events diverged rapidly and dramatically from this programme. In November 1979 the import deposit scheme was indeed relaxed. However, the ceiling on bank credit to the government proposed by the IMF was greatly exceeded, even during the second half of 1979. When bank credit eventually fell within the ceiling in the middle of 1980 the government tried to draw its fund credit but was refused. The refusal was on the grounds that the government had enhanced the export subsidy scheme by doubling the subsidy. The credit negotiated with the IMF in 1979 was thus never used.

Simultaneously pursuing options besides borrowing, the government tightened its wage guidelines in February 1979, and also directed a major effort to raising revenue. In June 1979 the sales tax, which had been 10 per cent, was increased to 15 per cent in general and 25–30 per cent on luxuries, with exemptions for capital equipment.

There was an initial restraint on money supply in 1979 owing to the credit squeeze and the deficit on the balance of payments, in spite of the fact that the government at the end of 1978 had resumed the practice of regular direct advances by the Central Bank to the government for the first time since 1976.

The Kenya government has never been strongly dependent on external loans and grants to finance its budget. Normally external financing has provided around 10 per cent of revenue, but in the period 1978–81 it increased to 15 per cent. Deficit finance was also considerable in the budgets of 1978/9 and 1980/1, as it had been during the mid-1970s. The aggregate budget deficit in 1978/9 was 8.2 per cent of GDP.

Although 1979 was thus a difficult year, until the oil price hikes the economy was still growing. The aggregate rate of growth was as high as 3.9 per cent, in spite of a decline in agriculture, and the basic balance was restored to zero. The oil price increases, however, changed the picture drastically for the worse. The terms of trade worsened by another 10 per cent between 1979 and 1980 and the basic balance was in deficit by over 5 per cent of GDP, in spite of continued heavy borrowing from abroad. Public foreign debt, sh.4,460 million at the end of 1973, had increased to sh.16,720 million by the end of 1980. The debt service ratio had risen to 13 per cent of GDP, from 3 per cent during the first half of the 1970s.

It was thus necessary to come up with further policy measures to deal with the economic crisis. In 1980 the government presented a structural adjustment programme in Sessional Paper no. 4 of 1980, *On Economic Prospects and Policies*, which was similar to the paper of 1975. Here it once again argued the case for fiscal stabilization and for measures to deal with the balance-of-payments problem. It proposed the elimination of quantitative restrictions on imports, to be replaced by equivalent tariffs, and the elimination of the No-Objection Certificates. There was also to be a standardization and reduction in the level of industrial protection and export stimulus. It envisaged a reduced dependence on administrative scrutiny of import licences, to be replaced by a system where foreign exchange was more automatically allocated according to demand and foreign exchange availability. A higher interest rate structure was also suggested.

The 1980/1 budget started the implementation of these measures. Import controls were liberalized and interest rates increased. However, the government was reluctant to introduce new tax measures. It was also largely unable to contain government spending and to achieve its incomes policy.

A new credit was negotiated with the IMF in October 1980 with less stringent policy conditions, except on one point, namely that import policy was to be changed from quantitative restrictions to tariffs. However, this agreement fared no better than its predecessor. This seems to indicate that the government tended to see the IMF money as easily available extra resources, rather than as a basis for long-term adjustment. This last agreement fell apart because government expenditures increased more rapidly than budgeted, partly because of a 30 per cent increase in civil service salaries and a food shortage, but primarily because of poor budgetary control. The latter may to some extent have been caused by the erosion of the budgetary procedures during the coffee boom.

According to the Report of the Controller and Auditor-General for 1980/1, expenditure by the ministries had consistently outstripped available resources, and the ministries continued to make unrealistic demands above spending ceilings. In the *Budget Speech* of 1982/3 the Finance Minister noted (p. 2) that 'sadly, one detects an apparent unwillingness of top managers in the government to appreciate the magnitude of the fiscal problem facing the nation. This together with the general lack of fiscal discipline in many ministries is very disturbing.' He further emphasized the need to restore the 'integrity and authority of the budget as the central framework for the allocation of Government financial resources'. The Philip Ndegwa Working Party report (Government of Kenya, 1982*b*) lists numerous sources of inefficiency in the public sector. As an example of poor financial control, the Annual Report and Accounts of the Industrial and Commercial Development Corporation (ICDC) for 1979/80 states that they had recorded receipts from the government of sh.506 million, while the government accounts showed that sh.745 million had been issued.

There were also large problems in connection with the parastatals, which had to be heavily subsidized. The Cereals and Sugar Finance Corporation had to provide money to a variety of parastatals concerned with agriculture to finance their losses. These were in part due to inefficiencies within these organizations, as shown in the *Review of Statutory Boards* (1979). The government had also guaranteed bad debts of parastatals. In addition, large sums had to be transferred to the National Cereals and Produce Board, which had been required to buy and sell cereals at prices which did not cover costs. Effectively this was a consumer subsidy.

Nelson (1984) attributes the continual failure of the Kenyan government to implement stabilization policies to three 'political economy' characteristics. First, a high proportion of urban wage and salary earners are actually employed by the government or parastatals, and these will be directly hurt by fiscal stringency. Secondly, the producers of key exports, who would benefit from a devaluation, are not as well organized or politically dangerous as the urban-based industrial groups, who would lose from it. Thirdly, the victims of a credit squeeze are the same urban élites. All these factors tend to delay adjustment or make it less efficient.

The efficacy of economic policy-making may also be influenced by the fact that Kenya's government is balanced to represent different areas and ethnic groups, and this means that cabinet members may be quick to stop measures hurting their constituents. This tends to delay the imposition of restrictive measures. Another factor is that, even though it has turned out to be difficult to manage the bureaucracy via budgeting, expenditure control, or personal or policy action, there has been relatively little interest in strengthening the financial and budgetary control mechanisms. The reason for this may be that the political leaders depend on their control over the allocation of resources for their political survival, and are therefore reluctant to relinquish control to a group of technocrats, even if that were to improve fiscal discipline. Finally, the fact that the political base of support is narrow may constrain the scope for action. Since President Moi does not have a large ethnic base he has had to rely on ethnic conciliation and appeals for national unity, populist gestures, and anti-corruption proclamations. Initially President Moi was able to build up widespread popular support, but as this has declined he has had to rely on the support of the political and administrative circles surrounding him.

Although the balance-of-payments situation was critical, growth in Kenya actually accelerated somewhat in 1980 to 4.5 per cent. The budget deficit, however, exploded and reached a record level of over 10 per cent of GDP in 1980/1 Money supply accelerated again, and inflation approached 20 per cent. In spite of the large deficits on the current account in 1979 and 1980 the government refused to devalue.[3] However, the food situation continued to be precarious in 1981, and further large food imports were necessary. Exports stagnated, and even though imports were reduced the basic balance showed an even larger deficit than in 1980. In the second half of 1981 the reserves had become depleted and were restored by expensive borrowing on the Euro-

---

[3] From 1974 the Kenya shilling had been pegged to the SDR.

currency market. The country was facing an acute balance-of-payments crisis. Belatedly, the government conceded a measure of liberalization under pressure from both the IMF and the World Bank and devalued twice, increasing the shilling price of the dollar by 36 per cent. The currency was further devalued in 1982 when the shilling price of the dollar increased by another 24 per cent.

Gulhati *et al.* (1985) estimate that this decline in the nominal exchange rate index, from 97.3 in 1975 to 65.4 in 1982, reduced the real effective exchange rate from 103.5 to 94.2. However, in Chapter 2 we question whether the concept of the real exchange rate used by Gulhati *et al.* is appropriate to the period considered.

Between 1980 and 1982 the outright bans on selected imports and the No-Objection Certificate procedure were abolished; tariffs were increased, as were export subsidies; and a new system of import licensing was put into effect from November 1981. The budget deficit was reduced a little, but was still huge (9.5 per cent of GDP). The public sector continued to expand at over 5 per cent and public investment increased. The total growth rate fell to 3.9 per cent.

In January 1982 a third stand-by agreement was reached with the IMF, with tougher conditions. Yet again the agreement was soon suspended: by the middle of 1982 bank credit to the government had broken through the agreed ceiling.

Sessional Paper no. 4 of 1982 marked a further attempt to plan the reform of import controls. Items would gradually be moved from quota-based schedules to quota-free ones at a rate to be determined by the availability of foreign exchange. It was expected that this process would proceed gradually up to 1985, when only 12 per cent of the items were to be left on the quota-based schedule. Those to be left on the schedule were to be goods which were to be controlled for health or moral reasons and goods of 'national import-ance'. The controls were also to be used to restrain demand for luxury goods.

In accordance with the plan the 1982/3 budget announced that 20 per cent of the items on the quota-based schedule would be shifted. However, because of the growing foreign exchange crisis this shift was never implemented. The individual scrutiny of import licences was reintroduced in mid-1982. In April 1983 a new mechanism for the shifting of items to the quota-free schedules was established, but when in early 1984 the time came at which the first shifts were to be made they were again delayed.

In December 1982 the shilling was depreciated by 15 per cent against the SDR, and severe restrictions on imports and foreign exchange use were introduced. The export compensation scheme (which was regarded as ineffi-cient) was abolished in the middle of 1982. The government was aware that expenditures had to be brought under control. In the *Budget Speech* of 1982 the Minister for Finance, Magugu, stated: 'the Budget deficit can now only be brought under firm control by curtailing government expenditure' (p. 2). However, the political process of implementation was precarious. The fragility of the position of the government was demonstrated by a coup attempt in August 1982 (a very rare event in Kenya), which might be seen as a concrete demonstration of the political constraints on retrenchment.

The budget deficit was reduced in 1982, but was still 6.7 per cent of GDP. Consequently, money supply growth was reduced and inflation fell to 13 per cent. Capital formation declined, gradually being squeezed out of the government budget during the economic crisis: the ratio of development to recurrent expenditure fell from 45 per cent in 1979/80 to 34 per cent by 1983/4. The basic balance deficit in 1982 was reduced to 3.4 per cent of GDP. This was achieved by reductions in imports, the long-term capital inflow being reduced considerably. GDP growth fell to 1.7 per cent, so that per capita incomes fell for the first time since the mid-1970s.

Thus, even with a more restrictive policy the external deficit remained large in 1982. During 1983, however, a zero basic balance was restored, in spite of considerably reduced long-term capital inflows. Export volume increased modestly, and coffee and tea prices were again increasing somewhat. The terms of trade improved by some 7 per cent. The major factor behind the improved external balance, however, was that the volume of imports had been reduced by over 40 per cent between 1981 and 1983.

This drastic reduction in imports, of course, had effects on the economy's potential for growth, though by 1983 the economy was again growing at a rate sufficient to preserve per capita incomes. By this time the public sector was not growing much faster than the rest of the economy. The budget deficit was reduced to 4 per cent of GDP. Domestic credit had been brought under control and inflation was down to about 10 per cent. Capital formation ceased to fall, but in both 1982 and 1983 its share of GDP was lower than at any time since 1975.

The Kenyan economy was thus still in a difficult economic situation in 1983, but it had managed to reduce both the external and internal deficits. The exchange rate had been brought down to a level that was probably sustainable, given the trade restrictions, and fiscal discipline had been at least partially restored.

6. Concluding Remarks

The first oil shock created a serious balance-of-payments crisis and a large domestic budget deficit in Kenya in 1974. A programme of structural adjustment was initiated, but this was side-tracked by the coffee boom. However, in view of the persistent failure of policy makers to implement adjustments under either favourable or adverse circumstances, we may doubt whether even without the boom the programme would have been implemented. During the boom government expenditure increased rapidly and when coffee prices fell back this expenditure was maintained.

With the second oil crisis both the basic balance deficit and the budget deficit reached record levels. The government borrowed heavily on the international capital markets until 1983, at the same time as it reduced imports through both administrative means and devaluations. By 1983 the government had managed to get both the budget and basic balance deficit under a measure of control, but the economy now had a much larger foreign debt to service. Growth prospects were therefore not as good as they once had been.

What was the root cause of the very serious crisis of 1981? As we noted before, Killick and Thorne (1981) interpret what happened in the aftermath of the boom as the 1974 crisis finally coming home to roost. They argue that the crisis had been under way since the first half of the 1970, and that the coffee boom just delayed the slide. Indeed, Killick (1984: 192) suggests that the government was on the whole fairly responsible, although it had not been so in short-run economic management. The Kenyan government, after all (he argues), made some adjustments to price incentives, taxation, government spending, and industrial protection.

Another possible interpretation of the 1981 crisis is that it was mainly caused by the second oil price shock of 1979. It is true, of course, that this was a contributory factor. Still, the economy could have coped more efficiently with this if it had not already been in a precarious situation, with extensive regulations and a government sector out of control. Imports were already extensively controlled by administrative means, foreign borrowing was large, and government expenditures were soaring. These basic imbalances were not caused by the oil price shock.

Our interpretation of the events is instead that the coffee boom was the root cause of the 1981 crisis, while the crisis of the mid-1970s was a smaller adjustment problem. The boom led to a breakdown of control over public expenditure, which was not restored until 1983. There was an expansion of the public sector considerably in excess of what was sustainable under normal circumstances, and additionally private demand expanded too rapidly. The coffee boom thus caused the serious disequilibrium of the economy. As a result of the boom the government became unable to handle its finances in an efficient and responsible way, and in consequence was unable to handle the second oil price shock efficiently. The behaviour of the government was characterized by a persistent refusal to adjust. Not until the situation developed into an unsustainable foreign exchange crisis was action taken, and then the government chose the option of introducing administrative control on imports, while devaluations and monetary policy were of secondary importance. Neither the control regime nor fiscal or monetary policies since the boom can be described as responsible.

We conclude that the coffee boom seriously disrupted the Kenyan economy, by leading to an unsustainable expansion. Two authoritative retrospective Kenyan views are provided by Duncan Ndegwa, the Governor of the Central Bank (Central Bank of Kenya, *Sources and Uses of Foreign Exchange in Kenya 1974–79*, 1981), and Philip Ndegwa in the *Report and Recommendations of the Working Party on Government Expenditures* (1982).

The Philip Ndegwa Working Party notes the loss of control of expenditure, described above, as the source of the financial crisis of the government. It notes (p. 15) that there has been a 'marked decline, over the years, in standards of management performance and financial control within the Government'. It further points out that there has been a 'systematic tendency in many ministries of ignoring financial regulation and instructions from the Treasury', and that there has been a 'collapse of financial discipline'.

This Kenyan view is in agreement with the interpretation suggested in this chapter. This official perception does not, however, mean that the government was quickly able to implement the changes needed. The restoration of financial control is a long-term and demanding task.

The Duncan Ndegwa report concluded (p. 34) that 'the next time a bonanza of the 1976 and 1977 magnitude occurs the authorities would be well advised to pay out the resulting incomes to society gradually in an orderly manner rather than in one season, as was the case at that time'. It suggested that precautionary foreign exchange reserves should be built up instead.

Whereas the Philip Ndegwa report correctly identifies an important element in the explanation of events, the Duncan Ndegwa report raises the issue of how best the windfall might have been handled. This central question of counterfactual policies we have investigated through the CGE model.

Appendix 2
The Computable General Equilibrium Model

1. *Introduction*

Here we describe the model used in the chapter for the simulation experiments.[1]

The model is a computable general equilibrium model (CGE). Firms maximize profits and households maximize utility at given product and

---

[1] An earlier version of the model was described in detail in Gunning (1979), was used for the World Bank Basic Economic Report, and was published (in a rather condensed form) as Gunning (1983). There are important differences between the model described here and its earlier version. First, rural wages and labour supply, which used to be exogenous, are in this version of the model determined endogenously: leisure is an argument of the utility function of peasants. Secondly, household savings rates are no longer fixed. Households distinguish between permanent and transitory income. Thirdly, there are no nominal rigidities in the model: all real variables are homogeneous of degree zero in wages and prices. Finally, goods and services produced by the formal and by the informal sectors are now modelled as imperfect substitutes in demand.

factor prices. Each market clears, excess demand (or supply) being eliminated either through price adjustments or through quantity adjustments (typically changes in exports or imports).

The model's solution is a general equilibrium with several non-Walrasian elements. First, there are real wage rigidities in urban labour markets. Secondly, investment is allocated (exogenously) over sectors in a way which does not equalize rates of return. Thirdly, credit market imperfections prevent peasants from adopting an optimal product mix. Finally, and most importantly, a trade policy which relies heavily on the use of quantitative restrictions creates large distortions.

The model is fairly disaggregated. There are 36 commodities, 48 groups of peasants, six types of urban labour, six types of rural labour, and eight types of urban households. One of the model's limitations is that it is a barter model: there are no financial assets in it. Only relative prices matter and there is no interest rate.

Kenya is modelled as a small open economy facing given world prices for its imports and exports and a given supply of foreign savings. The government's interventions consist of taxes, tariffs, control over producer prices, and import controls.

There are two reasons why in this model a commodity boom strongly benefits groups other than farmers producing the commodity, even if producer prices are tied to world prices. First, a considerable part of the extra income is spent by the initial beneficiaries, the farmers, on goods which are either non-tradable (e.g. services) or which are non-traded (because of import controls). As a result, large rents are created in the urban sector. Secondly, the mechanism of investment allocation is such that extra savings (whether by rural or urban groups) largely end up as an increase in the urban capital stock.

2. *Commodity Markets: Price and Quantity Adjustments*

In a general equilibrium model supply must be equal to demand for each commodity. Hence the balance equation

$$x = Ax + c + g + i^s + e - m \qquad (1)$$

must be satisfied, where A is an $n \times n$ input–output matrix and x, c, g, i^s, e, and m are n-vectors denoting production, private consumption, government consumption, investment (by sector of origin[2]), exports, and (competitive) imports. Hence the balance equation imposes the equality of total supply (domestic production, x, and competitive imports, m) and total demand (intermediate demand, Ax, plus domestic final demand, $d = c + g + i^s$, plus exports, e).

In the model, agents take prices as given,[3] producers maximize profits, and households maximize utility. The solution of these maximization problems

---

[2] The superscript s stands for 'source'.
[3] Except in sectors 17 and 18 (discussed below), where there is mark-up pricing.

consists of the quantities demanded or supplied by each agent. If we sum these quantities over agents we obtain an excess demand vector for the economy. In equilibrium all elements of this vector should be equal to zero; equation (1) is then satisfied. In the textbook general equilibrium model of a closed economy this is achieved through price changes: one solves for a price vector such that (1) is satisfied. All sectors are then assumed to be in the same 'regime', in which price changes clear the market. Conversely, in the standard model of trade theory, equilibrium is achieved through quantity adjustments: domestic prices are then tied to world prices and net domestic supply (demand) is exported (imported). The balance equation (1) is then satisfied because the term $(e - m)$ is treated as a residual.

In the Kenya model there are both price and quantity adjustments: commodities differ in regimes. In most cases, the regime is predetermined, i.e. we assume that price adjustment, for example, is always the equilibrating mechanism for a particular commodity. In some other cases, however (the most important cases from the point of view of trade theory), regime switches are possible: whether the market is cleared through price or quantity adjustments is then determined endogenously.

The commodities distinguished in the model are listed in Table 5A2.1. There are 36 commodities, divided over ten commodity groups. There are three groups of tradables (A, B, C); four groups of non-tradables (D, E, F, G); and three groups of commodities which cannot be produced domestically (H, I, J). The specification adopted for these ten groups is summarized in Table 5A2.2.

Before discussing the specification we introduce the price concepts used in the model. Associated with the balance equation (1) is a vector of domestic prices, pd. Producer prices (pp) are domestic prices net of indirect taxes, and net prices (π) are producer prices minus the costs of intermediate inputs (valued at domestic prices). Indirect tax rates (δ), import tariff rates (τ_m), and export subsidy rates (τ_e) are given. Domestic prices must lie within an interval determined by a price floor ($\underline{pd}$), which is determined by world prices, and a price ceiling ($\overline{pd}$), which is an instrument of trade policy. Hence:

$$\underline{pd} \leqslant pd \leqslant \overline{pd} \tag{2}$$
$$\underline{pd}_i = (1 + \tau_{mi})\,pw_{mi} = (1 + \tau_{ei})\,pw_{ei} \tag{3}$$
$$pp' = pd'\,(I{-}D) \tag{4}$$
$$\pi' = pd'\,(I{-}A{-}D) \tag{5}$$

where

$$pd = \text{the domestic price}$$
$$\underline{pd} = \text{the price floor}$$
$$\overline{pd} = \text{the price ceiling}$$
$$pw_{mi} = \text{the c.i.f. import price of the ith commodity}$$
$$pw_{ei} = \text{the f.o.b. export price of the ith commodity}$$

TABLE 5A2.1.   *Commodity classification in the model*

TRADABLES

A. *Exportables*

1. coffee
2. tea
3. cotton
4. sugar
5. other export crops
6. mining

B. *Importables (no QRs)*

7. maize
8. other food crops
9. livestock products
10. manufactured food products

C. *Importables (subject to QRs)*

11. non-food manufactured products

NON-TRADABLES

D. *Services (price adjustments)*

12. construction
13. trade
14. transport
15. housing
16. other services

E. *Services (quantity adjustments)*

17. electricity and water supply
18. government

F. *Commodities supplied by the informal sector (high-income self-employed)*

19. non-food manufactured products
20. trade
21. transport
22. other services

G. *Commodities supplied by the informal sector (low-income self-employed)*

23. non-food manufactured products
24. trade
25. transport
26. other services

NON-COMPETITIVE IMPORTS

H. *Consumer goods and services*

27. non-food manufactured products
28. trade
29. transport
30. housing
31. government
32. other services

I. *Imports for investment*

33. livestock
34. machinery and transport equipment
35. construction

J. *Other non-competitive imports*

36. imported intermediate goods and services

τ_{mi} = the tariff rate of the ith commodity
τ_{ei} = the export subsidy rate of the ith commodity
pp = the producer price
π = the net price
A = the input–output matrix
I = the identity matrix
D = a diagonal matrix of indirect tax rates $(d_{ii} = \delta_i)$.

World prices (expressed in domestic currency) are given. If pd equals $\underline{pd}$ any difference between the domestic price and the c.i.f. or f.o.b. price appears in the government budget as tariff revenue or as a payment of export subsidy. If pd exceeds $\underline{pd}$ then the difference accrues to firms as rents. Finally, it may be

TABLE 5A2.2. *Price and quantity adjustments: summary of the specification*

Commodity group[a]	Regime[b]	Domestic prices[c]	Adjusting quantity[d]
A: exportables	Q	tied to world price	exports
B: importables (no QRs)	Q	tied to world price	imports
C: importables (QRs)	Q^e	tied to world price	imports
	P^e	market-clearing	—
	Q^e	price ceiling	imports
D: services	P	market-clearing	—
E: services	Q	mark-up	output
F, G: informal sector	P	market-clearing	—
H, I, J: non-competitive imports	Q	tied to world price	imports

[a] See Table 5A2.1.

[b] Price adjustment (P) or quantity adjustment (Q).

[c] When the domestic price (pd) is tied to the world price, it is given by equation (3); when it is market-clearing it is the adjusting variable; and in the mark-up case pd is given by equation (14).

[d] Variable ($e, m,$ or x) which is determined residually from equation (1) in case of quantity adjustment.

[e] Switches between the three regimes are endogenous: cf. equation (12) and Fig. 5A2.1.

noted that the definition of the net price π corresponds to the concept of GDP at factor cost in national accounting.

This may be seen by writing out equation (5) for commodity i:

$$\pi_i = pd_i - \sum_j A_{ji} pd_j - \delta_i pd_i \tag{6}$$

Hence π_i is defined as the commodity's domestic price, net of indirect taxes paid by the producer per unit of output ($\delta_i pd_i$) and minus the cost of intermediate inputs, valued at domestic market prices.

We now turn to the adjustment mechanisms in the model (cf. Tables 5A2.1 and 5A2.2). We distinguish six exportable commodities (group A): five non-food agricultural products (of which coffee and tea are the most important) plus the output of the (tiny) mining sector. For these commodities there are no imports, there is no domestic final demand, the domestic price is tied to the world price, and all production net of intermediate demand is exported. Hence for this group of commodities we assume a regime of quantity adjustment: exports are residual. Therefore,

$$x_i = \sum_j A_{ij} x_j + e_i \tag{7}$$

$$pd_i = (1 + \tau_{ei}) pw_{ei}. \tag{8}$$

Food commodities (group B) are modelled as importables which are not subject to quantitative restrictions (QRs). For this group imports rather than exports clear the market and the domestic price is determined by the c.i.f.

price and the tariff rate:

$$x_i = \sum_j A_{ij} x_j + d_i - m_i \tag{9}$$

$$pd_i = (1 + \tau_{mi}) pw_{mi}. \tag{10}$$

Note that domestically produced and imported food are treated as perfect substitutes and, hence, traded at the same price (pd). Non-food manufactured products (group C) account for the bulk of Kenya's merchandise imports. These products are modelled as importables subject to QRs. In this case the type of adjustment mechanism is endogenously determined: the model may switch from one regime to another. We assume that the import control policy defines a level of imports ($\bar{m}$) which cannot be exceeded, unless the domestic price has reached its ceiling ($\overline{pd}$). When prices reach the ceiling, the QRs are relaxed: competitive imports are then allowed to clear the market. When imports are equal to $\bar{m}$, the domestic price is adjusted until the market clears (subject, of course, to the constraint $pd \leqslant \overline{pd}$). Hence, for group C:

$$x_i = \sum_j A_{ij} x_j + d_i - m_i \tag{11}$$

$$\underline{pd}_i = (1 + \tau_{mi}) pw_{mi} \tag{12}$$

$$\left. \begin{array}{lll} & m_i < \bar{m}_i, & pd_i = \underline{pd}_i \\ or & m_i = \bar{m}_i, & \underline{pd}_i \leqslant pd_i < \overline{pd}_i \\ or & m_i \geqslant \bar{m}_i, & pd_i = \overline{pd}_i. \end{array} \right\} \tag{13}$$

Equation (13) is illustrated in Fig. 5A2.1. In equilibrium imports are equal to excess domestic demand z (where $z_i = \sum_j A_{ij} x_j + d_i - x_i$), which is shown as decreasing in the price pd. Three possible positions of the excess demand curve are shown in the diagram. In the first case the solution is at A. Import controls are then not effective ($m < \bar{m}$) and the domestic price is tied to the world price by the tariff policy. If the demand curve shifts from z_A to z_B then a switch from quantity to price adjustment occurs.

At B the QRs are effective ($m = \bar{m}$) and the domestic price must rise above $\underline{pd}$ for the market to clear. At a still higher level of demand imports again take over the role of clearing the market. At C the domestic price has reached its ceiling ($pd = \overline{pd}$) and imports are determined residually from (11). Note that the import control policy creates a rent (corresponding to the price difference $pd - \underline{pd}$), which, since tax and tariff rates are fixed, accrues to private agents.

In the case of services, we treat domestic production and imports as complements in demand. Hence domestically supplied services are modelled as non-tradables (groups D and E), with balance equations

$$x_i = \sum_j A_{ji} x_j + d_i. \tag{14}$$

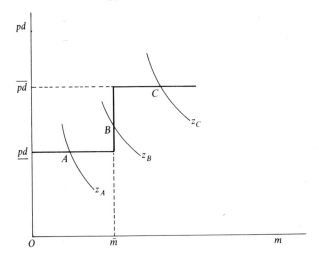

FIG. 5A2.1. *Price and quantity adjustments for importables subject to QRs*

For most services (those in group D) we assume a regime of price adjustment: pd adjusts until excess demand is eliminated. For two types of services (those in group E) this would not be a realistic assumption. Here we assume instead mark-up pricing and quantity adjustment. The adjustment applies to domestic production (x), rather than, as in the case of tradables, to international trade. Hence supply adjusts to demand: x is determined residually from (14).

In the case of commodity 18 (government services) the government is the sole agent on each side of the market. Since this sector's output is non-tradable, since demand is exogenous, and since there is no scope for factor substitution (wages and salaries account for 99 per cent of value added), it would make no sense to assume profit maximization and market-clearing prices: the demand curve is completely and the supply curve would be virtually completely inelastic. We assume therefore that supply adjusts to demand. Demand for the sector's output amounts to a demand for labour and, since only one agent is involved, it is therefore realistic to let any change in demand spill over into the labour market, which is what the specification amounts to.

In the case of electricity supply our reason is a technical one. There is no factor substitution in this sector. Past investment determines capacity (in, say, MW). This does not, however, imply a vertical supply curve. Output in the sector consists of energy (a capacity-times-time concept, measured, say, in GWh) and the supplier has no control over output as long as demand does not exceed capacity: an electrical network is a perfect example of output being determined by demand. Therefore we assume (as for the government, but for a quite different reason) that the balance equation is satisfied through changes in x.[4]

In both cases the domestic price is determined by a fixed mark-up (ρ) over unit costs (wages, intermediate inputs, and indirect taxes). Hence for group E, x is residual in (14) and the domestic price is given by:

$$pd_i = (1 + \rho_i)\left(\sum_k n_{ki} w_k + \sum_j A_{ji} pd_j + \delta_i pd_i \right) \tag{15}$$

where

n_{ki} = employment of type k labour per unit of output of sector i
w_k = wage rate for type k labour
ρ_i = mark-up rate.

Imports have appeared so far only in the balance equations (9) and (11), i.e. as perfect substitutes for the importables in groups B and C (commodities 7–11). In addition to these five categories of competitive imports, ten foreign goods play a role in the model as non-competitive imports (commodities 27–36). These imports are distinguished according to the source of demand: consumption (group H), investment (group I), and intermediate demand (group J). Hence the balance equations take a very simple form:

$$m_i = c_i \qquad \text{(G)} \tag{16}$$
$$m_i = i_i^s \qquad \text{(H)} \tag{17}$$
$$m_i = \sum_j A_{ij} x_j \qquad \text{(I)} \tag{18}$$

and in all three cases the domestic price is tied to the c.i.f. price:

$$pd_i = (1 + \tau_{mi}) pw_{mi}. \tag{19}$$

The goods and services considered so far (groups A–E and H–J) correspond to the coverage of the Kenyan National Accounts. This leaves out the production of the informal sector. Within this sector we distinguish a free-entry sector (the low-income self-employed) and a sector with barriers to entry (the high-income self-employed). The informal sector produces non-food manufactured goods and supplies three types of services: trade, transport, and other services. We assume that the output of the two groups of self-employed are imperfect substitutes for each other and for the output of the corresponding activity in the formal sector. For example, transport services may be supplied by all three groups of agents (commodities 14, 21 and 25 in Table 5A2.1) but a train, a taxi, and a matatu are treated as intermediate between complements and perfect substitutes. We assume that

---

[4] Implicitly we thereby assume that there is always excess capacity in the electricity sector. Our assumptions on investment in the sector ensure that this is the case.

the informal sector produces only for final (domestic) demand. Hence for groups F and G:

$$x_i = d_i \tag{20}$$

and this equilibrium is reached through price adjustments.

3. *Macro-balances and Homogeneity*

In the previous section we considered the equality of supply and demand at the level of the individual commodity. If each of the sectoral balance equations is satisfied, then, obviously, supply also equals demand for the economy as a whole, i.e. the balance equations imply the GDP identity (at current prices). To see this, we first define net government income from indirect taxes paid by domestic producers:

$$t_d = \sum_i \delta_i \, pd_i \, x_i \tag{21}$$

net revenue from tariffs and export subsidies:

$$t_t = \sum_i (\tau_{mi} \, pw_{mi} \, m_i - \tau_{ei} \, pw_{ei} \, e_i) \tag{22}$$

and net rents accruing to private agents when they sell (net) imports at a price exceeding the c.i.f.-cum-tariff price $(pd > \underline{pd})$:

$$r = \sum_i (pd_i - \underline{pd}_i)(m_i - e_i). \tag{23}$$

Substituting $d = c + i^s + g$ in (1) and multiplying by domestic prices we obtain

$$pd'x = pd'Ax + pd'd + (pd' - \underline{pd}')(e - m) + \underline{pd}'(e - m) \tag{24}$$

or, using (3), (21), (22), and (23):

$$pd'(I{-}A{-}D)x + t_d = pd'd - r + (pw'_e e - pw'_m m) - t_t. \tag{25}$$

Substitution of (5) gives

$$(\pi'x + r) + (t_d + t_t) = pd'd + (pw'_e e - pw'_m m). \tag{26}$$

This is the GDP identity. On the right-hand side the first term $(pd'd)$ represents total domestic final demand (consumption and investment) at current market prices, while the term in brackets is the difference between exports and imports valued respectively at f.o.b. and c.i.f. prices. On the left-hand side, the first term in brackets equals total GDP at factor cost, consisting of value added in domestic production $(\pi'x)$ and the value added (the rents r) generated by external trade to the extent that differences between domestic and world prices are not taxed away.

It should be noted that the term r on the left-hand side of (26) represents only part of the rents created by trade controls. Fig. 5A2.2 illustrates the point. In the absence of quantitative restrictions, the domestic price would be equal to $\underline{pd}$, domestic production would be equal to q_1, demand to q_4, and imports would be equal to the difference $(q_4 - q_1)$. If QRs restricted the volume of imports to $\bar{m}$, then the domestic price would rise to pd^*, demand would fall to q_3, and production would increase to q_2. Net income of domestic producers and importers would then rise: they would receive the rents corresponding to the shaded areas A and B. Area B (equal to $(pd^* - \underline{pd})\bar{m}$) is accounted for by the second term in (26); but area A is not. This part of the rents created by the import control policy is included in the term $\pi'x$ in (26), as an increase in the profitability of domestic production.

Hence the left-hand side of (26) is equal to GDP at market prices: the first term in brackets stands for GDP at factor cost and the second term for total (net) indirect taxes. Hence the GDP identity is indeed satisfied in the model.

If Walras' law holds then (26) implies balance-of-payments equilibrium. All agents are indeed on their budget constraints so that aggregate expenditure equals aggregate income. Aggregate income consists of GDP at market prices plus foreign savings (s_f): the total of net transfers received, net factor services income, and net capital imports. Hence, summing budget constraints over agents, we obtain:

$$(\pi'x + r + t_d + t_t) + s_f = pd'd \qquad (27)$$

and substitution in (26) gives:

$$s_f = (pw'_e e - pw'_m m) \qquad (28)$$

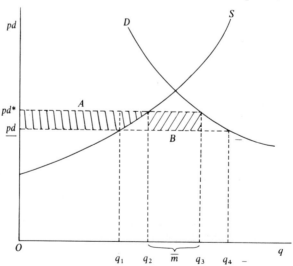

FIG. 5A2.2. *Import controls and rents*

and this implies external equilibrium: the difference between exports and imports (valued at world prices) is equal to foreign savings.

Foreign savings are given exogenously in this model (on the basis of e.g. detailed forecasts of external borrowing and repayment of outstanding debt). Provided this given total adds to the income of domestic agents,[5] the model's solution will satisfy (28). While in many other CGE models (28) is imposed as a balance-of-payments constraint, in the Kenya model balance-of-payments equilibrium is a result rather than an assumption.

The third macro-relation: the equality of total savings and investment in current prices is, of course, also satisfied. Following National Accounts conventions, gross domestic savings (s_d) are defined as the difference between GDP at market prices and total (private and public) consumption:

$$s_d = (\pi'x + r + t_d + t_t) - pd'(c + g) \tag{29}$$

and, since d is equal to $c + g + i^s$, substitution in (27) gives

$$s_d + s_f = pd'i^s \tag{30}$$

or: total (domestic and foreign) savings are equal to total investment $\left(\sum_i pd_i i_i^s\right)$.

The Kenya model is a barter model: there is no money or any other financial asset in it. This has two implications which should be noted: only relative prices matter (all real variables are homogeneous of degree zero in prices) and, secondly, exchange rate policies cannot be modelled.

The model's homogeneity property means that if a vector (say ξ) of all the real variables $(x, c, i^s, g, e, m, \ldots)$ is a general equilibrium solution, supported by a price vector (say p) consisting of all prices (including factor prices w) and foreign savings $(pd, pw_e, pw_m, pp, \pi, \ldots, w, s_f)$ then ξ is also a solution for $p = (\lambda pd, \lambda pw_e, \ldots, \lambda s_f)$, where λ is a positive scalar. Less technically: if all prices (and the value of foreign savings) were to be doubled, none of the model's real variables would be affected. This is so because all microeconomic relations in the model have this property and because parameters and exogenous variables are fixed in real terms (so that the fact that some variables are given does not rule out an equilibrium with all prices doubled and all quantities unchanged). In particular:

— trade taxes (import tariffs and export subsidies) are fixed in terms of *ad valorem* rates: a doubling of world prices and domestic prices is consistent with constancy of τ in equation (3);
— similarly, indirect tax rates are fixed in real terms: $pp_i = pd_i(1 - \delta_i)$;
— public consumption is fixed, but in real (g_i) rather than nominal $(pd_i g_i)$ terms;

[5] In the model foreign savings are allocated to firms and to the government, not to households. This may not be completely realistic. In particular, households are undoubtedly the recipients of part of the transfers received from abroad.

— urban wages are rigid in real terms, they change in proportion to an index of urban consumer prices;

— finally, as a last example, the introduction of the price ceiling $\overline{pd}$ in equation (13) does not introduce a nominal rigidity: $\overline{pd}$ is defined relative to world prices.

Hence there are no nominal rigidities in the model: only relative prices matter. We do not have to choose a numeraire since world prices are exogenous:[6] exogenous forecasts of world prices and foreign savings (in terms of current dollars) enter the model as the c.i.f./f.o.b. prices pw_m, pw_e, and as s_f (in terms of current Kenyan shillings) after conversion through a given (but not constant) exchange rate. Clearly, because of the model's homogeneity, a change in the conversion factor can have no real effects. This is why exchange rate policies cannot be modelled.[7]

4. *Agriculture: Smallholdings*

Peasants are distinguished by the size of their holding and by province. There are eight size classes (indexed by i)[8] and six provinces (index j). The disaggregation is introduced partly to allow for differences in land quality and in altitude and rainfall, and partly to capture differences in access to non-farm sources of income, especially remittances and wage income.

Peasants are involved in both agricultural and non-agricultural activities. They can grow any of the seven crops distinguished in the model;[9] they can keep livestock; they can work on other smallholdings; and they can have other wage employment, either in the large farm sector or in non-agricultural sectors.[10]

We model peasants as maximizing a household utility function (with current consumption and leisure as arguments),[11] subject to various constraints: production functions for crops and livestock; time and budget constraints; the size of the holding; the predetermined number of cattle and the allocation of land between crops; and, finally, the household's access to formal employment.

This optimization problem determines endogenously crop and livestock production, the amount of time devoted to leisure or spent by household

---

[6] Any one of these given world prices might be considered as the numeraire. In fact, world prices appear in the model as price indices (1972 = 1). No useful purpose would be served by normalizing any one of these.

[7] The point is simply that since there are no domestic and foreign currencies, one cannot talk of an exchange rate as the price of one currency in terms of another. The real exchange rate of trade theory is, of course, a meaningful concept in the context of this model.

[8] The eight classes are those distinguished in the IRS1 survey (Government of Kenya, 1977).

[9] Recall from section 2 that there are five non-food crops (including the two most important export products: coffee and tea) and two food crops (cf. Table 5A2.1).

[10] Henceforth, we shall refer to wage employment on smallholdings as informal employment and on large farms or outside agriculture as formal employment.

[11] Inter-temporal issues are ignored: savings rates are exogenous (cf. section 7).

members working on their own holding or in (formal or informal) employment, the amount of labour hired in, the household's farm and wage income, and consumption expenditures.

The household utility function has the form:[12]

$$u = \sum_j \beta_0 \ln(l_j - \bar{l}) + n \sum_i \beta_i \ln(c_i - \bar{c}_i) \qquad (l > \bar{l}; c_i > \bar{c}_i) \qquad (31)$$

where

$n =$ the number of household members
$l =$ leisure time of household member j
$c_i =$ per capita consumption of good i

and $\bar{c}_i, \bar{l}$ ('committed expenditures'), and β are parameters.

There are n_1 household members who divide total available time (t) between leisure (l) and hours worked (h); the remaining n_2 members of the household do not work. Hence, substituting the time constraint, (31) may be written as:

$$u = n_1 \beta_0 \ln(t - h - \bar{l}) + n_2 \beta_0 \ln(t - \bar{l}) + n \sum_i \beta_i \ln(c_i - \bar{c}_i). \qquad (32)$$

Total work time (h) is largely spent working on the own holding (h_0), partly in informal or formal employment (h_i, h_f):

$$h = h_0 + h_i + h_f. \qquad (33)$$

For crops (index k) we assume Cobb–Douglas production functions in land area devoted to the crop (a), and total labour input ($\tilde{n}$; this includes both family and hired labour):

$$x_k = \gamma_k a_k{}^{\alpha_k} \tilde{n}_k^{\beta_k} \qquad (k = 1, \ldots, 7). \qquad (34)$$

In the production of milk and other livestock products we assume fixed coefficients:

$$x_k = \delta_k c \qquad (k = 8) \qquad (35)$$
$$n_0^l = \varepsilon_0 c \qquad (36)$$
$$n_h^l = \varepsilon_h c \qquad (37)$$

where x is output; c the number of cattle;[13] n_0^l work of family members; and n_h^l hired labour used for livestock.

The balance equation for work on crops may now be written as:

$$\sum_k \tilde{n}_k = (n_1 h_0 - n_0^l) + (n_h - n_h^l) \qquad (38)$$

[12] We simplify the notation by supressing the superscripts for size of holding and province; hence, for example, the parameters in (31) are not the same for all 48 groups of peasants.
[13] Different forms of livestock are converted to cattle 'equivalents'. Hence we allow for e.g. the differences between improved and unimproved cows. Cf. Gunning (1979: 172–3, 304).

where n_h stands for the total use of hired labour on the holding.[14] Farm production requires intermediate inputs (e.g. seed, fertilizer, feeds) in fixed proportions, e.g. crop k requires a_{ik} units of commodity i per unit of output. Household income is now defined by:

$$y = \bar{y} + \sum_k \left(pd_k - \sum_i pd_i a_{ik} \right) x_k + n_1(w_i h_i + w_f h_f) - w_i n_h \qquad (39)$$

where w_i, w_f are the wage rates in informal and formal employment and $\bar{y}$ is exogenous income (e.g. remittances). Hence income consists of exogenous income, of the value of farm production, and of wage income; minus the costs of intermediate inputs and hired labour. The relative importance of various income components is indicated in Table 5A2.3.

The budget constraint is simply:

$$\sum_i pc_i c_i + s = y \qquad (40)$$

where s stands for savings (discussed in section 7) and pc for consumer prices.

TABLE 5A2.3. *Sources of peasant income 1974/1975* (Ksh./year)

	Province					
	Central	Coast	Eastern	Nyanza	Rift Valley	Western
Value of production[a]	3,171	1,271	3,115	2,270	3,676	1,482
Sales of crops	780	170	758	1,186	590	311
Sales of livestock	711	379	576	2	1,316	239
Farm costs in kind[b]	150	52	114	40	85	36
Own consumption	1,530	670	1,667	1,047	1,686	896
Farm costs	1,019	392	576	314	950	335
Crops[c]	516	107	359	187	423	169
Livestock	257	26	47	15	217	31
Labour	246	259	170	112	310	135
Non-farm income	2,122	2,495	1,574	1,123	1,491	1,307
Non-farm enterprises	326	626	491	365	303	126
Wages	1,286	923	721	523	931	724
Remittances[d]	510	946	362	235	257	457
Household income	4,272	3,374	4,113	3,079	4,217	2,454

[a] Excludes valuation changes.
[b] Output used as seed, fed to stock, or given to labour.
[c] Includes 'farm repairs'.
[d] Includes 'other gifts'.

[14] Note that family and hired labour are treated as complements in the case of livestock, and otherwise (somewhat unrealistically) as perfect substitutes. For a specification which allows for differences in efficiency between the two types of labour, see Gunning (1982).

Finally, formal sector jobs are rationed so that the household faces a constraint:[15]

$$h_f \leqslant \bar{h}_f. \tag{41}$$

This constraint will bind, provided w_f exceeds the wage rate in informal employment (w_i) and the return to family labour in work on the holding. Past investment decisions determine the allocation of land between crops and the household's livestock ownership: a_k in (34) and c in (35)–(37) are predetermined.[16]

Maximization of the utility function (32) subject to the constraints (33)–(41) determines, *inter alia*, h_0, h_i, h_f, and n_h.[17] Hence the model generates for each

TABLE 5A2.4. *Peasant land use, 1974/1975* ('000 ha)

Crop	Province					
	Central	Coast	Eastern	Nyanza	Rift Valley	Western
Maize	359	121	495	343	126	254
Other food	506	87	821	342	27	300
TOTAL FOOD CROPS	865	208	1,316	685	153	554
Coffee	50	—	68	15	—	1
Tea	60	—	12	6	6	2
Sugar	5	1	11	47	1	8
Cotton	—	1	25	28	2	22
Other	—	106	—	—	—	—
TOTAL INDUSTRIAL CROPS	115	109	116	96	9	33
GRAND TOTAL	980	317	1,432	781	162	587

Note: The table involves double-counting in two senses: (*a*) pure and mixed stands are added together; (*b*) areas planted in both long and short rains are counted twice. Since for the model only the proportions matter, this double-counting is not serious as long as the effect of the two factors does not change over time.

Source: Government of Kenya, *Integrated Rural Survey 1974–75, Basic Report* (1977), p. 79.

[15] The ration $\bar{h}_f$ is endogenously determined by the model. As explained in section 6, formal sector employment is generated by location, so that total labour demand in each of the six provinces is known (equation (48) in section 6). As in the case of urban employment, there is excess supply of peasant labour in the formal sector at the given real wage rates. Jobs are rationed on the basis of the skills and educational attainments of the applicants. As a proxy for this we use the data on h_f in the survey year. Households who then had access to formal employment apparently had the right qualifications. For later years we assume that the total number of jobs in a province is distributed over peasant households in proportion to the number of jobs they had in the initial year. This determines $\bar{h}_f$ in (41) endogenously.

[16] Table 5A2.4 illustrates land use in the initial year.

[17] The solution gives a linear expenditure system for consumption (c_i), which is discussed in section 7.

peasant group its demand for and supply of labour in the informal sector (n_h and $n_1 h_i$). Summing over households in the same province we obtain peasants' excess demand for hired labour at the given wage rate w_i (which is province-specific).[18] The model solves for a market-clearing wage rate, the level of w_i at which peasants' excess demand is equal to zero.[19]

5. Agriculture: Large Farms

The specification of large farms differs from that of peasants in several ways. First, within each province there is only a single, representative agent, engaged only in agricultural activities. Secondly, there is no informal labour market with market-clearing wages: there is only formal sector employment, and real wage rates (the w_f of the peasant model) are, as in the case of the non-agricultural sectors (section 6), given in real terms. Finally, while peasants retain a considerable part of their production for own consumption, all output of large farms is marketed.

Large farms produce the same eight commodities (two food crops; five non-food crops; livestock products) as peasants. The technology is again linear in the case of livestock (cf. equations (35)–(37)) and Cobb–Douglas for crops:

$$x_k = \gamma_k a_k{}^{\alpha_k} n_k^{\beta_k} \qquad (k = 1, \ldots, 7). \tag{42}$$

Land areas (a_k) are given and output (x_k) and employment (n_k) are determined by maximization of profits:

$$\text{profits} = \left(pd_k - \sum_i pd_i a_{ik} \right) x_k - w_f n_k \tag{43}$$

subject to (42).

The output of large farms is a perfect substitute for that of peasants: summation over large farms and all types of peasants determines aggregate output, which enters the balance equation.[20]

6. Urban Production, Factor Markets, and Income Distribution

We have seen in section 2 that there are 18 non-agricultural activities. While in the case of agriculture the same commodity is produced by different groups of agents (on large farms and on the various groups of smallholdings), using

---

[18] Equilibrium in the informal labour market is defined at the level of a province. Hence, implicitly, labour is assumed to be perfectly mobile within a province, while inter-provincial labour mobility is ruled out. Wage rates are therefore not equalized.

[19] Landless rural households fall outside the model's coverage. Hence, in the model peasants' payment for labour accrues entirely to other peasants, while in practice part of it accrues to landless labour.

[20] One complication is ignored in that equation but not in the model: peasants and large farms use different technologies and therefore have different input requirements. Hence for the agricultural commodities ($i = 1, \ldots, 5, 7$–9) there is not just a single row (a_i) in the input–output matrix, but different ones for different suppliers.

different technologies, for each of the non-agricultural activities there is only a single representative agent. The behaviour of this agent is summarized in Table 5A2.5.

In the case of mining the technology is linear in capital and labour. Since the capital stock is predetermined by past investment, output is determined by capacity and employment by output. Hence supply is completely inelastic (denoted as IS in the table). This is also the case for housing (where capital is the only factor) and for the production of the self-employed (which requires only labour). For two other sectors (government and electricity) we also assume a Leontief technology, but, as discussed in section 2, output is determined by demand in these cases. This is consistent with the production function, because in both sectors the investment programme assumed guarantees that the capital constraint is not binding:

$$y_i = \min[\alpha k_i, \beta l_i] = \beta l_i \qquad (i = 17, 18). \qquad (44)$$

The mark-up pricing assumption (equation (15) in section 2) implies that the supply curve is horizontal for these two sectors.

TABLE 5A2.5. *Non-agricultural sectors: production functions and pricing rules*

Commodity[a]	Production function[b]	Pricing[c]
Formal sector (6, 10–18)		
6: mining	L: $y = \alpha k, l = y/\beta$	IS
15: housing	L: $y = \alpha k$	IS
17: electricity and water	L: $l = y/\beta < \alpha k/\beta$	MUP
18: government	L: $l = y/\beta < \alpha k/\beta$	MUP
12–14, 16: all other services	CES	PM
10, 11: manufacturing	CES[d]	PM
Informal sector (19–26)		
19–22: high-income self-employed	L: $y = \beta l^e$	IS
23–6: low-income self-employed	L: $y = \beta l^f$	IS

[a] Cf. Table 5A2.1.

[b] L: Leontief technology. Capital (k) is used in mining, housing, and electricity. There is excess capacity in the electricity sector. In the cases of government and electricity, output is predetermined (supply adjusts to demand: cf. section 2); CES: CES production function in capital and labour.

[c] IS: inelastic supply (vertical supply curve); MUP: mark-up pricing (horizontal supply curve); PM: profit maximization subject to given prices and capital stock, hence upward-sloping supply curves.

[d] A single CES production function for the two commodities, which are assumed to be produced in fixed proportions.

[e] Labour supply predetermined.

[f] Labour supply price-elastic.

In the remaining urban activities we allow for factor substitution: we postulate CES production functions for manufacturing and for construction, trade, transport, and other services.[21]

$$y_i = (\alpha_i k_i^{-\rho_i} + \beta_i l_i^{-\rho_i})^{-1/\rho_i} \qquad (i = 10+11, 12, 13, 14, 16) \qquad (45)$$

where the elasticity of (factor) substitution is given by

$$\sigma_i = 1/(1 + \rho_i). \qquad (46)$$

Maximization of profits subject to (45) and for given values of the capital stock, wages, and prices gives value added and employment. There is (for all sectors) no substitutability between production factors and intermediate inputs. Hence in all cases value added (y) is proportional to gross output (x), both measured in constant base years prices (chosen to equal unity):

$$y_i = \left(1 - \sum_j A_{ji}\right) x_i \qquad (47)$$

where A is the input–output matrix.[22]

This completes the specification of urban production. We now turn to factor markets. Capital is sector specific and its stock is predetermined. It is assumed to be fully used, except in the electricity and government sectors. There is no market for capital services: the return to capital is determined effectively as a rent to a fixed factor.

We distinguish six types of labour: the two groups of self-employment and four types of wage employment ($j = 1, \ldots, 4$; in descending order of wage levels and skill or educational requirements).

We treat labour of different skills and at different locations[23] as complements in labour demand of sector i:

$$n_{ijp}^D = \gamma_{ijp} l_i \qquad (i = 6, 10, \ldots, 18; j = 1, \ldots, 4; p = 1, \ldots, 7) \qquad (48)$$

where l_i is the labour aggregate which enters the production functions. Note that the coefficients γ are sector specific: sectors differ in their skill requirements and in the locational distribution of employment. Total urban labour demand for skill j follows immediately:

$$n_j^D = \sum_i \gamma_{ij7} l_i. \qquad (49)$$

Real wages ($\bar{w}_j$) change over time, but they are given exogenously. At these

---

[21] Data limitations prevented estimating CES production functions separately for food and non-food manufacturing. We adopted the (rather unsatisfactory) solution of estimating an aggregate production function and assuming that food and non-food manufactured products are produced in fixed proportions.

[22] Recall that domestically produced and imported intermediate inputs are treated as complements: they appear in different rows of the input–output matrix.

[23] For rural locations $p = 1, \ldots, 6$ (depending upon the province); $p = 7$ indicates an urban location.

wages there is excess labour supply. Hence firms realize their labour demand (n^D equals employment), households are rationed in their supply of labour to the formal sector, and the vectors n^D and $\bar{w}$ determine the size distribution of wage income. In a detailed model employment is allocated to different groups of households (on the basis of their educational endowments). The function of this submodel is to map from the size to the household distribution of wage income. This submodel is not important for our present purpose and is therefore discussed only briefly.[24]

We assume that those who seek formal sector wage employment have different probabilities of being employed, depending on their educational attainment. Jobs are allocated over job seekers according to the following three equations:

$$
n_{ik} = \begin{cases} n_k & \text{if } i = 1 \\ n_k - \sum_l^{i-1} \pi_{lk} n_{lk} & \text{if } i = 2, 3, 4 \end{cases}
\tag{50}
$$

$$
n_{ik}^c = \sum_\kappa^{k-1} \pi_{ik} n_{i\kappa} + p_{ik} n_{ik}
\tag{51}
$$

$$
\pi_{ik} = \begin{cases} p_{ik} & \text{if } n_{ik}^c \leqslant n_i^D \\ (n_i^D - n_{ik-1}^c)/n_{ik} & \text{if } n_{ik-1}^c < n_i^D < n_{ik}^c \\ 0 & \text{if } n_{ik-1}^c \geqslant n_i^D \end{cases}
\tag{52}
$$

where

i = the wage class ($i = 1$ is the highest level)
k = educational attainment ($k = 1$ is the highest level)
n_k = job seekers with education k
n_{ik} = job seekers with education k who apply for type i jobs (including those who failed to get higher-wage jobs)
n_{ik}^c = cumulative labour supply of type i jobs (including applicants with higher educational qualifications)
p_{ik} = employment 'probability' in the absence of rationing
π_{ik} = fraction of applicants who are successful.

Job seekers try their luck first in the market for the highest-paying jobs ($i = 1$) and then, if unsuccessful, move to lower-wage jobs. Hence, in the first equation, labour supply n_{ik} is defined as all job seekers with that level of education minus those who have obtained jobs at higher wage levels ($i = 1, 2, \ldots, i-1$). Cumulative labour supply for type i jobs is then defined in the second equation by multiplying n_{ik} by the *ex ante* 'probability' p_{ik} and taking into account those jobs already allocated to job seekers with higher

[24] For a detailed description, see Gunning (1979: 191–201, 272–81).

qualifications. The difference between supply and demand then determines the *ex post* 'probability' π_{ik} in the third equation. Given labour demand (n_i^p), labour supply by level of education (n_k), and the matrix p (which is estimated from 1974 survey data), the three equations determine the distribution of job seekers over wage groups $(n_{ik} \pi_{ik})$ and, residually, the number of unsuccessful job seekers $\left(n_k - \sum_i n_{ik} \pi_{ik} \right)$.

In the model we distinguish eight types of urban households $(h = 1, \ldots, 8)$, which differ in the number of household members who are in the labour force, and in educational attainment. Using the 1974 Household Budget Survey, these types were defined by occupation and income of the head of household:

$h = 1, \ldots, 4$ head of household regular wage earner with wages: up to 400; between 400 and 1,000; between 1,000 and 2,000; and over Ksh.2,000 per month (in 1974 prices);

$h = 5, 6$ head of household self-employed, with incomes of up to and over Ksh.400 per month, respectively;

$h = 7$ head of household unemployed;

$h = 8$ 'other occupation' (basically: head of household not in the labour force).

All labour force members (except the high-income self-employed, who are discussed later) are assumed to seek wage employment.

There are γ_h households of type h, each with e_{hk} job seekers of education level k. Then n_k in equation (50) is given by summation over households:

$$n_k = \sum_h \gamma_h e_{hk}. \tag{53}$$

The fraction π determined in (52) may then be used to derive the number of wage employees by household type and wage group (n_{ih}^W):

$$n_{ikh} = \begin{cases} e_{hk} & \text{if } i = 1 \\ e_{hk} - \sum_i^{i-1} \pi_{ik} n_{ikh} & \text{if } i = 2, 3, 4 \end{cases} \tag{54}$$

$$n_{ih}^W = \sum_k \pi_{ik} n_{ikh}. \tag{55}$$

Since wage employment accounts for two-thirds of the urban labour force (Table 5A2.6) and for almost three-quarters of urban incomes, the most important part of the household income distribution is described by the equations (50)–(55). But it remains to consider the self-employed and the unemployed.

TABLE 5A2.6. *The urban labour force,*
Nairobi 1974 ('000)

Wage-employed	206.1
High-income self-employed	23.8
Low-income self-employed	18.7
Unemployed	40.4
Others (including casuals)	20.2
TOTAL	309.3

We assume that the group of high-income self-employed are protected by barriers to entry: the number of people in these activities is related to the growth of real urban incomes and their distribution over household types remains constant. We assume, rather arbitrarily, that the distribution of the total number of high-income self-employed (n^H) over the four activities in which they are engaged is fixed. Hence, for these activities employment (l) is given by

$$l_i = \lambda_i n^H \qquad (i = 19, \ldots, 22). \qquad (56)$$

Similarly, for the low-income self-employed

$$l_i = \lambda_i n^L \qquad (i = 23, \ldots, 26). \qquad (57)$$

but in this case total labour supply n^L is *not* exogenous: it follows from the equilibrium condition for the free entry sector.

In this sector all those who have not yet succeeded in getting a wage job $\left(\text{i.e. the number } \sum_h \gamma_h \left(e_{hk} - \sum_i n_{ih}^W \right)\right)$ continue to search, either while unemployed (the number n^U) or while in low-income self-employment (n^L). If those who choose self-employment are θ times as efficient as the unemployed in job search, then the probability p of an unemployed person getting a job is determined by

$$\theta p n^L + p(n^U + n^W) = n^W. \qquad (58)$$

This equation is similar to the Harris–Todaro definition of the probability of employment as the ratio of the number of jobs (n^W) and the number of job seekers ($n^W + n^L + n^U$), except that the self-employed are less efficient in job search.[25] Within the free entry sector, labour allocation is determined by equalization of expected incomes:

$$\theta p y^W + (1 - \theta p) y^L = p y^W. \qquad (59)$$

For given values of θ per capita incomes y^W and y^L, n^W and n^L plus n^U, these two equations may be solved for n^L, n^U, and p.

[25] Cf. Fields (1975) and Collier (1979). See, however, Collier and Lal (1986).

Within a household, the unsuccessful job seekers are allocated between unemployment and low-income self-employment in the same ratio as determined for the aggregate:

$$n_h^L / n_h^U = n^L / n^U. \tag{60}$$

This completes the allocation of each household's labour force members between activities: there are n_h^H in high-income self-employment; n_{ih}^W in wage employment in wage group i ($i = 1, \ldots, 4$), n_h^L low-income self-employed; and n_h^U are unemployed.

Note that household types are not defined in terms of their members' activities and earnings but in terms of their endowment. The number of households in each type is given (γ_h), but within a household labour force members can move between activities.

A household can receive income from four sources: from wage employment; from the two types of self-employment; and from formal sector firms in the form of distributed profits. The first three sources have been discussed already; the only change we introduce at this point concerns income differentials between households for the same activity. The survey data indicate that these differentials can be substantial. The model does not explain them: we keep the differentials fixed, thereby leaving part of the inequality of the distribution of income unexplained.

Formal sector firms retain most of their profits. A constant fraction (in current prices) is, however, distributed. Households of different types share in this total according to the distribution of 'other income' in the survey data. Household income is now determined as:

$$y_h = n_h^H \xi_h^H y^H + \sum_i n_{ih}^W \xi_{ih}^W y_i^W + n_h^L \xi_h^L y^L + \mu_h \Pi \tag{61}$$

where

y^j = per capita income in activity j ($j = H, L, W$: high-income self-employment, low-income self-employment, wage employment)

n_h^j = the number of household members engaged in activity j in households of type h

ξ^j = a vector of income differentials (fixed)

μ = a vector of shares in distributed profits

Π = distributed profits.

It should be emphasized that the equations which apply to the wage-employed and high-income self-employed form the most important part of the urban model: the two activities account for almost three-quarters of the labour force and for almost 90 per cent of household income (Tables 5A2.6, 5A2.7).

It may be useful to summarize the way in which urban incomes and their distribution are determined in the model. First, within a period, real wages

TABLE 5A2.7. *Household composition and income, Nairobi 1974*

	Labour force members (mean per household)	Contribution to household income (Ksh./month)
Head of household	0.95	1,008
Of which:		
wage-employed	0.71	779
high-income self-employed	0.08	189
low-income self-employed	0.09	23
unemployed	0.33	—
other	0.04	16
Other labour force members	0.58	258
Of which:		
wage-employed	0.31	225
self-employed[a]	0.04	23
unemployed	0.17	—
other	0.06	12
Others[b]	—	92
TOTAL	1.53	1,358

[a] Of these, three-quarters are in the low-income group.
[b] Earners not covered by our definition of the labour force.

Source: Our calculations based on unpublished raw data of the 1974 Nairobi Household Budget Survey.

are given. At these wages there is excess supply and jobs are rationed on the basis of educational qualifications, so that the distribution of wage income is determined by the distribution of educational endowments over households. Secondly, prices for the output of the high-income self-employed are predetermined, reflecting barriers to entry (e.g. capital requirements, which are not modelled explicitly). Thirdly, those who do not succeed in finding a job in the formal sector allocate themselves between unemployment and low-income self-employment in such a way that expected incomes are equalized. Finally, the high-income self-employed do not compete for wage employment, but all other labour force members do.

7. Consumption, Saving, and Investment

The peasant model generates a linear expenditure system. For urban households we also assume a Stone–Geary utility function,[26] so that, for a given

[26] But in this case leisure is not an argument of the utility function: labour supply of urban households is exogenous. This difference reflects data limitations: for urban households we have no information on the number of hours worked. The rural and urban demand systems also differ in their commodity disaggregations.

household with income y and savings s, facing consumer prices pc, consumption of good i is given by:

$$pc_i c_i = pc_i \bar{c}_i + \beta_i \left(y - s - \sum_j pc_j \bar{c}_j \right) \qquad (i = 1, \ldots, 7). \qquad (62)$$

We have used data from the 1974 Nairobi Household Budget Survey to estimate the parameters $\bar{c}$ (committed expenditure) and β (marginal propensities to consume) for three categories of goods (livestock products; other food; non-food) and four categories of services (housing; electricity and water; transportation; other services). The elasticities implied by these estimates are given in Table 5A2.8, for three values of total consumption ($y - s = 1{,}000$, 1,500 and 2,000 Ksh./month, 1974 prices).[27] It may be noted that demand for food is inelastic with respect to both prices and income, especially at low income levels, and that the income and price elasticities of the demand for services are high. Income inelasticities increase with income in the case of goods ($i = 1, 2, 3$) and decrease for services ($i = 4, \ldots, 7$).

In the case of peasants the LES applies to six groups of expenditures:[28] own produced food crops; purchased food crops; own-produced livestock products; purchased livestock products; other food; all non-food consump-

TABLE 5A2.8. *Urban household consumption: income and price elasticities*

	Price elasticities			Income elasticities		
	1,000[a]	1,500[a]	2,000[a]	1,000[a]	1,500[a]	2,000[a]
1. Livestock products	−0.70	−0.78	−0.83	0.76	0.83	0.87
2. Other food	−0.69	−0.77	−0.82	0.72	0.79	0.83
TOTAL FOOD	−0.73	−0.80	−0.84	0.73	0.80	0.84
3. Non-food goods	−0.65	−0.74	−0.79	0.66	0.74	0.80
4. Housing	−1.09	−1.06	−1.04	1.28	1.17	1.12
5. Electricity and water	−1.57	−1.30	−1.20	1.82	1.42	1.29
6. Transportation	−1.14	−1.08	−1.06	1.30	1.18	1.13
7. Other services	−1.13	−1.20	−1.14	1.59	1.33	1.23
TOTAL NON-FOOD	−1.00	−1.00	−1.00	1.13	1.08	1.06

[a] Total consumption (Ksh./month).

[27] Since all households are assumed to face the same prices there is an identification problem. We impose the restriction that committed expenditures for non-food items sum to zero ($\bar{c}_3 + \ldots + \bar{c}_7 = 0$). This implies unitary price elasticity (as indicated in the last line of Table 5A2.8).

[28] In this case too we have assumed that committed expenditures for non-food items are zero ($\bar{c}_6 = 0$). This is why the last price elasticity in Table 5A2.9 is equal to one.

TABLE 5A2.9. *Rural household consumption: income and price elasticities*

	Price elasticity	Income elasticity
1. Food crops (own)	−1.04	1.25
2. Food crops (purchased)	−0.41	0.43
3. Livestock (own)	−1.14	1.38
4. Livestock (purchased)	−0.68	0.63
5. Other food	−0.71	0.80
TOTAL FOOD	−0.94	0.94
6. Non-food	−1.00	1.17

tion. Income and price elasticities (evaluated at the mean) are given in Table 5A2.9.

Note that own-produced and purchased food items are treated as imperfect substitutes in demand.

The classification used in the rural and urban consumption functions does not match the sectoral classification used in the model. Hence there is a mapping from the vectors c^R, c^U, giving total rural and urban consumption according to the classification used in the two LES systems to total private consumption according to the model's commodity classification (i.e. the vector c used in the balance equations):

$$c = M^R c^R + M^U c^U \tag{63}$$

(where the dimensions of the matrices are 36 × 6 for M^R and 36 × 7 for M^U). Many rows of the two conversion matrices contain only zeros (e.g. because there is no domestic consumption of coffee) and most non-zero elements are constants. The urban demand for 'other food' (c_2^U) is, for example, distributed in fixed proportions over the three food commodities distinguished in the model (c_7, c_8, c_{10}; cf. Table 5A2.1) and (to account for trade and transportation margins) over two services. The corollary is that the price vectors pc associated with c^R and c^U are weighted averages of the domestic prices pd associated with aggregate consumption c (with the elements of the conversion matrices as weights).

There is one case in which the coefficients are not constant. This concerns the activities in which the self-employed compete with the formal sector. For example, demand for non-food manufactured products is distributed over c_{11}, c_{19}, c_{23}, and c_{27}: consumption demand for the products produced by the formal sector and by the two groups of self-employed, and imported goods, respectively (cf. Table 5A2.1). Imports are non-competitive but the three types of domestically produced non-food manufactured products form a CES aggregate. Hence the coefficients which divide total demand for this CES aggregate between the three sources of supply are endogenously determined (from the dual of the CES function) as functions of relative prices.

Hence some elements of the matrices in (63) change with prices, and consumer prices are derived from the domestic price vector pd by applying the dual of (63).

In the absence of large income changes (such as occurred during the coffee boom) households consider their income as permanent income and save a constant fraction of it. We denote these given savings rates as σ_i^R, σ_h^U for rural households of type i and urban households of type h, respectively.

The coffee boom affects savings rates in two ways. First, both rural and urban households consider the difference between their current income (y) and the income they would have earned in the absence of the boom (y^*) largely as transitory: out of this extra income they save a large fraction $(\hat{\sigma})$. Secondly, during the boom, controls on imports of consumer groups were relaxed. Urban groups which correctly foresaw that this liberalization would be temporary took out consumption loans in order to benefit from it. These loans were repaid in the post-boom period.

Consider first rural households (of type i; $i = 1, \ldots, 48$). In the case of the boom period $(t = 1976, \ldots, 1979)$, total consumption expenditure $(\tilde{c})$ is given by:

$$\tilde{c}_{it} = y_{it} - s_{it} \tag{64}$$

$$s_{it} = \sigma_i^R y_{it}^* + \hat{s}_{it} \tag{65}$$

$$\hat{s}_{it} = \hat{\sigma}(y_{it} - y_{it}^*). \tag{66}$$

If there are γ_i households of type i, boom-related rural savings are:

$$\hat{s}_t^R = \sum_i \gamma_{it} \hat{s}_{it}. \tag{67}$$

The banking system is implicitly assumed to use a fraction δ of savings for consumption loans, the remainder for capital formation. The consumption loans are repaid after the boom and rural households then withdraw the corresponding part of their deposits.[29] The proceeds are entirely consumed. Hence, in the post-boom period $(t = 1980, \ldots, 1983)$:

$$\tilde{c}_{it} = (y_{it} - s_{it}) + \delta(\hat{s}_{i1976} + \ldots + \hat{s}_{i1979})/4.0 \tag{68}$$

$$s_{it} = \sigma_i^R y_{it}. \tag{69}$$

Hence, in the early 1980s, rural households save a 'normal' fraction σ^R out of their current incomes, but increase their consumption as they withdraw their bank deposits. At the end of the day, a fraction $(1 - \delta)$ of their extra savings is left deposited with the banking system and this corresponds to capital formation. Since interest rates are zero the savings behaviour of

---

[29] Note that from (68) this part of the deposits is assumed to be withdrawn in equal annual instalments.

farmers during the boom adds to the economy's capital stock but not to their own post-boom incomes.

For urban households of type h ($h = 1, \ldots, 8$), we have for the boom period ($t = 1976, \ldots, 1979$):

$$\tilde{c}_{ht} = (y_{ht} - s_{ht}) + \delta(\varepsilon_{ht}\hat{s}_t^R + \hat{s}_{ht}) \tag{70}$$

$$s_{ht} = \sigma_h^U y_{ht}^* + \hat{s}_{ht} \tag{71}$$

$$\hat{s}_{ht} = \hat{\sigma}(y_{ht} - y_{ht}^*) \tag{72}$$

$$\varepsilon_{ht} = y_{ht} / \sum_h \gamma_{ht} y_{ht}. \tag{73}$$

Equations (71) and (72) are analogous to (65) and (66). Equation (70) indicates that consumption is temporarily higher than the difference between income (y) and savings out of current income (s): the household takes out a consumption loan equal to a fraction δ of its own extra savings[30] and a proportional part of total rural savings.[31]

If there are γ_h households of type i, boom-related savings are:

$$\hat{s}_t^U = \sum_h \gamma_{ht}\hat{s}_{ht}. \tag{74}$$

After the boom urban savings rates return to their original value (σ^U), but consumption loans must be repaid. Hence, for $t = 1980, \ldots, 1983$:

$$\tilde{c}_{ht} = (y_{ht} - s_{ht}) - \delta[\varepsilon_{ht}(\hat{s}_{1976}^R + \ldots + \hat{s}_{1979}^R)$$
$$+ (\hat{s}_{h1976} + \ldots + \hat{s}_{h1979})]/4.0 \tag{75}$$

$$s_{ht} = \sigma_{ht}^U y_{ht}. \tag{76}$$

Finally, it may be noted that if we aggregate savings, defined as the difference between current income and consumption, $y - \tilde{c}$, over all households, we obtain total nominal household savings (s^H) as:[32]

$$s_t^H = \sum_i \gamma_i(y_{it} - \tilde{c}_{it}) + \sum_h \gamma_h(y_{ht} - \tilde{c}_{ht}) =$$

$$\sum_i \gamma_i \sigma_i^R y_{it}^* + \sum_h \gamma_h \sigma_h^U y_{ht}^* + (1 - \delta)(\hat{s}_t^R + \hat{s}_t^U) \qquad (t = 1976, \ldots, 1979) \tag{77}$$

where the last term indicates that a fraction δ of boom-related savings ($\hat{s}^R + \hat{s}^U$) does not add to s^H, which measures households' contribution to capital formation. Similarly, for the period after the boom:

$$s_t^H = \sum_i \gamma_i \sigma_i^R y_{it} + \sum_h \gamma_h \sigma_{ht}^U y_{ht} + \delta(\hat{s}_{1976}^U + \ldots + \hat{s}_{1979}^U)/4.0. \tag{78}$$

---

[30] In fact, the lending and borrowing was, of course, done by different households. We cannot model this and therefore let each household borrow from banks part of what it deposited.

[31] Note from (73) that the fractions ε sum to one.

[32] Equation (77) may be derived from (64)–(67) and (70)–(74).

Taking the two periods together, (77) and (78) indicate that the extra savings of urban households ($\hat{s}^U$) eventually all lead to capital formation. The only complication which the introduction of consumption loans introduces is that this effect is not instantaneous: a fraction δ of the total effect on the capital stock is realized only after the boom, when loans are being repaid. There is no such offsetting effect in the case of rural savings: a fraction $(1 - \delta)$ leads to capital formation in the boom period. The remainder never does; it adds to urban consumption rather than to investment.

The savings of peasants are in part used for investment on their own farms to increase their cattle ownership or to increase the acreage under coffee or tea.[33] The remainder is added to foreign savings, corporate savings, and government savings. This gives total investment in current prices (other than in coffee, tea, or livestock), $\hat{i}$. The sectoral allocation of this total is fixed. This gives a vector i^d of investment by sector of destination, which is used to update the capital stock between periods. The composition of capital formation in terms of the sectors of origin is also fixed. This gives the vector i^s which enters the balance equation (1), representing investment demand for a sector's output (as opposed to investment in the sector, which is what i^d stands for). Hence:

$$i^s = Bi^d \tag{79}$$

$$i_i^d = \lambda_i i \tag{80}$$

$$p^c = \sum_j \sum_i pd_i b_{ij} \lambda_j \tag{81}$$

$$ip^c = \hat{i}. \tag{82}$$

The vector λ gives the allocation of total (real) investment i. Investment in sector j requires b_{ij} units of output of sector i (capital goods, construction services, etc.). Hence the matrix B is used in (79) to map from investment by sector of destination to the i^s vector used in the balance equations. Finally, an aggregate price of capital goods p^c is defined in (81) and used in (82) to relate total real investment to the nominal total $\hat{i}$, which is determined by savings.

Public consumption in real terms is an exogenous variable in the model ($\bar{g}$), and its sectoral composition is assumed to remain unchanged. Therefore:

$$g_i = \mu_i \bar{g}. \tag{83}$$

---

[33] The expansion of tea acreage is exogenous in the model, while investment in the other two assets is a function of the household's income. On this, see Gunning (1979: 172–3). In all three cases the cost of this asset acquisition is subtracted from the household's total savings; the remainder is added to the common pool of investable resources (which is allocated between sectors without regard to the source of the savings). Investment in coffee and tea increases the land allocated to these crops (a_1 and a_2) and (since the total area of the holding is given) subtracts from the area available for the other crops ($a_3, \ldots, a_7$). The model does not go further in endogenizing product mix: the proportion in which the rest of the holding is used for the other crops is fixed.

Government revenue is endogenously determined by tax, tariff, and subsidy rates. Since government consumption in current prices $\left(\sum_i pd_i g_i \right)$ follows from (83), this determines government savings. Abstracting from general equilibrium effects (e.g. induced changes in prices or government revenues), the exogeneity of public consumption means that the public sector's marginal savings rate is equal to unity. As to corporate savings, firms retain a fixed percentage of profits (distributing the remainder to urban households). These retained earnings form the model's concept of corporate savings.

This completes our description of the model's structure, which started with the balance equation (1). In earlier sections we discussed production (x), intermediate demand (Ax), external trade, and the various adjustment processes which ensure that the balance equation is satisfied. The equations in the present section determine the remaining variables: the final demand components c, g, and i^s.

6

An Application to the Tanzanian Economic Decline of 1975–1984

1. Introduction

In Chapter 5 two different approaches, an analysis of National Accounts data and a CGE model, were used to investigate the macro and general equilibrium effects of the coffee boom windfall. This combination of techniques both increases our confidence in certain results that were common, and enables a wider range of questions to be addressed. Unfortunately, the descriptive account of the Tanzanian economy given in the Appendix to this chapter, and the theoretical analysis of Chapter 3 suggest that this dual approach would be inappropriate for Tanzania. When the commodity market is in sustained disequilibrium, agents optimize subject to expectations of quantity rationing. This invalidates a CGE model, in which, of course, prices adjust to clear markets and agents optimize subject to those prices. A general equilibrium model which took expectations of quantity rationing into account would necessarily be highly experimental and therefore contribute little to our confidence in the results, while requiring a considerable diversion of effort from other areas. We have not attempted to construct such a model. Our analysis of the effects of the boom is therefore confined to National Accounts data, these being presented in section 2. To substantiate the disequilibrium analysis of Chapter 3, in section 3 we summarize our analysis of changes in the availability of consumer goods, which is more fully reported in the companion volume, *Peasants and Governments*. The Appendix provides a narrative of macroeconomic events.

2. An Analysis of National Accounts Data

2.1. *Changes in Prices and Quantities*

In repeating the National Accounts analysis of Chapter 5, we encounter the problem that statistics are generally less complete. In Table 6.1 we apply the same definitions used in Chapter 5 to construct proxies for import substitutes and non-tradables, and report price and quantity series for 1975–84.

The coffee boom is again identifiable as an improvement in the terms of trade during 1976–9. However, an important peculiarity of the Tanzanian trade unit value series is that the terms-of-trade improvement appears to be much less pronounced than in Kenya. The proximate reason for this lies in the differing behaviour of the c.i.f. import series. In Table 6.1 we include the Kenyan c.i.f. non-oil imports unit cost index expressed in Tanzanian shillings, this being the cost at which Tanzania could have purchased imports with the same composition as Kenyan imports. As the table reveals, there is a substantial discrepancy between this series and the reported unit cost of Tanzania's non-oil imports. There are two credible explanations for this divergence: either import composition differs in a way which caused a more rapid increase in Tanzanian unit costs, or Tanzanian importers increasingly over-reported the true cost of imports. We investigate the import composition explanation first. In both countries, but especially in Tanzania, the composition of imports changed over the period. However, these changes cannot account for any part of the divergence between the indices, since by construction they measure the cost of a bundle of imports of constant composition. Hence, it is not compositional changes, but rather differences in the composition of the bundles used in the Kenyan and Tanzanian indices which might explain divergent trends. For the period 1975–9 both countries report unit value indices disaggregated at the one-digit level. We were therefore able to construct reaggregated non-oil unit value indices in which the weights that define the two bundles were each applied to both sets of indices.[1] Using the nine Kenyan unit value indices and Kenyan weights, by 1979 the aggregate non-oil index is 153.5. When Tanzanian weights are used instead the index is 154.8. Thus, differences in import composition by 1979 indeed account for some increase in Tanzanian unit costs relative to Kenya, but only of the order of 0.8 per cent. However, analogous to the standard index number problem, an equally valid comparison is to apply the two sets of weights on the nine Tanzanian indices. This calculation results in the opposite conclusion, namely that differences in composition should by 1979 have reduced the unit cost of Tanzanian non-oil imports by 8.2 per cent relative to Kenyan unit costs. Averaging these two results implies that correcting for compositional differences would increase the divergence between the series in 1979 by 3.7 per cent. While it is possible that differences in composition within the nine aggregates could offset this so strongly as to account fully for the divergence, we do not have data by which to investigate this hypothesis, nor can we find grounds for believing it might be the case. We therefore conclude that the most likely explanation for the divergence in non-oil unit values is the increasing, systematic misreporting of c.i.f. import costs by Tanzanian agents relative to their Kenyan counterparts. Recall that such a tendency towards growing overinvoicing was predicted by our theoretical analysis of a price-control regime (see Chapter 3, section 3). If this is correct it has two powerful

---

[1] The sources were for Tanzania, *Statistical Abstract 1973–79*, table E15, and *Foreign Trade Indices*, tables 7 (b) and (c); and for Kenya, *Statistical Abstract, 1980*, table 68.

TABLE 6.1. *Prices and quantities, 1975–1984*

	1975	1976	1977	1978	1979	1980	1981	1982	1983	1984
Prices										
(Kenyan) all imports[a]	1.00	1.15	1.25	1.31	1.67	2.00	1.96	2.07	2.37	
(Kenyan) non-oil imports[a]	1.00	1.15	1.26	1.36	1.67	2.07	2.20			
Tanzanian non-oil imports[b]	1.00	1.18	1.36	1.51	1.84					
Import substitutes[c]	1.00	1.12	1.24	1.38	1.55	2.01	2.81	3.30	3.76	4.44
Non-tradables[c]	1.00	1.06	1.20	1.31	1.48	1.79	2.11	2.52	2.95	3.36
Exports[d]	1.00	1.37	1.92	1.69	1.90	2.31	2.80			
Exports (non-oil)[e]	1.00	1.38	1.95	1.69	1.89					
Capital goods[f]	1.00	1.05	1.22	1.35	1.41	1.62	1.66	1.88	2.02	2.22
All imports[g]	1.00	1.18	1.36	1.49	1.84					
Prices relative to (Kenyan) non-oil imports										
Import substitutes	1.00	0.97	0.98	1.01	0.93	1.00	1.43	1.59	1.59	
Non-tradables	1.00	0.92	0.95	0.96	0.89	0.89	1.08	1.22	1.24	
Capital goods	1.00	0.91	0.97	0.99	0.84	0.81	0.85	0.91	0.85	

Quantities

Imports (all)[h]	1.00	0.85	0.94	1.41	1.36	1.11	1.18	0.62	0.56	0.49
Import substitutes[i]	1.00	1.18	1.25	1.31	1.18	0.95	0.75	0.95	0.85	0.88
Non-tradables[i]	1.00	1.01	1.02	1.02	1.01	1.02	0.96	0.95	0.85	
Export crops[j]	1.00	1.12	1.05	0.93	0.94	1.06	0.84	0.82	0.81	
Exports (all)[h]	1.00	1.12	0.92	0.81	0.93	0.84	0.88			
GFKF[k]	1.00	1.19	1.32	1.32	1.48	1.30	1.40	1.40	1.06	0.98

[a] Derived from Government of Kenya, *Statistical Abstract, 1984*, table 66, and IMF, *International Finance Statistics*, using the period average exchange rates between the Kenyan and Tanzanian shillings. The series shows the c.i.f. (to Kenya) unit cost of Kenya non-oil imports in Tanzanian shillings.

[b] From Government of Tanzania, *Foreign Trade Indices* (1974–81), table S(iii).

[c] GDP deflator for sectors as defined in chapter 5, plus the construction sector derived from Government of Tanzania, *National Accounts of Tanzania* (1976–84), and Government of Tanzania, *Statistical Abstract, 1973–79* (for 1975).

[d] From *Foreign Trade Indices*, tables 7(b) and S(xii).

[e] Derived from *Foreign Trade Indices*, table 7(b).

[f] The GFKF deflator from tables 14 and 15 of *National Accounts of Tanzania* (1976–84) and corresponding tables in *Statistical Abstract 1973–79* (for 1975).

[g] From *Foreign Trade Indices*, table 7(c).

[h] *Foreign Trade Indices*, table S(x).

[i] Sources and methods as in note c.

[j] Weighted series covering coffee, cotton, sisal, tea, cashew, and tobacco derived from Bank of Tanzania, *Economic and Operations Report* (1982 and 1983), table 26(b), and *Quarterly Statistical Bulletin* (July 1985), p. 18.

[k] Sources and methods as in note f.

implications for our analysis. First, it suggests that the true magnitude of the windfall should be estimated using not the Tanzanian import unit value series but the Kenyan one (converted into Tanzanian shillings). Second, it enables us to quantify the magnitude of the extra overinvoicing as the divergence between the two series. An alternative or additional explanation of the exceptional rise in unit import costs (which leads, however, to similar conclusions) is that the centralized bureaucratic purchasing organizations (notably the Board of External Trade) became progressively less competent in selecting sources of supply.

In Table 6.2 we present three different measures of the windfall over the period 1976–9. As a measure of the true actual windfall we take the difference between the 1975 terms of trade and the actual terms of trade as defined by the ratio of Tanzanian export unit values to Kenyan import unit values converted into Tanzanian shillings. This terms-of-trade improvement is then applied to actual export volumes. The resulting magnitude, Tsh.3,720.6 million, is 21.9 per cent of 1975 GDP. This is slightly smaller than the Kenyan windfall, which was 24 per cent of 1975 GDP. However, this is explicable because of the substantially worse performance of Tanzanian export volumes during the boom. Had the trend in export volume followed that in Kenya, the windfall would have been 25.3 per cent of GDP, (Tsh.4,305 million). Since the shortfall in export performance was, we shall argue, endogenous to economic policy, this is a not unreasonable estimate of the potential value of the

TABLE 6.2. *Measures of the windfall, 1976–1979*

	1975	1976	1977	1978	1979	Total
'True' terms of trade[a]	1.00	1.19	1.54	1.29	1.14	—
Actual export quantities[b]	1.00	1.12	0.92	0.81	0.93	—
True windfall at 1975 prices[c] (Tsh.m)	—	736.7	1,719.9	813.2	450.8	3,720.6
Kenyan export quantities[d]	1.00	1.08	1.10	1.03	1.04	—
True windfall with Kenyan export performance	—	710.4	2,056.4	1,034.1	504.1	4,305.0
'Apparent' terms of trade[e]	1.00	1.16	1.41	1.13	1.03	—
Apparent windfall at actual quantities (Tsh.m.)	—	620.4	1,305.9	364.5	96.6	2,387.4

[a] From Table 6.1, Kenyan all imports unit value/all exports unit value.

[b] From Table 6.1 (all exports).

[c] Exports in 1975 were Tsh.3,462m. (Government of Tanzania, *Statistical Abstract 1973–79*, table Q1), the windfall being calculated as $3,462 \cdot \sum_{i=1976}^{1979} (1-t_i)q_i$, where t is the terms of trade from row 1 and q is the quantity from row 2.

[d] From Government of Kenya, *Statistical Abstract, 1984*, table 67.

[e] From Table 6.1, all imports unit value/all exports unit value.

windfall under changed policies. The apparent windfall, that is measured using the Tanzanian import unit value index and actual export quantities, was only Tsh.2,387.4 million or 14.1 per cent of GDP.

Returning to Table 6.1, there is a dramatic change in domestic relative prices, starting in 1981. In that year relative to the 'true' c.i.f. unit cost of imports, the price of non-tradable goods rises by 21 per cent and that of import substitutes by 43 per cent. These large changes are then amplified between 1981 and 1983, by which time the relative price of import substitutes has risen by 59 per cent from its 1980 (and 1975) level. As discussed further in Chapter 7, these changes in relative prices are radically different from those which occurred in Kenya. However, it must be borne in mind that prices in Tanzania were largely administered. The quantity changes are extraordinary; by 1984 output of the import substitutes sector has declined by 63 per cent from its peak (1978) and the non-tradables sector by 17 per cent. Export crop production is 24 per cent below its 1980 peak. Indeed, this contraction continued into 1984, with the import substitute sector declining by a further 12.5 per cent. Finally, despite a large increase in gross fixed capital formation (GFKF) over the period 1976–82, there appears to be no increase in the relative price of capital goods (unlike Kenya). Probably this is because a large proportion of Tanzanian capital goods was imported.

Table 6.1 suggests that the price level rose rapidly. However, it would have risen far faster had not the velocity of circulation declined. Table 6.3 provides series on non-bank holdings of cash, deposits at commercial banks excluding government agencies[2] and the EAC, and monetary GDP at market prices. The velocity of circulation, roughly constant 1973–7, halved between end-1977 and end-1981. Thereafter, owing to changes in presentation of the national accounts, the series cannot be continued. However, an approximation, the ratio of GDP to the money supply, shows no further decline between 1981 and 1984. Table 6.4 focuses on the period 1977–81, during which velocity fell. The annual increase in the money stock is decomposed into that part due to the growth in monetary GDP given the velocity which prevailed in the previous year, and that part due to the fall in the velocity given an unaltered monetary GDP (leaving a small residual).

The fall in the velocity of circulation made a considerable contribution to non-inflationary government financing, especially in the period end-1978 to end-1980, during which the increase in the money stock from this source amounted to 10 per cent of monetary GDP (or about 25 per cent of total government recurrent expenditure). However, incremental holdings then appear to have diminished: in 1980/1 the fall in the velocity contributed government resources of only 3.8 per cent of monetary GDP.

Virtually the entire increase in the money supply, not just the increase in fiat money, can be regarded as a government resource, because the banking

---

[2] Defined as central and local government, schools, hospitals, the university and public enterprises (which account for about 20% of the total).

TABLE 6.3. *Money balances, 1973–1981 (end of year) (Tsh. millions)*

	1973	1974	1975	1976	1977	1978	1979	1980	1981
(1) Monetary GDP at market prices[a]	9,892.0	12,189.0	13,758.0	16,799.0	20,890.0	21,385.0	23,618.0	25,468.0	28,081.0
(2) Cash with non-banks[b]	1,199.0	1,517.0	1,756.0	2,071.0	2,380.0	2,915.0	4,065.0	5,246.0	6,611.0
(3) Commercial bank deposits (excluding govt. agencies and EAC)[c]	1,719.3	2,178.6	2,660.7	3,238.3	4,160.9	4,982.0	7,275.3	9,784.5	11,127.5
(4) Money stock: (2)+(3)	2,918.3	3,695.6	4,416.7	5,309.3	6,540.9	7,897.0	11,340.3	15,030.5	17,738.5
(5) Velocity:(1)/(4)	3.390	3.298	3.115	3.164	3.194	2.708	2.083	1.694	1.583

[a] Government of Tanzania, *Statistical Abstract 1973–79*, tables Q1 and Q2, and Government of Tanzania, *Economic Survey* (1981), tables 1 and 20. Table 1 gives GDP in the monetary sector for 1980 and 1981 only at factor cost. This is converted to market prices using the increases in 'customs and excise' shown in table 20 and applying the same percentage increase to net indirect taxation of the monetary sector.

[b] Bank of Tanzania, *Economic and Operations Report* (various years), tables 2 and 10.

[c] Ibid., table 15: total minus cols. (1), (2), (3), (4).

TABLE 6.4. *Accumulation of money balances, 1977–1981*

Year	Increase in money stock		Increase due to rise in money GDP				Residual increase due to rise in money GDP and change in velocity[d]	Increase due to fall in velocity			
	Annual	Annual % growth	Total[a] (1)	As % GDP	On 1977 velocity[b] (2)	Inflation tax on balances held owing to rationing		Annual[e]	As % GDP	Cumulative on velocity[f] in 1977	As % GDP
1977/8	1,356	(20.7)	155		155	0	28	1,173	(5.5)	1,202	(5.6)
1978/9	3,443	(43.6)	825		699	126	249	2,369	(10.0)	3,946	(16.7)
1979/80	3,690	(32.5)	888	(3.5)	580	308	200	2,602	(10.2)	7,056	(27.7)
1980/1	2,708	(18.0)	1,543	(5.5)	818	725	107	1,058	(3.8)	8,946	(31.9)

[a] (money GDP$_t$ − money GDP$_{t-1}$)/velocity$_{t-1}$
[b] (money GDP$_t$ − money GDP$_{t-1}$)/3.194. (From Table 6.3, 3.194 is the velocity of circulation in 1977.)
[c] Col. (1) − col. (2).
[d] Residual.
[e] (Money GDP$_{t-1}$/velocity$_t$) − money stock$_{t-1}$
[f] (money stock$_t$ − money GDP$_t$)/3.194.

Source: Table 6.3.

system consists only of one nationalized bank, which lends predominantly to public agencies administering components of government expenditure. For example, between 1975 and June 1983, 67 per cent of incremental net bank lending accrued to the crop-marketing parastals. In effect, the food subsidy to urban consumers was financed through money creation achieved by directives to the banking system to issue loans on non-commercial criteria. For this reason, variations in the controls on the banking system discussed in Chapters 4 and 5 did not apply in Tanzania. Throughout the period private agents operated in a regime of virtually total financial repression, enabling increases in the money supply to accrue entirely to the government.

Since the observed reduction in the velocity of circulation is important for our analysis, being consistent with the 'honeymoon' monetary behaviour discussed in Chapter 3, it is appropriate to consider explanations other than that of a response to stochastic rationing. Potentially, the increase in financial assets relative to GDP could reflect an accelerated process of financial deepening, or the growth of idle balances held by government agencies funded in excess of their expenditure. However, neither of these appears plausible. Claims of commercial banks and other financial institutions (other than the Central Bank) rose only from sh.68.3 million in December 1977 to sh.79.7 million in December 1981,[3] whereas total commercial bank deposits rose from sh.6,254 million to sh.14,868 million over the same period. Indeed, non-bank holdings of cash grew more rapidly than any other monetary aggregate, precisely the opposite of the pattern to be expected had the explanation of monetary growth been greater financial intermediation.[4] Probably Tanzania experienced the reverse of deepening, for during this period the largest financial intermediary, the East African Community, was dissolved. Deposits of the EAC at commercial banks in Tanzania declined from 5.8 per cent to 0.1 per cent of total bank deposits between 1977 and 1981.[5] Idle balances held by government agencies rose from sh.1,959 million to sh.3,845 million over the period,[6] that is at a slower rate than the growth of cash or bank deposits.[7]

An alternative explanation for the apparent rise in velocity might be that the demand for money had been increased by high prices on black markets and by unrecorded monetary transactions on parallel markets. There are grounds for suspecting that the official consumer price index understates the increases in the price level experienced by peasants through an underrecording of black market transactions. Indeed, the underlying process of information gathering about prices is confined to urban areas. We conducted

---

[3] Bank of Tanzania, *Economic Bulletin*, 13/3 (1983), table 12.

[4] Nominal interest rates, the conventional explanatory variable of the ratio of cash to bank deposits, were constant or rising over the period.

[5] Bank of Tanzania, *Economic Bulletin*, 13/3, table 15.

[6] Ibid.

[7] Government agencies are here defined to cover central and local government, schools, hospitals, the university, and public enterprises.

a rural survey which gathered data on prices and quantities for 18 basic consumer goods on both official and black markets. As described in more detail in the companion volume, *Peasants and Government*, from these data a rural price index was constructed which could be compared with the official consumer price index (CPI). Taking as our base 1976/7 and assuming that at that time availability at official prices was sufficient for there to be no black market, our index indeed reveals a larger increase in price level than shown by the official CPI. However, even by the end of 1983 this divergence in indices was only 23 per cent, so that were the National Accounts data understating the increase in the price level by this amount while correctly estimating changes in quantities, the true velocity of circulation would still show a massive decline. Further, as discussed in Chaper 3, section 3, higher black market prices do not necessarily increase the transactions demand for money by as much as their impact on the price level. Unrecorded parellel market activity would undoubtedly mean that actual monetary GDP was higher, and therefore the velocity of circulation higher, than their apparent level. However, our survey found that only 18 per cent of crop sales were through unofficial markets. Although our survey may itself have understated such sales (which were not, however, illegal), even were the National Accounts constructed on the assumptions of zero unofficial marketings (which they were not) there seems no evidence for regarding actual monetary GDP to be double the estimate in the Accounts (which it would need to be to invalidate the apparent decline in velocity).

Other financial policy instruments, interest and exchange rates, were not actively used. Table 6.5 shows that until 1983 nominal exchange and interest rates were broadly constant. The real interest rate on savings deposits was highly variable but always negative, being as low as -25 per cent. Holdings of cash attracted increasingly negative real interest rates. This provides some guide as to which types of agents were acquiring the large extra money balances noted above. For example, between the beginning of 1980 and the end of 1982 the real value of a unit of domestic currency more than halved. This suggests that the demand for increased real money balances could not have been derived from an increased asset demand except by agents whose asset choices were very severely constrained. Our own explanation, of course, rests not upon an increased asset demand but on a change in the transactions demand due in effect to the technical regress in commodity exchange generated by price controls: because of the random nature of shortages and hence of opportunities to make purchases, consumers needed to hold larger money balances per unit of achieved expenditure.

As in Chapter 5, we now attempt to derive from the National Accounts data some quantification of the responses of private agents and the public sector to the windfall. Again, though for rather different reasons, our private sector analysis of section 2.2 focuses on the period 1976–9. In the case of Kenya this was because the windfall triggered a public expenditure bonanza

TABLE 6.5. *Interest rates and exchange rates, 1975–1984*

	1975	1976	1977	1978	1979	1980	1981	1982	1983	1984
Nominal exchange rate										
Sh. per SDR end year	9.66	9.66	9.66	9.66	10.83	10.43	9.69	10.55	13.04	17.75
Normalised on 1975	1.00	1.00	1.00	1.00	1.12	1.07	1.00	1.09	1.35	1.84
National consumer price index	100.00	106.90	119.20	132.80	151.10	196.70	247.10	318.70	404.80	549.80
Annual inflation	26.40	6.90	11.50	11.40	13.80	30.20	25.60	30.00	27.00	35.80
Nominal interest rate on										
bank savings deposits (%)	4.00	4.00	4.00	5.0	5.0	5.0	6.0	7.5	—	—
Real interest rate on bank savings deposits	−22.40	−2.90	−7.50	−6.4	−8.8	−25.2	−19.6	−22.5	—	—

Sources: IMF, *International Financial Statistics*, and Bank of Tanzania, *Economic and Operations Report* (1983).

the repercussions of which rapidly came to dominate private sector behaviour. In Tanzania, as we shall show in section 2.3, the windfall did not trigger a similar increase in public expenditure. Rather, it enabled a fundamentally unsustainable policy stance which was largely put in place in the years immediately before the windfall to survive through to about 1980. Hence, from about 1980 onwards private sector behaviour is to be understood not as post-windfall planning, but as part of the slide into implosive decline.

2.2. *Private Sector Response to the Windfall, 1976–1979*

Again it is necessary to postulate as a counterfactual how the economy would have behaved in the absence of the boom. In estimating counterfactual income, the absence of substantial relative price changes in the period 1976–9 suggests that transfers accruing as rents are (unlike the Kenya case) not an important part of the analysis for this sub-period (although rents from black market activities were probably important after 1979). Further, the general decline in output suggests that extra capital formation merely raised the capital/output ratio. However, since in 1975 the economy was quantity-constrained in the foreign exchange market, the windfall may have had a multiplier effect through the increased availability of imports. One such effect appears likely from Table 6.1, namely output of the import substitutes sector. This sector is indeed likely in the short run to operate under a technology with close to fixed coefficients between imported inputs and output. It is therefore possible that the bulge in manufacturing production 1976–9 over both its 1975 and post-1979 levels is attributable to the windfall.[8] On this interpretation we derive counterfactual GDP in Table 6.6.

One use to which private agents probably put the windfall was illegal capital exports achieved through overinvoicing. We can make a tentative estimate of the order of magnitude involved through extending the analysis of Table 6.2. Had exports and imports been of equal value the difference between the first and last figures of Table 6.2—the boom at 'true' and 'apparent' terms of trade—would be the measure of extra overinvoicing. However, this condition is not met. In Table 6.7 we quantify the value of extra overinvoicing for the period 1976–81 (the latest available data) for non-oil imports. Over this period the total value was sh.2,978.2 million. However, not all of this can be attributed to the boom. Our preceding theory has suggested that over the whole period 1975–84 two distinct pressures to increase overinvoicing might be operating. Recall that one pressure is the incentive to inflate costs under conditions of rationing in commodity markets. As noted in our discussion of the prices and quantities series of Table 6.1, there is an abrupt onset of this incentive in 1981, consequent upon a spectacular collapse

---

[8] This procedure may overestimate the windfall by ruling out substitution effects among inputs.

TABLE 6.6. *Counterfactual GDP, 1975–1979* (Tsh. million)

	1975	1976	1977	1978	1979
Apparent terms-of-trade windfall[a]	0	620.4	1,305.9	364.5	96.6
Manufacturing multiplier[b]	0	382.9	531.7	659.4	382.9
Total apparent windfall	0	1,003.3	1,837.6	1,023.9	479.5
Actual GDP[c]	18,613	19,801	20,359	20,950	21,210
Counterfactual GDP	18,613	19,418	19,827	20,291	20,827
Total true windfall[d]	0	1,119.6	2,251.6	1,472.6	833.7

[a] From Table 6.2.

[b] From Table 6.1, import substitutes quantity series minus 1975 level.

[c] Our estimate of 1975 GDP is derived from *National Accounts of Tanzania* (1976–84) (for 1976) and *National Accounts* (1970–82) for the change 1975/6, all at 1975 prices.

[d] From Table 6.2 plus the manufacturing multiplier.

TABLE 6.7. *A quantification of overinvoicing, 1975–1981*

	1975	1976	1977	1978	1979	1980	1981
Tanzanian non-oil import unit values[a]	1.00	1.18	1.36	1.51	1.84	2.07	2.20
Kenyan non-oil import unit values[b]	1.00	1.15	1.26	1.36	1.67	2.00	1.96
% overinvoicing[c]	0.00	2.6	7.9	11.0	10.2	3.5	12.2
Non-oil imports (volume)[d]	1.00	0.79	0.94	1.40	1.41	1.09	1.22
Value of overinvoicing (Tsh.m.)[e]	0.00	106.5	382.5	789.7	736.7	196.5	766.2

[a] From Table 6.1.

[b] From Table 6.1 (in Tanzanian shillings).

[c] Row 1/row 2.

[d] Derived from Government of Tanzania, *Foreign Trade Indices*, tables S(iv) and S(x).

[e] The value of 1975 imports is subject to slight reporting variations according to source, with a range of Tsh.5,694m. to Tsh.5,885m. We adopt the estimate of Tsh.5,823m. derived from the *National Accounts*, (1976–84) (for 1976) and *Foreign Trade Indices*, these being the most recent sources available. Non-oil imports are then derived for 1975, using table S(iv) of the latter source, as Tsh.5,132.9m. The value of overinvoicing is thus at 1975 prices.

in manufacturing output and a consequent increase in its relative price. The second pressure is the incentive to acquire illegal foreign assets during a period of windfall income if all legal saving and investment avenues are regarded as highly unattractive. Clearly this operated primarily during the windfall phase, 1976–9. Interestingly, the pattern of extra overinvoicing, both as a percentage of the true price and by value, displays just this profile: a trajectory with low values in 1976 and 1980 and a peak in 1978, followed by a large increase in 1981. It may therefore not be unreasonable to attribute the overinvoicing which occurred in 1976–9 to windfall-induced asset behaviour. During this period sh.2,015 million was illegally sent abroad through extra overinvoicing, this being 54 per cent of the true value of the windfall. These numbers must, of course, be treated only as orders of magnitude because of the fragility of the underlying data and assumptions.

The other major asset accumulation by private agents out of windfall income was presumably real domestic capital. Table 6.8 presents data on capital formation by sector and ownership using various deflators. The last two rows of the table show the divergence between counterfactual GDP growth and private and public sector GFKF.

It is apparent that there was a considerable boom in private sector GFKF unrelated to GDP between 1976 and 1982, with its peak in 1979. Conversely, there is no increase in public sector GFKF, and indeed, starting about 1980 there is a precipitate decline relative to GDP. Table 6.9 brings together our estimates of the windfall (including the multiplier effect in manufacturing) and its uses for asset formation. By the end of 1979, 78 per cent of the windfall was invested, made up of 35 per cent held illegally overseas in financial assets, 63 per cent held by the private sector as extra GFKF, and − 18 per cent being a reduction in public sector GFKF.

The considerable private sector real asset accumulation during and after the boom may be a response to the income windfall or, additionally, to changes in the structure of incentives. Interestingly, there is a close relationship between private sector domestic investment and the accumulation of illegal holdings of foreign exchange through extra overinvoicing. Although we only have pairs of observations for 1975–81, the regression of private sector GFKF on foreign exchange overinvoicing suggests a significant association:

$$\text{GFKF} = 1,589 + 1.23\text{FX}$$
$$(15.6) \quad (6.4)$$
$$\bar{R}^2 = 0.87$$
$$\text{F} = 40.5$$
$$\text{DW} = 2.08$$

where ( ) = t-statistic; GFKF = private sector GFKF in sh. million (1975 prices) (Table 6.8); FX = extra overinvoicing in sh. million (1975 prices) (Table 6.7).

There are two explanations for this association. First, both assets might be chosen in relatively constant proportions as total desired savings fluctuated owing to the boom, and subsequently perhaps due to constraints upon the ability to make purchases. Second, purchases of imported capital goods might be an important mechanism for achieving the illegal export of capital. In either case the regression implies that marginal asset choices were split 55:45 between real domestic capital and illegal foreign financial assets.

TABLE 6.8. Capital formation, 1975–1984 (1975 = 1.00)

	1975Tsh	1975	1976	1977	1978	1979	1980	1981	1982	1983	1984
Public sector GFKF nominal	2,885[a]	1.00	1.02	1.36	1.37	1.53	1.69	1.65	2.07	1.62	1.65
Public sector deflated by Kenyan non-oil imports		1.00	0.87	1.08	1.01	0.92	0.85	0.84	1.00	0.68	
Private sector GFKF nominal	1,330[a]	1.00	1.66	2.06	2.54	3.15	2.82	3.67	3.65	3.14	3.15
Private sector deflated by Kenyan non-oil imports		1.00	1.44	1.63	1.87	1.89	1.41	1.87	1.76	1.32	
Private sector deflated by Tanzanian non-oil imports		1.00	1.41	1.61	1.68	1.71	1.36	1.67	2.25	1.87	
Manufacturing (nominal)	1,343[b]	—	1.00	1.66	1.24	1.39	1.46	1.91	1.91	1.34	
Manufacturing (deflated by Kenyan non-oil imports)	—	—	1.00	1.22	1.54	1.61	1.32	1.49			1.15
Non-tradables (nominal)	1,949[b]	—	1.00	1.52	1.05	0.96	0.84	1.12	1.25	0.91	
Non-tradables (deflated by Kenyan non-oil imports)	—	—	1.00	1.12	1.30	1.11	0.76	0.88	1.06	0.65	
Total GFKF (nominal)	4,129	1.00	1.25	1.61	1.78	2.08	2.09	2.33	2.62	2.14	
Total GFKF (deflated by Kenyan non-oil imports)	1.00	1.00	1.09	1.28	1.30	1.25	1.05	1.19	1.27	0.90	
Counterfactual GDP	1.00	1.00	1.04	1.07	1.09	1.12	1.15	1.14	1.15	1.15	1.17
GDP deflator	1.00	1.00	1.14	1.28	1.36	1.53	1.81	2.14	2.56	2.85	3.15
Private GFKF (deflated by GDP deflator minus GDP trend)	0	0	0.42	0.54	0.78	0.94	0.41	0.57	0.28	-0.05	-0.17
Public GFKF (deflated by GDP deflator minus GDP trend)	0	0	-0.15	-0.01	-0.08	-0.12	-0.22	-0.37	-0.34	-0.58	-0.65

[a] The National Accounts are reported in two internally consistent but mutually inconsistent series, 1970–82 and 1976–84. We use the latter as the more definitive. This however, leaves 1975 as a problem year. Our solution has been to apply the 1975–6 percentage change calculated from the 1970–82 series, to the 1976 figure from the 1976–84 series. Source tables are *National Accounts* (1970–82) table 16, and *National Accounts* (1976–84), table 14.
[b] 1976.

TABLE 6.9.   *The windfall and asset formation, 1976–1979* (Tsh. millions at 1975 prices)

	1976	1977	1978	1979
(1) Total true windfall[a]	1,119.6	2,251.6	1,472.6	833.7
(2) Overinvoicing[b]	106.5	382.5	789.7	736.7
(3) Windfall private GFKF[c]	558.6	718.2	1,037.4	1,250.2
(4) Windfall public GFKF[d]	−432.8	−28.9	−230.8	−346.2
(5) Windfall unspent on assets[e]	887.3	1,179.8	−123.7	−807.0
(6) Cumulative unspent windfall[f]	887.3	2,067.1	1,943.4	1,136.4

[a] From Table 6.6.
[b] From Table 6.7.
[c] From Table 6.8, penultimate row times private GFKF in 1975 (third row).
[d] From Table 6.8, last row times public GFKF in 1975 (first row).
[e] Row (1) minus rows (2), (3), and (4).
[f] Sum of row (5),

Source: Tables 6.6, 6.7, and 6.8.

2.3. Public Sector Response

This section uses the analytic procedure developed in Chapter 5.[9] Public sector data are much less complete and up to date for Tanzania. It did not prove possible to construct a consistent data set directly from Tanzanian published sources, and indeed the only consistent data set available is that published by the International Monetary Fund in the *Government Finance Statistics Yearbook*. This series starts in fiscal year 1972 and is currently complete only up to fiscal year 1981. The tables below are therefore restricted to calendar years 1972–80, though some piecemeal information[10] is available for later years.

Table 6.10 indicates the overall fiscal pattern. It differs from the corresponding table for Kenya in three respects (other than the shorter period). First, it is not possible to separate interest payments between the domestic and foreign components. Second, it is possible to disaggregate capital expenditure into direct capital formation by central government and capital transfers to parastatals only in the years 1972–7. Hence the exhaustive expenditure and surplus categories now include these capital transfers.[11] Third, the table includes two memorandum items, coffee export duty and defence expenditure. The former is of interest because the Tanzanian authorities made a concerted effort to obtain a large share of the windfall; the latter

[9] Minor variations are noted in the text where they occur.
[10] Notably on indirect taxes: see below.
[11] The equivalent financing activity in Kenya would have been recorded within the 'investment' category, which we have consolidated with net domestic borrowing.

TABLE 6.10. *Fiscal aggregates, 1972–1980 (Tsh. millions)*

	1972	1973	1974	1975	1976	1977	1978	1979	1980
(1) Indirect tax	1,104.0	1,590.0	2,054.5	2,272.5	2,668.0	3,393.5	3,977.5	4,278.0	4,847.0
(2) Direct tax	575.0	673.5	880.5	1,068.0	1,272.5	1,578.5	1,677.0	2,055.0	2,595.5
(3) Total revenue	2,043.5	2,735.5	3,707.0	4,315.0	5,149.5	6,348.0	7,085.5	7,960.0	9,425.0
(4) Consumption	1,348.0	1,915.5	2,838.5	3,286.0	3,710.5	4,550.5	6,033.0	6,719.5	6,853.5
(5) Capital expenditure	718.5	980.0	1,412.0	1,686.0	1,925.5	2,721.0	3,901.0	4,551.0	4,323.5
(of which GFKF)	(348.5)	(482.5)	(705.5)	(845)	(969)	(1,194.5)			
(6) Total expenditure: (4)+(5)	2,066.5	2,895.5	4,250.5	4,972.0	5,636.0	7,271.5	9,934.0	11,270.5	11,177.0
(7) Surplus: (3)−(6)	−23.0	−160.0	−543.5	−657.0	−486.5	−923.5	−2,848.5	−3,310.5	−1,752.0
(8) Interest payments	130.0	152.5	190.5	253.0	311.5	329.0	452.0	702.5	916.5
(9) Current unrequited transfers	363.5	410.0	592.0	797.5	739.0	667.0	557.5	456.0	505.5
(10) Total current transfers: (8)+(9)	493.5	562.5	782.5	1,050.5	1,050.5	996.0	1,009.5	1,158.5	1,422.0
(11) Financing: (12)+(13)=(10)−(7)	516.5	722.5	1,326.0	1,707.5	1,537.0	1,919.5	3,858.0	4,469.0	3,174.0
Of which:									
(12) Foreign	379.5	429.5	543.0	612.5	651.5	761.0	756.0	788.0	729.0
(13) Domestic	137.0	293.0	783.0	1,095.0	885.5	1,158.5	3,102.0	3,681.0	2,445.0
Memorandum items									
Defence	274.0	391.0	612.0	728.0	818.0	1,129.5	2,323.5	2,204.0	1,361.0
(Of which capital)							(763)	(567)	(327)
Coffee export duty	40.5	86.5	81.5	76.5	409.0	597.0	428.0	386.0	271.5

Sources; IMF, *Government Finance Statistics Yearbook*, 1985, IMF, *International Financial Statistics*, Dec. 1985.

is of interest because the war with Uganda was very expensive and complicates the counterfactual.

Table 6.11 gives the same information as a percentage of GDP at market prices. The Central Bureau of Statistics has recently revised the GDP series, but only back to calendar 1976. Unfortunately the new and old series appear to be remarkably divergent. Here the GDP figures for 1972–5 have been altered in the same ratio as the new/old values for 1976. The broad conclusions reached below do not appear to be sensitive to this treatment, but the detailed calculations certainly are.

(a) Fiscal patterns

These patterns are quite different from the Kenyan patterns. Despite the direct (and successful) attempt to tax the windfall coffee income, total revenue was remarkably stationary relative to GDP over the period 1974–80. The expenditure side of the story is rather different. It had already increased dramatically between 1972 and 1974, with the consequence that the exhaustive deficit had jumped to 3 per cent of GDP, and the total financing requirement to about 8 per cent of GDP.

The position in 1975 was clearly unsustainable. There was a mild improvement in the overall position during the boom itself, 1976–7, followed by a massive deterioration in 1978–9. The exhaustive deficit was running at about 9 per cent of GDP in these years, and the total financing requirement at about 12 per cent. The cause was the very large increase in expenditure; this was partly attributable to the war, but by no means entirely, as will emerge below.

This huge increase in the government's financing requirement was not met by foreign borrowing; on the contrary, the relative contribution of this fell over the period. The consequence was a very dramatic rise in domestic financing, primarily in the form of expansion of the money supply. Table 6.12 reproduces the figures for the increase in money stock given in Table 6.4 and sets them alongside the total domestic financing requirement of the central government (on a fiscal year basis).

The table demonstrates very clearly that the government's domestic financing requirement was wholly monetized over the four-year period.[12] Since this requirement was running at about 10 per cent of GDP in the middle two years, it would normally have led to a very dramatic rise in inflation. The reason why it did not has been discussed at length earlier in this chapter and in Chapter 3. Here we need only note again the large scale of the phenomenon and the great difficulty of eliminating the overhang via fiscal means. The cumulative totals of Table 6.12 amount to nearly 30 per cent of GDP; it is inconceivable that the government should run a large enough surplus for long enough to eliminate these liabilities.

---

[12] This accounts for the very small increase in interest payments over the period.

TABLE 6.11.　*Fiscal pattern as percentage of GDP, 1972–1980*

	1972	1973	1974	1975	1976	1977	1978	1979	1980
(1) Indirect tax	9.1	11.2	11.8	11.0	10.5	11.6	12.2	11.7	11.2
(2) Direct tax	4.7	4.7	5.1	5.2	5.0	5.4	5.2	5.6	6.0
(3) Total revenue	16.9	19.3	21.4	20.9	20.3	21.8	21.8	21.9	21.8
(4) Consumption	11.1	13.5	16.4	15.9	14.6	15.6	18.6	18.5	15.9
(5) Capital expenditure	5.9	6.9	8.1	8.2	7.6	9.3	12.0	12.5	10.0
(of which GFKF)	(2.9)	(3.4)	(4.1)	(4.1)	(3.8)	(4.1)			
(6) Total expenditure:(4)+(5)	17.1	20.4	24.5	24.1	22.2	24.9	30.6	30.9	25.9
(7) Surplus:(3)−(6)	−0.2	−1.1	−3.1	−3.2	−1.9	−3.2	−8.8	−9.1	−4.1
(8) Interest payments	1.1	1.1	1.1	1.2	1.2	1.1	1.4	1.9	2.1
(9) Current unrequited Transfers	3.0	2.9	3.4	3.9	2.9	2.3	1.7	1.3	1.2
(10) Total Current transfers: (8)+(9)	4.1	4.0	4.5	5.1	4.1	3.4	3.1	3.2	3.3
(11) Financing:(12)+(13)=(10)−(7)	4.3	5.1	7.6	8.3	6.1	6.6	11.9	12.3	7.3
Of which:									
(12) Foreign	3.1	3.0	3.1	3.0	2.6	2.6	2.3	2.2	1.7
(13) Domestic	1.1	2.1	4.5	5.3	3.5	4.0	9.5	10.1	5.7
Memorandum items									
Defence	2.3	2.8	3.5	3.5	3.2	3.9	7.1	6.1	3.2
Coffee export duty	0.3	0.6	0.5	0.4	1.6	2.0	1.3	1.1	0.6

Source: Table 6.10.

TABLE 6.12. *The domestic financing requirement, 1977/8–1980/1, (Tsh. millions)*

	1977/8	1978/9	1979/80	1980/1	Cumulative
Increase in money stock	1,356	3,443	3,690	2,708	11,197
Domestic financing requirement	1,558	4,646	2,716	2,174	11,094

(b) *The impact of the boom*

Inspection of Table 6.11 suggests that the 1975 pattern is again reasonably representative of the immediate pre-boom pattern. However, there are reasons why it is somewhat less satisfactory as a counterfactual for the whole boom episode.

First, there is the war with Uganda. At one extreme it might be argued that only the amelioration of the fiscal situation due to the boom permitted the Tanzanian government to embark on this exercise. In that case the war expenditure would be seen as directly contingent on the boom. At the other extreme, it might be argued that the war would have occurred anyway, so the war expenditure should be treated as included in the counterfactual case. This is the treatment adopted here; it has the effect of minimizing the expenditure consequences of the boom.

Second, there is the question of whether the 1975 fiscal pattern was a sustainable one, given the financing requirement, already noted, of 8 per cent of GDP. In the abstract this might seem implausible; however, the (un-weighted) financing requirement averaged nearly 9 per cent over the following five years, so it does indeed appear to have been sustainable, at least in the medium term.

Table 6.13 presents estimates of the boom's impact on the main fiscal aggregates measured at 1975 prices. Once again, the estimated manufacturing multiplier is subtracted from constant price GDP to achieve a counterfactual GDP series. The 1975 fiscal pattern is then used to generate counterfactual fiscal aggregates. These are amended by adding back the increment in defence expenditure attributed to the war, and these amended aggregates are subtracted from the actual figures (deflated using the implicit GDP deflator) to obtain the impact estimates.

The pattern that emerges from Table 6.13 differs in some crucial respects from the Kenyan pattern. While there again appears to have been an explosion of spending following the boom, it peaked very rapidly in Tanzania (in 1979) and there does not appear to have been the same ratchet effect and general loss of expenditure control as in Kenya. Recall that the figures in Table 6.13 assume that the war would have taken place (and at the same intensity) anyway; otherwise the surge of spending in 1978/9 would have been still sharper, and the subsequent reduction back towards the counterfactual still more remarkable. Unfortunately, the further development of the pattern

TABLE 6.13. *Fiscal changes due to the boom, 1976–1980* (Tsh. million at 1975 prices)

	1976	1977	1978	1979	1980	Cumulative
Indirect tax	1	345	403	230	54	1,033
(of which coffee						
export duty)	(274)	(382)	(220)	(159)	(55)	(1,090)
Direct tax	10	143	43	130	194	520
Total revenue	72	578	423	328	221	1,622
Consumption	−100	74	264	248	77	563
Capital expenditure	−55	407	608	874	435	2,269
Exhaustive expenditure	−155	481	872	1,120	511	2,829
Exhaustive surplus	228	98	−448	−793	−289	−1,204
Interest payments	18	5	58	179	221	481
Other current transfers	−181	−297	−475	−612	−655	−2,220
Total current transfers	−164	−291	−417	−432	−434	−1,738
Financing	−392	−388	31	360	−144	−533
Of which:						
Foreign	−67	−34	−128	−185	−315	−729
Domestic	−324	−354	159	545	170	196
Memorandum item						
Apparent windfall	1,003	1,838	1,024	480	—	4,345

after 1980 cannot be traced in the integrated form of Table 6.13, but some partial evidence is presented below.

A second major difference is the much larger extent to which the Tanzanian government's increased expenditure was concentrated in capital expenditure (80 per cent of the total, compared with 24 per cent over the same period in Kenya). Furthermore, only 57 per cent of the increase in expenditure was covered by increased revenue, the remainder generating a large increase in the exhaustive deficit in 1978 and 1979. As already noted, by 1980 this position had been substantially rectified.

A third difference is in the pattern of revenue. In both countries this largely involved increased indirect taxes, but whereas in Kenya these primarily reflected increased general tax rates, and were accordingly a permanent change, in Tanzania they were entirely accounted for by the coffee export duty. Indeed, this accounted for 67 per cent of total incremental revenue and 25 per cent of the total apparent windfall.

To summarize the estimates in the table, the principal conclusions are that the Tanzanian economy was already following a path which was unsustainable in the long run, and that the windfall slightly postponed the cumulative consequences of this policy. Whether the net impact was harmful or beneficial depends primarily on whether the additional Tsh.2,269 million of spending on capital assets generated an addition to the country's assets with a true value in excess of the Tsh.1,204 million deterioration in the exhaustive surplus.

3. The Effect of Price Controls on the Availability of Consumer Goods

Before 1975 price control theoretically applied in rural areas, but probably was not effectively enforced. In that year Operation Maduka extended state control to the retail level by replacing private, typically Asian-owned, shops by village- or state-owned co-operatives. Transitional problems (e.g. private shops being closed before collectively owned replacements could be organized) plagued this system for several years, but in the early 1980s the vast majority of villages had at least one shop. By then a village-level national rationing system had been introduced. The rules which governed this system caused access to goods at the village level to be a matter of luck. In *Peasants and Governments* we report detailed survey evidence on the severity of shortages of consumer goods in rural areas, both at official prices and on the black market. Using time series data disaggregated by region, we demonstrate that the decline in peasant sales of crops can be explained by the deteriorating availability of consumer goods.

4. Dismantling the Control Regime

In Chapter 3 we discussed the theory of escaping from an imploding controlled economy. Recall that even though the central problem was declining crop sales, raising crop prices would not, by itself, provide a solution and was indeed liable to make matters worse. Rather, what was required to switch the economy out of a rationed environment was both a reduction in demand, by means of a large increase in the price level, and a temporary increase in goods supply. Without the latter, since delay in implementing policy change increased the magnitude of the price increase required to clear the market, the price level would have to overshoot.

In Tanzania there were three possible routes by which the availability of consumer goods in rural areas could be temporarily increased. Donors could have temporarily switched aid from investment projects to the funding of consumer imports; the government could have encouraged the return of the foreign exchange illegally held abroad by Tanzanian citizens who, we have seen, used overinvoicing as a means of capital flight; or the allocation of foreign exchange could have been redistributed from government expenditure and urban workers towards rural consumer goods. Each of these routes was problematic. Reliance upon foreign donors would have required an addition to non-project aid on a scale which donors were unlikely to countenance. While the limited success of much past project aid might appear to reinforce the case for a switch in funds to a recovery programme, it also increased the resistance of donors to any new funding initiative. To attract the return of illegally held foreign exchange requires that the government grant credible amnesties to those agents it has previously characterized as enemies of the state, and moreover, permit them to enjoy many of the fruits of their illegal acts through the importation of consumer goods. It may be politically difficult for the government to make such a large reversal, and it may be technically difficult to do so in a way that convinces such foreign exchange holders that they are safe from future prosecution. As we shall see, in fact the Tanzanian government was able to overcome these difficulties. Redistribution from government expenditure and urban workers would have required a politically powerful group to suffer losses while a politically weak group experienced gains, an implausible scenario. In Bevan *et al.* (1987*a*) we discuss a variation on such a redistribution strategy which, by defending the real incomes of key groups, might have been politically feasible.

Even if one of these three routes were feasible, as we have seen, an increase in availability may well not be sufficient to secure a short-term positive supply response, because peasants may react by running down their money balances. The precondition for a powerfully positive short-run supply response is that peasants should wish to increase their cash balances at the same time as they encounter improved availability. Hence, increased availability must be synchronized with policies which reduce the real value of these balances. Such policies can be grouped into those offering something in exchange for the excess balances and those that default on them.

The difficulties associated with the former category make them impractical. The problem would be to find a good or an asset with two attributes: peasants must want it and the economy must be capable of supplying it without using foreign exchange or other scarce inputs. Accordingly, currently produced goods are ruled out, leaving government bonds and the entitlements to existing real assets. It is not clear that peasants would have voluntarily exchanged cash for bonds. The only real asset they might have chosen to acquire was land: the government could have sold back to peasants the land which it had previously taken into national ownership. However, this would have been politically highly sensitive.

There are two strategies for default by the government on the claims upon it held by peasants, namely inflation and currency reconstruction. A proportionate increase in the domestic prices of consumer goods and crops virtually constitutes a devaluation in the Tanzanian context, for these two categories largely encompass the set of internationally tradable goods. A currency reconstruction may involve the exchange of new currency for old, but with limits on the magnitudes which can be converted (such limits either being per capita or over a certain time period). Both methods of default succeed in reducing real cash balances, but each has different advantages. The advantage of raising the price level is that it enables the relative prices of goods and factors whose nominal price is rigid downwards to be lowered. The classic example of this is the wage rate. In Tanzania it is by no means clear whether by the mid-1980s real wages were too high once the economy had returned to market clearing, even though wages were too high relative to the official price level for the duration of repressed inflation. The advantages of currency reconstruction are that the rules of conversion can be made distributionally progressive, and that being a discrete and unusual event it is perhaps less likely to generate expectations of policy repetition. Since the expectation of default lowers the demand for real money balances, which in turn depresses crop sales, it is desirable that peasants should hold exclusive unrevised expectations (in the terminology of Chapter 2) with respect to the default event.

The above discussion has considered hypothetical possibilities open to the Tanzanian government. We now describe and evaluate the course actually chosen. Per capita GDP continued to contract, falling in each successive year until the Tanzanian government accepted the need for policy change in early 1986. An agreement was negotiated with the IMF and initiatives were taken both to increase the supply of consumer goods and to default upon monetary obligations. The IMF agreement ostensibly triggered donor funding for extra imports, and by 1987 imports were some 50 per cent above their low-point of the early 1980s. However, it is striking that this increase in imports was not, in fact, funded by extra aid. Rather, the key policy reform was the granting of permission for 'own-funded' imports, that is, the repatriation of illegally held foreign exchange.

Recall from Table 6.7 that we estimate that between 1976 and 1981 overinvoicing at a rate above the (unknown) 1975 level accounted for around sh.3 billion at 1975 prices. At the 1975 exchange rate this was $400 million of illegally held foreign exchange. By 1986 the true amount of illegal holdings would have been substantially larger than this. First, the outflow presumably continued: had the flow during 1982–5 continued at its 1981 rate this would have amounted to a further $400 million. Second, the above calculations are over and above the rate of capital flight experienced through overinvoicing in 1975. Third, overinvoicing was by no means the only mechanism for capital flight: some exports were smuggled over the border unrecorded, and foreign exchange could be purchased from tourists on the black market. Finally, the illegal holdings of foreign exchange were earning interest and so accumulating. It therefore seems likely that by 1986 illegal holdings of foreign exchange were in excess of $1 billion, perhaps substantially so.

Although the policy change was announced in the 1984/5 budget, it took some time for own-funded imports to materialize, perhaps because of lingering uncertainties. However, by 1986 and 1987 the flows of such imports were estimated to be $400 million per annum (Economic Research Bureau, *Tanzanian Economic Trends*, 1/1 (1988), 29). As noted there: 'Own funded imports at such levels are sufficient to account for the increase in imports.' There are three possible interpretations for an inflow of this magnitude. One is that it reflects the counterpart of a flow of unrecorded exports induced by the opportunity to import. Although this is possible it seems somewhat unlikely. In 1986 and 1987 recorded exports were only $350 million per annum, so unrecorded exports would have exceeded recorded exports. A second possibility is that capital flight has been so large that the own-funded imports represent the sustainable income flow from the foreign capital stock. For this to be the case illegal holdings would need to amount to around $8 billion, which is implausibly large. The third interpretation, to which we incline, is that own-funded imports of $400 million represent a stock-adjustment: the foreign assets accumulated in the period 1975–85 are being run down as agents rationally satisfy their previously repressed expenditure. As long as the inflow is indeed sufficient to switch the economy out of rationing for long enough to change the expectations of peasants, such a stock-adjustment is desirable. Indeed, this accumulation and subsequent decumulation of foreign financial assets has certain parallels with asset management of the temporary trade boom in Kenya.

The main default mechanism chosen by the Tanzanian government was devaluation, although a modest currency reconstruction was also undertaken. Between the first quarter of 1986 and the first quarter of 1988 the rate against the SDR was depreciated from sh.18.2 to sh.126.0. Over the same period the price level rose by about 70 per cent, thereby defaulting upon about 40 per cent of the monetary liabilities of the government.

This conjunction of extra consumer goods and monetary default was, in itself, an appropriate response to the acute problems of implosion. However, at the time of writing it is far from clear that these measures have been sufficient to return the economy to a compatible policy set. As of 1986/7 the government was running a deficit in excess of 12 per cent of GDP. It seems possible that while the above measures have been sufficient to switch the economy out of implosive rationing, there remains an incompatibility between exchange rate, trade, and budgetary policies. If so, such an incompatibility will be resolved either by further policy reforms which at last secure a compatible policy set, or by a degeneration of the economy on to its previous ruinous course.

5. Conclusion

The preceding analysis has identified several events which are consistent with the theories developed in Chapter 3. In *Peasants and Governments* we demonstrate that both official and unofficial markets were subject to quantity rationing and that this had set in and intensified subsequent to the coffee windfall. This substantiates the quantity-rationing assumption which underlies the model of Chapter 3. Three consequences predicted by the model were then shown to be consistent with the evidence. First, the predicted implosion in marketed output, a powerful and bizarre feature of the model, was unfortunately borne out in section 2.1. Not just relative to the trends of population or Kenyan output, but in absolute terms, there was a severe and accelerating decline in all sectors of marketed output. Secondly, the predicted increase in the demand for real money balances and consequent decline in the velocity of circulation is consistent with the actual halving of velocity, despite accelerating inflation, reported in section 2.1. Thirdly, the predictions of increases in overinvoicing both during the boom phase as a means of asset accumulation out of transient income, and during the implosive phase as a response to cost-plus pricing, were supported by the estimate of a large actual increase in overinvoicing relative to Kenya. Finally, in section 2.3 it was demonstrated that the policy stance adopted immediately before the boom was unsustainable even without the second oil shock. Hence, our interpretation of the post-windfall period as the deferred consequences of pre-boom policy errors is at least consistent with the evidence. We are conscious that the model developed in Chapter 3, being an extension of recent fix-price macro-theory, would fall by Occam's razor to a less complex account of the same phenomena. However, the model of Chapter 4, which retained commodity market clearing but introduced various other government interventions, while it captured rather well the Kenyan experience, fits Tanzanian experience badly. The fix-price model is therefore justified in our view as an extension of the incremental analysis of controls developed in Chapter 4 which provides a coherent account of apparently dramatically irregular economic events.

Appendix
A Narrative of Macroeconomic Events

[The chosen course] avoided the erosion of the credibility of and popular basis for the political system.

(Reginald Green, adviser to the Tanzanian government, 1980)

I can't just sign [the IMF agreement] and have riots in the streets.

(President Nyerere, 1984)

1. Introduction

Whereas in retrospect the coffee boom became publicly recognised by Kenyan policy makers as a major missed opportunity, there appears to have been no similar perception in Tanzania. This is not because the windfall was either significantly smaller or better handled, but rather because the boom became a brief respite in a gathering macroeconomic débâcle of tragic proportions. The origin of this débâcle was an overriding political commitment to an unsustainable public expenditure programme. The public decision process was unable to respond to evidence of failure. This appendix provides an account of events as seen by policy makers and other commentators. Again we set the scene with an account of the macroeconomy before the boom.

2. The Period up to 1975

During the first years after the attainment of independence in 1961 the Tanzanian government concentrated on the Africanization of the public sector. There were no major policy initiatives. In rural areas some village settlements were encouraged, but on the whole the government relied on conventional policies of promoting peasant agriculture. Industrial policy was to encourage import substitution, with reliance on private investors. Tanzania remained an open economy highly dependent on primary exports. Growth was fairly rapid, capital formation high, prices stable, and the balance of payments satisfactory.

However, the period up to 1967 was perceived by the government as one of increasing inequalities and disappointing industrial growth, with the foreign capital inflow not meeting expectations. The Arusha Declaration was President Nyerere's reaction to this perceived pattern of development. Augmenting the pursuit of growth, the official objectives of Tanzanian economic policy became equity, broad access to public services, popular participation in economic decision-making, self-reliance, and public sector leadership. The Declaration was followed by extensive nationalizations, increased government control of the economy, and the resettlement of the rural population into villages. In the modern sector the share of public enterprises grew rapidly from 27 per cent in 1962 to 66 per cent by 1974.

Owing to the expansion of government activities and the parastatal sector, the public sector borrowing requirement started to increase rapidly in the late 1960s. The price level started to rise and by the end of the decade the inflation rate was 4 per cent.

Expanding public sector expenditure raised imports and there was a sharp deterioration in the trade balance in 1970 and 1971. This could not be compensated by increased aid, and extensive loans and credits were required. Having exhausted its borrowing opportunities, the government reacted to the foreign exchange crisis mainly by trying to control imports. In 1971 it introduced a system of import licensing and exchange control which remained in force throughout our period. Import requirements were estimated at the level of individual firms or projects, and licences allocated on the basis of guidelines decided by the cabinet. Imports of capital goods received priority treatment, followed by intermediate goods, while imports of consumption goods were gradually squeezed out. Within a priority category there was a tendency to allocate foreign exchange in proportion to demand: for example, all textile mills received some of their requirements, but none sufficient to operate at full capacity. This may well have increased capacity underutilization. The nominal exchange rate was not actively varied, the shilling being pegged initially to the dollar and subsequently to the SDR.

A second aspect of the government's response to the crisis was the establishment of a domestic credit policy encompassing all commercial lending, and regulations on the use of enterprise surpluses. The sectoral direction of credit from now on was laid down in the Annual Finance and Credit Plan. The entire financial system in Tanzania consists of public institutions, and most flows occur within the public sector, their direction and magnitude often being determined as a by-product of non-financial policies.

Finally (and crucially, for our analysis), in 1973 a price commission was established. This came to regulate a wide array of prices in the economy on a cost-plus basis, firms being allowed a fixed mark-up over total costs. The Board of External Trade was established to regulate foreign trade, while the Board of Internal Trade with regional trading companies was to handle wholesale trade. Major crop parastatals such as the National Milling Corporation (NMC) and the Cotton Authority were also established. There was a strong political commitment to this system because of the ideological suspicion among Tanzanian leaders of the market as an allocative mechanism. Party officials tended to acquire an interest in the preservation of the administrative allocative system in which they participated. In the food grain market both consumer and producer prices were set by the government, and inter-district trade was the legal monopoly of marketing boards. The marketing of export crops was largely handled by public monopoly authorities, which controlled both purchases of output and delivery of inputs. The domestic prices of export crops were not closely related to world market prices, but were set by the cabinet on the basis of recommendations of the Marketing Development Bureau. This attempted to equalize the return to a day's labour on different crops, both export and food, so that crop prices, like manufactures, were determined on a cost-plus basis. Thus, it was in the aftermath of the 1971 foreign exchange crisis that much of the system of regulations and controls, which characterized Tanzania until the late 1980s, was created.

In 1972 the economy recovered somewhat, but in 1973–4 there was a marked deterioration. To a degree this was due to exogenous events: the weather was poor in both 1973 and 1974 and agricultural output fell. This made food imports necessary at a time when world market prices for grains were high, and on top of this came the first oil shock. The terms of trade deteriorated and the import bill almost doubled between 1972 and 1974 at current prices. These exogenous events were compounded by domestic political decisions. In 1972 the government had initiated a decentralization to regional bureaucracies which generated large additional costs. In 1974, impatient with the pace of voluntary villagization, the government launched a compulsory mass resettlement programme involving some 60 per cent of the population (see Collier *et al.*, 1986 for an account of the effects of this initiative).

The volume of agricultural exports stagnated, by 1973 being lower than in 1968. Real GDP growth declined, the only dynamic component of the economy being the public sector. To a considerable extent this was financed by accelerating inflation and the use of reserves. The current account deficit in 1974 was 19 per cent of GDP, and although part of this was made up by large increases in foreign aid, the foreign reserves were virtually exhausted.

The strategy which was pursued by the government in response to the oil shock had four proclaimed goals, namely, to maintain the pace of development, to protect the consumption of the weakest groups, to preserve the base for future growth, and to mobilize external finance. The policy package presented in April 1974 included considerable increases in agricultural producer prices, large increases in retail food prices, some curtailment of public investments, and tax increases. The effects of these changes on the living standards of urban wage earners—if not economically the weakest group, certainly the strongest politically—were more than offset by a 40 per cent increase in the minimum wage. Credit and foreign exchange budgeting was made more restrictive and efforts were made to mobilize foreign exchange. Public service levels were maintained. An indication of the government's thinking may be found in the writings of their principal economic adviser of the time, Reginald Green:

> A classical retrenchment with massive consumption cuts would deter recovery, destroy the demand basis for resumed growth and wipe out faith in the seriousness of the leadership's commitment to the transition to socialism. [The course chosen] avoided the erosion of the credibility of and popular basis for the political system. (Green *et al.*, 1980: 44).

Whether despite or because of this modest restraint, economic performance in 1974 was poor. The growth rate dropped, domestic savings fell drastically, the current account deficit remained massive, the budget deficit was increasing, and the money supply growth was accelerating together with the rate of inflation.

Now let us consider in some detail the situation in 1975, the last year before the coffee boom.

3. *The economic situation in 1975*

The modest retrenchments instituted in 1974 were intended to carry the country over until supply increased, and meanwhile Tanzania sought bridging finance.[1] It was assumed that the financial resources would be invested in activities generating output which could earn foreign exchange, that the

---

[1] SDRs, gold tranche, first credit tranche, oil facility, and compensatory financing facility drawings were all used.

weather would be better than it had been in 1973 and 1974, that the higher food crop prices would stimulate food production, and that a speedy completion of ongoing projects would lead to increased manufacturing output.

In spite of being in a situation in which the existing level of government activity was difficult to sustain, in early 1975 the government advanced the target dates for universal primary education and universal rural water supply. However, there were some concessions towards economic circumstances. The government had put together a compendium of its expenditure ambitions in the format of the Third Five Year Plan. This was due to be implemented in mid-1974. Even had the economy been in budgetary and foreign exchange equilibrium and had there been no oil shock, this compendium could not have been fully implemented. Its manifest lack of relevance to the post-oil-shock era might have suggested abandonment. While the government could not bring itself to outright abandonment, the plan was at the last possible moment postponed, and without the onset of the coffee boom might have remained so.

At the end of 1975 the government's view was that the adjustment had been fairly successful, with the exception of the attempts at speedy completion of projects and export rehabilitation (Green, 1983:114). This view of the situation was optimistic. In effect the country was still in a fundamental disequilibrium both internally and externally, and there had been little real, permanent improvement. Since the generation of export incomes was to become the major constraint on long-term growth, it was fanciful to regard performance as successful when no progress had been made on export production. Domestically, the budget continued to be precarious. The economy (we have argued) was liable to deteriorate unless some extraordinary positive exogenous event occured. Such an event was, of course, forthcoming: the coffee boom rapidly increased foreign exchange earnings. This sustained the economy until 1979, but during those years policy makers lost sight of the large underlying structural imbalances.

4. *The boom, 1976–1979*

The economy of Tanzania was thus in a serious disequilibrium in 1975, with both public sector and balance of payments suffering large and unsustainable deficits. At the same time the government was committed to a rapid expansion of its own expenditures, a foreign exchange intensive industrialization strategy, and a villagization programme. Against this background the world market coffee price quadrupled, increasing export incomes dramatically in 1976 and 1977 (see Table 6A.1). The terms of trade apparently increased by about a third between 1975 and 1977 (see our qualification in the main body of the chapter).

The first response was that the postponed Third Five Year Plan was allowed to be launched from mid-1976. In this plan the Basic Industries Strategy was set out. This was a highly ambitious programme of broad-based

TABLE 6A.1. *Coffee statistics, 1975–1984 (1975 = 100)*

	Deflated export price (A)	Deflated producer price (B)	(B)/(A)	Producer's share of price [a]	Export tax share [a]	Coffee's share in exports	Deliveries	Exports
1975	100	100	1.00	72.4	16.0	17.5	100	100
1976	233	106	0.45	69.1	18.9	31.2	106	92
1977	374	110	0.29	48.2	43.5	41.4	86	107
1978	217	75	0.35	46.2	41.7	35.2	93	93
1979	199	63	0.32	45.5	36.6	31.1	83	83
1980	153	58	0.38	48.7		26.9	79	94
1981	106	47	0.44			28.4	94	113
1982	80	43	0.54			30.8	101	87
1983	79	42	0.53			35.2	94	88
1984	91						96	

[a] Data on producer's share and export tax share in price refer to crop years—e.g. the entry in the line for 1975 refers to 1974/5. Export taxes on coffee were waived in 1981.

Sources: Tables 15, 16, and 40 in Government of Tanzania, *Economic Survey* (1981) and *Haifa ya Uchumi wa Taifa katika Mwaka* (1984), *Statistical Abstract 1982*, *Quarterly Statistical Bulletin*, 35/1 (1984), and Ellis and Hanak (1980: 14–15).

industrialization, which implied large investments. The programme would be a substantial net *user* of foreign exchange well into the 1980s. To sustain the strategy Tanzania would have to earn large amounts of foreign exchange or receive unprecedented amounts of foreign aid. Increased export production seemed highly unlikely given the relative price policy of the government, and the scope for increased aid was limited. The foreign exchange situation had been strongly exacerbated by the shocks of 1973–4, so that the economy already relied heavily on foreign savings.

Faced with this increase in world coffee prices the government chose, in contrast to the Kenyan government, to impose a coffee tax, which was intended to divert the windfall directly into government revenue. The domestic producer price was permitted to rise only by 10 per cent in real terms, even at its peak in 1977.

As a political decision the imposition of this coffee tax reflected both the urgent desire of the government for extra revenue with which to finance its industrial capital formation ambitions, and the low value which the government placed upon extra income for coffee farmers. The latter were regarded as a peasant élite, whereas the major thrust of the Arusha Declaration had been to arrest and reverse perceived tendencies to the formation of such an élite. Further, coffee farmers had not participated in the major policy instrument designed to implement this objective, namely the villagization programme.

As an aspect of macroeconomic stabilization policy the decision appeared well justified. We have seen in Chapter 5 that the levying of a coffee tax during the boom can be an appropriate policy response in conjunction with other policies. However, the Tanzanian coffee tax was rapidly converted from an instrument by which the government pre-empted windfall income to a claim on non-windfall income: by 1978 the real producer price was already 25 per cent below its 1975 level.

As a result of the new industrialization strategy investment was shifted from infrastructure and agriculture to directly productive activities (see Table 6A.2). In 1976–7 both intermediate and capital goods imports increased rapidly (see Table 6A.3). The large foreign exchange claims of the Basic Industries Strategy were thus accommodated by the boom in conjunction with a significant transfer of resources from agricultural to industrial programmes, industry increasing its share of investment from around a seventh to a third. Owing to a break in time series in 1976 we cannot be certain about the rate of growth of manufacturing output in this period, but it was clearly rapid.

There are serious problems with the data on agricultural production for this period, but it seems likely that the relative importance of food crops increased, for there was a prolonged stagnation in export crop production. Green *et al.* (1980: 84) attribute this stagnation to major policy errors. They point to the neglect of price incentives, tea and tobacco projects which should have been completed faster, the ineffectiveness of the marketing system, and

Two African Applications

TABLE 6A.2. *Capital formation and savings, 1975–1984 (%)*

	Directly productive[a]	Economic infrastracture[b]	Commercial services[c]	Government administration and social services	Investment rate[d]	Savings rate[e]
1975	35.3	47.5	13.1	4.1	20.3	17.8
1976	37.8	38.7	10.9	12.7	22.8	22.1
1977	43.9	31.5	13.1	11.5	22.5	10.2
1978	36.7	37.5	12.2	13.6	23.6	13.6
1979	34.7	35.6	8.9	20.9	20.0	8.3
1980	37.1	31.2	9.7	22.0	18.9	14.4
1981	41.6	28.3	9.1	21.0	17.9	9.4
1982	45.8	23.7	12.8	17.7	13.4	7.8
1983	47.6	20.4	14.1	17.9	16.8	4.7
1984	44.0	21.4	15.6	19.0		

[a] Agriculture, mining, manufacturing, construction.
[b] Electricity and water supply, transport and communications.
[c] Wholesale and retail trade, finance, insurance, real estate and hotel services.
[d] Capital formation as percentage of GDP.
[e] Savings as percentage of GDP.

Sources: National Accounts of Tanzania (1976–84), and Ndulu and Hyuha (1984).

TABLE 6A.3. *Composition of imported goods by end use, 1975–1983* (%)

	Consumer	Intermediate	Capital
1975	31.4	41.4	27.2
1976	20.8	49.2	29.7
1977	18.6	45.5	35.9
1978	19.4	40.4	40.2
1979	14.6	40.4	45.0
1980	14.2	40.0	45.8
1981	10.7	39.4	49.8
1982	11.0	40.0	49.0
1983	16.1	44.3	39.6

Sources: Mbelle (1988) and informal ILO-mission estimates.

the lack of commodities for the farm sector. Indeed, in addition to the policy stance being pro-industry and hence anti-agriculture, there was a shift within agricultural policy towards the support of food production, through the ujamaa programme, marketing, rural credit, input supply, research, and pricing.

The government sector continued to grow rapidly in 1976 and 1977, at 12 to 13 per cent. This was at least in part a response to extra revenue: revenue overshot the 1976/7 estimates owing to rapidly increasing incomings from the coffee export tax, income tax, and various indirect taxes. In response, the government decided that there was room for a more expansionary stance, so that the budget for 1977/8 allowed considerable expenditure increases without any tax increases, and domestic credit formation targets were increased.[2] Additionally, the determination of wages and salaries was returned to the industrial tribunal system, with the expectation of an increase in the level of awards. With the rapid growth of the public sector the borrowing requirement was large. An indication of how fast the parastatal sector had grown is that the parastatal financing requirement was equal to 25 per cent of monetary GDP in 1976/7, compared with the budgetary financing requirement of 13 per cent. The parastatal borrowing requirement was growing rapidly and constituted the bulk of the increase in the public sector's borrowing requirement in that year.

In 1976/7 the government did not have to borrow from the Bank of Tanzania or commercial banks, and the rate of growth of money supply was

[2] The allocation of financial resources in Tanzania is not governed by interest rates to any significant degree. The interest rates, which remained more or less unchanged through the 1970s until 1978, were thus not used to control credit. Real interest rates became increasingly negative after 1971–2 and in 1980 they had fallen to about − 20% (Kimei, 1985: table 6.4.b). Credit was allocated mainly through credit planning in the form of the annual Finance and Credit Plan. This set both overall ceilings and allocated funds to the various sectors of the economy.

halved compared with 1975. The inflation rate dropped from 26 per cent in 1975 to 7 per cent and 12 per cent in 1976 and 1977. Both domestic and external balances improved significantly in these two years.

Green *et al.* (1980: 102) argue that the policy stance of 1974–7 was 'macro-efficient', even if there were numerous examples of 'micro-inefficiency'. It may be questioned, however, to what extent the stabilization achieved in 1976/7 was due to changes in policy. Most of the improvement was due to the unanticipated terms-of-trade windfall. Import licensing was eased in the second half of 1977, with priority being given to spares and inputs going to manufacturing. The exchange rate was not altered, and export volumes continued to stagnate while imports rose sharply. The liberalization of foreign exchange budgeting was continued through 1978, and the Foreign Exchange Plans of 1977/8 and 1978/9 were optimistic. Moreover, the government planned considerable real increases in its expenditures. This was in part due to the desire to meet the deferred needs of maintenance, in part due to the demands of the Third Five Year Plan. A further major public expenditure commitment entered into in late 1978 was the invasion of Uganda. Completely justified morally following an invasion of north-west Tanzania by Amin's forces, the response was, however, arguably among the more expensive of a range of options. The war is thought to have incurred direct costs of up to $700 million, of which a large component was in foreign exchange. It is not known to what extent this was externally funded. Thus, through 1978 policy was expansionary in spite of the fact that the balance of payments was continually deteriorating. Green *et al.* (1980) describe the stance in the plans for 1978/9 as a 'firm commitment to further expansion'.

The coffee price started to fall in 1977, and in 1978 export incomes consequently fell considerably, while import expenditures increased dramatically. In 1978 Tanzania also started to feel the effects of the collapse of the EAC and the war against Amin started. There was a huge and unsustainable deficit on the basic balance of 8 per cent of GDP and foreign exchange reserves were falling rapidly.

The share of foreign savings in GDP jumped to 15 per cent (Table 6A.4). Imports grew by some 25 per cent, being Tsh.600 million larger than the already ambitious Foreign Exchange Plan target. There was, however, a substantial change in the composition of imports. Consumption imports were reduced, while remarkably the government maintained investment throughout the period up to 1982 and thus had large imports of capital goods. A factor which contributed to this was that much of the foreign aid was tied to capital goods imports.

Green (1983: 116) is critical of the agricultural policy of this period, suggesting that agricultural policy and institutional performance have been the major domestic 'contribution' to the crisis. Large changes in relative prices over 1975–9 led to a fall of two-thirds in output (or, more accurately, gathering) of the most promising export crop, cashew. At the same time, there

TABLE 6A.4. *Expenditure shares of GDP, 1975–1984* (current prices)

	Public sector cons.	Private cons.	Gross fixed capital formation	Exports	Imports	Exports minus imports	Domestic savings
1975	17.1	74.5	18.6	18.2	31.0	-12.8	
1976	15.7	64.4	20.3	20.9	23.0	-2.1	17.8
1977	14.8	62.7	22.8	19.3	22.5	-3.2	22.1
1978	17.2	72.9	22.5	14.4	29.4	-15.0	10.2
1979	16.4	70.4	23.6	14.1	26.8	-12.7	13.6
1980	12.7	77.7	20.0	12.8	25.7	-12.9	8.3
1981	12.0	74.0	18.9	11.6	19.5	-7.9	14.4
1982	13.3	77.9	17.9	8.0	17.7	-9.7	9.4
1983	11.7	79.5	13.4	8.7	16.7	-8.0	7.8
1984	12.2	82.4	11.8	8.4	17.5	-9.1	4.7

Sources: For 1975, Government of Tanzania, *Statistical Abstract 1982*. For 1976–84, the revised data from *National Accounts of Tanzania* (1976–84).

were large switches to several traditional drought-resistant crops,[3] whose surpluses from 1976 to 1978 could be neither stored nor exported except at massive losses. There was a severe decline in the relative price of export crops, and in the case of coffee the share of export taxes and marketing margins by 1978/9 had increased to 55 per cent of the coffee export price[4] (Table 6A.1). Most of this was due to the increase in export taxes.

GDP growth in 1978 was 2.9 per cent, with agriculture growing by only 1.4 per cent. The estimates for agriculture are very uncertain, but it is probable that many peasants were withdrawing from the monetary economy. Public services continued to grow rapidly through 1978 and 1979 (see Tables 6A.5 and 6A.6). The rate of growth of the manufacturing sector fell in 1978, but the Basic Industries Programme of investment was not cut back. Consequently a large number of new firms was established in spite of increasing spare capacity. The ambitious investment programme also meant that co-ordination and project analysis was neglected. To be able to run the new industries large amounts of foreign exchange would have been needed, but there was no strategy for the realization of this aim. There was an ambition to expand the processing of primary exports, but the results were poor (and probably net foreign exchange users). The scarcity of foreign exchange led to shortages of raw materials, intermediate inputs, spares, and replacement machinery.[5] This

TABLE 6A.5. *Growth rates, 1970–1984* (%)

	GDP	Agriculture	Manufacturing	Public services
1970–4 (av.)	4.5	1.5	6.1	12.1
1975	5.7	8.5	0.3	16.1
1976	2.8	0.2	6.2	12.2
1977	2.8	0.2	6.2	12.2
1978	2.9	1.4	4.8	12.2
1979	1.2	1.2	−10.2	14.0
1980	0.8	3.0	−18.6	5.8
1981	−1.1	2.3	−21.5	7.7
1982	1.3	2.6	−17.9	7.9
1983	−0.4	1.1	−8.8	9.8
1984	2.5	2.6	−13.3	6.5

Sources: For 1970–5 estimates are computed from Government of Tanzania, *Statistical Abstract 1982*, and *Economic Survey* (1977/8). For 1976–84 the estimates are taken from *National Accounts of Tanzania* (1976–84).

[3] Cassava, millet, sorghum and pigeon peas.

[4] In the late 1970s about 245,000 peasants were growing coffee, i.e. about 9.5% of all peasant households. The peasants produced 83% of output in 1978/9 against only 17% for the estates. During the 1970s coffee income constituted 27% of total producer income from sales through official channels.

[5] The ratio of foreign exchange allocation to requests fell from 56% in 1977 to 49% in 1978, 21% in 1979, 24% in 1980, and 6% in 1981 (Ndulu and Hyuha, 1984: 9).

TABLE 6A.6. *Economic structure by sector, 1975–1984* (%)

	Production (current prices)			Modern sector employment		
	Agric.	Indust.	Services	Agric.	Indust.	Services
1975	41.3	14.7	44.0	27.0	28.8	44.2
1976	44.4	16.0	39.6	28.6	24.6	46.8
1977	44.5	16.0	38.9	26.6	23.9	49.5
1978	44.6	16.6	38.8	22.6	28.4	49.0
1979	46.1	15.3	38.6	28.6	24.6	46.8
1980	46.2	14.1	39.7	27.2	23.6	49.2
1981	47.6	13.2	39.2	23.9	26.6	49.5
1982	51.7	11.1	37.2			
1983	53.0	9.6	37.2			
1984	52.9	8.8	38.3			

Sources: As for Table 6A.5.

in turn had knock-on effects in the public utilities, leading to shortages of electricity and water. As a result, capacity utilization in manufacturing began a rapid decline. Ndulu (1985: 17) claims that as much as 92 per cent of the variation in capacity utilization over the period 1975–8 is explained by variations in intermediate imports. He also concludes that much of the investment that was undertaken was wasteful.[6]

Money supply was held in check in 1978, but of course this was due in part to the very large balance-of-payments deficit (see Tables 6A.7 and 6A.8). Non-government credit expanded by 39 per cent and government credit by 51 per cent. The rate of inflation remained about 12 per cent as 1977. This was partly due to the low rate of monetary expansion, but also to the fact that the Tanzanian shilling was actually appreciated against the dollar.

Towards the end of 1978 it was becoming apparent that there was a serious economic crisis, with dwindling reserves, a recurrent budget deficit, and inflationary credit expansion. Some contractionary measures were undertaken. In November, taxes on drinks and cigarettes were increased, and in December the credit plan was adjusted and import licences were cut back. The latter exacerbated shortages of inputs and spares and this in turn led to a decline in manufacturing output.

5. Crisis 1979–1981

In 1979 the nominal coffee price was more or less constant, but oil prices were raised again and exports were stagnant. On top of this the costly war against

[6] Access to foreign finance was often tied to the capital content of development projects. This part could not be shifted to meet recurrent costs or the demand for intermediate inputs, and this may have contributed to the lowering of capacity utilization.

TABLE 6A.7. *The balance of payments, 1970–1984* (Tsh. million)

	Trade balance	Service balance	Transfer balance	Balance on current account	Net long term capital movements[a]	Basic balance	Basic balance as % of GDP
1970	−422	226	92	−105			
1971	−737	209	41	−487			
1972	−538	256	30	−252			
1973	−871	190	35	−646			
1974	−2,433	182	351	−1,899			
1975	−2,860	481	759	−1,620	1,027	−593	−3.1
1976	−1,162	518	464	−180	885	705	+2.8
1977	−1,697	666	962	−69	924	855	+2.9
1978	−5,127	209	1,273	−3,645	1,051	−2,594	−8.0
1979	−5,006	307	1,447	−3,252	1,399	−1,853	−5.1
1980	−5,816	157	1,055	−4,604	1,363	−3,241	−7.5
1981	−4,747	579	1,888	−2,280	1,694	−586	−1.2
1982	−6,472	361	1,107	−5,005	2,456	−2,549	−4.2
1983	−5,905	435	1,146	−4,324	2,148	−2,176	−3.3
1984	−7,624	548	1,427	−5,649			

[a] In long-term capital movements are included governmental, private, and parastatal medium- and long-term borrowing.

Sources: For 1967–75, Government of Tanzania, *Statistical Abstract 1982* and *Economic Survey* (1977/8). For 1976–84, *National Accounts of Tanzania* (1976–84), and Bank of Tanzania, *Economic and Operations Report* (June 1984).

TABLE 6A.8. *Monetary data, 1970–1984*

	Rate of change in the national consumer price index (%)	Exchange rate Tsh./$US (end period)	Rate of growth of Money supply (%)	
			M1[a]	M2[b]
1970–4 (av.)	9.2	7.14	20.0	18.0
1975	26.5	8.26	34.3	25.0
1976	6.9	8.32	15.6	13.3
1977	11.6	7.96	14.3	18.5
1978	11.4	7.41	11.6	13.7
1979	13.8	8.22	38.8	37.7
1980	30.3	8.20	34.1	31.7
1981	25.6	8.32	21.3	21.6
1982	28.7	9.57	20.2	21.7
1983	27.3	12.46	9.4	17.2
1984	29.7	18.11	20.1	18.3

[a] M1: currency in circulation plus demand deposits, except those of the central government.
[b] M2: currency and demand, time, and savings deposits, except those of the central government.

Sources: Bank of Tanzania, *Economic and Operations Report* (June 1984), Kimei (1985), and IMF, *International Financial Statistics*.

Amin continued. While contributing to the economic crisis, the war drew the attention of policy makers from the economy.

Perhaps because of this diversion of attention there were few economic policy initiatives during 1979, despite a conjunction of negative foreign exchange shocks on top of an unsustainable existing stance. Additionally, large losses of the agricultural parastatals were uncovered. Only towards the end of 1979 did policy makers finally become aware of the seriousness of the crisis. Negotiations were held with the IMF and IBRD, but these broke down and the government failed to implement a workable strategy. A new foreign exchange crisis occurred, during which the entire reserve of foreign exchange was exhausted. This at last provoked a policy response, but primarily this took the form of a reversal of the previous liberalization of commercial policy: imports were again strictly controlled by quantity restrictions. The contraction in monetized GDP consequent on the reduction in imported inputs eroded the tax base, and customs and excise duties also declined drastically. Despite this decline in the revenue base, government expenditures continued to increase, and to finance this expenditure the government increased sales and income taxes. However, these extra sources of revenue fell far short of requirements, and the government resorted to increased bank borrowing and external grants and loans. During the 1980s debt service has been the principal increasing component of government expenditures.

The measures which were undertaken did not in any significant degree improve the balance of payments, the balance of trade continuing in large deficit. The transfers that were received from the rest of the world only made up for a small part of this deficit, Tanzania's favoured position among donors having been eroded because of the disillusionment with economic policy. The basic balance was in huge deficit, which was only financed by the government borrowing heavily on the international capital markets. Clearly such a strategy was unsustainable since the limits of creditworthiness were rapidly approaching. The rate of economic growth in 1979–80 slowed down to about 1 per cent per year in spite of the rapid expansion of the public sector. Although manufacturing output had increased during the boom, from 1979 it suffered an amazingly rapid contraction. Output fell in some years by more than 20 per cent, and by 1984 it was 63 per cent below its 1977 peak.

From 1979 foreign exchange availability was too low to make possible a high degree of capacity utilization and good maintenance. The government had used all of its low-conditionality IMF facilities, but since it failed to come to terms with the IMF, it could not get more finance from that source.

Domestic savings declined rapidly, and Tanzania continued to rely on foreign savings at a rate of 13 per cent of GDP in 1979 and 1980, and after this at near 10 per cent. Money supply growth was rapid, as implied by the combination of a rapidly growing public sector and contracting monetized private sector.

Changes in the money supply and the price level were not closely matched. The large balance-of-payments deficits absorbed a considerable proportion of monetization: during the period 1974–78 deficits absorbed as much as 68 per cent (Rwegasira, 1983). Further, the velocity of circulation (monetary GDP/M1) decreased significantly after 1978. Between 1971 and 1978 it was fairly stable at around 3.0, but in 1979 it fell drastically from 2.9 to 2.1, falling further to 1.7 in 1980 (Kimei, 1985: annex 8.8). Such a large acceleration in domestic credit would normally have implied a more than proportionate increase in the price level (as agents refused to hold increased real money balances). However, the government was acutely sensitive to the political implications of price increases, especially wishing to be seen to protect the living standards of urban wage earners, who were indeed largely its own employees. This concern was in part manifested in the government's repeated reluctance to devalue the currency, causing in the process a massive real appreciation. However, more directly it led the government to activate the apparatus of price control, which, we have seen, had been formally established in 1973.

Prices of consumer goods were now held down and rapidly became substantially lower than market-clearing levels. In consequence, consumer shortages became endemic and unofficial (or 'parallel') markets emerged, on which prices were considerably in excess of official prices. In *Peasants and Governments* we show that the officially estimated consumer price index indeed understates the true increase in the cost of living during this period. Even correcting for this bias in the official estimates of the price level it remains true that the velocity of circulation declined, so that money was hoarded as shortages of consumer goods became more acute. The demand for money under conditions of shortage is a component of the theory developed in the main body of the chapter.

This reduced availability of goods at official prices differed between areas. On the whole it seems that Dar es Salaam received priority over the rest. Amani *et al.* (1984) computed the per capita supply of preferred cereals (maize flour, rice, wheat flour), and found that rural areas were given lowest priority (see Table 6A.9). Little NMC grain was sold outside the major urban centres. In many small urban areas consumers were forced to rely on the parallel markets.

Keeler *et al.* (1981) estimate that by 1980 some 30 per cent of urban food needs were served from the parallel markets. Their estimates of the parallel prices relative to the official ones are given in Table 6A.10. In the parallel market unground maize was selling at two to four times the official price. It is

TABLE 6A.9. *Per capita supply of preferred cereals[a]: NMC deliveries by destination, 1974/5–1980/1 (kg).*

Destination	1974/5	1975/6	1976/7	1977/8	1978/9	1979/80	1980/1
Dar es Salaam	176.0	147.2	156.0	178.7	201.8	190.0	197.7
Up-country towns	198.6	122.0	111.5	94.6	92.7	83.3	105.0

[a] Maize flour, wheat flour, rice.
Source: Amani *et al.* (1984: 7).

TABLE 6A.10. *Parallel market prices relative to official prices for thirteen lake-region villages, 1979/80–1980/1.*

	1979/80	1980/1
Maize	3.08	4.98
Paddy	1.54	2.42
Cassava	3.06	4.58
Sorghum	2.96	4.68
Millet	2.37	4.63

Source: Keeler *et al.* (1982: 81).

thus not surprising that NMC purchases from domestic farmers declined and that some 70 per cent of NMC sales in 1980/1 was based on imported grains (Sharpley, 1983: 39). The urban population, particularly that of Dar es Salaam, was thus fed largely through imports at heavily subsidized prices. Official food procurement halved between 1976/7 and 1983/4.

Inflationary pressure, though repressed, was thus building up again after the boom, and the fiscal deficit was a key factor behind this. The defiantly optimistic policy stance of the government in the response to the 1979–81 crisis corresponded closely to its behaviour during the previous crisis episode of 1974–5, only this time no coffee boom ensued. The government did not consider liberalization measures or drastic expenditure reductions or tax increases. Policy makers again tried to acquire bridging finance, and the Basic Industries Programme was continued into 1981.

As a consequence of the rapid expansion of the public sector relative to the import potential of the country, maintenance deteriorated and there was an imbalance between personnel and complementary inputs. The ratio of recurrent expenditures to development expenditures in economic infrastructure declined from 1.32 in 1965/6 to 0.35 in the 1980s (Ndulu, 1984: 11). This was particularly serious for the rural water supply programme (Green *et al.*, 1980: 69), though many poorly integrated and inefficient rural programmes were attempted.

We have seen that from the mid-1970s agricultural prices were largely set on the basis of costs of production plus marketing costs. When the sum of marketing parastatals payments to producers and marketing costs exceeded export earnings at the official exchange rate, the government absorbed the losses in the budget. In the early 1980s subsidies to the crop-marketing parastatals as well as their bank overdrafts increased dramatically. Increases in nominal agricultural producer prices were thus largely financed by increases in the government budget deficit. Subsidies and related costs rose from about Tsh.150 million in the 1979/80 budget to Tsh.1,427 million in the 1981/2 budget (see Table 6A.11). This contrasts with surpluses of public enterprises in the early 1970s of 5 to 6 per cent of GDP. Under this system the determination of producer prices depended in part on the ability of the government to absorb the losses of the parastatals. During the late 1970s the income per unit of output for export crop producers was drastically reduced (see Ellis (1982) and Bevan *et al.* (1988)) and this was to a large extent a consequence of budgetary constraints ensuing from the exchange rate policy. In particular, the exchange rate adopted by the government had become increasingly overvalued.[7] At the same time the prices of inputs had risen, as had real transport costs—if transport was at all available. Thus access to

[7] Kimei (1985) estimates the ratio between the black market rate and the official rate to have increased from 2.4 in 1979 to 4.3 in 1980, 6.0 in 1981, and 6.9 in 1982. Keeler *et al.* (1981) have a somewhat lower estimate than Kimei for their last year, 1979, which was 1.6.

TABLE 6A.11. *Agricultural parastatal indebtedness, 1980–1981*

	Overdraft at 31 March 1981 (Tsh. Million)	Overdraft as % of annual purchases	Change from previous year (%)
National Milling Corporation	2,826	530	16
Tanzania Cotton Authority	654	160	39
Coffee Authority of Tanzania	602	90	125
Tobacco Authority of Tanzania	337	260	103
Tanzania Sisal Authority	297	100	27
Cashew Authority of Tanzania	187	100	76
Sugar Development Corporation	106	30	18
GAPEX	58	60	57
Tanganyika Pyrethrum Board	42	210	74
Tanzania Tea Authority	25	20	35
TOTAL	5,134	180	32

Source: Marketing Development Bureau (1981).

markets became much less reliable, among other things owing to the inefficiency of the crop marketing parastatals. Keeler *et al.* (1981: 31–2) point to their inadequate accounting practices and the inefficient use of lorries.

As an indication of the magnitude of policy-induced relative price changes, between 1971/2 and 1983/4 the real price of food fell by 8 per cent while the real price of cash crops fell by 42 per cent. Over this long period there had been a strong relative price shift in favour of food crop production. However, this had occurred between 1971 and 1976. Between 1976/7 and 1983/4 the relative price remained more or less constant, while the real price of both categories fell by about a third. Since the major proximate cause of the rapid contraction in manufacturing output was the shortage of foreign exchange, and enhanced export crop production the most feasible means by which the government could increase the supply of foreign exchange, its export crop-pricing policies must be regarded as unfortunate even in terms of its industrial objectives.

By the early 1980s most household goods had become scarce or nonexistent in the rural areas and the government recognized that this might be adversely affecting crop marketing. A decision was therefore taken to divert extra supplies to rural areas, particularly the coffee-growing areas. However, the decision was never implemented, being overtaken by the accelerating decline in goods availability nationally. Although the major factor behind the scarcity of goods was the foreign exchange shortage, it was aggravated by government distribution policy. This aimed at reducing the role of private traders and replacing them by regional trading corporations and co-operative village shops. The role of private transport was also reduced in favour of public sector transport companies. Sharpley (1983: 40) notes that

> the relative inefficiency of public transport has cut down on the flow of consumer items to rural areas, and some of these goods do not reach the villages since it is easier to sell on the parallel market in towns which are more accessible and less closely controlled. Even when villages do get their allocations these are often hopelessly small in relation to demand.

6. *Adjustment attempts from 1982 to 1984*

For several years of crisis the government maintained its broad policy stance, but eventually changes were forced upon it by the course of events. In 1981 policy makers finally decided that there should be a shift away from general investment promotion, and the investment budget of 1981/2 was 20 to 25 per cent below that of the year before, though still being 18 per cent of GDP. Attention was now instead to be focused on bottlenecks and the restoration or completion of existing projects through maintenance, re-habilitation, and working capital.

Indications of this rethinking are evident in the National Economic Survival Plan (NESP), drafted in 1981, the main emphasis of which was to concentrate efforts on projects which either generated or saved foreign exchange. Some projects which did not meet these demands were shelved for the time being (e.g. the Mufindi Paper and Pulp Mill, the Kidatu Mufindi Transmission Line, and the Dar es Salaam Electric Bulbs Factory). The NESP also put higher priority on micro-efficiency, and it stated the ambition to control inflation through control of the budget deficit and money supply. The NESP evolved in 1982 into a Structural Adjustment Programme (SAP). It had two main purposes. One was crisis management, to get inflation under control and to increase production. This was to be facilitated by international injections of foreign exchange. The second aim was structural adjustment. The goals were improved incentives and support for exports, retrenchments in government expenditures, improved allocation of foreign exchange, the liberalization of internal trade, and the rationalization of pricing.

In the section on agriculture the SAP proposed various measures to enhance efficiency in production and marketing, but little was said about the relative prices of cash crops. Instead in 1982–3 the relative prices of maize, beans, and cassava were raised in the interest of food security.

The section on industry contained similar broad proposals, together with an espousal of import substitution in inputs and increased exports. However, there were few specific policy measures other than a rebate scheme for exporters, and permission for corporations and companies to open external accounts and retain a portion of their export earnings.

With regard to parastatals it was realized that there was inadequate accountability and motivation, but the proposed solution was increased central control. Two presidential commissions were appointed to suggest reforms of parastatals and government ministries. Although these reported in 1983, few changes were made.

As with all previous government plans and programmes, the SAP assumed that there would be a speedy inflow of foreign funds. It was believed that this would lead to a rapid turn-around for both manufacturing and export crop production. Whether or not this belief was realistic, the assumption about external funding, on which it was predicated, was not: funds were not forthcoming, and a major reason for this was that Tanzania could not reach an agreement with the IMF.

Since the late 1970s the government had been in continual disagreement with the IMF, which proposed a standard package with a large devaluation, large cuts in government expenditures, especially food subsidies, and increased interest rates, which had been negative in real terms since 1971. It was admitted by the IMF that a devaluation would lead to inflation in the short run, but it was argued that the increased availability consequent upon devaluation would subsequently restrain prices. It was also argued that higher relative prices of export crops would increase their output and thereby improve the balance of trade.

The government on their side claimed that an increase in export crop prices was not enough to increase supply, but that there also had to be improved availability of goods. It also feared that the inflationary effect would be stronger than suggested by the IMF, and that the demand for imports would not be reduced since in Tanzania the price system did not determine allocation. It also argued that the shift of income from urban to rural inhabitants was unjustified, and that the elimination of food subsidies would be socially disruptive, this perhaps revealing the binding political constraint. President Nyerere explained his resistance to an IMF agreement as follows: 'I can't just sign and have riots in the streets. We say, how much will the people take?' (*The Times*, 24 Nov. 1984).

The government proceeded to implement the SAP without the level of external funding assumed in the original plan. The shilling was devalued by some 80 per cent in the two years after the SAP was presented, but it still appreciated in real terms; and between 1979 and 1982 the real effective import weighted exchange rate had appreciated by 92 per cent. Most of the adjustment measures were of a macro nature, while sectoral programmes were slow to develop.

The acute shortage of foreign exchange did not improve. The decline in export volume continued, and there was a gradual increase in debt service following the years of deficit. The deficit on the basic balance decreased somewhat, but that was due to a large reduction in imports. In spite of this, export income covered a declining fraction of imports. Between the end of the boom and 1984 the share of imports financed by exports fell from about 75 per cent to about 40 per cent. Over the period 1979–82 Tanzania built up $300 million in trade arrears, took $100 million in short-term commercial bank credits, $200 million in suppliers credit, and $20 million in delayed payments on long-term debts.

However, since such finance is limited, imports declined both absolutely and relative to GDP (Table 6A.12). The lack of foreign exchange had multiplier consequences on output. For example, there was a lack of fuel and of funds for road maintenance.[8] Vehicles were therefore liable to break down quickly, while there was no foreign exchange to replace them or buy spares. Hence transport deteriorated further, so that it became yet more difficult to get export commodities to the market or goods to the countryside. In 1982 per capita GDP declined by 2 per cent, with manufacturing output falling by 18 per cent. Productivity declined markedly: while industrial production was reduced by more then half between 1979 and 1982, employment increased by 13 per cent. The extra industrial employment should therefore be regarded as unproductive and hence an additional claim on public expenditure. Investment in the sector also continued to expand despite capacity utilization being only about 35 per cent, accommodated by a sharp decline in the ratio of

TABLE 6A.12.   *Exports and imports, 1976–1984* (%)

	Merchandise		Goods and services	
	Export/import	Import/GDP	Export/import	Import/GDP
1976	77.8	20.6	90.7	23.0
1977	72.5	21.1	85.6	23.5
1978	41.7	27.1	49.1	29.4
1979	44.3	24.7	52.6	26.8
1980	41.9	23.2	50.0	25.7
1981	47.9	17.9	59.7	19.5
1982	36.8	16.9	45.1	17.7
1983	43.6	15.9	52.2	16.7
1984	40.2	16.9	47.8	17.5

Sources: Government of Tanzania, *Statistical Abstract 1982, National Accounts of Tanzania* (1976–84).

[8] The same is true for railway and water transport. See Kasungu and Ndulu (1984).

intermediate imports to capital goods imports. In spite of the low level of domestic activity the trade balance deteriorated further, and foreign savings relative to GDP approached 10 per cent.

Modern sector employment continued to increase rapidly in 1982 and 1983: even during 1983 government employment grew by 3.5 per cent. However, there was a drastic decline in real wages. According to ILO estimates, by 1983 minimum and average wages had fallen to about a third of their peak levels. The official rate of inflation was close to 30 per cent. The drastic decline in the availability of manufactured goods and some foods contributed to inflationary pressure, but this did not show fully in the official inflation rate, partly because it was repressed by price controls and converted into shortages, and partly because of the emergence of black markets, transactions on which were under-recorded.

There was some slow-down in the growth of the public sector from 1982, but it still continued to increase its share of GDP. Although there were for the first time real cuts in government expenditures, there were three growing bureaucracies to be financed: the government itself, the parastatals, and the party (the CCM), which received large subsidies. In 1967 there had been 64 parastatals, while in 1984 there were 433. Shimwela (1984: 98) writes that

> unfortunately the majority of them have miserably failed the viability test and have contributed significantly to the current economic crisis. Inefficient operators transfer their overheads to the final consumer of whatever little they produce. This is often done with the consent of the National Price Commission, whose cost-plus method of price setting does not encourage cost cutting, competitiveness and increased productivity. The result is cost-push inflation hitting everybody. In more severe cases such as the NMC they fall back on the government for both capital and recurrent support. Hence, in part, explosion of the budget is actually to subsidise their inefficiency.

In spite of attempts at controlling government expenditures the public sector deficit remained enormous. Export taxes, which constituted a significant part of government revenue through the 1970s, were virtually eliminated in 1981/2 when the government attempted to make export crop production more advantageous. In January 1983, in an attempt to offset the revenue loss, the rates of import and sales taxes were increased for selected items, and there were attempts also to intensify revenue collection. From June 1983 a freeze on government employment was proclaimed, but there were exceptions to this rule.

The Bank of Tanzania had allocated foreign exchange on a six-monthly basis, but this was discontinued during 1982/3 owing to the tightness of the foreign exchange situation. Instead the Bank started to grant licences on a selective basis (*Economic and Operations Report*, 1983: 26). Exporters were given preferential treatment, but overall the foreign exchange allocation was only 17.8 per cent of that requested.[9] Only 38 per cent of the foreign exchange allocated to imports in 1982/3 was a free resource, the remainder being tied to item-specific external finance.

There were also steps to restrain the access to credit. Rather than use interest rates for this purpose, the government attempted to ration credit using planning criteria. This was not a simple procedure. For example, the Bank of Tanzania (*Economic and Operations Report*, 1983: 36) noted that there should be no slackness in credit supervision just because the borrower was a parastatal organization, which suggests that this may have been the case earlier. The Bank of Tanzania further regretted the erosion of confidence in the financial system, which had led to refusals to accept cheques and an increased use of cash transactions. It noted, however, that an extra Tsh.800 million compared with April 1982 was deposited with the NBS after the 'crack-down' in April 1983 (a campaign of police scrutiny). Since financial resources were rationed according to non-market criteria, there was a tendency to self-financing and the emergence of informal credit markets.

In 1984 economic decline continued and the crisis deepened. The government was caught in a debt trap, since the budget deficit generated a rapidly increasing debt burden, the servicing of which constituted an ever increasing proportion of the budget. Export income was stagnating, and fewer imports could be purchased. Action was necessary, indeed long overdue, but delay had foreclosed some options.

A further economic package was adopted in June 1984, which attempted to contain the budget deficit and to effect changes in relative prices, so as to stimulate export production. It had the following elements (Svendsen, 1984: 11–12):

— increased sales taxes on beer, soft drinks, cigarettes, and petroleum products;
— a shift in the financial responsibility for major services (such as education, rural health, and rural roads) to district or urban councils, requiring them to raise the money needed on their own through flat-rate poll taxes;
— cuts in subsidies to parastatals, especially crop authorities, owing to the reintroduction of the co-operatives;
— some shift in the sectoral allocation of foreign exchange in favour of agriculture;
— a complete removal of the Tsh.375 million maize flour subsidy;
— a removal of the fertilizer subsidy of Tsh.215 million;
— an increase of export crop prices in the range 46–55 per cent;
— a devaluation of the shilling from Tsh.12.6 per dollar to Tsh.17 per dollar;

[9] Over the period 1980–2, 60% of the foreign exchange requested for petroleum was granted. Between the first half of 1981 and the first half of 1982 the same shares for spare parts fell from 9% to 2%, for consumer goods from 25% to 8%, and for medicine from 56% to 25%. See Kimei, (1985: 74).

— measures to improve foreign exchange earnings: an expanded export rebate scheme; an external accounts scheme; and a scheme for some industries to retain foreign exchange to be used for their own imports;
— airport tax to be paid in foreign exchange;
— foreign-exchange shops open for all—with no questions asked;
— fees for secondary school pupils.

To offset the immediate impact of these measures on the living standards of the most powerful interest group, there was a 30 per cent increase in government salaries and an increase in the minimum wage from 600 to 810 shillings per month. These changes were in many respects directly contrary to long-cherished government objectives, but major policy changes had become inevitable. The government decided that it would over a period repay parastatal debts, and relieve itself of the financial burden of crop authorities. The role of the NMC was to be reduced. There would be no subsidies at all to the re-created co-operatives. The central target for the 1984/5 budget was to keep bank borrowing at the 1983/4 level.

At the end of 1984 private importation was liberalized. Individuals or firms with foreign exchange available abroad were now allowed to bring freely into the country goods such as textiles, bicycles, and building materials. The system of price controls was still in force, but its scope had been drastically reduced, with many fewer commodities being price-controlled. The argument for price control has been that it was necessary to protect poor people and to promote a more equal income distribution. This argument can be questioned. Lipumba (1984: 42) notes that

> Only a minority of consumers, mainly well connected urban elite and Government institutions are able to get supplies of most essential goods at the controlled prices. Most don't get the industrial goods or they purchase them at exorbitant prices in the parallel markets. Even maize flour is available at the controlled prices mainly in Dar es Salaam. Most other consumers in urban centres purchase maize in the 'free' markets.

7. Concluding Remarks

Since the policy changes ushered in by the Arusha Declaration the living standards of most Tanzanians have fallen drastically. According to the National Accounts, per capita GDP fell by 14 per cent between 1976 and 1984, declining in every year. In *Peasants and Governments* we quantify the decline in living standards through the comparison of five household budget surveys spanning the period 1969–84.

Despite being a large windfall, the coffee boom appears as no more than an intermission in this unfortunate period. Although there was one policy response (the coffee tax) that might be construed as windfall management, since it was in effect never revoked it is perhaps more accurately seen as part of a wider set of policies designed to divert resources from agriculture to the public sector and industry. That is, while the coffee tax was indeed belatedly removed, more than the equivalent depressing effect on the domestic producer price was accomplished through the increasing overvaluation of the exchange rate and widening parastatal operating margins. Thus, far from inducing nimble macroeconomic policy adjustments appropriate for a temporary windfall, the coffee boom, the answer to Micawber's prayer, retarded policy responses needed to cope with the prior foreign exchange crisis.

An array of policies, of which the coffee tax was a minor component, caused the stagnation of agricultural exports. Coupled with foreign-exchange-intensive public expenditure programmes, stagnation gave rise to a gradual build-up of a foreign exchange shortage, which first surfaced in 1970–1. The shocks of 1973–4 converted this into an acute crisis which was promptly concealed for a few years by the coffee boom. As a result structural adjustments were postponed, and instead the boom induced the government into a liberalization of foreign trade at an exchange rate that was quite unrealistic once the boom was over. Above all it encouraged the government to launch and persist with a huge industrial investment programme, which absorbed large sums of foreign exchange.

The boom thus led to a rapid increase of imports and a rapid expansion of government expenditures. Unfortunately, the boom did not last for ever. When coffee prices fell the latent structural crisis re-emerged with greater force than before, since there were now much larger government expenditure commitments (including an expanded industrial work-force). As the crisis surfaced donors started to question the Tanzanian strategy, and the scope for using aid to make up for the deficits was diminished.

The government first used up its foreign reserves, then borrowed on the international capital market, and finally reduced domestic demand for imports. It was highly resistant to devaluation and instead increased the stringency of import controls, especially on consumer goods, which were virtually eliminated. At the same time the government resorted to deficit financing of the budget. Since prices were controlled and the official price increases were less than those required to clear markets in a situation where goods were in very short supply, shortages developed and parallel markets flourished. The economy was thus in a situation of serious disequilibrium, from which it was bound to be difficult to escape.

The government had embarked upon a path of development which was not sustainable. The coffee boom concealed this and thus delayed the necessary policy changes. Moreover, the boom encouraged policy makers into adventures which drove the economy further away from a sustainable development path. By the end of our period (1984), although politically painful policy changes had begun to be made, the results had at best been meagre.

7

Macroeconomic Experience Compared

1. From Unregulated Private Behaviour to Public Intervention

The preceding chapters examined macroeconomic responses to a trade shock in three steps. Section 2 of Chapter 4 developed a theory of optimal response in the absence of controls. This is an important first step in the analysis, since it establishes both what should have happened and what would actually have happened if responses had been determined by well-informed and unconstrained private agents. However, it is inadequate as a theoretical foundation for the study of trade shocks, since controls are in fact pervasive and important. For convenience, we may call this the theory of unregulated behaviour, to contrast it with the more complex theory that takes explicit account of these controls. The latter theory was developed in the remainder of Chapter 4 and is the second step in the analysis. The third step was the application of the theory of regulated behaviour, and the demonstration that it was helpful in illuminating what happened during and after the coffee boom. The application was conducted in Chapters 5 and 6. This chapter summarizes our account in these chapters, and draws some conclusions from the comparison between the experience of the two countries.

The theory of the domestic effects of a commodity boom is relatively simple if there are no controls and if the government reacts passively. First, incomes rise and are redistributed in favour of the producers of the export good. Secondly, to the extent the boom income is not spent entirely on tradables, there will be the familiar 'Dutch Disease' effect of a rise of the price of non-tradables relative to that of importables. Thirdly, public expenditure will rise, and subsequently fall, in line with the induced changes in revenue from existing taxes. Finally, if agents directly perceive the boom as temporary, savings rates will rise temporarily. Initially, much of the savings will be held in the form of foreign financial assets, part of the return on which comes from the trajectory of the relative price of domestic capital goods over the boom from which delayed real investment benefits. At the end of the boom the financial assets are gradually converted into domestic real assets, the return on which represents the boom's long-run effect, in the form of an increase in permanent income.

It will have become clear that what actually happened in Kenya and Tanzania during, and in the wake of, the coffee boom differs in many respects radically from the predictions of the theory of unregulated behaviour. The reasons for the differences can be grouped under four headings: the pre-boom control regime, the policy response to the boom, the irreversibility of public expenditure increases, and the unsustainability (in both countries, but particularly in Tanzania) of the pre-boom policy stance.

The pre-boom control regime included, in both countries, foreign exchange controls, import controls, and financial repression. As we emphasized in Chapter 4, foreign exchange controls and the absence of alternative domestic financial assets force agents to use their savings inefficiently, allocating more to the acquisition of domestic real assets in the boom period than would otherwise be optimal. This, as we saw in Chapter 5, led in the Kenyan case to large increases in the relative price of capital goods; increases in rents, which implied a redistribution of income from rural to urban groups; and an erosion of the real value of boom-induced savings, that is a reduction of the enhancement to permanent income. This would have happened in Tanzania as well, if it were not for the Tanzanian system of price control, one of the major differences between the two countries. In the theory of unregulated behaviour there are, of course, no import controls, but these were in force in both Kenya and Tanzania. Under constant import quotas 'Dutch Disease' affects not just non-tradables but also importables: the relative prices of importables rise since extra demand for importables must be met by an increase in domestic supply due to quantitative restrictions on imports. In the extreme case all imports are controlled and a boom causes a fall in export volumes accompanied by large relative price changes, which induce shifts in the allocation of resources from exportables to importables and non-tradables. In Kenya these effects operated, although not in this extreme form since controls never applied to all imports and the quantitative restrictions were temporarily relaxed during the boom. Relative prices of some importables rose and this was one of the reasons discussed in Chapter 5 why Kenyan coffee growers benefited surprisingly little from the boom. In Tanzania price control prevented this effect. With relative prices fixed, controls were initially maintained (leading to a short-lived build-up of foreign exchange reserves) and then briefly relaxed (which increased industrial output: capacity utilization improved as more intermediate inputs were imported).

While foreign exchange restrictions, financial repression, and import controls were common to Kenya and Tanzania, Tanzania differed in its ideological commitment to, and use of price control. Price control completely changes the effects of the other distortions: there is, for example, no counterpart in Chapter 6 to the rural–urban income redistribution and the growth of rents of Chapter 5. But, in addition, since Tanzania controlled prices at nonmarket clearing levels and black markets could not fully compensate for this, the boom had an effect completely different from anything that happened in Kenya: it postponed a switch into a rationing regime.

In the policy response to the boom there are, again, similarities and differences. Kenya passed the price increase on to coffee growers, imposing a coffee tax only after the boom was already over and then only at a very low rate. In Tanzania coffee was taxed so heavily that coffee growers experienced only a minor terms-of-trade gain, most of the boom income accruing directly to the government.

Neither country pursued a stabilization policy, though our analysis in Chapter 4 implies that, given the restricted choice of assets available to private agents, there was a case for one. In Kenya foreign borrowing fell dramatically in the early years of the boom, but this did not amount to stabilization. As documented in Chapter 5, the changes in external borrowing and public expenditure were adversely phased, actually increasing the instability of domestic capital formation. Hence, the government's policies reinforced rather than damped the relative price changes induced by the investment boom. Further, even to the extent that the policy succeeded in reducing investment in the early years of the boom, it did not succeed in raising investment later, since by then savings had been pre-empted as a result of the loss of fiscal control. As we concluded in Chapter 5, it would have been extremely difficult to devise an effective stabilization policy in any case.

The Tanzanian coffee export tax should not be seen as a stabilization policy. It was motivated not by the desire to stabilize the income of coffee growers but by the wish to deny the boom income to that (politically unpopular) group altogether. Indeed, taxation was not reduced during the downswing: the ratio of domestic to world prices for coffee after the boom was far below its pre-boom level. Whereas public expenditure should probably rise during a commodity boom and fall back thereafter, we have seen that there were powerful ratchet effects in both countries. This is the 'Dutch Disease' in the original sense of the term: increases in public revenue trigger increases in expenditure which prove very difficult to reverse when the extra revenue ceases. We observe this in both countries but most strikingly in Kenya, where, as we saw in Chapter 5, budget procedures were abandoned during the boom and the Minister of Finance openly admitted that he had lost control.

Finally, the initial policy stance was not, in the sense developed in Chapter 4, a sustainable one. In Kenya the fiscal stance, if maintained, would have implied a rising debt/income ratio. Hence the ratchet effect operated in a regime in which fiscal discipline had, in that sense, already been lost. The thesis of Chapter 3 was that in Tanzania the pre-boom situation was unsustainable in a much more fundamental way. Price control, the import control policy (favouring intermediate and, especially, capital goods over consumer goods imports), the concern with the protection of urban living standards, and the commitment to high (and rising) levels of public expenditure, including investment under the Basic Industries Strategy, formed a disastrous combination. In Chapter 3 we have shown that the rigidity imposed on the economy by price and import controls implies a special form of vulnerability: an adverse shock can plunge the economy into a rationing regime. The economy then implodes, peasants reducing their export crop production as they encounter reduced availability of consumer goods at given prices: these reduced exports (and hence imports) further reduce availability. One adverse shock had already occurred: export crop production was already falling before the boom, partly because producer prices were shifted dramatically in favour of food crops, partly because of the villagization programme. In addition, there were large increases in public expenditure which had not yet occurred but to which the government had already committed itself. In particular it was committed to an industrial investment programme which, at least in the medium run, would be a net user of foreign exchange. Only fairly minor policy changes had been adopted in response to the 1974–5 crisis. Had nothing else happened the economy would have switched into rationing as exports fell, public expenditure rose, and foreign exchange became increasingly diverted to industry. But something else did happen: the coffee boom postponed the regime switch. The time thus bought was not used to avert the switch into rationing. In Chapter 5 we considered whether the boom induced any increases in public services, such as health and education. Broadly, our conclusions were that public services did not share in the expansion of public spending. Here we note that to the extent that the boom income was used for industrial investment it did not generate an increase in permanent income. For under rationing, if industrial output is constrained by the availability of imported intermediate imports, additions to the capital stock do not increase output (which, in spite of massive investment, was by the mid-1980s far below the level reached in 1975) but simply reduce capacity utilization.

2. Relative Prices

The differences between the two countries are strikingly reflected in the changes in relative prices (Fig. 5.2 and Table 6.1). In the case of Kenya four changes may be noted. First, the price of non-tradables rose during the boom, relative to the price of (non-oil) imports. This is the traditional 'Dutch Disease' effect, reinforced, however, in two ways by the control regime. The Kenyan trade policy led to a huge redistribution of income, from the boom's initial beneficiaries, the coffee growers, to urban groups, and this redistribution increased the demand for non-tradables. Further, the control regime led to an investment boom since the acquisition of financial assets was (for private agents) illegal in the case of foreign assets and unattractive in the case of domestic assets. The investment boom implied an enormous increase in the demand for non-tradables (trade and transportation, but particularly construction) and this is reflected in the relative price series. Secondly, the relative price of importables also rose. This reflects import controls which were relaxed, but not abolished during the boom. Thirdly, since capital goods were only partly imported, the relative price of capital goods also rose, again a reflection of the investment boom.

Finally, the relative price of importables fell in the 1980s after the boom. This is because investment during the boom was heavily biased in favour of importables (basically: non-food manufacturing). When these investments came on stream they lowered industrial prices. This result is important because it means that the real value of the quantitative restrictions on industrial imports was eroded, without a change in trade policy. In fact, we suggested that such an effect (specific, of course, to an economy with the Kenyan combination of investment bias and import controls) complicates the design of trade liberalization programmes: trade liberalization may fail because, paradoxically, protection would have been reduced more if controls had been maintained. The relative price change is also important for its distributional effect: it means that, while peasants lost some 40 per cent of this income gain during the boom as a result of adverse relative price changes, in the post-boom period they benefited from an improvement in the rural–urban terms of trade.

The price series for Tanzania are entirely different. First, if we measure the boom as an increase in the ratio of export prices and (recorded) import prices then the terms-of-trade improvement is very much smaller than in Kenya. This is because recorded import prices rose relative to world prices and, as we argued in Chapter 6, this is evidence of overinvoicing. We estimated that more than half (54 per cent) of the windfall was lost to the rest of the economy through overinvoicing. While in Chapter 6 we used Kenyan import prices (as a proxy for world prices) in order to calculate the true value of the windfall, in the present context it is appropriate to calculate relative prices in terms of recorded Tanzanian import prices.

Secondly, the prices of import substitutes, non-tradables, and capital goods are very stable relative to the price of imports and relative to each other, and they were in 1976–80 lower (in terms of import prices) than in 1975. The relative stability reflects the price control policy. Hence we have the remarkable phenomenon of a massive increase in investment (recall from Table 6.1 that gross fixed capital formation was 30 to 40 per cent higher in real terms than in 1975 throughout the period 1977–82) which was not accompanied by

TABLE 7.1. *Tanzanian relative price indices, 1976–1981* (1975 = 100; prices are relative to the prices recorded for non-oil imports)

	1976	1977	1978	1979	1980	1981
Exports	116	141	112	103	112	127
Import substitutes	95	91	91	84	97	128
Non-tradables	90	88	87	80	86	96
Capital goods	89	90	89	77	78	75

a rise in the relative price of capital goods. In the Kenyan case we considered the price rises for capital goods excessive (being accentuated by the control regime), and hence a problematic symptom of the boom, since they implied that savings were partly lost by adding to transient rents rather than to permanent income. In Tanzania, by way of contrast, it is the absence of any such price increases that is problematic: price rises might have reduced the speed at which the government implemented its investment programme. That the relative prices of all three categories (import substitutes, non-tradables, and capital goods) are lower in terms of import prices than in 1975 also reflects, presumably, the price control policy. Overinvoicing increased during the period and under a cost-plus pricing system this must have led to a fall in the price of domestic goods relative to imports (the size of the fall depending upon the import content of domestic goods). An additional reason is probably that wages fell in terms of import prices.

Thirdly, the relative price of capital goods is much lower in 1979–81 than in 1976–8. The most likely explanation for this change is that overinvoicing increased in 1979–81 for imports generally but was made more difficult to achieve on imports of capital goods because of the reimbursement procedures of loans which finance most of these imports.

Finally, the most remarkable change is the substantial increase in the relative price of import substitutes after 1980 (shown only for 1981 but increased thereafter, as we shall see). Note that this is the opposite of what happened in Kenya. Hence, while in Kenya the effect on the real income of peasants of the post-boom fall in the coffee price was mitigated by favourable relative price changes, in Tanzania the fall in the coffee price was reinforced by an increase in prices of manufactured goods. Again, the reason is to be found in the priorities for foreign exchange allocation and the cost-plus pricing system. As the demand of firms for imported intermediate inputs became rationed, capacity utilization fell. In 1984 industrial output was (after a decade of heavy investment) only half of what it was in 1975. As capacity utilization falls, controlled prices must be raised to maintain a fixed rate of return.

We now relate the observed changes in the domestic relative prices of exports, importables, and non-tradables to the geometric analysis of compatible macroeconomic policies developed in Chapter 2. In Fig. 7.1 we graph the path of relative prices for each economy in the double relative price space devised in Chapter. 2. The graph highlights two important features: first, that in both economies relative prices changed very substantially over this eight-year period, and secondly, that relative prices followed radically different paths in the two economies. The underlying data for Fig. 7.1 are again from Table 6.1 and Figs. 5.1 and 5.2. However, because the Tanzanian price series for non-oil exports end in 1979, for later years we have assumed that unit values followed changes in the Kenyan index corrected for changes in the cross-exchange rate. Similarly, the series for Tanzanian non-oil imports ends

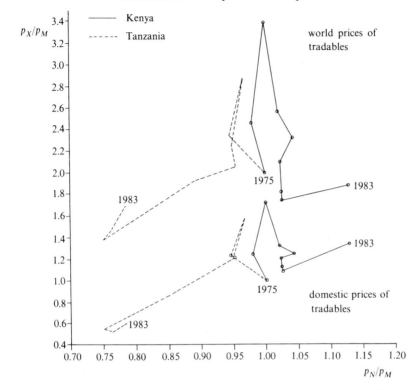

FIG. 7.1. *The path of relative prices in Kenya and Tanzania, 1975–1983 (official unit cost of Tanzanian non-oil imports)*

in 1981, and we have likewise assumed that in the last two years it followed the Kenyan series. The latter assumption is contentious, because, as discussed in Chapter 6, the Kenyan and Tanzanian unit import value series diverge between 1975 and 1981, which has been the basis for our estimate of overinvoicing. Since there is reason to believe that the official Tanzanian unit import value series overstates the cost of imports, the path of prices is repeated in Fig. 7.2 using the exchange-rate adjusted Kenyan series. In all cases we have normalized on the rate of tariff-equivalent protection in 1975, setting $(1 + t_t)(1 + t_q) = 2$.

First, consider the change in Kenyan relative prices between the two end-points, 1975 and 1983, and whether this can be related to the analysis of Chapter 2. Fig. 7.3, which follows Fig. 2.1, provides such an account. Recall that the major long-term effect of the boom in Kenya was import-substituting investment. As discussed in Chapter 2, such investment shifts the locus of non-tradable goods equilibrium to the right, from $N–N$ to $N'–N'$. In an economy with constant world prices, free trade, and compatible policies,

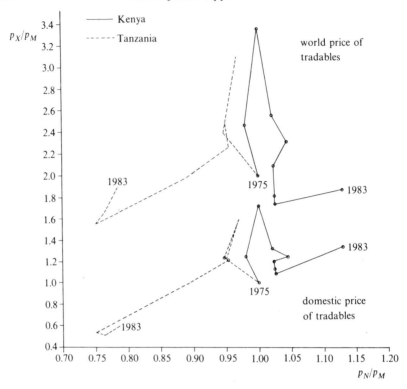

FIG. 7.2. *The path of relative prices in Kenya and Tanzania, 1975–1983 (our estimate of unit cost of Tanzanian non-oil imports)*

relative prices would change from F to F', that is, there would be an increase in the relative price of non-tradables to import substitutes. By 1983 this relative price is indeed 13 per cent above its 1975 level in Kenya. However, Kenya did not start from free trade, nor were its trade restrictions of a constant level of severity. We have noted that import-substituting investment has a trade liberalization effect if quantitative restrictions upon imports are held constant. In Fig. 7.3 this is shown as a reduction in the implicit tariff rate from t_q to t'_q.

With constant world prices and compatible policies, domestic relative prices would therefore change from E to E', with both p_X/p_M and p_N/p_M rising. This is indeed what happened in Kenya, for there was a pronounced trade liberalization effect, the price of import substitutes falling by 30 per cent relative to the c.i.f. cost of non-oil imports. This simple account characterizes the change in Kenyan relative prices well, because the underlying assumptions of common world prices in the two years and compatible policies are reasonable approximations. The relative prices of non-oil exports and

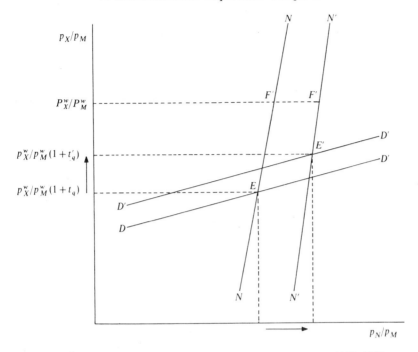

FIG. 7.3. *The geometry of relative price changes in Kenya, 1975–1983*

non-oil imports differed by only 6 per cent in 1975 and 1983, and the balance of payments, though unsatisfactory, was not chronically unsustainable.

Whereas Fig. 7.3 provides a simple analytic account of changes in Kenyan relative prices over the period, it clearly cannot be the explanation of what was happening in Tanzania, since prices moved in the opposite direction. Our geometric account of why Tanzanian relative prices changed is set out in Fig. 7.4. To a considerable extent the story is simply the converse of Kenya's. Although there was an enormous amount of import-substituting investment in Tanzania, as we have stressed, this was worse than useless, since by diverting foreign exchange from intermediate inputs it caused an accute reduction in manufacturing output. Tanzanian expenditure on investment was thus analytically equivalent to a reduction in the manufacturing capital stock, which shifts the non-tradable goods locus to the left, from N–N to N''–N''. The same policy of giving absolute priority to imports of capital goods involved an even more acute squeeze on imported consumer goods, sharply increasing the implicit tariff rate from t_q to t''_q. Further, the Tanzanian shilling appreciated relative to the Kenyan shilling by 25 per cent between 1975 and 1983. In terms of Fig. 7.4 this shifts the monetary equilibrium locus from D–D to D''–D''. Thus, with compatible policies and constant world prices, relative prices would change from E to E''. To some extent this indeed

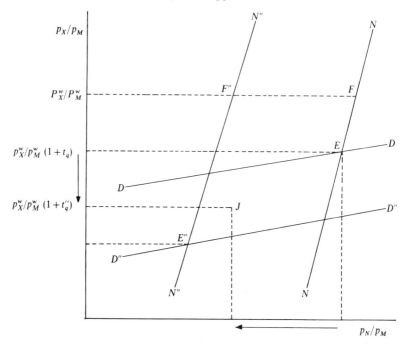

FIG. 7.4. *The geometry of relative price changes in Tanzania, 1975–1983*

captures what happened in Tanzania: p_N/p_M indeed fell by a massive 28 per cent, and p_X/p_M fell by an even more dramatic 40 per cent. However, large as these changes were, they were insufficient to clear markets. Far from being in the vicinity of a compatible policy set such as E'', the economy was deep within the disequilibrium zone of excess demand for tradable goods and excess supply of money, at a point such as J. In Chapter 2 we described the manifestation of this zone as being an unsustainable balance-of-payments deficit, which was indeed the case in Tanzania. However, an alternative manifestation would be shortages in goods markets combined with upward rigidities in nominal prices. As we have seen, this was how Tanzanian goods markets were characterized. Hence, the full analytic description of how relative prices changed in Tanzania is of a partial adjustment from E to J, further relative price changes required for equilibrium being suppressed.

Thus, although relative prices changed powerfully and differently in the two economies during our period, each pattern is explicable within the framework of the same simple analytic model. The relative prices of 1983, and their sustainability, were the outcome of the commercial, investment, exchange rate, and budgetary policy decisions taken during the boom and its aftermath.

3. Fiscal Patterns

In both countries the boom induced a large increase in public expenditure. In Tanzania this led to a large increase in the deficit: only 57 per cent of the extra expenditure (excluding the cost of the Uganda war, which we assume would have been incurred anyway) was covered by increased revenue (mainly the coffee export tax). Three aspects of the Tanzanian experience deserve to be emphasized. First, while there was a ratchet effect, public expenditure peaked in 1979 and by 1980 the explosive increase in the exhaustive deficit had been substantially rectified: there was no general loss of fiscal control, as there was in Kenya. Secondly, a very high proportion (80 per cent) of the extra spending was used for investment. This implies that Tanzania would have converted the windfall income into a substantial increase in permanent income if only the investment had been efficient. Given the concentration on capital-intensive heavy industry this would have been doubtful, however, even if the new capital stock had been fully utilized. At least until the economy breaks out of the rationing regime this is not the case: in that sense the investment effort was largely wasted, its main effect being an addition to idle capacity. Thirdly, the huge increase in the government's financing requirement was met not by foreign borrowing but largely by an increase in the money supply. In four years the money stock rose by the equivalent of 30 per cent of GDP and velocity halved. This development, which we documented in Chapter 6 was remarkable in itself. In the Tanzanian case it was extraordinary, because, as we pointed out in Chapter 3, price control imposes fiscal discipline by eliminating the use of the inflation tax. The Tanzanian policy stance was possible only because private agents were willing to increase their real money balances at the very time when the budget deficit increased. This was a response to the onset of rationing and was (according to a theoretical model which we developed in Chapter 3) by its very nature temporary. In that sense the government was lucky twice in a row, the need for domestic policy changes being postponed first by the coffee boom itself and then by the adjustment of private agents to the onset of rationing. In Kenya, by contrast, public expenditure rose much more, was not brought back under control after 1979, was largely used for consumption rather than investment, and was financed by a combination of tax increases (particularly the sales tax) and foreign borrowing. In Chapter 5, section 2, we argued that the net impact of the government on domestic capital formation was positive in 1979 and 1980 and heavily negative thereafter. Our simulation experiments in section 3 supported this conclusion: the phasing of public expenditure and foreign borrowing was pro-cyclical. It thereby reinforced rather than offset relative price changes, which adversely affected the real value (in terms of capital goods) of savings. In that sense the boom was afterwards correctly described as a missed opportunity. Because of the control regime, the responses of private agents were sub-optimal. A second-best policy involving stabilization through direct taxation and foreign asset acquisition (an option we explored in Chapter 5, section 4) could have offset part of the resulting loss in permanent income. What the government actually did, however, made matters worse, in fact wiping out most of the long-run gains from the boom which would have been realized if it had remained passive.

4. Conclusion

In 1975 Tanzania had just completed its first, limited, policy adjustments in response to the first oil price increase, the 1974/5 drought, and the fall in export volumes, which was beginning to be perceived as a problem. The government was considering further changes, having postponed the Third Five Year Plan when the coffee boom appeared to remove the need for them. Because of the coffee tax the boom did not benefit coffee growers substantially. The extra income was either siphoned off into importers' foreign accounts by overinvoicing, and so denied to the rest of the economy, or it largely accrued to the government and was converted into domestic capital goods. Much of the newly created industrial capacity remained idle after the boom. The main effect of the boom was to postpone the switch into a rationing regime to the 1980s. As in Kenya, the opportunity of the boom was not used to liberalize controls at a time when that could have been done relatively painlessly. We argued that postponement of policy changes which were inevitable (since under rationing the economy would continue to implode under the existing combination of policies) made the problem far less tractable. In particular, once agents had adjusted to rationing, the government faced a monetary overhang and black markets, which are difficult to eliminate.

Tanzania is certainly not *sui generis*, for a sizeable group of countries can be identified in whch peasants face quantity constraints in the official markets for consumer goods. That such cases are unfamiliar to most economists merely reflects the fact that they are largely unresearched. However, the Kenyan experience is manifestly widely applicable. Indeed, there are grounds for regarding it as the usual, if not the general, case. It shows that even under fairly mild distortions, the effects of a boom can depart dramatically from the optimal responses depicted in the theory of unregulated behaviour. An important reason is the ratchet effect in public expenditures. In addition, the Kenyan controls made stabilization both desirable and difficult to implement, and led to huge redistributions of income between rural and urban groups, eroding both the income gain of coffee growers and the real value of savings.

8

Conclusion: And a Manifesto

Many, though by no means all, developing countries are controlled open economies. In the preceding chapters we have attempted to construct models with sound micro-foundations which incorporate the constraints which agents face in such countries; that is, we have embarked upon the task of constructing a theory of controlled open economies. Within this set we have drawn a sharp distinction between those in which the controls are compatible and those in which they are incompatible.

We have analysed one variant of the latter, the excess demand peasant economy, both theoretically and empirically. It has alarming properties: the economy implodes, yet conventional marginal reforms, which may work well in a market-clearing environment, are actually counter-productive. Fortunately, not many developing economies are currently characterized by this model. However, because of the disastrous course on which such an economy is charted, they are naturally over-represented in the set of countries facing macroeconomic crises. Our analysis therefore serves, we hope, two functions: first as an aid to restoring these few crisis-ridden countries to sustainable policies, and second as a warning to other countries to avoid the policy configuration which generates the implosion.

Within compatible control regimes we focused upon the effects of a temporary trade windfall, taking the example of the Kenyan coffee boom. Although most discussion of policy during trade shocks focuses upon 'management' of the shock, this is probably less important than three other dimensions of government behaviour. First, we have stressed that the response of private agents to a windfall is conditioned by the initial policy environment: if agents are constrained by controls their behaviour will be socially inefficient. Second, actual changes in the level of public expenditure are probably best regarded not as the implementation of planned stabilization measures, but as the unintended consequence of a slackening in the public sector budget constraint. Finally, we have seen that not all types of public expenditure were expanded uniformly.

Our analysis of public expenditure yielded two major conclusions. First, the path of total public spending rose dramatically as a consequence of the boom. Second, those components which are most likely to be productive or to yield utility were very little affected by the boom: the increase was concentrated in unproductive sectors like general administration and defence. Yet in *Peasants and Governments* we demonstrate that the neglected sectors, such as education and health, were highly valued by households on average and yielded positive benefits at the margin.

These considerations suggest two types of policy counterfactual which it would be useful to pursue in respect of public expenditure. One simply involves leaving the 'productive' sectors to follow the same path, while holding down the expansion of the unproductive sectors. In effect, this amounts to reducing the level of public expenditure while assuming no direct adverse effects of the reduction. This case has already been considered in detail, in two of the CGE simulation experiments of Chapter 5.

The other type of counterfactual is where public expenditure did indeed rise, but with this increase occurring in the productive sectors. Since we do not possess the sort of information to permit any detailed cost-benefit analysis, we cannot draw any conclusions as to whether increased (productive) public expenditure would have been a more or less beneficial use of windfall income than comparable increases in private expenditures. But it is quite clear that this type of expansion would have been preferable to what actually took place.

The fact that coffee-growing peasants saved such a high proportion of their windfall income (over 60 per cent by our estimate) suggests both that they must have recognized that the price change was temporary, and that they have a high regard for future well-being. When the behaviour of peasants is juxtaposed with that of their government, the thesis that government stabilization is desirable in order to prevent myopic peasants from squandering the windfall looks somewhat inaccurate. As long as peasants are presented with the elementary information on the causes and likely duration of the price boom, which in Kenya they were through the co-operative societies, our analysis demonstrates that there is no reason to doubt their ability to infer appropriate asset behaviour. Conversely, we have found grounds for doubting the capacity of government to replicate this behaviour. The Tanzanian policy of introducing a windfall coffee tax cannot be justified on the basis of planning an appropriate aggregate savings propensity.

The trajectory of peasant asset formation in Kenya, as opposed to its magnitude, might well have been socially inefficient. For private agents as a whole this has, of course, been one of our major themes: in a regulated environment asset choices will be distorted into less efficient patterns. As other private agents, peasants clearly suffered from restricted asset choices. During 1977 inflation was 18 per cent, the rate of interest paid on co-operative savings deposits was 5 per cent, and many peasants were probably unable to access even this rate of interest, which was generous in local terms.[1] The heavily negative real interest rate on financial assets presumably accelerated peasant investment in real assets.

---

[1] There was a sharp decline in the proportion of savings to demand deposits, as banks often refused to accept money into the former. (The interest rate they themselves could earn on rediscounted Treasury Bills averaged only 1.5% during the year.)

The composition of peasant asset formation was concentrated in the export and non-tradable sectors. Coffee and tea planting, and the other agricultural investments, augmented the export capacity of the economy, whereas improvements to housing augmented the flow of non-tradables services. Since in both countries investment outside the peasant sector was heavily concentrated in the import substitute sector (as a result either of government direction or of trade and financial controls), peasant investment tended to offset this bias. Hence, a coffee tax would have further skewed the composition of investment towards import substitutes even had the government succeeded in matching the peasant savings rate.

The only sense in which such investment might have been socially inefficient is if the export quota negotiated through the International Coffee Agreement imposed large differences in social and private returns to marginal coffee production. In the short term, with the onset of a second world coffee boom in 1986, the extra planting had a high social pay-off. In the longer term in Kenya extra coffee output is likely to be valuable because Kenya probably has an interest in gradually increasing its quota by means of stock accumulation, which is feasible under the ICA rules. However, the workings of the coffee cartel are beyond the scope of our study, so that we accept as a possibility that the marginal social value of coffee production is considerably below its price. If this were the case, further production could be discouraged either by decentralizing the national production quota (the policy in force until the early 1970s) or imposing a coffee tax to bring the domestic price to that level at which production is equal to the national quota (which we might term a virtual production price by analogy with the concept of virtual prices in consumer theory). The former policy is probably the more costly to enforce, but the latter involves a transfer from peasants to the government. However, neither should be confused with a stabilization policy. If production quotas are used to regulate output, a coffee boom calls for a clearly signalled temporary suspension of the production quota (with the information that quotas will revert to their initial household-specific levels after the boom). If virtual producer prices are used, peasants similarly need to be informed that the domestic price will revert to that level at which only initial production is profitable. There is no more reason to believe that peasants would be myopic about quotas or virtual producer prices than about world prices. The coffee boom induced planting because it occurred at a time when production was regulated neither by quotas nor by taxation, and we suspect that this was in fact the appropriate policy stance.

In the 1950s many economists and policy makers were worried by the economic consequences of commodity price instability for developing countries. They believed that such instability was liable to be harmful, in particular reducing the growth rate, and proposed international price stabilization as an appropriate intervention. Subsequent work, especially that of MacBean (1966), appeared to discredit the premise that export price instability reduced the rate of growth, though the basis for this conclusion was highly aggregated multi-country regressions. By the 1980s the broad consensus of the consequences of agricultural trade shocks was probably that, whereas at the macroeconomic level instability in export prices did little harm, at the level of the peasant economy such price fluctuations were highly detrimental, leading peasants on the wild-goose chase of the cobweb cycle, and dissipating windfall income in transient orgies of rural consumption. Hence, the academic consensus was that international commodity price stabilization was not worthwhile but that national stabilization, through windfall taxes, was desirable: the government of Kenya was advised to impose a windfall coffee tax and the government of Tanzania did so.

Our analysis of the Kenyan coffee boom failed to bear out this consensus in three respects. First, more critical than the policy response to a trade shock is the policy environment in which the shock occurs. Our theory of unregulated private behaviour (Chapter 4) made the simple point that if private agents are well informed and unconstrained their responses will be socially appropriate. However, if asset and goods markets are controlled, so that choices are constrained, they will deploy a windfall inefficiently. If the controls are sufficiently severe, the windfall will be so badly deployed that it may even reduce social welfare.

Secondly, the Platonic guardian role for the government implied by nationally implemented stabilization is clearly at variance with how the Kenyan government actually behaved. There was indeed an orgy of consumption in response to the coffee boom, but this decision was taken not on the shambas of coffee growers but in government ministries. For each K£1 of extra revenue an extra K£1.35 was spent. Potentially, of course, this massive transfer to the public sector could nevertheless have been productive, and raised the living standards of peasant households. We have seen that it did not do so. This was not because all public expenditure is useless, which is a common implicit assumption in macroeconomic models. We have established in *Peasants and Governments* that there is a range of public services received by peasants—education, extension, health facilities, roads, and water—all of which are valued by the recipients and have discernible effects upon peasant incomes. Rather, these were not the components of public expenditure that increased during the boom: as public expenditure soared these items in aggregate declined from about 60 per cent to about 47 per cent. Had public expenditure been targeted on services received by peasants, it is an open question whether this would have raised living standards by more or less than if peasants had spent the income on their own behalf. However, public expenditures fully covered by extra revenue, targeted on to useful services which were well designed, take us rather far into the domain of the counterfactual.

Thirdly, we have established that peasants responded to the windfall, where they were permitted to receive it, in a manner which closely resembles the behaviour allotted to the Platonic guardian government, namely, they saved a very high percentage of it.

Our conclusion is thus that whether or not a trade windfall is efficiently used depends first and foremost upon the initial policy environment. If controls are extensive then private agents will badly misallocate windfall resources. However, national stabilization policies can be detrimental for two reasons. First, if a government is sufficiently capable to 'manage' the boom it may well already have in place a set of policies which make 'management' unnecessary, whereas when 'management' goes wrong it can more than dissipate the entire beneficial opportunities of the trade windfall. Secondly, peasants may not need to be protected from price variations. Price crashes might, of course, be highly damaging: the ability of peasants to convert windfall income into assets tells us nothing of their capacity to divest themselves of assets, and the occurrence of famines indicates that there are constraints upon rapid divestment. However, large temporary falls in the world prices of agricultural commodities are much less common than large temporary rises. Price fluctuations are not symmetrical about the mean but consist of short, sharp peaks and long, shallow troughs. An implication of recent analysis (Deaton and Laroque, 1989) is that this is intrinsic to such markets. Hence, a hypothesis suggested by our results is not that peasants can cope with anything, but rather that they can benefit from those price fluctuations likely to be encountered.

Were the temporary trade shock experience in Kenya representative, it would suggest an alternative to the consensus. If all agents behave wisely, neither international nor national stabilization policies are necessary. However, the agent who made the major mistakes in handling the trade shock was the government, rather than peasants. In such a case the ideal intervention would stabilize prices for the macroeconomy while retaining fluctuations for peasants, but neither national nor international policies would have achieved this combination. A national policy would have achieved fluctuating prices for the macroeconomy and stable prices for peasants and would therefore have been useless in Kenyan circumstances. An international policy would have achieved stable prices for both. Therefore, international stabilization, which would have prevented the windfalls ever arising, would have had beneficial effects in that the scope for government error would have been reduced. Thus, an international Platonic Guardian would at best have protected Kenyan citizens from their government.

The question which cannot be answered by this study is whether the Kenyan experience is indeed representative of the consequences of temporary trade shocks. However, Kenyan and Tanzanian experiences were nevertheless so divergent (in apparently similar economies) that our prior expectation must be of diversity. The research challenge is to model that diversity.

References

AHAMED, L. (1986), 'Stabilization Policies in Developing Countries', *World Bank Research Observer*, 1: 79–110.

AMANI, H. K. R., MBELE, R., RUGUMISA, S., and MSAMBICHAKA, L. A. (1984), 'Agriculture in Economic Stabilization Policies', in Lipumba *et al.* (eds).

BANK OF TANZANIA (annual), *Economic and Operations Report*, Dar es Salaam.

——(1983), *Economic Bulletin*, 13/3, Dar es Salaam.

——(1984), *Tanzania: Twenty Years of Independence (1961–1981): A Review of Political and Economic Performance*, Dar es Salaam.

BEAN, C. R., LAYARD, P. R. G., and NICKELL, S. J. (1986), 'The Rise in Unemployment: A Multi-Country Study', *Economica*, 53, Supplement.

BELL, C., HAZELL, P., and SLADE, R. (1982), *Project Evaluation in Regional Perspective*, Johns Hopkins, Baltimore.

BEVAN, D. L., BIGSTEN, A., COLLIER, P., and GUNNING, J. W. (1987*a*), *East African Lessons on Economic Liberalization*, for the Trade Policy Research Centre, Thames Essay no. 48, Gower: Aldershot.

——, COLLIER, P., and GUNNING, J. W. (1987*b*), 'Consequences of a Commodity Boom in a Controlled Economy: Accumulation and Redistribution in Kenya, 1975–1983', *World Bank Economic Review*, 1: 489–513.

——, BIGSTEN, A., COLLIER, P., and GUNNING, J. W. (1988), 'Incomes in the United Republic of Tanzania during the "Nyerere Experiment"', in W. van Ginneken (ed.), *Trends in Employment and Labour Incomes: Case Studies on Developing Countries*, ILO: Geneva, pp. 61–83.

——, COLLIER, P., and GUNNING, J. W., with BIGSTEN, A., and HORSNELL, P. (1989), *Peasants and Governments: An Economic Analysis*, Clarendon Press: Oxford.

——, COLLIER, P., and GUNNING, J. W. (1989*a*), 'Black Markets: Illegality, Information and Rents', *World Development*, 17/12.

——, COLLIER, P., and GUNNING, J. W. (1989*b*), 'Fiscal Response to a Commodity Boom: The Kenyan Coffe Boom', *World Bank Economic Review*, 3/3.

BIGSTEN, A. (1984), *Education and Income Determination in Kenya*, Gower: Aldershot and Brookfield, Vt.

BRUNO, M. (1976), 'The Two-Sector Open Economy and the Real Exchange Rate', *American Economic Review*, 66: 566–77.

CENTRAL BANK OF KENYA (1981), *Sources and Uses of Foreign Exchange in Kenya 1974–79*, Government Printer: Nairobi.

—— *Quarterly Economic Review*.

COLLIER, P. (1979), 'Migration and Unemployment: A Dynamic General Equilibrium Analysis Applied to Tanzania', *Oxford Economic Papers*, 31.

—— and LAL, D. (1986), *Labour and Poverty in Kenya*, Clarendon Press: Oxford.

——, RADWAN, S., and WANGWE, S. (1986), *Labour and Poverty in Rural Tanzania*, Clarendon Press: Oxford.

COOKSEY, B., FOWLER, A., and KWAYU, C. (1987), *Incentive Goods for Development in Tanzania*, Afro-Aid: Dar es Salaam.

CORDEN, W. M. (1984), 'Booming Sector and Dutch Disease Economics: Survey and

Consolidation', *Oxford Economic Papers*, 36/3: 359–80.

——(1985), *Protection, Growth and Trade*, Blackwell: Oxford.

DAVIS, J. M. (1983), 'The Economic Effects of Windfall Gains in Export Earnings, 1975–78', *World Development*, 11/2: 119–39.

DEATON, A., and LAROQUE, G. (1989), 'On the Behavior of Commodity Prices', Discussion Paper 145, Woodrow Wilson School, Princeton.

DICK, H., GUPTA, S., VINCENT, D., and VOIGHT, H. (1984), 'The Effects of Oil Price Increases in Four Oil-Poor Developing Countries: A Comparative Analysis', *Energy Studies*, January.

DORNBUSCH, R. (1984), 'Tariffs and Non-Traded Goods', *Journal of International Economics*, 4: 177–85.

ECONOMIC RESEARCH BUREAU (1988), *Tanzanian Economic Trends*, 1/1, University of Dar es Salaam.

ELLIS, F. (1982), 'Agricultural Price Policy in Tanzania', *World Development*, 10/6.

——and HANAK, E. (1980), *An Economic Analysis of the Coffee Industry in Tanzania 1969/70: Toward a Higher and More Stable Producer Price*, Economic Research Bureau: Dar es Salaam.

FIELDS, G. S. (1975), 'Rural–Urban Migration, Urban Unemployment and Under-Employment and Job Search Activity in LDCs', *Journal of Development Economics*, 2: 165–87.

GOVERNMENT OF KENYA (annual), *Budget Speech*, Government Printer: Nairobi.

——(annual), *Economic Survey*, Government Printer: Nairobi.

——(annual), *Statistical Abstract*, Government Printer: Nairobi.

——(various), *Development Plan* (1966–70), (1970–4), (1974–8), (1979–84).

——(1965), *African Socialism and its Application to Planning in Kenya*, Sessional Paper no. 10, Government Printer: Nairobi.

——(1975), *On Economic Prospects and Policies*, Sessional Paper no. 4, Government Printer: Nairobi.

——(1977), *Integrated Rural Survey 1974–75, Basic Report*, Government Printer: Nairobi.

——(1979), *Review of Statutory Boards*, Government Printer: Nairobi.

——(1980), *On Economic Prospects and Policies*, Sessional Paper no. 4, Government Printer: Nairobi.

——(1981), *The Integrated Rural Surveys 1976–79, Basic Report*, Government Printer: Nairobi.

——(1982a), *On Development Prospects and Policies*, Sessional Paper no. 4, Government Printer: Nairobi.

——(1982b), *Report and Recommendations of the Working Party on Government Expenditures* (Ndegwa Working Party), Government Printer: Nairobi.

GOVERNMENT OF TANZANIA (various), *Economic Survey*, Government Printer: Dar es Salaam.

——*Statistical Abstract 1973–79*, Government Printer: Dar es Salaam.

——*National Accounts of Tanzania, (1976–84)*, Government Printer: Dar es Salaam.

——*Statistical Abstract 1982*, Government Printer: Dar es Salaam.

——(1983), *Foreign Trade Indices 1974–81*, Government Printer: Dar es Salaam.

——(1984), *Quarterly Statistical Bulletin*, 35/1 (June), Government Printer: Dar es Salaam.

GREEN, R. H., RWEGASIRA, D. G., and VAN ARKADIE, B. (1980), *Economic Shocks and*

National Policy Making: Tanzania in the 1970s, Institute of Social Studies, Research Report Series, 8, The Hague.

GREENE, D. G. (1983), *Kenya: Growth and Structural Change*, World Bank: Washington, DC.

GULHATI, R., BOSE, S. and ATUKORALA, V. (1985), 'Exchange Rate Policies in Eastern and Southern Africa 1965–83', World Bank Staff Working Paper, 720, Washington, DC.

GUNNING, J. W. (1979), 'Income Distribution in Models for Developing Countries: Kenya and Tanzania', D.Phil. thesis, University of Oxford.

——(1982), 'Dual Decision Taking on Smallholdings', mimeo, Free University: Amsterdam.

——(1983), 'Income Distribution and Growth: A Simulation Model for Kenya', in D. G. Greene (principal author), *Kenya: Growth and Structural Change*, 2 vols., World Bank: Washington, DC, pp. 487–621.

——(1987), *De geschokte economie* ['The Shocked Economy'], inaugural lecture, Free University Press: Amsterdam (in Dutch).

HOLLANDER, M., and WOLFE, D. A. (1983), *Non-Parametric Statistical Methods*, Wiley: New York.

IMF (International Monetary Fund) (annual), *Government Finance Statistics Yearbook*, Washington, DC.

——(quarterly), *International Financial Statistics*, Washington, DC.

JOHNSON, G. E. (1971), 'The Determination of Individual Hourly Earnings in Kenya', Discussion Paper 115, IDS, Nairobi.

KASUNGU, R. S., and NDULU, B. J. (1984), 'Potential Solutions to the Critical Problems in the Transport Sector in Tanzania', in Lipumba *et al.* (eds.).

KEELER, A. G., SCOBIE, G. M., RENKOW, M. A., and FRANKLIN, D. L. (1981), *The Economic Effects of Agricultural Policies in Tanzania*, Research Triangle Institute for US AID.

——(1982), *The Consumption Effects of Agricultural Policies in Tanzania*, NC Sigma One Corporation, Report prepared for US AID.

KILLICK, T. (1981a), '"By their fruits shall ye know them": The Fourth Development Plan', in Killick (1981b).

——(1981b), *Papers on the Kenyan Economy: Performance, Problems and Policies*, Heinemann Educational Books: Nairobi and London.

——(1984), 'Kenya, 1975–81', in T. Killick (ed.), *The IMF and Stabilization*, Heinemann Educational Books: London.

——and THORNE, M. (1981), 'Problems of an Open Economy: The Balance of Payments in the 1970s', in Killick (1981b).

KIMEI, C. S. (1985), 'Tanzania's Financial Experience in the Post-War Period', mimeo, Department of Economics, University of Uppsala.

KNIGHT, J. B., and SABOT, R. H. (1990), *Education, Productivity, and Inequality: A Comparative Economic Analysis of the East African Natural Experiment*, Oxford University Press: New York.

LIPUMBA, N. I. H. (1984), 'The Economic Crisis in Tanzania', in Lipumba *et al.* (eds.).

——, MSAMBICHAKA, L., and WANGWE, S. (eds.) (1984), *Economic Stabilization Policies in Tanzania*, Economics Department and Economic Research Bureau, University of Dar es Salaam.

MACBEAN, A. (1966), *Export Instability and Economic Development*, George Allen and

Unwin: London.

MALINVAUD, E. (1977), The Theory of Unemployment Reconsidered, Blackwell: Oxford.

MARKETING DEVELOPMENT BUREAU (1981), *Price Policy Recommendations for the 1982–83 Agricultural Price Review*, Government Printer: Dar es Salaam.

MBELLE, A. V. Y. (1988), 'Foreign Exchange and Industrial Development: A Study of Tanzania', Ph.D. thesis, Department of Economics, University of Gothenburg.

MUSSA, M. (1976), 'Tariffs and the Balance of Payments: A Monetary Approach', in J. A. Frenkel and H. G. Johnson, *The Monetary Approach to the Balance of Payments*, George Allen and Unwin: London.

NDULU, B. (1984), 'The Current Economic Stagnation in Tanzania: Causes and Effects', Discussion Paper 2, African–American Issues Center, Boston.

——(1985), 'Investment, Output Growth and Capacity Utilization in an African Economy: The Case of the Manufacturing Sector in Tanzania', Paper presented at the Eastern Economic Association Convention, Pittsburgh.

—— and HYUHA, M. (1984), 'Investment Patterns and Resource Gaps in the Tanzanian Economy, 1970–82', mimeo, Workshop on Economic Stabilization Policies in Tanzania, Dar es Salaam.

NEARY, J. P. (1978), 'Short-Run Capital Specificity and the Pure Theory of International Trade', *Economic Journal*, 88.

——(1985), 'Real and Monetary Aspects of the "Dutch Disease"', in K. Jungenfelt and D. Hague (eds.), *Structural Adjustment in Developed Open Economies*, Macmillan: London.

—— and STIGLITZ, J. E. (1983), 'Toward a Reconstruction of Keynesian Economics: Expectations and Constrained Equilibria', *Quarterly Journal of Economics*, 98, Supplement.

—— and VAN WIJNBERGEN, S. (eds.) (1986), *Natural Resources and the Macroeconomy*, Blackwell: Oxford.

NELSON, J. M. (1984), 'The Political Economy of Stabilization: Commitment, Capacity, and Public Response', *World Development*, 12.

PHELPS, M. G., and WASWO, B. (1972), 'Measuring Protection and its Effects in Kenya', Working Paper 37, IDS, Nairobi.

PRACHOWNY, M. F. J. (1984), *Macro-Economic Analysis for Small Open Economies*, Oxford University Press: Oxford.

RWEGASIRA, D. (1983), 'Adjustment Policies in Low-Income Africa: An Interpretation of the Kenyan and Tanzanian Experiences 1974–78', mimeo, IMF, Washington, DC.

SHARPLEY, J. (1983), *The Impact of External and Domestic Factors on Tanzania's Agricultural Surplus and Foreign Exchange Earnings in the 1970s*, Development Centre, OECD.

SHIMWELA, N. N. P. (1984), 'Tanzania: Some Reflections on the Deepening Economic Crisis', in Lipumba *et al.* (eds.).

SVENDSEN, K. E. (1984), 'Tanzania's Recent Macroeconomic Policies', mimeo, Report to the Swedish International Development Authority, Stockholm.

INDEX

Note: Pages in **bold** refer to Tables; pages in *italics* refer to Figures.

rents (*cont.*)
  quota, tax increase and compatible trade
    and fiscal policies model **36**
  representative agent and Kenyan coffee
    boom 146–55
  repression, financial, Kenyan coffee boom
    and 178–82
revenue composition in Kenya **163**, 164
  see also fiscal policies
risk aversion and consumption path in tempo-
    rary windfall *104*
rural areas
  availability, changes in 85–8
  black market equilibrium *74*, 75
  household consumption, income and price
    relations in Kenya **280**
  see also agriculture; peasants

savings
  Kenya: and CGE 279–85; foreign, actual
    and counterfactual **148**, 152, 172; private
    out of transient income **203**; ratios and
    asset changes 146–50
  Tanzania 317, **318**, 326
  windfall, allocation of 106, *107*
scale, *see* economies of scale
seigniorage 30
shocks
  exclusive, *see* Kenya: coffee boom
  see also oil prices; temporary windfall
  short-run effects of replacing import con-
    trols by tariffs in Kenya **230**
shortages, dynamics of 70, *71*, 72, 82
  see also rationing
simulation experiments
  in general equilibrium analysis of Kenyan
    coffee boom 195, **196**, 197–8
  parameters in **93**
smallholders in Kenya
  and CGE 268–72
  income sources in Kenya **270**
  see also Kenya: coffee boom
special cases of compatible regimes 31–5
  free trade equilibrium 32–3
  import controls 33–4
  logarithmic preferences 35
  tariffs 34–5
stabilization and taxation
  income tax in Kenya **235**
  optimal tax and expenditure policies 123
  policies in Kenya 218, **219**, 220–7
stochastic rationing and money stocks 57–62
structural adjustment 8
subsistence, *see* food
sugar 247, 329, 605
supply response to changes in prices or availability in case of rationing 77, **78**

Tanzania in economic decline (1975–84) 2–3,
    286–336
  comparison with Kenya, *see* macro-
    economic experience compared
  control regime dismantled 313–16
  effect of price controls on availability of
    consumer goods 307, 308
  narrative of economic events 311–36
  see also national accounts and Tanzanian
tariffs 9, 252
  in compatible trade and fiscal policies
    model 34–5; replacing quotas 37, **38**, 39
  constant in temporary windfall model *118*
  import controls in Kenya replaced by **230**
  reduction in Kenya 233, **234**, 235–6
  reductions and tax changes in compatible
    trade and fiscal policies model **38**
  see also imports; trade
taxation, *see* fiscal; income tax; optimal tax
    and expenditure policies
tea 143, 245, 317, 329
  prices in Kenya 198, **199**
temporary windfall 2, 3, 4, 97–140
  in controlled economy 125–40; fiscal policy
    137–40; foreign exchange controls 125–7;
    import controls with fixed exchange rate
    130–5; managed exchange rate 127–30;
    monetary control 135–6
  effect of *102*, 103
  see also booms; uncontrolled economy
terms of trade
  Kenya **240**
  rationing as result of deterioration in 65, 66
  shocks temporary windfall
  see also exports; imports; trade
theory of controlled open economies, *see*
    compatible control regimes; incompati-
    ble control regimes; temporary windfall
time path
  of public expenditures and Kenyan coffee
    boom 166, *167*, 209–14
  of relative price of capital goods in tempo-
    rary windfall model 118
tobacco 317
total budget deficit by market prices 242, **243**
tradables in models, *see* compatible control
    regimes; temporary windfall
trade
  barriers to, *see* imports, quotas
  equilibrium: in compatible trade and fiscal
    policies model 32–3, **40–1**
  and fiscal policies model, *see* compatible
    trade and fiscal policies model
  liberalization in trade policy model 21–6
  monetary and exchange rate policies
    model, *see* trade policy model
  policies, *see under* policies
  shocks, *see* temporary windfall